ABOUT THE EDITOR

Michael J. Rosen is the perpetrator of some fifty books for both adults and children, including cookbooks, young-adult novels, illustrated anthologies, and three collections of his own poetry. Many of his collaborative books benefit Share Our Strength's anti-hunger efforts or the Company of Animals Fund, a granting program he began in 1990 that assists animal welfare agencies. For nearly twenty years, he served as literary director of Thurber House, the cultural center in James Thurber's restored home in Columbus, Ohio. He can be contacted through his website, www.michaeljrosen.com or www.mirth-of-a-nation.com. Alas, all but the most undemanding letters languish in the Inbox for weeks. Any submissions for a subsequent volume of the biennial, which are more than welcome, must be sent to P.O. Box 35, Glenford, OH 43739.

MORE MIRTH OF A NATION

READER'S AGREEMENT

You agree not to reproduce, reprint, or replicate any of the following pieces without the author's written consent, unless, of course, you find yourself imprisoned in a Peruvian jail and one of the guards says "Reprint that piece this instant or I will feed your elbows to the rats." Then, by all means, reprint it or whatever else he wants you to reprint for God's sake. You agree for verification purposes to cite your mother's maiden name, her Maidenform bra size, and whether or not she's familiar with the band Iron Maiden. When reading this book, you agree to give it your undivided attention, or if you must divide it, make sure it is divisible by 3, keeping in mind all principles of pi. At the end of each sentence, you agree to thrust your arms upward and grunt a loud, staccato "Hey!" just like they do at the end of each stunt in a circus. You agree that, on any given weekend, there are way too many mattress sales. You agree to sing Yiddish lullabies while tweezing your eyebrows with your nondominant hand. You agree to refrain from banal office chat (e.g., complaining on Monday about it being Monday; acknowledging on Thursday that it is almost Friday). You agree to refrigerate and marinate overnight. You agree to give me your Visa number (please include expiration date) and approval to spend up to $500 on merchandise from the Summer 2002 Anthropologie catalog. You agree that it would neither be kind nor appropriate to throw a heart-healthy cinnamon bran muffin at a sailor. You agree that yes, we all suffer, perhaps even daily and deeply, but who wants to hear it? You agree that some women look sophisticated wearing a shawl, others foolish. You agree not to overdo it with the e-mail petitions, bad metaphors, and catnip.

Yes, I agree to these terms.

_____
Name
_____
Date
_____
Visa #   **Exp. Date**

—A.K.R.

MORE MIRTH OF A NATION

The Best Contemporary Humor

Edited by
MICHAEL J. ROSEN

Perennial
An Imprint of HarperCollins*Publishers*

Copyright acknowledgments appear on pages 545–552.

HarperCollins books may be purchased for educational, business, or sales promotional use. For information please write: Special Markets Department, HarperCollins Publishers Inc., 10 East 53rd Street, New York, NY 10022.

FIRST EDITION

Designed by Christine Weathersbee

Library of Congress Cataloging-in-Publication Data
More mirth of a nation: the best contemporary humor / edited
    by Michael J. Rosen.—1st ed. p. cm.
  ISBN 0-06-095322-5
    1. American wit and humor. I. Rosen, Michael J.
  PN6165 .M67 2002
  817'.608—dc21

                                                    2002072817

02 03 04 05 06 ❖/RRD 10 9 8 7 6 5 4 3 2 1

The Short Essay That Conquered the Planet

It started quietly. The writer finished the short essay and sat back, pleased. He sent it off for publication, and the essay was distributed into the world. A few people read it. They showed it to others. Others began reading it. Soon, they noticed changes: They felt younger, more alive. Their warts and blemishes disappeared. Their reproductive organs swelled. Their hearts were filled with song.

They began to tell others about the essay. Soon, the essay was being copied—e-mailed around the world (with an appropriate copyright fee always, always being sent back to the author), and placed on websites. It was tacked up in offices, schools and churches. It was read from pulpits and from podia, and from the balcony of the Vatican. It was appropriated by a columnist for the *Boston Globe*.

The essay was set to music; it became an opera, a play, a blockbuster film. It became a well-received ballet, and an avant-garde production at the Brooklyn Academy of Music, staged by Robert Wilson, with music by Tom Waits—whose music seemed happy for quite possibly the first time ever. The essay became the shortest piece of writing ever to receive the Pulitzer Prize and the National Book Award. It went on to win the Caldecott Medal, the Nobel Peace Prize, and the Jean Hersholt Humanitarian Award. Then it swept the Grammies.

Miraculous reports began to trickle in: The essay had closed an unclosable wound. It had brought peace where there had once been strife. It scratched the places that could not be itched. It tamed lions.

Word of the essay spread to other lands. It was translated into many languages. Relief organizations stopped shipping food, and began simply dropping the essay on blighted areas, which miraculously revived. The essay created droughts where there were floods, and floods where there were droughts. It converted water to wine, and vice versa. It partitioned those parts of the world that had hitherto been thought to be unpartitionable. It sowed peace and love. It raised the dead and smote the wicked.

After months of planning, the people of the world, at a given hour on a given day, all stood in the streets and read the essay aloud, in unison, billions of voices mingling into one as the essay soared out into the heavens in a fantastic global murmur. The heavens parted and the sun shone on the entire world at once, in a cataclysmic expression of joy, and all animals were given the power of speech, and all humans were given the ability to fly, and the unicorns returned.

The writer beheld all this and smiled. "This," he thought to himself, "is a fine beginning."

—Tim Carvell

Contents

Now here we are, gloating over all the glories compounded in this new volume, thinking back over the last volume's introduction, and dreaming of (read: dreading) all the introductions of the biennials to come. Being shy of fifty, and, hoping health, luck, and the publishing business all continue in favorable manners, we realize this might indicate the possibility of a dozen such prefatory remarks. A dozen chances to offer a "state of the nation's humor" address.

Well let's dispel that occasion right away: We will hardly presume to know more than the state of our own minds, and, as clever readers have already quipped, even that is a dubious assessment. So what does this mean to you, the reader? (Hello, reader!) You who are simply eager to see your favorite authors and to meet new favorites. (And also you who are already asking yourself why you aren't included here.) It means this: You are being spared a separate introduction in exchange for a table of contents capriciously annotated with italics, as well as supplementary book-whacking by the likes of Henry Alford, Amy Krouse Rosenthal, and the loquacious Davis Sweet, who offers this volume's "Submission Guidance" at the end of the book, before the copious offers from our sponsoring merchants (don't forget to mention Mirth of a Nation to receive a special rolling-of-the-eyes discount).

Once again this anthology selects and honors writing where the humor itself is the achievement and not simply something, like grammar or spicy dialogue, that keeps your interest. Here, humor is the show dog (and we've got representatives from all the groups, from the mutts to the toy breeds, from the nonsporting dogs to the rough-and-tumble terriers); humor is not merely the linty bits of biscuits you dole out to your puppy (read: reader) just to keep him (read: you) (also read: apologies for using the accepted simplicity of the masculine pronoun to stand in for everyone) heeling on a walk. Yes, this is the Best of Show in humor writing. In somewhat less metaphorical terms, we're only showcasing work where humor is the spectacle itself rather than the glitter a writer adds to give the unspectacular a little sparkle. In still plainer terms, hoping to wel-

come even the metaphorically impaired, here the humor is the ham and not the little wedges of pineapple and the maraschino cherries stuck on with frill picks. Humor is the feature presentation and not just the big box of Jujyfruits you eat all through the first half of the movie so that you can spend the second half of the movie wondering why on Earth you ate such junk as you discreetly try to pry the sticky bits from your teeth. Please hold any questions you may have about this policy until after reading this entire volume; if you remain still uncertain as to what we have been trying to say about humor, just let us know and we can posit further metaphors in the next edition.

DAVID M. BADER

We are delighted to be publishing this mini-book by Mr. Bader in this volume. Think of it as a sort of bonus we're throwing in, like some nifty booklet of fifty things you can do to prevail upon everything from crabgrass to indigestion that magazines like Men's Health and Prevention and [your favorite fanzine here] send you as a way of saying, "Hey, thanks for subscribing." Truth to tell, "How to Meditate Faster" came to us in a much longer—or, to be more direct—much slower version, which we convinced the author to expedite for your benefit. Alas, no one convinced the editor to follow suit.

RICHARD BAUSCH

ANDY BOROWITZ

TIM CARVELL

Speaking of rating, this seems as good a time as any to offer up a simple method for rating your own sense of humor. This comes to us compliments of an Amazon.com reader/reviewer from New York who proclaimed this about Mirth of a Nation: "Don't drink milk while reading!" Sure, it might have been swell had his name been Michiko Kakutani, but that small chagrin is offset when you that note that "11 out of 11" potential book buyers browsing Amazon's site found that review helpful. And so, what could be simpler: Got milk? As you read each entry in this new volume, sip your milk, be it skim, 2 percent, rice, lite soy, what have you. And then, once you've finished the book, count the number of milk-spattered pages and divide by the total page count. Feel free to devise your own rating system for calibrating blot size, sprayed area, and so forth (you, after all, understand your nose best, and its propensity to propel beverages when surprised by laughter).

We have not yet designed a means of calibrating or assessing the naso-lacto index, so you may, on the basis of anything you like, declare yourself a person with a Very Fine, Fine, Good, or Average sense of humor and no one here will think the worse of you. (Heaven help the lactose- and humor-intolerant.)

A word about this contribution. Readers may remember from our introduction to the previous edition that we attended medical school. Yes, six months, even twenty-four years ago, does count. So when I might have been discussing the classics of the world's literature around a table at some neighborhood Hungarian pastry shop, I was seated across from the periodic table on the wall of the lab extracting caffeine from tea and precipitating unknowns from cloudy solutions. (If I'd only understood how much that latter process actually describes the very murky science of writing itself!) Anyway, in recognition of those lost years, we are including a new periodic table here. An addendum, if you will. And, as always, readers are invited to nominate their own new elements for yet another supplementary chart. Depending on how many of your submissions receive a high naso-lacto score, we'll offer a few prizes and report the collective "findings" in the next volume of our biennial.

Which is another way of saying thank you to Messrs. Gerber and Schwarz for rekindling our lack of interest in all things that remotely possess the smell of chemistry, physics, math, psychology, bodies, pain, cadavers, or live human beings.

We have selected five offerings from the pen of Lewis Grossberger, media critic for Media Week, his most recent tenure after years of reporting, surveying, and assessing for a slew of esteemed magazines in the last decades. Already we've received some heat for his first entry, since it seems NASCAR has become a phenomenon you can now admit to enjoying, much like the Weather Channel or World Wrestling Entertainment or The Pretender reruns, which were once the clandestine pleasures of the few, the underserved, and the bored. No, people have stopped saying that NASCAR is just one stroke and an extra "a" shy of "mascara." Or maybe they haven't started—whatever. Anyway, Mr. Grossberger's explanation of the phenomenon struck us as important, and if some readers object to his opinions, well, surely the role of journalism has always been to spark dialogue and we must fan the spark, ever hopeful of a conflagration.

Yes, yes, attentive types, Mr. Harris did contribute his "clarifications" to our last volume, Mirth of a Nation. But doesn't the world feel ever more in need of such painstaking differentiation? For instance, future confusions that ought to be charted by Mr. Harris include one we think about most mornings, swallowing our 20 mgs. of Lipitor: Is it a prescription drug or is it an archnemesis of one of the Superfriends in the Justice League?

Even our nephews Ben and Louie have tried their hand at clarifications: Is it a kind of Greek column or is it a word for someone stupid? (Moronic? Ionic? Idiotic? Asinine? Dorkic? Corinthian?) Or my favorite: Is *it a beverage or an ice-skating maneuver? (Triple Salchow? Single Lutz? Chai? Double Decaf Skinny Latte? Camel? Brown Cow?)*

  If Poets Wrote Poems Whose Titles
  Were Anagrams of Their Names

And now, readers, another gift to you. Having, for five years, resisted the beguilements of "light verse," and even weathered the berating of their authors, we are proud to present out first chapbook of poetry: an even dozen poems by Francis Heaney. It is a lonely little petunia of verse volunteering among the onion patch of prose.

But a curious question begs to be asked: How many humorists are also poets, or (pause for dramatic effect) were poets? Perhaps all future submissions to the biennial should come with a cover-page affidavit admitting that the writing of poetry either has or has not played a significant part in the would-be contributor's own life. We will endeavor to make this bill become a law before Congress adjourns.

  "Skinny Domicile"
    by Emily Dickinson
  "Toilets" by T. S. Eliot
  "I Will Alarm Islamic Owls"
    by William Carlos Williams
  "Likable Wilma" by William Blake
  "Hen Gonads" by Ogden Nash
  "nice smug me"
    by e. e. cummings
  "Is a Sperm Like a Whale?"
    by William Shakespeare
  "Halt, Dynamos" by Dylan Thomas
  "DH" by H.D.
  "Kin Rip Phalli" by Philip Larkin

GREGORY HISCHAK

About Mr. Hischak, we cannot resist mentioning the fact that he is not only a writer, champion poetry-slam participant, and a graphic designer, but also an artist. An Official Artist, no less, of the Etch A Sketch company, Ohio Art. He himself created the five Van Gogh drawings reproduced here (go ahead and skip ahead to page 169 and the little gallery of reproductions we've included) by twisting those two clumsy dials himself. He writes, "I drew them myself."

To be good at so many things takes so much work! It's just pitiful that kids today, with tools like gel pens and glitter sticks and KidPaint, can make art so easily they hardly appreciate craft, apprenticeship, and hard work. In Mr. Hischak's day, when the Etch A Sketch proved to be a childhood favorite, art was long and summers were short, and you usually had poison ivy and chigger bites and all, and there wasn't any instant messaging either. But let's not go down that path.

CYNTHIA KAPLAN

MARK KATZ

MARTHA KEAVNEY

Time for another note in passing: Apparently the author has a videotape of the firemen. A recent e-mail from her described it as "two hours of guys soaping up the trucks, which is not a euphemism, that I'm having converted to digital stock for posterity." We have inquired on behalf of interested readers about the future availability of the tape, but at press time, no details were available. Feel free to contact Ms. Lawless directly at the corner of Eighth and Forty-eighth.

Mr. Martone, in fact, lives very near Cedar Point, on Lake Erie, which boasts not one, not two, not three, not four, not nearly enough roller coasters, because usually for the whopping price of admission you can stand in line for about three of the popular rides in a whole day, and they last a couple minutes each, so you have to figure that you're paying 95 percent of the admission price just to stand around waiting for the fun you wanted to have. I know, it sounds a lot like sex, and maybe it's really supposed to help kids understand how life is like a roller coaster. In our next volume, perhaps we will ask our contributors to offer up examples of how life is like a roller coaster or to propose other metaphors, not necessarily associated with amusement parks. Readers waiting in one sort of line or another should certainly feel encouraged to share their own metaphors. These may be sent to the editor, in care of Cedar Point Amusement Park. We don't have the address right here, but it should be easy enough to find.

And now, we are pleased to announce a new feature in the biennial, our Discovery Prize in American Humor (working title). The parameters of this distinction, the judging process, as well as the distinction itself, are somewhat cloudy, like most things that can't be divided nicely into two categories. But it is our heartfelt attempt to put a little foil star (represented below by the illustrations of the gold bar) beside the name of Alysia Gray Painter in the canonical role book. (We chose the gold bar because, guess what? Not only is "Au" the copy editor's notation for "Author," but it's also the symbol for gold on the periodic table! Coincidence? Not hardly.) Now, certainly McSweeney's Internet Tendency should claim to have actually discovered Ms. Painter, if one accomplishes such a thing by selecting the author's first work to appear on their site. And no one here wants to get into the old Louis Leakey v. those other doubting paleontologists poking around Olduvai Gorge claiming to be the real discoverer of the genuine—

shoot, all we mean to do is to say this is the author's first appearance in print, and to shout, "Hey, Cozy Canon of American Humor: Everybody scootch together and make room for someone else to sit down." Which is also a way of saying, "Hey, literary agents: Sign up this writer for the big six-figure advance now, while flattery still means something!" On the more pragmatic level, we hope readers everywhere will welcome Ms. Painter into their fold of favorites.

So without further ado, prize money, or paperweight sandblasted with winner's name and date, here are four works by this volume's big winner.

While we are on the subject of Zagat's and rating things, we thought it might be of interest to share a partial list of people, products, or other nouns that, after two solid years of reading submissions for this volume, no longer possess the capacity to amuse (us? or anyone?) in a humorous piece of writing. This is another service to would-be contributors. We are putting a moratorium on the following: Dharma and Greg, people pretending not to know who Dharma and Greg are/were, Ally McBeal, anything vaguely Sopranos-related unless having to do with actual music, Zima, Pez, Ozzy Ozbourne, Ross Perot, Yanni, Depends, AARP, John Tesh, Sonny Bono, Amy Grant, Britney or Barbra or Mariah or J.Lo or Ricky, phlegm, Feng Shui, Star Wars, "titillation" (even without quotes), Regis Philbin and Kathie Lee Gifford, Regis without Kathie Lee, Kathie Lee with or without her exploitative merchandise, anyone whose name begins with Kathie or Kathy or even a "K," Bruce Lee, anyone or anything (i.e., cigars, stains, food, ovals, tape recorders) having to do with the Clinton scandal, any Brady person or reinvented Brady actor, Strom Thurmond, the Pleistocene, pit bulls, Pluto (the impugned planet, not the dog), polka (with or without dots), dot-coms (especially failing ones), Mary Tyler Moore, Oprah, and nearly any other word beginning with O or having an "o" sound, like "Rosie O'Donnell" or J.Lo or Mariah-O or Britney-O or

Quentin Tarantino, David Copperfield, extremely skinny actresses (your choice), rap singers who shoot/shoot-up/punch-out/bark (your choice), Dan Quayle (seemingly always in humor's West Wing), Barbara Walters, Sam Donaldson, Al Roker and Willard Scott and any other affable heavyset guy, Michael Eisner, Michael Bolton, Florence Henderson (come on, she's suffered enough), annual Christmas letters, people with cell phones, power bars, Bowflex, Barcaloungers, gingko biloba, haggis, Bill Gates, and everyone else with enough money to make the rest of us go away. There are others, many others, but we must conserve our energy. Oh, and there's nothing that can, or should, stop the Bushisms ahead. (Updates to this list will sporadically appear on our website www.mirth-of-a-nation.com. And, by all means, readers may submit their own exhausted candidates.)

Once again, just as Dave Eggers generously provided in our last volume, we are offering even more suggestions by Davis Sweet (not his real name, apparently) on nurturing your own humorous inclinations. While we did have the chance to read over some of his remarks, the editor, publisher, and 67 other contributors to this volume are not in any way responsible for the ideas expressed by Mr. Sweet. Likewise, the author himself claims none. Nor has any other party shown any particular responsibility for the ideas expressed hither and thither throughout these pages. (Guess what? Spell-check let us get away with "hither" and "thither!" We thought, for sure, we'd end up having to use "here" and "there.")

Just for the record, we were not overwhelmed with unsolicited manuscripts sent in response to the last volume's proclamation of our open-door submission policy. Perhaps the subjects listed in our submission policy were intimidating. Sorry. The fact is, we welcome all submissions. They should be sent to the editor, in care of P.O. Box 35, Glenford, OH 43739. Of course, you are welcome to visit our website as well: www.mirth-of-a-nation.com, because we feature swell things there and readers tend to like swell things. Submissions cannot be sent by e-mail. Nor can would-be contributors pout about this inexorable delaying of the response process. Maybe everyone doesn't recall those bygone years (say, five years ago), but it used to be that submissions had to go through the U.S. Mail, had to sit on some editor's desk (or floor) for five weeks or five months, and then had to be either returned in an SASE, or, equally often, lost en route. But now, the expectation is that the work can be sent via e-mail and since it's instantly received, the decision should bounce back even before the submitting party has logged off. Our policy here is: humor must stand the test of time. We also believe in supporting philately, patronizing stationery stores, and taking the dogs for a ride to the post office to be nice.

And speaking of visiting websites, is there any reason why everything must petition us to visit its website? The packet of Sweet'n Low in the motel coffee kit beseeches us to stop by. The folks that make the bags of charcoal briquettes urge us to visit. (What, so the while the coals burn down, we can download safety tips?) And Tums! Yes, Tums wants us to browse its World Wide Web of all things Tum-escent. And so does Juicy Fruit. Don't we all have time to browse the website of the chewing gum where, as of this writing, one can see (click here!) the winners of their sweepstakes that ended in 1999, or download nifty "wallpaper" screen savers (click here!), which consist of precisely two billboards for the chewing gum that can fill one's computer screen as though subliminal advertising has lost its appeal? Sorry, but isn't chewing gum the thing you *can do while doing something else, such as walking? If we had time to loiter about the Sweet'n Low and Tums and Juicy Fruit websites, we'd have time to download submissions from the Web. But, at the risk of repeating ourselves, we don't.*

QUESTIONS FOR READING GROUPS

INDEX

NOTES ON CONTRIBUTORS

Now we must confess an oversight. Biographical notes come, as most things do, in two varieties: the straightforward credential listing sort, and the tongue-in-cheek sort that's peppered with drollery and lies, and garnished with chervil. We neglected to advise our many contributors which sort we wanted here. And so, in order that no one feels stranded on one side or the other, we added (actually, Roger Director did) some other biographical notes to the stable. However, we did not feel up to including yet more work from these improbable characters.

NOTES ON CONTRIBUTORS

PERMISSIONS

*Wait, there's more. Throughout this volume, independent of the alphabetical arrangement of authors, are works by four other talents. This is not to suggest that they do not play nicely with others. They are not in time-out. **AMY KROUSE ROSENTHAL** has supplied various pieces influenced by the very format of a book; they appear on pages iii, xxvii, 231, 540, 553, and 555. We have dispersed **CHIP ROWE**'s "55 Bad Fortunes" as if these were subscription cards blown among the pages as well as ads from **CHRIS WARE**'s Acme Novelty Co. as if these were, well, ads.*

   To determine which fortune would be yours, use this ancient formula we learned from Crossing Over with John Edward: Add the numbers in your year of birth, and multiply by your age. Subtract this from the total number of pages in the book and then turn to that page in the book and see if there's a fortune. If so, it's yours. If not, that's your misfortune.

Now, if you like playing these sorts of numerological games, you might like to try these two formulae, which we learned during the commercial break while watching The Jeff Corwin Experience—you know, the program on Animal Planet with the other, sillier, sexier zoology-guy who runs around the globe squealing about "gorgeous rattlesnakes" and "beautiful rhinos." Here's how to calculate your own perfect drag name: Take your first pet's name and add that to your mother's maiden name. Go ahead. You don't have to put on women's clothing just to try it. You can write your name here on the blank we've provided:_____. (By the way, we are Freckles Mindell.)

Now, dear readers, here is how you can calculate your porn star name: Write down your middle name and follow it with the name of the street on which you were born. Here's another blank:_____. (We were Joel Geers. Too hot!)

We have also scattered into the mix here a dozen contributions by **RANDY COHEN** (porn name: Sandy Greenberg—he wanted to name his cocker spaniel "Big Penis"; drag name: Steve Brighton). His compacted and brilliant "Unnatural Histories" seemed a bit too rich to consume at one sitting, as ill-advised as eating too much foie gras, or any foie gras, to speak candidly. Here at Mirth HQ, where there are not enough people even to constitute a "we," we say to hell with the gourmet purveyors and superchefs and all the worshippers of force-fed geese! We've asked Randy to give us a one-minute history of fattened goose liver for the next volume. He'll also be taking on Latvia (since we want to know why humorists always choose that as the "funny" country), and also the origin of those orange circus-peanut candies your grandma used to serve when the girls came over to play canasta. You can find "Unnatural Histories" by Randy Cohen on pages 26, 67, 107, 158, 215, 250, 270, 307, 351, 398, 447, and 473.

SPECIAL FEATURE

Index, Lists, and Incomplete Sentences

In this issue we are also publishing, in further defiance of the alphabetical march of authors, some very short works by some very other authors. Given that published humor is blithely considered filler by many magazines and periodicals, we realize it appears to be a further compounding of the injustice to suggest that the following pieces are fillers, but such are the indignities of the genre. It's not like we told these authors they couldn't use whole sentences and sit at the grown-ups' table. It's simply because, unlike most publications, we do not fill our odd tenth-of-a-page remaindered spaces with advertisements for B&Bs on Nantucket, SunCatchers, herbal arthritis remedies, and ultimate cat toys.

And this brings us, at last, to the close of the Contents pages. What more needs to be added, dear readers? Perhaps a pledge to drop the "dear reader" salutation in the next volume? Here's to all things mirthful. Keep us posted. Come visit.

Subject: New Virus Alert
Date: Jan 2001 17:36:18 0500
From: "amy k.r." amy@suba.com
FYI, forward this to everyone on your list. . . .

— —Original Message— —

There is a new virus called Cobbler. It will arrive on e-mail titled
"BEST PEACH COBBLER EVER." AOL has announced that it is very
powerful, even more so than CHLOE SEVIGNY. There is no remedy. It is a virus that will ERASE YOUR WHOLE SEX DRIVE, and
misplace your G-spot. DO NOT OPEN. DELETE RIGHT AWAY.

It will eat ALL YOUR LEFTOVER CHINESE FOOD, even the almond
cookies you put in your pantry last October and totally forgot
about. It will send an e-mail to everyone in your address book
telling them, in no uncertain terms, what you really think of them,
citing dates and times of when you found them at their self-
absorbed/dull peak. It will make you wait 40 minutes at Nobu
EVEN THOUGH YOU HAD RESERVATIONS. THIS IS THE MOST
DESTRUCTIVE VIRUS YET.

It removes all the beautifully sculpted, trainer-enhanced definition
in your upper arms. It programs your cell phone ringer to play "La
Bamba." It makes you weep.

Opening this deadly e-mail also ensures that on your next flight you
will a) sit on the runway for three hours; and b) be seated next to
an earnest 20-year-old who has just discovered Huth Prather's
Notes to Myself and can't contain herself from sharing the "most
unbelievably amazing" passages with you. It makes you use big
words when normal ones would do. It erases the entire plot of Cider
House Rules from your memory, which may be the only beneficial
fall out of the virus.

It destroys your sense of humor. We know of one man who was
not warned about this virus in time, and while he used to be pretty
funny after an apple martini or two, he now only talks about his
cold, his new porch, and his children's afterschool activities.

I repeat, DO NOT OPEN. DELETE AT ONCE.

It finds the most sophisticated painting in your living room—the one that you think really reflects who you are, the one you subtly glance at when a new guest arrives because you want them to notice it and think things about you—and then replaces it with a cheaply framed college poster, most likely that one that was so popular in the mid-80s, with the ballet slipper standing on the egg.

It mutates your subscription to WALLPAPER magazine (granted this only affects 120 people or so) into a 52-week subscription to all the 1997 back issues of U.S. NEWS & WORLD REPORT. It makes your left eyelid twitch. It mocks you.

It will make your son (a sophomore at Brown) major in eighteenth-century Portuguese philosophy, with a minor in late twentieth-century craft fair collectibles (his thesis: "The Socio-Political Role of the Walnut Shell Figurine in Post Cold War America").

It will turn you into the kind of person who constantly has little drops of spit collecting on the sides of his mouth but doesn't know it (or doesn't care), and so talking to you is both unappealing and distracting because all one can think about is telling you to wipe the spit away.

It makes you constantly and acutely aware of the parts of your life which are false, ridiculous, and dreadfully inconsistent with the (better) life you can envision, the one you know you can and should lead.

It makes you INTERESTED IN ASTROLOGY !

Also, BTW, if you receive an e-mail with the subject "7-ELEVEN'S NEW FALAFEL'N'COFFEE COMBO" don't open that either. We won't even go into what that one does.

MORE MIRTH OF A NATION

How to Meditate Faster

DAVID M. BADER

As hard as they try, most people never quite manage to achieve Enlightenment. Some have sat motionless, in silent meditation, and wondered, "Are we done yet?" Others have truly wanted to achieve Perfect Patience and Equanimity, but already had plans for the weekend. Few actually find time to attain complete Oneness, or even Two- or Threeness. Fortunately, help is at hand. Based on centuries of the most sacred and profound Buddhist and Taoist writings and influenced by several recent kickboxing movies, this convenient guide for the serenity-impaired will have you spiritually awakened and seeing into the essential nature of reality in no time at all.

Step 1.
How to Sit in the Lotus Position,
or Not Sit in the Lotus Position,
As the Case May Be

You will never achieve Enlightenment with terrible posture. This is the reason for the Lotus Position or *padmasana* (Sanskrit for "I have just dislocated my femur"). Recite to yourself, "I am supple."

Then, crossing your legs, bend your knees and position your feet on top of your thighs, pulling your toes in toward your kidneys. Then recite the following: *"Yaiiiiieeeeee!!!"* (Sanskrit for "I am not supple. I am in need of urgent medical attention.") Interestingly, according to emergency room statistics, "patient sat in full Lotus Position" is the leading cause of meditation-related injuries, ahead of "patient inhaled way too much incense" and "patient dropped Buddha statue on foot." Not to worry—you are now in perfect harmony and balance.

Step 2.
How to Breathe (Important!)

The classic *Sutra on Breath to Maintain Mindfulness* lists no fewer than 16 different types of meditative breathing techniques, not even including hiccuping, burping, and having an asthma attack. Begin with the very simple Meditation of Contemplation of the Breath. With each in-breath, think, "Experiencing a breath, I am breathing in. Calming the breath, I am breathing in." If you become aware of a thunderous pounding in your ears and sharp pains in your sides, breathe out. This is a key point of *The Sutra on Not Turning Blue and Fainting.*

Then try the Meditation of Counting the Breath. Tell yourself: "I am ever mindful to number each breath consecutively, for no particular reason." If you have been breathing for a long time and the number is not getting bigger, something is wrong. This is explained more fully in *The Sutra on Not Really Being a Math Person.*

Finally, don't forget the Meditation of Freshening the Breath. As the Buddha himself often said, "Breathing out a whole breath, I am ever mindful to eat a Tic Tac." This advice can be found in *The Sutra on Garlic Tofu.*

Step 3.
How to Stare into Space

One of the most ancient meditation techniques involves sitting and staring at a blank wall, a practice known as *pi-kuan* ("wall-gazing" or, literally, "no commercials"). Legend has it that the sixth-century Zen master Bodhidharma sat in this position for nine years until, finally, his legs fell off. Legend also has it that this was a pretty clever practical joke by the standards of the time and that all the Zen monks had a good laugh, though perhaps you had to be there.

Start by closing your eyes, though not all the way. Closing them completely could lead to napping or snoring, not to mention the whole problem of peeking. With your eyes partly open, pick a spot on the wall at which to gaze. Think about the spot. Ask yourself, "How did the spot get there? Will it come out? Who is responsible for this mess?" When you are finished with that spot, move to another spot. Then another. When you are done, ask yourself whether it is time to repaint.

Step 4.
Koans: Unanswerable Questions
of the East and the Answers!

Throughout history, students of Zen have been known to devote countless meditation sessions to contemplating a single puzzling question such as "What is the sound of one hand clapping?" (a whooshing noise, but you have to clap really quickly) or "Does a dog have Buddha nature?" (Probably not, but could the Buddha jump and catch a frisbee in his mouth?) Unfortunately, most koans are completely inscrutable. For example, a monk could spend years wrestling with the question, "What's the deal with Richard Gere?" For this reason, when presented with a koan, you should simply answer, "Gee, that's a puzzler. I'm stumped!" Then try to change the subject.

Step 5.
Movement Meditations, Unless You've
Already Been on Your Feet All Day

There's no need to sit still as you meditate, particularly if you are running late. For example, try the Walking Meditation. As you walk, think "I am shifting, I am lifting, I am placing; I am shifting, I am lifting, I am placing." This technique also works quite well for jaywalking. In a crowd, think "I am elbowing; I am shoving; I am putting my needs first." All that matters is that you take joy in every step, up to the point when you find a taxi. Remember that the path is the goal and the journey is the destination, especially in traffic.

Step 6.
Achieving Perfect Emptiness,
Though Not After a Heavy Meal

One of the most commonly asked questions about meditation is, "What does Enlightenment really feel like?" The answer is that true Enlightenment transcends verbal expression. This in turn raises the question, "Yes, of course. So, seriously, what does Enlightenment really feel like?"

Enlightenment is sometimes described as "No-Self"—the absence of any separation between the Self and other phenomena. (This is not to be confused with simply bumping into other phenomena). In other words, it is the feeling that the Self is part of a borderless continuum in which everything can be broken down into smaller and smaller parts. Even the smallest part can be broken further so that, in the end, a stolen BMW can be smuggled into South America completely undetected. Looked at another way, the nonexistence of the Self may mean that your psychiatrist is an even bigger waste of money than you thought.

A Zen master once explained it to his pupils this way: "After much meditation, I ascertained my Self to be void, and all external phenomena to be empty and without essence. It was an awakening." His pupils were in awe.

He went on to say, "Of course, this was shortly after my divorce. A few months later, I began to feel much better about my Self and all external phenomena and started dating again."

Step 7.
The Dropping Away of Body and Mind: How to
Tell If Your Body and Mind Are Still There

Paradoxically, the attainment of "No-Self" begins with self-awareness. Only when you achieve full awareness of your self-awareness can you then progress to a lack of self-awareness. This will, ideally, yield to the lack of awareness of even the awareness that you lack self-awareness. It is in this state of complete and utter unawareness that many Buddhists have allowed their heads to be shaved.

This process is sometimes called "the dropping away of body and mind." To determine whether your own body and mind have dropped away, look for these telltale signs:

1. Your clothes seem extremely roomy.
2. The doctor who did your CAT scan is deeply puzzled.
3. You cease to see yourself as a distinct person and instead identify yourself simply as "a transient wave in the surging sea of universal phenomena."
4. As a result, restaurants can never find your reservation.

In the end, you may think you have attained "No-Self" only to wake up with a start in the middle of the night wondering. "If I have no Self, to whom have I been muttering all these years?"

This is a good question. In the future, try to be more discreet.

Step 8.
The Way of Tea: Will That Be for Here or to Go?

Sipping and savoring tea has been part of the meditation experience ever since the fifth century, when the *Holy Scripture of Tea* was published to rave reviews—"The scroll on how to boil water was riveting . . . impossible to put down!" In the tea ceremony, still practiced today, the tea master brews and serves the tea in ceramic bowls amid votive candles and silk, bamboo, and lacquer ornaments. The color, flavor, and aroma of the steaming tea all aid in dissolving the artificial boundaries of the mind. Guests focus instead on tranquil thoughts inspired by the surroundings, such as "Nice tea room!" and "I really, seriously hope I don't break anything." In medieval Japan, it was not uncommon for a tea drinker to wipe his mouth accidentally on a priceless wall-hanging and end up having to commit hara-kiri.

The inspirational power of tea can be seen in the lesson of the venerable tea master who often filled his guests' tea cups well past overflowing. "Your mind is like this cup," he would say. "Too full to accept new teachings!" Some of his guests became enlightened, while others felt that having hot tea intentionally spilled on them was grounds for a massive lawsuit. The venerable tea master went bankrupt and ended his days frothing milk and grinding beans in a venerable coffee bar.

Step 9.
Practicing Nonattachment: Attaining No-Stuff

Attachment to material possessions, the Buddha repeatedly emphasized, is the source of most of our craving, desire, and unhappiness. "Owning," "wanting," "getting," and "possessing" are all artificial constructs, delusions that anguish and enslave us, he taught. The Buddha often spoke instead of the Four Divine Abodes: the Abode of Lovingkindness, the Abode of Compassion, the Abode of Sympathetic Joy, and the Abode of Equanimity. "As far as I'm concerned," he would say, "Four Abodes just means four times as many repairs. I mean, who needs that kind of headache?" Still, when it comes to a small, single-family abode, from a tax standpoint, it may be better to own than to rent.

Step 10.
Mantras and Other Catchy Phrases

Some people meditate while reciting mantras—sacred formulas of words or sounds, repeated over and over—because they believe them to possess magical powers. Popular mantras typically consist of monosyllables, words, or entire phrases. These include *"Om Mani Padme Hum"* ("All Hail the Jewel in the Lotus"), *"Namu Dai Butsu"* ("I Am One With the Great Buddha"), and *"Brong, Brong . . ."* ("I Am Imitating a Gong"). Skeptics often ask, "Can the constant intoning of meaningless syllables and noises possibly have any influence or importance?" And yet, as many monks have pointed out, it seems to work for Sam Donaldson. You may find that reciting a mantra simply helps to quiet the mind. Or you may conclude that, after many long periods of silent meditation, a mantra is not really all that bad a conversation.

Step 11.
Martial Arts: How Not to Die of Natural Causes

Meditation and the practice of deadly martial arts have complemented each other throughout history. Both involve developing powers of physical and spiritual discipline. Both emphasize calm acceptance of fate, as embodied in the Samurai Code of Bushido: "Face death unflinchingly! Behead your adversaries! Never surrender! Have a nice day!"

There are many types of martial arts, most dating back to feudal Japan—unarmed fighting (judo), swordsmanship (kendo), archery (kyudo), and swimming in armor (drowning). Whichever one you pursue, try to follow the advice of a great Zen archery instructor: "You must aim without aiming, for the more obstinately you try to strike your target, the less you will succeed." Also remember his famous last words, "Aah, I'm hit, I'm hit!"

Generally it is a good idea to be careful around people who claim to take martial arts classes "for the exercise." Other, less dangerous Zen arts to consider include calligraphy (shodo) or the Japanese art of flower arrangement (ikebana). For fastest arrangements, dial 1-800-FLOWERS.

Step 12.
Suggestions for Further Meditation

The best way to explore more advanced techniques is to find a Zen teacher to guide you. For information on Zen teachers in your area, contact the Zen Teachers Union. If no teachers are available, see if you can find a Zen substitute teacher. Or consider going away on a Zen mountain retreat. Many seekers of wisdom have experienced profound moments of Enlightenment on remote, craggy peaks, such as "Wow. This is some view!" Some have fallen thousands of feet to their deaths, yet were grateful for the experience. Others have returned many times, for the skiing. For more about this, consult the definitive treatise in the field, *What to Chant During an Avalanche*.

Whatever you do, the important thing is to be serene at all times. Live mindfully. Seek the path of Enlightenment. As the Buddha taught, it is important to practice self-restraint, cultivate higher levels of consciousness, and live more reflectively. Still, there is no point in overdoing it.

Top 100 Foods

1. Gruel
2. Potatoes
3. Mud
4. Soup
5. Stew
6. Goulash
7. Paella
8. Gravy
9. Chowder
10. Mush
11. Gumbo
12. Cioppino
13. Consommé
14. Bouillon
15. Yosenabe
16. Gazpacho
17. Bouillabaisse
18. Poi
19. Borscht
20. Shoes
21. Grubs
22. Algae
23. Baba ganoush
24. Grass
25. Berries
26. Seeds
27. Nuts
28. Roots
29. Mushrooms (good)
30. Scum
31. Eggs Benedict
32. Turnips
33. Bacon double cheeseburgers
34. Rocks
35. Boogers
36. Squirrel
37. Rocky Mountain oysters
38. Carrots
39. Jerky
40. Apples
41. Bourbon balls
42. Mushrooms (bad)
43. Bananas
44. Corn
45. Rice
46. Oats
47. Wheat
48. Couscous
49. Polenta
50. Crab bisque
51. Chicken
52. Cow
53. Sheep
54. Pig
55. Frog
56. Carp
57. Clam dip
58. Microwave butter-flavored popcorn
59. Ice cream
60. Haggis
61. Rumaki
62. Kim chee
63. Balut
64. Fudge brownies
65. Coq au vin
66. Nutria
67. Beets
68. Chow chows
69. Meat-lovers stuffed-crust pizza
70. Cheese Danish
71. Kreplach
72. Dumplings
73. Matzoh
74. Gyoza

75. Garlic Parmesan croutons
76. Fritters
77. Jujyfruits
78. Sesame noodles
79. Pigs in a blanket
80. Chiccarones
81. Fresh Cook'd Potato Chips
82. Memphis barbecue
83. Cousin's Special
84. Almond windmill cookies
85. Thasos olives with red pepper flakes
86. Mashed potatoes with wasabi, caramelized onions, and roasted garlic
87. Fettucine carbonara
88. Thanksgiving dinner
89. Broiled oysters
90. Diana's Meat Pie at Hunan on Sansome in San Francisco
91. Mr. Beef's Italian Beef
92. Crawfish étouffée
93. Stilton cheese
94. Usinger's Bratwurst
95. Lobster Thermidor
96. PB&J
97. Philly cheese steaks
98. Horse
99. Tinfoil
100. Prunes

(Will Durst admits this list may get a little personal near the end.)

While you are giving an important speech, someone in the audience will ask, "Are you imagining us in our underwear?"

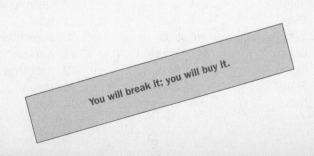

You will break it; you will buy it.

Representative Government:
A Correspondence

RICHARD BAUSCH

This e-mail correspondence was conducted in the winter of 2000 between the author and Senator John Warner (R., Va.).

Dear Senator Warner,

The impeachment of President Clinton is going to be remembered as the manner in which the radical right finally brought the Republican Party, the party of Lincoln, down. Nothing Clinton did or didn't do endangers the republic; this trial does. I urge you to seek an end to this madness, this nearly McCarthyesque vendetta by a group of zealots who seem willing to trample everything in order to accomplish their purpose—what Senator Bumpers called "wanting to win too badly."

Sincerely,
Richard Bausch

Dear Fellow Virginian:

It is important that you have provided me with your views concerning the impeachment of President Clinton. I share your deep concern, and I assure you that I am proceeding in a manner that aims to preserve the integrity of the United States Constitution and to provide fairness and due process to all involved parties. I am listening carefully to the views of the people of Virginia, and I commit to you that I will reach decisions based not on politics but rather on the best interests of the nation.

Sincerely,
John Warner
United States Senator

Dear Senator Warner,

Is it to be the contention of the party that ONLY Republicans are following the Constitution, and that the entire Democratic Party is trying to circumvent it? Americans are not the dupes some of your colleagues apparently think they are. The people, quite clearly, see this for what it is: a partisan attack on the presidency. It is very difficult to suppose that the lines of conflict would fall so sharply along party lines if EVERYBODY were voting his conscience. I believe you are. I very much admired your refusal to support the election of Oliver North a few years back. I believe you have the courage to stand against the kind of animus toward a man that may end up changing this government against the expressed will of the people.

Sincerely,
Richard Bausch

Dear Fellow Virginian:

It is important that you have provided me with your views concerning the impeachment of President Clinton. I share your deep concern, and I assure you that I am proceeding in a manner that aims to preserve the integrity of the United States Constitution and to provide fairness and due process to all involved parties. I am listening carefully to the views of the people of Virginia, and I commit to you that I will reach decisions based not on politics but rather on the best interests of the nation.

Sincerely,
John Warner
United States Senator

Dear Senator Warner,

I see from this answer that your writers have crafted a global response letter to be used in all cases. The letter THIS letter answers was the SECOND letter I sent, and was in response to THIS letter. So it is as though I am addressing one of those Chatty Cathy dolls, where you pull the string, and the same words come out, no matter what ELSE is said. In fact, I'm sure I'll get this same form letter in answer to THIS e-mail. I hope you are true to form.

Richard Bausch
(Fellow Virginian)

Dear Fellow Virginian:

It is important that you have provided me with your views concerning the impeachment of President Clinton. I share your deep concern, and I assure you that I am proceeding in a manner that aims to preserve the integrity of the United States Constitution and to provide fairness and due process to all involved parties. I am listening carefully to the views of the people of Virginia, and I commit to you that I will reach decisions based not on politics but rather on the best interests of the nation.

Sincerely,
John Warner
United States Senator

Dear Senator Warner,

This is so much fun, this very direct and concerned correspondence. Let me say here that I think walla walla and didda didda and booka booka poo. Also, I think you should doola doola obla obla dip de dip dip. And it seems to me that our country badda bing badda boom badda ling ling ling, and that even so your responses show such pesty in flamma lamma ding dong.

So in these times when democracy is at breakfast, asleep in the arms of the alimentary bood, that you are certainly bendicky to the concerns of your liperamma damma fizzle foodee dingle dangle dreb of our society, and the good thing is that ordinary citizens can actually get the pring that you have their fandaglee doodity in mind as you press forward with the concerns of government.

Sincerely,
Richard Bausch

Dear Fellow Virginian:

It is important that you have provided me with your views concerning the impeachment of President Clinton. I share your deep concern, and I assure you that I am proceeding in a manner that aims to preserve the integrity of the United States Constitution and to provide fairness and due process to all involved parties. I am listening carefully to the views of the people of Virginia, and I commit to you that I will reach decisions based not on politics but rather on the best interests of the nation.

Sincerely,
John Warner
United States Senator

Dear Senator Warner,

It really is time to call this off, since our relationship has moved to a state of such intimacy. When you say "Fellow Virginian," I know you mean so much more. I know this is more of your unusual reserve, your—how shall I put it?—sausage and eggs. I really am unable to continue, being married and a Catholic. So regretfully I say farewell. One concerned citizen to a clambake; one Virginian to a baked Alaska. I remain ever faithful, ever the liver and onions, my lover, my poppyseed, my darling.

With sweat socks and deep appreciation,
Richard Bausch

Dear Fellow Virginian:

It is important that you have provided me with your views concerning the impeachment of President Clinton. I share your deep concern, and I assure you that I am proceeding in a manner that aims to preserve the integrity of the United States Constitution and to provide fairness and due process to all involved parties. I am listening carefully to the views of the people of Virginia, and I commit to you that I will reach decisions based not on politics but rather on the best interests of the nation.

Sincerely,
John Warner
United States Senator

Dear Senator Warner,

May I request here, with all due respect and with full appreciation of our long-held affection for each other, that you stop harassing me with these letters. I have said that we must call this off, and I now again respectfully adjure you to cease. I am especially troubled by your persistence in using your little endearment for me— do you mean it ironically? I only let my closest friends and associates call me "Fellow Virginian," and would think that, since we are going our separate ways, you would know that I wish you to revert back to your old term for me, the one that used to amuse you so much—oh, remember? You'd say it and then laugh so hard: "voter," you'd say, and then guffaw guffaw. It used to make you so silly, that word. You'd laugh and laugh. Remember? And then I'd say "representative government," and you'd have to run to the bathroom.

But that is all past. We have to move on now. Oh, well, all right, once more for you, for old times' sake, I'll use our endearment in closing.

I remain, then, trusting you to adhere to my wishes, your little "voter," your "Fellow Virginian,"
Richard Bausch

Dear Fellow Virginian:

It is important that you have provided me with your views concerning the impeachment of President Clinton. I share your deep concern, and I assure you that I am proceeding in a manner that aims to preserve the integrity of the United States Constitution and to provide fairness and due process to all involved parties. I am listening carefully to the views of the people of Virginia, and I commit to you that I will reach decisions based not on politics but rather on the best interests of the nation.

Sincerely,
John Warner
United States Senator

Dear Sentor Warner,

My daddy is very busy, so could I please have a bicycle for Christmas?

Love,
Darlene

Dear Fellow Virginian:

It is important that you have provided me with your views concerning the impeachment of President Clinton. I share your deep concern, and I assure you that I am proceeding in a manner that aims to preserve the integrity of the United States Constitution and to provide fairness and due process to all involved parties. I am listening carefully to the views of the people of Virginia, and I commit to you that I will reach decisions based not on politics but rather on the best interests of the nation.

Sincerely,
John Warner
United States Senator

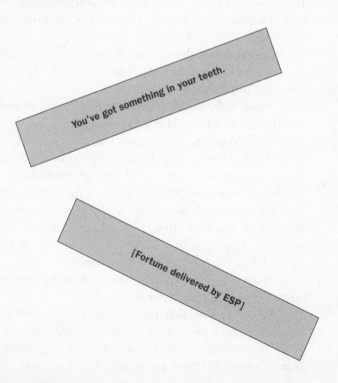

You've got something in your teeth.

[Fortune delivered by ESP]

Diva Checklist

ANDY BOROWITZ

*Posted backstage at VH1's "Divas 2000: A Tribute to Diana Ross,"
with Mariah Carey, Donna Summer, and Faith Hill*

1. Miss Ross requests that she be addressed at all times as "Miss Ross."
2. In the event that crew members forget to address Miss Ross as "Miss Ross," Miss Ross requests that she be addressed as "Your Serene Highness, Queen of the Universe."
3. Miss Ross requests that she not be spoken to, touched by, or sung along with by Mariah Carey, Donna Summer, or Faith Hill.
4. Miss Ross requests that somebody explain to her exactly who this Faith Hill person is again.
5. Miss Ross requests that video trickery be used to make Mariah Carey's legs look forty percent shorter.
6. Miss Ross requests that, in her onstage introduction, her performance as Dorothy in *The Wiz* be referred to as both "critically acclaimed" and "Oscar-winning."
7. Miss Ross requests that the audience greet Ms. Summer's singing with a derisive chant of "Na na na na, na na na na, hey hey hey, good-bye."
8. Miss Ross requests that the other divas be served meals consisting entirely of Hot Pockets.
9. Miss Ross requests that the onstage introduction of Ms. Carey make prominent use of the word "ho."
10. Miss Ross requests that no reference be made, onstage or off, to the existence of other Supremes.

The Inaugural Address of President George W. Bush

ANDY BOROWITZ

Bush . . . has confused Slovenia and Slovakia, called Kosovars "Kosovarians" and called East Timorese "East Timorians."

—*Salon,* September 28, 1999

My fellow Americanians:

Over the past two years, I had the special privilege of travelling this great land of ours. I shook hands with Kansanians and South Dakeutians, picked potatoes with Idahovians, and ate barbecued po'boys with Alabamaniacs.

I met the young and the old, the rich and the poor, Jewstaceans and Gentillia. I met Hawaiiticians, Alaskalopians, and Puerto Ricordians.

And, everywhere I went, the Americanian people sent the same message, loud and clear: the era of big governmentariantudinism is over.

My friends, as we begin a new millenniarium let us pledge to defend freedom everywhere, from the Montezumian halls to the Tripolistic shores.

Let us send the message of freedom to all the peoples of the world: not just the Kosovarian and the East Timorian, not just the Slovakian and/or the Slovenian, but the Perugian, the Brazilliantine, the Russianomatic, and the Chineezish.

Let us work together in Washingtopolis, both Democresiacs and Republicateers. Let us recognize the issues that unite us, and stop using the labels that divide us, like "conservaticious" and "librarian."

It is time to recognize that we are all Americanians, whether we be Caucastic, Africanoodian, Asiadontic, or Hispanicky. Together, as one, we can make this country a better place—not just for us, not just for our children, but for geraniums to come.

God bless each and every one of you. And God bless Americanistan.

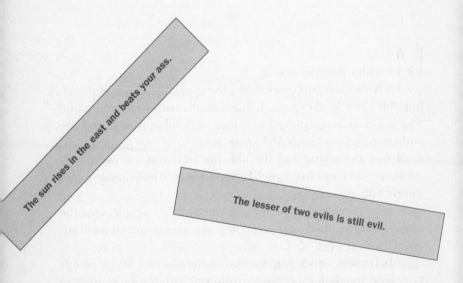

Election 2000

ANDY BOROWITZ

With a Bush and a Dole already in the race, it was only a matter of time before someone decided to roll the dice and see if the Dukakis name still had its magic. Newly announced candidate Olympia Dukakis has been crisscrossing Iowa spreading her gospel of Liberalism Without Being Too Liberal, and pledging that, if elected, she will stop playing annoyingly eccentric aunt roles.

Campaign experts believe that Dukakis may be riding high in the early polls because she has the same last name as 1988 Democratic nominee Michael Dukakis, but warn that those numbers could sink later on when people remember who Michael Dukakis actually is.

The name-recognition factor may have jump-started the Dukakis campaign, but it has not scared away another formidable candidate: George Clinton, the leader of the nineteen-seventies band Parliament/Funkadelic, who currently sits atop several surveys of likely Iowa voters. Clinton believes that his message of Conservatism the Way You Like It, Baby, is catching on with voters, and denies that his poll ratings are in any way tied to the fortunes of President Clinton, to whom he is not related.

"George has his own body of work," said Clinton campaign spokesperson Sandy Grunwald. "Look at 'Atomic Dog.' Look at

'Cosmic Slop.' I think the American people would be hard-pressed to elect a President funkier than George."

Already deluged with appeals from Clinton and Dukakis, Iowans were not prepared for the introduction of yet another aspirant to the race: Merchant-Ivory regular Helena Bonham Carter. Ms. Bonham Carter, of course, is not related to former President Jimmy Carter, and claims not to have heard of him, but the confusion alone has given her a considerable bounce in the polls.

The acclaimed actress, whose political philosophy is called Centrism with a Wee Touch of Fascism, brushed aside criticism that she has no right to run for President since she is not an American citizen. "Blimey," she said. "I'm not going to get my knickers in a twist over that, you wanker."

Which candidate will Iowa choose? All bets may be off with the expected announcement this week of a new candidate: Torrance Ford, a car dealership in Southern California. While not technically a relative of former President Gerald Ford, nor technically a human being, Torrance Ford has successfully advanced a political philosophy called Moderation with Cash Back at Inception, which calls for no money down and a 3.9 percent A.P.R., especially popular with suburban soccer moms.

Emily Dickinson, Jerk of Amherst

ANDY BOROWITZ

It was with great reluctance that I decided to write about my 30-year friendship with Emily Dickinson. To many who would read my book, Miss Dickinson was a cherished literary icon, and any attempt to describe her in human terms would, understandably, be resented. And yet by not writing this book I would be depriving her most ardent admirers of meeting the Emily Dickinson I was privileged to know: more than a mentor, she was my anchor, my compass, my lighthouse.

Except when she was drunk. At those times, usually beginning at the stroke of noon, she became a gluttonous, vituperative harpy who would cut you for your last Buffalo wing. Once she got hold of her favorite beverage, Olde English malt liquor, the "belle of Amherst" would, as she liked to put it, "get polluted 'til [she] booted." This Emily Dickinson would think nothing of spitting chewing tobacco in a protégé's face, blithely explaining that she was "working on [her] aim."

Who, then, was the real Emily Dickinson? Daughter of New England in chaste service to her poetry, or backstabbing gorgon who doctored your bowling score when you went to get more nachos? By exploring this question, I decided, I had a chance not only to learn about Miss Dickinson but also to learn about myself, and to learn even more about myself if the book went into paperback.

When I first met Miss Dickinson, I was a literary greenhorn with a handful of unfinished poems, struggling to find my voice and something that rhymed with "Nantucket." Believing that she would be more likely to take me under her wing if I appeared to be an ingénue, I entered her lace-curtained parlor in Amherst dressed as a Cub Scout. But she took no note of my attire as she read over that day's work: "Parting is all we know of heaven,/And all we need of hell." Putting down her quill, she brushed the bonnet-crowned curls from her forehead. "Well, it beats stealing cars!" she croaked in a husky baritone.

Declaring that "quittin' time is spittin' time," she reached into her sewing box for a pouch of her favorite "chaw," as she called it, and pulled a "tall and foamy" out of the icebox. She generously agreed to look over my poems, pork rinds spilling from her mouth as she read. Finally, she anointed my efforts with words of encouragement that would sustain me throughout my early career: "You're a poet and you don't know it. Your feet show it. They're long fellows. Now I gotta hit the head."

Years passed before I saw another, less merry, aspect of Miss Dickinson's character, at a book party for Ralph Waldo Emerson. Miss Dickinson was experiencing a trough in her career; she had been reduced to writing advertising copy, most notably, "Nothing is better for thee / Than me," for Quaker Oats. At the party, Miss Dickinson sat alone at the bar, doing tequila shooters and riffing moribund, angry couplets that often did not scan. I sensed that it was time to take her home.

In the parking lot, she stopped abruptly near Emerson's car. "Let's key it," she said, her eyes dancing maniacally. I assumed that this was just "Emily being Emily," and tried to laugh it off. "Don't be such a wuss," she said, scratching "Waldo sucks" into the passenger door. I gently upbraided Miss Dickinson for her actions, which only served to inflame her: "Emerson's trying to steal my juice, baby. It took me years to get where I am, understand what I'm saying? I used to run three-card monte on the streets of Newton. And I ain't goin' back!" At this moment, I found myself confronted with a possibility that I had never wanted to consider in all our years of friendship: Emily Dickinson was a real jerk.

Some years later, Boston University asked me to moderate a panel including Miss Dickinson, William Dean Howells, and the author, long since forgotten, of the verse "Finders, keepers/Losers, weepers." I was by this time a successful poet in my own right, having become renowned for my series of "Happiness Is . . ." gift books and pillows. Seated next to Miss Dickinson, I attempted to mend the breach that had developed in our relationship; I went on at some length about my debt to her work. She took a sip of water, cleared her throat, and replied, "Bite me, you self-aggrandizing weasel."

The last time I saw Emily Dickinson, she said she didn't have time to speak, as she was on her way to the greyhound races in Taunton. But I could not let her go without asking what had happened to our friendship. Her eyes downcast, she said, simply, "You've got ketchup on your tie." Quizzically, I lowered my head and took a right uppercut to the jaw. As I crumpled to the pavement, Miss Dickinson unleashed a profane tirade, along with a pistol-whipping that was startling for both its vigor and its efficiency.

As I review this last memory, it occurs to me that some readers might conclude that I am trying to cast Emily Dickinson in a negative light. Nothing could be further from my intentions. In fact, when I regained consciousness I realized that Miss Dickinson, in her tirade, had given me a final, precious gift. True, I no longer had my wallet, but I had, at long last, a separate identity, a voice. And, perhaps most valuable of all, a rhyme for "Nantucket."

Istanbul

Istanbul, the largest city in Turkey, was once known as Constantinople; before that it was ancient Byzantium. Most cities get along fine with one name, but the bright and talented actress, Barbara Hershey—not, of course, a metropolitan area—was formerly known as Barbara Seagull, when the spirit of that bird passed into her body. It was the sixties. Before that, she was Barbara Hershey, creating a pleasing feeling of symmetry. Under its various names, Istanbul has been the capital of the Byzantine Empire, of the Ottoman Empire, and, until 1923, of the Turkish Republic. Barbara Hershey was very good in those Woody Allen movies. Istanbul was in that James Bond movie where he takes the Orient Express, back before Sean Connery ever thought he'd wear a hairpiece. (I think it was *From Russia, with Love.*)

The name Byzantium may derive from that of Byzas, who, according to legend, was leader of the Greeks from the city of Megara who captured the peninsula from pastoral Thracian tribes and built the city about 657 B.C. Hershey, Pennsylvania was named for the popular candy bar and not the attractive actress. In A.D. 196, having razed the town (Byzantium) for opposing him in a civil war, the Roman emperor Septimius Severus rebuilt it, naming it Augusta Antonina in honor of his son. (Although in our time, a boy named "Augusta" or "Antonia" would probably have it tough in high school, even in Hershey, Pennsylvania.) In A.D. 330, when Constantine the Great dedicated the city as his capital, he called it New Rome. The coins, nevertheless, continued to be stamped Byzantium until he ordered the substitution of Constantinopolis. Sometimes you just have to spell things out for people in no uncertain terms. In the thirteenth century Arabs used the appellation Istinpolin, a "name" they heard Byzantines use—*eis ten polin*—which actually was Greek for "in the city." Transformed over the centuries, this name became Istanbul. Similar mishearings occur to this day with the lyrics to rock songs—Excuse me while I kiss this guy!—but, perhaps like Barbara Hershey in the sixties, there may be drugs (and candy bars) involved.

—Randy Cohen

I Was Alan Greenspan's Roadie

TIM CARVELL

Hello, Detroit!"

Technically, it was the Palace of Auburn Hills, but no one corrected him. No one ever did. For he was Alan Greenspan, he was on tour, and 22,000 eager fans had paid up to $125 apiece to see him, not including the Ticketmaster surcharge. They roared their approval as one. They'd been patient through the opening acts—Alice Rivlin and her trained dogs, Kid Rock, Cokie Roberts' amusing anecdotes from *This Week* (her David Brinkley impersonation was uncanny)—but now, the place just went fucking nuts.

Alan let them go on a little while, then finally spoke: "I hope there isn't any irrational exuberance going on!" That, of course, just set them off again. Looking closely at Alan from the wings, I could see him slump a little. It was clear that, ten cities into a twelve-city tour, the grind was getting to be a bit much. What's more, this wasn't even the tour he'd envisioned: He'd wanted to devote this one to acoustic performances, in smaller venues. But the promoters had come to him and patiently explained that he could make much, much more money with another swing through the big showplaces. They calculated the work-to-revenue ratios for everyone involved; they showed him bar graphs that tallied up the difference. The promoters knew their man: Alan had always been a sucker for bar graphs. He sighed, smiled wanly, and announced that he'd do the arena tour. "It seems like the more prudent course," he said, trying to convince himself as much as anyone else.

Prudent it may have been, but at this point, I couldn't help but wonder if it had been worth it. Not that I had much time to ponder the question: I had to set off the flash pots. They went off, and while the audience was distracted by the light and smoke, the other roadies quickly lifted the scrim that had hidden the conference-room set; it was all done so seamlessly that it looked like the set had materialized out of thin air.

It's funny: The conference-room scene was more or less the same as it had been during the past three tours, but the crowd still loved it. Essentially, it consisted of the Fed governors trying to persuade Alan to raise rates, and him gallantly fighting them off. The governors took turns being the heavy in this scene, so as not to prejudice the public against any one of them. We learned our lesson on the '97 tour, when Ed Kelly played the bad guy, night after night; by the end of it, his family was receiving death threats. Tonight, it was Ed Gramlich's turn; Gramlich was always my favorite, the most natural actor of the bunch. "Mr. Greenspan," he said in his big moment, "we simply cannot afford to play dice with the nation's economy."

"Well, Ed," Greenspan replied, "I've always been a bit of a riverboat gambler."

It wasn't even an especially snappy comeback, but the audience always roared at the line. Then they started the chanting, sort of a low rumble, sounding like an enormous collective "Moo." Obviously, they were trying to replicate the "Bruuuuuuuce" familiar to Springsteen concertgoers, but it was apparent that the crowd was split between "Aaaaaalllaaaaaaan" and "Greeeeeeeeenspaaaaaaaaan," with a few diehards going with "Buuuuuuuuuck," Greenspan's lesser-known Phi Psi nickname.

Anyway, the diverging chants blended together and didn't make much sense, but it was the spirit of it that mattered, I supposed.

Surveying the crowd, I could see that it was much the same as always: A thick clot of pinstriped bankers and fund managers near the stage, and, in the distance, individual investors in the cheaper seats. I once pointed out to Alan that it seemed unfair that the small investors, who'd been responsible for much of his popularity, weren't closer to the stage; I even suggested that we bring a couple of folks from the nosebleed sections and put them in the front row, the way Springsteen does. He fixed me with that stern but patient look of his and said, "It's a free market economy." I felt like a fool.

The rest of the evening went according to plan—the conference room scene giving way to a set consisting of a table and a glass of water, as Greenspan defended his policies to the Joint Economic Committee. When he got to the big money line— "Betting against markets is usually precarious, at best"—a few fund managers threw their underpants onto the stage. The underpants-tossing had begun as a joke a few years back, at a show in Dallas, but it had now become a nightly ritual, one that always discomfited Alan. Then came the medley of Alan's best-known speeches, with the other governors each getting a solo of their own finest moments.

Then Alan announced that he was going to "slow things down a bit," pulled out his guitar, and began the four-song set that he'd insisted he be allowed to do every night; tonight, he did "Kentucky Rain," "Always on My Mind," "Daydream Believer," and—a surprise fourth choice—Warren Zevon's "Accidentally Like a Martyr." The crowd got restless during the singing—they always did—but I sensed that it was the one part of the show that Alan actually looked forward to, and he didn't really give a rat's ass whether the crowd enjoyed it or not. That was Alan.

After that, there came a bit of padding—a performance from Cirque du Soleil, with Alan giving some witty patter about how this acrobat represents interest rates, while that one represents housing starts, etc.—and then the big finale, when Alan took questions from the audience. The first question, as always, was "So, are you going to raise rates?", to which Alan gave the exact same answer he always did: "Yes." (Pause, wait for gasp.) "Oh, I'm sorry, did you ask about raising rates? I thought you asked if I like Yeats." Again, not a great line, but the audience howled.

Then came the usual three or four or five additional attempts to weasel the information out of him—"Should I be buying stocks right now?"; "What would you invest in these days, cyclical or noncyclical stocks?" and so on, followed by a few softballs on the Latin American economy and, this time, a Detroit-specific question about the auto industry. Then, as always, they started asking the weird stuff—"What do you eat for breakfast?"; "How's Andrea doing?"; "Can I kiss you?"—before Alan finally thanked them for their time and waved good night. After standing in the wings for about two minutes of applause, he straightened his jacket, smoothed down his tie, and came back for the encore—where he did the usual, a magic trick in which he appeared to levitate his "surprise" special guest Robert Rubin.

Then, finally, Alan was hustled out the back door before the applause even ended. The crowd milled around for a little while, hoping he'd come back for another encore, or maybe they'd catch a glimpse of him grabbing a favorite towel off the stage. And then, the part of the job I liked the best: I cleared my throat, picked up the microphone and spoke into the P.A. system.

"Ladies and gentlemen," I announced. "The Fed chairman had left the building."

Not very original, I realize, but Alan liked sticking to the script, and who was I to argue? I was a mere roadie, and I would have followed him anywhere.

The Talent Competition

TIM CARVELL

The talent portion of the Miss America pageant got off to a rousing start last night, when Miss Alabama annexed the Sudetenland. The applause was deafening.

Her turn was followed by Miss Alaska's bravura performance as Jake LaMotta in her stage adaptation of *Raging Bull*, supported by Miss North Dakota as Vicky and Miss South Dakota as Joey. The judges, impressed, granted Miss Alaska a perfect score, which nearly compensated for the fact that, in gaining 40 pounds for the role, she had pretty much ceded the swimsuit competition.

Miss Arizona, who was premed at her junior college, then removed Miss Arkansas' kidney, using her bare hands. For her part, Miss Arkansas attempted to survive despite the removal of said kidney. She received a warm ovation.

In an unusual departure from form, Miss California gave birth to a litter of beagles, which Miss Colorado then suckled. Miss Connecticut—whose platform is the need to have pets spayed or neutered—then euthanized the pups, amid general outcry.

Miss Delaware—as have all Miss Delawares before her—pointed out the state of Delaware on a map. Miss District of Columbia granted Miss Puerto Rico statehood, amid much crying and hugging.

Ever topical, Miss Florida reenacted Section II, portions (B) through (E) of the Starr Report to Congress, leaving several of the judges impressed and visibly flushed.

Miss Georgia recited "The Love Song of J. Alfred Prufrock," then dared to eat a peach.

Miss Hawaii presented her cure for polio. Upon being informed that polio had already been cured, she burst into tears.

In a feat both impressive and stultifying, Miss Idaho sat alone onstage for three hours and took the SAT, as the audience fidgeted. Later in the evening, it was announced that she had received 690 in the verbal portion, and 730 in the math, to scattered applause.

Miss Maine made a mockery of the Holocaust, and received seven Academy Award nominations.

Miss Maryland got her groove back.

Miss Michigan—who was accompanied by an identically attired midget, representing, she said, "my state's Upper Peninsula"—assisted an elderly woman's suicide, although it was later disclosed that the woman was in perfect health, and had not requested the service.

Miss Minnesota blamed Ted Hughes for everything.

Miss Missouri, with the help of Miss Montana and Miss New York, reenacted the assassination of Archduke Ferdinand. (Miss Montana's performance as the carriage received particularly high marks.)

In the competition's most dramatic moment, Miss Iowa attempted to escape from handcuffs and a straitjacket while chained underwater. She failed, and was awarded the Miss Congeniality title.

Miss New Hampshire built a life-size replica of herself out of suet. Miss New Jersey ate said replica.

Miss New Mexico told the old chestnut about the priest,

the rabbi, the minister, and the syphilitic prostitute, which is not fit to be shared in mixed company, but which, rest assured, brought down the house.

Miss Ohio devised a fair and equitable partition of Bosnia, while Miss Oklahoma blew saliva bubbles until she was forced to stop.

As the competition entered its sixth hour, Miss Pennsylvania, who is Amish, churned butter, and Miss Rhode Island hit 62 home runs in a row. In rapid succession, Miss South Carolina disclosed which of her fellow contestants had "had work done," and where; Miss Utah ate five pounds of raw veal in under five minutes; Miss Vermont bought Dell when it was at 12½.

Through a prior arrangement with the New Jersey courts, Miss Louisiana, Miss Indiana, Miss Kansas, Miss Texas, Miss Nebraska, Miss Nevada, Miss Washington, Miss Tennessee, Miss Mississippi, Miss Iowa, Miss North Carolina, and Miss Oregon comprised the jury for a capital murder case. They voted for conviction, and the death penalty.

Later, with the help of a group of students from Northwestern, Miss Illinois proved the executed man's innocence. Muted applause ensued.

Lending a brief moment of levity to the proceedings, Miss Virginia impersonated Miss West Virginia. And vice versa.

And finally, Miss Wyoming sprouted pink furry wings, and flew around the arena. The other contestants quickly followed suit, creating a thunderous noise as they flapped away and shed their sashes, which fell like streamers upon the amazed audience. They were last seen above the Atlantic Ocean, flying in formation, slowly receding into the sunset, until they disappeared entirely.

My Week As a Nielsen Family: A Memoir

TIM CARVELL

Some kids want to be an astronaut or a fireman when they grow up. Not me. I always wanted to be part of a Nielsen family. I imagined Nielsen families as clean-scrubbed. With Mom in pearls, Dad with pipe and cardigan, and two adorable little kids named Junior and Sis. Their last name was Nielsen. And their mission in life was to watch TV and decide what the rest of us got to watch. It seemed like the best job on Earth.

As I grew older, that dream faded. But it all came back last October when a postcard arrived in my mailbox: "It is my pleasure to tell you that your household has been chosen to be a Nielsen family." I did a dance of joy. The card, however, attempted to whip me into even more of a frenzy: "In a few days," it continued, "you will receive a long-distance phone call from us to explain this exciting opportunity." I loved that adjective "long-distance," placed there, it seemed, as a further enticement. It was as if I were living in the 1950s. (Ma! Pa! Stay off the phone! I'm gonna get a long-distance phone call!)

The phone call, oddly, never came, but I did eventually receive a Nielsen diary and a dollar bill, in payment for my services. The diary itself was a flimsy, stapled set of pages. It was made up almost entirely of a grid, which I had to fill out to denote times when my TV was off, times when it was on, and what I was watching at 15-minute intervals. This was beginning to look suspiciously like work. The diary also asked questions like "If you watched no TV at all this week, please check a reason: ( ) went on vacation; or ( ) TV was broken." The notion that I might have a rich social life, filled with other leisure activities, was effectively ruled out as a possibility. I mean, I don't. But it would have been nice for them to pretend.

Nonetheless. I began filling out my diary with a sense of purpose: I had been summoned to TV jury duty. But I soon realized that the task before me was impossible: I don't watch TV in 15-minute increments. Most shows are lucky if they get more than ten seconds. I don't like to watch specific programs: I just like to watch television. Pretty soon I'd had enough. I decided I wasn't under oath and certainly wasn't being paid enough for the amount of work Nielsen was expecting of me. I became a rogue Nielsen home.

It started when I looked at the top of the page, where I had neatly written my name under "Male head of household." But that looked so lonely next to "Female head of household." So I wrote in "Gladys." Gladys, I decided, likes the sight of blood. During commercial breaks I started hunting through TV listings for shows she might want to watch, and within minutes, she had taken in an NHL game and a documentary on sharks on the Discovery Channel.

Once Gladys was sated, I realized that there was nothing keeping me from having the Nielsen family of my dreams. I inked "Junior" and "Sis" into two of the slots. Junior, I figured, watched cartoons in the afternoon when he came home from school, while Sis liked the morning talk shows. And we all watched the *Today* show religiously, because we like that nice Katie Couric. During commercials, I filled out the diary's questions about my income, favorite shows, and so on. I happened

on a box for my family's ethnic group, and with a flick of the
pen, we were all suddenly Eskimos.

For the rest of the week, my Eskimo family and I watched
TV together—cozy, I imagined, in our whale skins, eyes glued
to the set as we gnawed on seal. Soon their tastes emerged: Sis
preferred Rosie O'Donnell to Roseanne, while Junior surprised
me by having a deep and abiding affection for anything on
UPN. On Monday night, PBS telecast a special performance of
Andrew Lloyd Webber's *Cats*, and in a brief fit of sadism, I
forced the whole family to watch it.

Around this time I began wondering about the effects my
family's choices would have on other viewers: Would *Friends*
add an Eskimo on my account? Would Katie Couric get another
pay raise? Nielsen had supplied a toll-free phone number to call
with questions, so I dialed it up (long distance!), and reached a
very nice lady who told me that the company mails surveys to
1.5 million homes. Given that the whole TV audience is something like 100 million homes, my family represented only something like 67 homes. I was disappointed: I had hoped to be the
TV equivalent of the electoral college, standing in for whole
states. I pressed on.

"Hey, would you be able to tell if I were to make stuff up?"

"Yes, we can usually tell if it's not correct," she said, adding
darkly. "You wouldn't consider doing that, would you?"

"Me? No. No, of course not."

"Good."

Now I was beginning to feel guilty. But not too guilty to keep
from having the whole family watch a rerun of *The Rockford Files*.

I knew, though, that our time together was drawing to an
end. That night I treated Gladys to a final game of hockey. I filled
out the portion of the diary that asked for "Any thoughts you
may have on TV." ("Scented television might be nice.") And then
I sealed my family into their postage-paid wrapper and mailed
them off to the Nielsen company. I'm going to miss them.

TEAS AND/OR PSYCHEDELICS I'M INVENTING

Precious Bacon
Cy Twombly
Calamari Soother
Office Crackpot
Mint & Dolphin Steamer
Liquid Apology
Milwaukee Bed Pan
David Hyde Pierce
Fried Onion Dilemma
Racquetball Almond
Vanilla Shot-Callin' Cracker-Ass Goodness
Plaque de Menthe
Boiling Anger
Passive-Aggressive Pleaser
Yannick Noah Aroma
Nightstalker Fogg
Zubaz Juice
Trig Teacher's Breakroom
Simpering Copy Editor
Uncle Gary's Anti–D.T.s Blend
Elderly Bathwater
Burbling Furnace Scrapings
Mountain Goat Pen

Premium Gift Teas for Which
I'm Offering Consulting Services

Forgiveness by Steak-Umm Corp.
My Chance by State Farm Insurance
Marmalade Tears by Denny's
Zoloft Oolong by Max Azria BCBG

—Jeff Johnson

The Self-Help Hot Line

CARINA CHOCANO

Hello! And thank you for calling the Feng Shui for the Cluttered Soul hot line. To ensure the quality of our service, this conversation and others you may have had in the past may be monitored and recorded.

For automated past-life regression, press 1. To rearrange your chakras, press 2. To reupholster your chakras, press 3. To contact your inner mover, press 4. *Para Español, oprima el cinco.*

Thank you. Please hold.

[Soothing wind chimes]

You have selected automated past-life regression. To confirm your selection, press 1. To feel at peace with your selection, press 2. To affirm that your selection is beautiful and loved, press 3. To let go of the emotional barriers that prevent you from accepting your selection, press 4. To stop the cycle of blaming your selection, press 5. To remove the toxic voices in your head that say your selection was really, really, stupid, press 6.

Thank you. Please hold.

[Soothing wind chimes]

You have confirmed your selection. To go the extra mile and

cherish your selection, press 1. To celebrate your selection, press 2. To learn to love your selection the way babies love, press 3. To clear your emotional body of toxic selections and make room for your new selection, press 4.

Thank you. Please hold.

[Soothing wind chimes]

For spirit attachment, spirit releasement, and soul-mind fragment retrieval, please enter your sixteen-digit Visa or MasterCard number and four-digit expiration date to receive a copy of our video, "Spirit Attachment, Spirit Releasement, and Soul-Mind Fragment Retrieval." Please allow six weeks for delivery.

To hear more about how Feng Shui can help you successfully rearrange your past lives in order to increase the positive flow of chi to your present life, press the pound key.

Thank you. Please hold.

[A bamboo flute]

The following menu contains useful information on how the ancient art of Feng Shui can help you successfully rearrange your past lives in order to increase the positive flow of chi to your present life. Please listen to all of the following options before making your selection.

To discover your present-life purpose by understanding past-life sofa placement, press 1. To recover past-life memories of north-facing ottomans, press 2.

You have selected to recover past-life memories of north-facing ottomans. You were specifically asked to listen to all of the following options before making your selection.

To discover your present-life purpose by understanding past-life sofa placement, press 1. To recover past life memories of north-facing ottomans, press 2. To discover the causes of fear, guilt, anger, and phobias under ill-placed foyer shrubs, press 3. To find out how past-life memories of sink-adjacent refrigerators may be affecting your health, press 4. To understand the role your past-life headboard played in the choice of your parents, press 5. To hear these options again, press 6. To hear a service representative celebrate your specialness, press the pound key.

You have selected violence. Slamming the phone against the wall does not constitute a valid selection.

To acknowledge your anger, press 1. To find healthy ways to vent your anger, press 2. To find alternative outlets for the pressure that builds up in your head, press 3. To play the blame game, press 4. To speak to an owner-representative, hang up and call back when you are ready to lose the unhealthy attitude and get moving on a positive life cycle.

Thank you for calling the Feng Shui for the Cluttered Soul hot line.

Om.

You will have one of those days for a year.

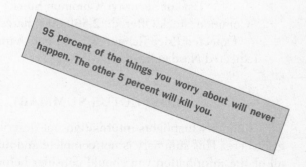

95 percent of the things you worry about will never happen. The other 5 percent will kill you.

My Own Private I.P.O.

CARINA CHOCANO

Carina Chocano (henceforth "The Company"), a California corporation, is pleased to announce she's going public. The Company is offering for sale ("Sale"), pursuant to this announcement, up to 2,500,000 shares at a price of U.S. $8 ("Cheap"). The offering is being underwritten by Morgan, Fairchild & Co. and Sayonara Securities.

The Issuer:	Carina Chocano
Type of Security:	Common Stock
Common Stock Offered:	2,500,000 shares
Expected Price Range:	U.S. $5 per share (OBO)
Expected Nasdaq Symbol:	MEME

PROSPECTUS SUMMARY

This summary highlights information not described more fully elsewhere. This summary is not complete and may not contain all of the information you should consider before investing in our common stock. Prospective investors should carefully consider then disregard the matters set forth in the section of this prospectus entitled "Risk Factors." This prospectus contains forward-looking statements based on our current expectations, assumptions, estimates, projections, fondest wishes, wildest dreams, psychic readings, and fraudulent intentions. These forward-looking statements involve risks and uncertainties like you would not believe. Our actual results could differ materially from those anticipated in these forward-looking statements as a result of certain factors, as well as others which are none of your ("Your") business.

PROSPECTUS

Our Business

Carina Chocano (henceforth "The Company") is a private concern focused on the manufacture and dissemination of her own unmerited celebrity and nonspecific notoriety. The Company is uniquely positioned to become a premier e-provider of Carina Chocano–related products and services, including, but not limited to: concepts; works in progress; inconsequential notions; self-involved monologues; lengthy, circuitous anecdotes; drunken proselytizing; and unsolicited, unwelcome advice. The Company does not otherwise produce salable goods or services of any kind, including, but not limited to: legal counsel; mole removal; shoe repair; or the delivery of fancy fruit, regular fruit, or hot lobster dinners.

Our Strategy

The Company's strategy is to call undue and unwarranted attention to itself through use of a premier network of authorized and unauthorized websites, cameo appearances, magazine interviews, docudramas, product endorsements, record contracts, multiple marriages, lucrative divorces, flagrant drug addictions, soft-focus workout videos, and other shameless displays that will appeal to users with high-value demographics, surplus time, and little contact with reality.

Our Market

The dramatic increase in Internet use provides a tremendous opportunity for online advertising, electronic commerce, and narcissists. We believe the scope of our intended éclat ("The Product") and the high-value demographics of our user base ("The Marks") offer a unique opportunity to adequately simulate a mutually beneficial arrangement wherein The Marks receive valuable unspecified goods and vaguely defined services in exchange for cash.

Risk Factors

1. Carina Chocano currently has a very limited user base, consisting at the present time of the issuer herself and, infrequently, her mother. While this situation is normal for a company in the prepublic stage, significant expansion must take place in order to attract advertisers and sponsors, generate additional revenue, and allow the issuer to purchase a 10-acre island outside the jurisdiction of the Securities and Exchange Commission's Fraud Division. The Company must increase its user base to attract advertisers and sponsors and to generate additional revenue. Failure to attract advertisers and sponsors could result in The Company's falling short of its goal of stratospheric fame, rendering The Company merely critically acclaimed, and therefore insolvent.

2. Failure to increase the size of our user base may result in an inability to generate additional revenue, which could leave us unable to maintain or grow our business. To increase our user base, we must:

    - expand our network of sycophantic hangers-on, including but not restricted to yes-men, brown-nosers, fluffers, and paparazzi

    - endorse a cause

- endorse a shoe

- endorse a check

If we do not achieve these objectives, our business could be severely harmed.

3. Valuation of The Company's stock is based on uncertain market, industry, and other conditions, including per capita bullshit consumption in our target geographical areas; it is subject to seasonal and cyclical fluctuations due to financial, environmental, hormonal, and bipolar mood swings.

4. We may be held liable for content on our websites. Despite the fact that we are completely uninformed, uninsured, and given to making knowingly false, defamatory, and malicious statements, we will be making frequent pronouncements on subjects including but not limited to the following: foreign and domestic policy; scientific advancements in the treatment of fatal diseases; high-end exercise equipment; skin care and how to have better orgasms in just two weeks. As a result, we face potential liability for libel; slander; negligence; ignorance, copyright, patent, or trademark infringement, and other claims based on the nature and content of the material that is published or distributed on our network of websites. This could severely harm our business and result in severe financial judgments.*

---

*By then The Company will have decamped with the proceeds, however, and this will no longer be our problem.

Do Svidannya, Baby!

CARINA CHOCANO

Oscar-winning *Titanic* director James Cameron is planning a stay on board the Russian space station *Mir* beginning next summer. U.S. businessman Dennis Tito already is planning a trip to *Mir,* and Hollywood producer Mark Burnett has a deal to create a *Survivor*-type series in which the winner would fly to *Mir*.

—*New York Post*

A Russian official said today that a committee of Russian designers had recommended ditching the aging *Mir* space station in the Pacific Ocean.

—*New York Times*

MOSCOW, JULY 5, 2001

Of course, we are regretting for the gruesome tragedy. We still cannot be believing it. Yet, it was wonderful dog and donkey show while it was lasting.

Mr. Cameron was being an uppermost film director and he will not be around anymore with much bereavement. To him we are saying, "Do svidannya, baby!" and "You are King of the Whales!"

Moneymaker Mr. Tito was also top breed of human, and the $20 million he is giving us to Russian space program will not be being spent all in one place, we are guaranteed. We are sorry his holiday was ending abruptly in a ball of flames.

We are also having the blues for nice game show contestant who was being crushed by falling debris behind security hatch number three. This was not topmost prize as was expected by him. For us, yet, he will always be the "Survivor" even when deceasing.

We cannot restate plenty our regretting of this unfortunate mishap. Number One capitalists who are wanting to bestow time and rubles to Russian space program in future are being told by us do not be afraid! One big boo-boo is not meaning two!

But we are not dwelling on flaming fireball as we are having too many fond memories of Hollywood twinkling and Fortune 50 fun aboard research vessel that is rust and too often smelling like vomit and urine. We are not being worthy!

Happy remembrances are involving Mr. Cameron who is later teasing that he would be preferring to be jettisoned into space orbit aboard set of *Alien* without a paddle. We are thinking he is a laugh rally. We are even joking that we are desiring Kate Winslet to come in his place, and if not, then at least Winona Ryder, because his breasts are leaving something to be fancied! And he is not taking it wrong way! Mr. Cameron was being a top-notch Hollywood cheeseball, but deep inside he is just a regular Boris. We are feeling the pain of his four widows and his agent in this time of losing.

Mr. Tito—who was being no relation to former Yugoslav apparatchik (ha, ha, as if being!)—was telling us often about how he is owning many luxury vehicles with leather interior and stereophonic sounds. We know he is stooping to visit crummy space station, so we are not minding when he is asking for room service and massage. He is wanting his dollars worth, after everything. Now he is being big tipper in the sky! God bless!

Confessional: At first, we are thinking, "Okay, before we were being pride-filled Soviet space station manned by utmost cosmonauts, and now we are being willy-nilly theme park for imperialist swine. No biggie!" We also are sometimes thinking that Mr. Cameron and Mr. Tito have oversized boastfulness and that *Mir* ain't not big enough for the couple of them. One time, they are telling game show contestant that one million dollars is only walnuts and is not making him a millionaire. This is making game show contestant cry, and we are telling him in Moscow, he is getting all the girls because they are hungry.

Explanation: We are telling this because so many persons are interrogating why we are leaving three rich Americans on space station that is going south. Coincidation? We are thinking yes. We are wanting to make crinkly clear there was no hanky-panky in the control room. We are only letting Mr. Cameron take charge because he is telling us he is number one helmer in Hollywood and Paul Verhoeven cannot lick his shorts. So we are believing him. So litigate us.

Frankly, we are also thinking exit signs are being better marked. Believe us: When we are saying, "Racing you to the capsule!" we are not thinking, "Oh boy, they are cooked pork!" No!

Even though they are treating us like space stewardess, we are not having any hard feelings, only laughs!

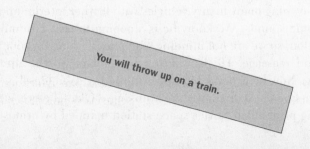
You will throw up on a train.

Losers' Auction

LAWRENCE DOUGLAS AND

ALEXANDER GEORGE

LOT #84 • ANONYMOUS
[Rudolf Nureyev: note from a friend]

Handwritten and signed, penned in ballpoint c. 1985. "Rudy, Rudy, Rudy. I'm not asking for much here. Love, Christophe." Such notes to Nureyev are common, but this one is unusual for its brevity and poignance. Scattered staining, with a tear running along the entire length of the letter; otherwise in good condition.

    Provenance: Unknown but its authenticity has been verified by the Trustees of the Estate of Rudolf Nureyev.

[$500/$750]

LOT #142 • THE ZUCKERMAN TAPE
[Assassination of President Kennedy]

Twenty-two inches of 8mm celluloid. Like Abraham Zapruder, Sydney Zuckerman was a home-movie enthusiast who chanced to film the motorcade on the fateful day in Dallas. Moments before the assassin's shots were fired, however, Zuckerman had his Paillard-Bolex camera yanked from his hand by his four-year-old son, Jacob. The film shows a dizzying kaleidoscope of grass, sky, and close-ups of Zuckerman's face. An unusually personal and peculiarly touching perspective on one of the most famous moments in our nation's history. Brittle.

[$40/$60]

LOT #179 • AMY STRUNK

[Greta Garbo: admirer]

Octavo notebook in which the author meticulously detailed every one of her sightings of Garbo in New York City over a period of thirty years. A sample entry: "Feb. 6, 1961, as seen from a moving bus: GG crosses south on 56th Street on the west side of Lexington Avenue; camel-hair, knee-length coat, no. 8 glasses, and hat no. 23 [reference to numbering in an appendix to the notebook describes and catalogs many of Garbo's accessories and outfits]; facial expression obscured; determined stride; gorgeous." A truly unique item no Garbo-mane will want to be without. Weathering and soiling consonant with age and use.

[$500/$750]

LOT #184 • MANUEL HERNANDEZ

[Jacqueline Kennedy Onassis: doorman]

Black-and-white photograph, 170mm × 140mm; 6¾ × 5½ inches, 1979. A photograph of Hernandez holding the door for an unidentified visitor to 1040 Fifth Avenue, the building in which Jacqueline Kennedy Onassis long resided. Inscribed in ballpoint: "Hey, Ricky! On the job! Besos, Mani." A touching, personal item. In excellent condition.

Provenance: Mr. Enrique Diaz.

[$200/$300]

LOT #203 • THE PAPERS OF HAROLD HEATH
[Annals of Publishing]

After his death in 1995, Heath left behind thousands of rejection letters from editors and publishers. Although none of Heath's fictional work survives—it was all burned by testamentary request—this rich trove of letters was spared. As a collection, they offer a fascinating cultural history of the publishing industry, including everything from form rejections from the leading magazines and publishing houses of the day (e.g., "Not quite right for us; we hope you will try us again") to handwritten notes from long defunct literary journals (e.g., "This must have been sent to us by mistake"). The collection comes with Heath's own original filing system that meticulously organizes the letters on a scale from "mildly encouraging" to "aggressively negative."

[$10/$15]

LOT #294 • FRED STILTSKY'S BASEBALL
[Sports memorabilia: Nolan Ryan]

In his only plate appearance in his major league career, Fred Stiltsky was beaned in the elbow by the legendary fastball of Hall of Fame pitcher Nolan Ryan. After recovering from his injury, Stiltsky was progressively demoted through the ranks of the minor leagues until a combination of astigmatism and a worsening allergy to grass drove him from professional baseball. Fine condition, slight scuffing on the ball.

Provenance: Mrs. Louise Stiltsky.   [$50/$75]

LOT #356 • THE LOVE LETTERS OF MARY LOU LANE
[Truman Capote: correspondence]

643 handwritten letters; various media, sizes, and shapes. Over a span of 42 years, Mary Lou Lane, a short-order cook in a diner in Syracuse, New York, wrote love letters to the famous novelist. Lane, who died last year in a work-related accident, never

mailed Capote any of the letters, and there is no evidence that they ever met. Of varying conditions: many bear crease marks as would result from crumpling.

[$80/$120]

LOT #417 • THE PRINTS OF VICTOR SKINK
[Modern Art: Andy Warhol and his circle]

An early collaborator of Andy Warhol's, Skink parted company with the father of Pop Art over artistic differences arising from Warhol's epochal series of Brillo box and Campbell's soup can images. Skink went on to become a founder (and perhaps the only member) of the self-styled "Grand Moments" movement. He taught art for many years in the Great Neck public school system before retiring in 1974. The lot comprises three lithographs: *The Construction of the Great Pyramid of Giza, The Coronation of Napoleon,* and *Moonwalk.* Signed and numbered. All in mint condition.

Provenance: The Creditors' Agency Incorporated, from the heirs of Mr. Skink. [$90/$130]

You will never know the magic word.

Portrait of the Postmodern Renaissance Man As Quilt Stitcher, Filmmaker, Deep Thinker, and Sculptor of Cubes of Tofu in Vats of Water

LAWRENCE DOUGLAS AND
ALEXANDER GEORGE

Inside a vast Chelsea loft, the pair of interviewers find Timothy Inca-Munch seated in a pink butterfly chair, snacking on pine nuts and sipping ginger beer. If he looks relaxed, five minutes with this one-man genre will convince you otherwise.

His video works are currently on display at the Guggenheim and his sculpture is featured at the Venice Biennale; a major show of his kinetic projects has recently opened at the Art Barge, which travels up and down the East River; and an unauthorized autobiography is on its way. Yet, Inca-Munch (unlike his distinguished Norwegian predecessor, his name, he insists, "rhymes with Cap'n Crunch") remains very much a controversial figure, best known for his weeklong performance piece in which Inca-Munch simply led his days as usual.

"People kept asking that old question, 'Yes, but is it *art?*'," Inca-Munch explains, his leg shaking with nervous energy. An athletic 38, he wears a troubadour's quilted doublet and a black Gap pocket-T. "Of course, that was the point. The term 'art' is too fraught, too tied to the canon, just too *too*. I think of myself as an 'omnist'; in my view the aesthetic is distinctly promiscuous."

His statement finds confirmation in his loft, an enviable space that is a cross between a painter's studio and a Toys "R" Us. As he rocks in his chair, now furiously stitching a quilt commissioned for a Sojourner Truth memorial, he lists the most powerful contemporary influences on his work: Ren and Stimpy, Pina Bausch, Karen Carpenter, and Charles Manson. He has even begun a work about the latter, an opera slated to premiere at BAM.

"These are figures who have dared to push the envelope, even Manson. Art—see how difficult it is to get away from that word?—if properly done, is itself a form of murder. And murder can be a form of art. Not always, but sometimes, like with de Sade or Tarantino."

Does his work kill?

"In a sense it does—it kills convention. I think I've been misinterpreted as embracing a wholesale chucking of the past, but nothing could be further from the truth. It's like what Freud said, you can't subvert the tradition without first putting it on the couch. I think too many of today's artists are overly swept up in the scene, the hype. It's still important to read, you know. I'm a voracious reader. Last week I read all of Kant—terrific stuff. Very dense. I suddenly understood Fassbinder and Kraftwerk."

"At the same time," he continues, now from behind a camera snapping close-ups of our ears, "I find all this 'decline and fall' talk nonsense. For example, I think TV has taught us a great deal about the organization of visual images. Especially commercials. Coke has done as much to define our environment as Cobain or Klee."

But is it possible to compare Coke to Kant?

Inca-Munch laughs at this question and tugs at the twin pigtails sprouting from the back of his head. "Obviously they're quite different. But let's not forget that in the name of 'high culture' African-Americans were enslaved all over medieval Europe. Now we're opening the field, inviting in the Other. Bazooka is not just one flavor anymore. Does that lead to dissonance? Sure, but even Bach was banned in his own lifetime by Bismarck. As Ice Pick has rapped, 'If it doesn't kill me, it'll make me richer.' "

Is he stung by the criticism that his most recent work lacks the vitality and the creative edge of his late-eighties pieces?

"I stopped reading the critics after the Jesus Herbert Christ show," Inca-Munch says. Dashing toward a massive window, he hollers to the street below and videos the response. "I mean, the praise got it wrong and now so does the criticism. All I can say is go and breathe the work. *Absorb* it. Then decide."

"Absorb" captures well what the viewer must do at the omnist's new installation on the Art Barge. A short film based on the life of Joan of Arc (written and directed by Inca-Munch) is projected against a backdrop of *Playboy* covers while water spouts from sprinklers above the spectator.

"I wanted to juxtapose Joan's immolation with the viewer's relative safety. And I was very pleased that we got Sandra Bernhard to play Joan. Sandra's a very focused performer, in her own way as focused as Joan. Unfortunately, all the critics could talk about were the sprinklers."

When asked about a sculpture now on view in Venice of large cubes of tofu floating in vats of water, the omnist's face brightens.

"That was a very important work for me. I had been thinking a lot about Beuys and how he changed my way of seeing fat. Every day I'd go into this Korean market down the block and buy some tofu. I needed to capture something about its presence, its ontology. In all its blandness, bean curd really is a very subversive foodstuff."

But should taxpayers' dollars support the making of self-consciously subversive art?

"I'm in the minority on this one, but don't get me wrong—I have nothing against welfare mothers. It's just that Kafka was right; the artist has to be hungry as a roach in order to achieve something lasting. It makes the work sharper."

"You see," he says, rebraiding his pigtails, "the omnist just does it."

OBSCURE CHURCHES
IN YOUR NEIGHBORHOOD

United Cafeterian

The Church Under the Stairs

Church of Bladder Day Saints

Holy Smokes Cool Menthol
  Congregation

Shirley Temple

St. Bernard's Church for Dogs

The Divine Order of Fries

The Frisbeeterians

Greek Orthodontic Church

The Scary Church in the
  Graveyard That No One
  Talks About

Pente-cost-you-less Church
  of Mega Savings

Holy Monks of Eric Roberts

The Presleybeterian Church

Dan's Church-in-a-Van

Miss Universalist

Holy Cows

Church of George Burns
  in That One Movie

Backstreet Boys Totally
  Awesome Buddhist Temple

That One Church with
  That Guy in the Hat

Quaker Shake Your Money
  Maker Reformed Church

First Confrontational

—John Moe

Packing for the Second Coming

MICHAEL THOMAS FORD

When I was seven years old, I packed for the Second Coming of Jesus Christ Our Savior. I did it in shoe boxes—seventeen of them—filled to near bursting with everything I thought I might need in the great hereafter. I even labeled them: PHOTOS, SOCKS, *CHARLIE'S ANGELS* trading cards. After watching my mother organize numerous moves, I knew how it was done, and I was a model of efficiency. When I got to Heaven, I would know exactly which box my toothbrush was in.

The impetus behind this frenzy of packing was a charming little song called "I Wish We'd All Been Ready," which I'd recently heard one of my sisters playing on her stereo. It was sung by a Christian rock singer named Larry Norman, and it was all about the unbelievers who were left behind when Jesus came to sweep up His chosen people before the world was burned up in the End Times.

It says something about the nature of Norman's cheery ditty that I can still remember most of it today. It isn't hard, really, because essentially each verse was a mini–horror movie about another unfortunate soul shocked into awareness of his or her sinful existence by the sudden disappearance of a more pious friend or loved one during the Rapture. My personal favorite line described the seemingly tranquil scene of a man and wife asleep in bed. Then, suddenly, the wife hears a noise and turns her head. *Poof!* Just like that—hubby's gone. Just in case the message was somehow lost, the chorus nailed it home with a refrain about how the singer wished we'd all been ready because there's no time to change your mind once the Son of God comes and you've been left behind.

Children, they say, are visual creatures to begin with. In my mind, I saw a woman rolling over in bed, only to find it empty because her husband (who of course had begged her for years to accept Christ in preparation for just this kind of thing) had flown up to Heaven, leaving her to face the tortures of Armageddon, not to mention the bills and hungry pets, all by herself. From there it was but a small leap to picturing myself waking up one sunny morning and going in search of my family, only to find the house empty and Satan himself knocking at the front door.

For several reasons I decided that the Fourth of July would be The Day. This was 1976—the Bicentennial—and everyone had been talking about it for months. I knew that the Fourth was the special occasion everyone was waiting for, and I was certain Jesus would want to make a big entrance. It made sense that he would surprise everyone by showing up in time for the fireworks and picnics I was told were in the planning.

When I'd packed everything and sealed it tightly with tape, I arranged the boxes in a pile. Then I sat on my bed and waited, although I wasn't entirely sure what I was waiting for. No one had ever explained to me exactly what would happen when the Rapture occurred. But based largely on Norman's song and my own interpretation of the Bible, I had some ideas. I believed that there would probably not be much warning, and that it would all be over rather quickly. Those who were left on Earth would suddenly discover themselves riding in cars without drivers, talking to companions who were no longer there, and becoming tangled in jump ropes as the turners on either side were whisked away to the Great Reward.

I confess I was secretly thrilled by the idea of unmanned cars skidding around the roads while the sinners inside screamed, and I hoped I'd get to see it. As for myself, I suppose I expected the heavens to open up and to feel myself being raised gently into the skies like a kite, giving me a good view of all the doubters below crying out for forgiveness as I hovered, saved, above their heads.

And so I sat and waited. After a few minutes, when everything seemed to be going on just as it had before I'd packed, I started to wonder if maybe something was a little off in my timing. I tried to remember whether Norman had specified precisely *what time* the Son was coming. I thought about going downstairs and getting my sister's record and checking the liner notes for clues, but I feared that being separated from my belongings when the Blessed Event occurred would be a tactical error.

After an hour had gone by with not the slightest hint of a Rapture, I decided that I'd been had. Jesus wasn't coming. I got up and looked out the window. Outside, kids were running up and down the street playing kick the can in the afternoon light. None of them seemed worried in the slightest about the Earth's imminent destruction. They were laughing and having a good time while I sat inside waiting for someone who clearly had no intention of keeping our date.

Then—suddenly—the skies clouded over with angry gray. There was a rumble of thunder, followed by a crack of lighting, and it began to pour. The kids scattered as the rain descended in sheets and darkness fell over the neighborhood. The whole world seemed to be surrounded by the storm. It certainly wasn't what I'd expected the Rapture to look like. I'd thought it would be more like *The Sonny and Cher Comedy Hour*, with bright lights and maybe some lively music.

Then a horrible thought entered my mind: What if Jesus had already come while I was packing. Perhaps, so worried about what to take, I'd missed the whole thing. Even worse, perhaps I'd been fooling myself all this time, and Jesus never had any intention of taking me with him. I reeled at the thought that somewhere along the line, I'd skipped a step in the process of salvation, and now I was doomed to burn with all the other sinners.

Filled with terror, I ran from my room screaming. I half expected the halls of my house to be overrun with lurching demons reaching out to drag me into Hell. Holding my arms in front of my face as protection, I dashed into the living room, wailing, "No, Jesus! I didn't mean it! Please, come back! Whatever I did, I'm sorry!"

Sitting on the couch were two women I had never seen before. They looked at me, pieces of cake paused in midair in front of their open mouths. I stopped, gasping in huge breaths, and stared at their anxious faces. They didn't look like demons to me, but I couldn't be sure. I knew the Devil and his ways well enough to know his minions appeared in many forms, even as cake-eating middle-aged ladies. "Be gone!" I shouted forcefully, recalling the words our pastor claimed Jesus used to vanquish the evil ones. I pointed my finger at them defiantly. "In the name of Jesus Christ, go back to Hell!"

The ladies looked at me, panting and wild-eyed before them. Then they screamed. Then I screamed. Then I fainted.

The next thing I knew, I was lying in my bed with my mother looking down at me worriedly. "Is this Heaven?" I asked hopefully, thinking maybe Jesus, impressed by my stand against the demons, had decided to come back for me after all.

"What?" she said.

"Where are the demons?" I asked.

"What demons?" she said. "What are you talking about? And why did you interrupt my garden club meeting? You scared Mrs. Whitley and Mrs. Hogan half to death."

Garden club? Then it wasn't really the Apocalypse after all. I breathed a sigh of relief. I started to get out of bed.

"Oh, no, you don't," my mother said. "You stay right there and take a nap. I think you have a fever."

She left, shutting the door behind her. I looked out the window. It was still raining, but the world wasn't ending. Larry Norman was a big, fat liar. I wasn't sure at first if I was comforted or saddened by this thought. On the one hand, it would have been fun to have seen Heaven and found out once and for all what it was really like. Never having met anyone who'd been there, all I had to go on was secondhand descriptions. I wanted to see it for myself. And I had done such a nice job of packing. It was a shame to see it all go to waste.

Then again, there were a few things to look forward to right here on Earth. It was summer. I'd just gotten a skateboard and new sneakers I hadn't even worn yet. My father had promised to take me and my friend Stephanie to *Star Wars* for the ninth time. My birthday was coming up, and I'd been hinting around for a bike. Besides, it was the Fourth of July, and I knew there were sparklers in my future when the rain stopped. There was a lot left to do; maybe Heaven could wait a while. Satisfied that I wasn't quite ready for Jesus to come back after all, I settled into the pillows and closed my eyes.

Before I drifted off, I looked at the stack of boxes next to the bed. Half asleep, I picked up the box with my favorite *Charlie's Angels* cards in it and tucked it behind my pillow. Just in case.

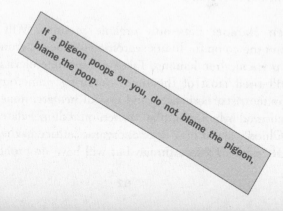

If a pigeon poops on you, do not blame the pigeon, blame the poop.

Ah-Choo! A Guide to the New Hankie Code

MICHAEL THOMAS FORD

For years, gay men searching for sexual fulfillment have been aided by the convenience of the hankie code, the wearing of different colored handkerchiefs in the back pocket to alert the careful observer to the wearer's particular fetishes. While this code has worked nicely for some, those of us who would like to identify potential partners by means other than what they do in the bedroom have been left to our own devices. This is not fair. So in an attempt to right this wrong, I have developed the following hankie code based not on sexual proclivities, but on general personality traits.

Green Hankie: Eats only organic produce. Will drag you around the co-op for hours searching for locally grown cilantro and pesticide-free lemons. Takes a multitude of vitamins, but is still tired most of the time, requiring numerous visits to acupuncturists, herbalists, and crystal healers, none of whom are covered by a health plan. When on a dinner date will complain loudly about how the nonorganic lettuce in the salad will surely result in a sore throat, but will have no problem eating the entire piece of chocolate cheesecake you ordered for your-self. Advantages: Always has homeopathic remedies on hand for sudden colds, interesting collection of New Age books, makes great smoothies. Disadvantages: Will ban meat from the refrigerator, spends most weekends at self-actualization retreats, listens to music by whiny girl singers.

Yellow Hankie: Amateur activist. Has a membership in every gay group you can imagine, from the Human Rights Campaign to the gay swimming club. Has memorized every acronym imaginable, believes in the educative power of the bumper sticker, and leaves articles clipped from the newspaper on your kitchen counter with salient points underlined. Frequently unavailable for dates due to a heavy schedule of petitioning and volunteering for local gay political candidates. Advantages: Gets invited to parties with pseudo-celebrities, able to converse on numerous subjects (as long as they're gay), enthusiastic in bed because sex is seen as a political statement. Disadvantages: Makes moviegoing difficult because of constant boycotts of allegedly homophobic films, tends to accuse friends of holding less evolved opinions, thinks Bette Midler is frivolous.

Red Hankie: Processing junkie. Enthusiastically codependent, and will not hesitate to reassure you that your personality defects are completely normal and most likely the fault of your parents. Has an entire library of self-help books, and knows the schedule and meeting location for every conceivable 12-step program. Generally has a degree in social work. Dates will involve talking about how you feel about the previous date. Advantages: Always concerned with your welfare, generally doesn't abuse any substance except Prozac, very organized. Disadvantages: The phrase "How do you feel about that?" quickly becomes tiresome, has many depressed friends who need constant attention and call at odd hours, worries that having sex more than four times a week constitutes an addiction.

Blue Hankie: Enjoys foreign films, particularly when playing in inconveniently located theaters with no parking and surrounded by ethnic restaurants of ill repute. Will frequently tell you that anything made in Hollywood is crap and insist on attending only movies featuring arcane plots, actresses with three names, and children carrying balloons. A typical date will consist of sitting through three hours of subtitles and an additional three hours of exposition, during which you are told as many times as possible that you "just don't get it." Advantages: Selecting a date activity is easy, extreme length of most foreign films renders conversation impossible, seldom recognizes sarcasm. Disadvantages: Wears too much black, refuses to attend Oscar night parties, seldom recognizes sarcasm.

Lavender Hankie: Overly fond of Siamese cats. Probably has at least two, who will sport unsuitable matching names like Melissa and kd or Joan and Bette, even if male. Will frequently cancel dates because one or the other of them is sneezing, and will not understand when you ask that the cats not be allowed to sleep on your face at night. Dates will involve neurotically prepared dinners followed by looking at high school yearbooks and hearing endless stories about all of the people in them. Advantages: Tends to be very loyal, enjoys giving backrubs, clean. Disadvantages: Likes to call you "Pussums" in bed, high-strung, allows pets to use sex toys as playthings.

Pink Hankie: Bad poet. Has an entire shelf filled with note-books of badly rhymed sonnets dating back to the sixth grade, and will spend hours reading each and every one of them to you. Easily breaks into tears while listening to Elton John or Jewel albums and says, "Can you believe how deep that is?" Dates center around poetry slams and exhibits of black-and-white photos of body parts with accompanying text from the work of Sylvia Plath. Advantages: Often has interesting friends, does just about anything sexually, will paint a mural on your dining room wall just for fun. Disadvantages: Works at Starbucks or the Gap because part-time work allows more time for "creating," has tentative grip on reality, will break up with you just to have something to write about.

Orange Hankie: Tanning booth aficionado and gym bunny. Insists that every season is swimsuit season, and always looks the part. Spends hours in the gym, and then even more time in front of the mirror. Comes with a startling array of hair and face care products, and considers the Abercrombie & Fitch catalog acceptable bedtime reading. Dates will involve shopping at J. Crew and repeatedly answering the question, "Does this make my ass look big?" Advantages: Takes a good picture, easy to shop for, likes just about anything. Disadvantages: Has many friends named Kyle, obsessive about fat intake, tends to go rapidly downhill after age 26.

Black Hankie: Depression queen. Medicine cabinet is filled with half-used prescriptions for every mood-altering medication known to science. Stays on each drug for a month before announcing, "It just isn't working," and trying another. Partial to career paths almost certain to result in failure, and frequently laments that it's too late to become a model, write a novel, or learn French, so why bother. Dates will consist of recounting everything said at the last therapy session and the therapist's reactions. Advantages: Loves Janeane Garofalo, makes your life seem comparatively wonderful, has low expectations. Disadvantages: Misery loves company, won't go outside if sunny, will blame you for the breakup.

White Hankie: Virgin martyr. Never does anything wrong, but makes sure that you know when you have. Is adept at sighing and looking disappointed, particularly on birthdays and anniversaries. Passive aggressive, and will answer almost any question about making plans with, "Well, if that's what you want to do," without suggesting an alternative. Favorite phrase is, "I don't want to talk about it," particularly when uttered while sulking over situations of unclear nature and origin. Dates will revolve around discussions of exes and everything they did to ruin the relationship. Advantages: None. Disadvantages: Reminds you of your mother.

CANCELED REGIONAL MORNING TALK SHOWS

Hot Coffee Thrown in Houston's Face

The Fort Wayne Morning Shed

Shame on You, Denver!

Tulsa Kills Itself

Why Won't You Love Me, Cincinnati?

A.M. Terrified Grin Detroit

The Ghost of Anwar Sadat Inexplicably Haunts Tacoma

Wake the Hell Up, Knoxville

Please, Phoenix, Let's Never Speak of This Again

Uncomfortable Portland Morning with the Sweaty Guy

I'm Sick of You, Wichita. I'm Sick of You, and I'm Sick of Your Shit

Billings Might As Well Be Dead

Boston Morning with Stabby and Shouty

Orlando Angst

I Said Wake the Hell Up, Knoxville! Jesus!

Percodan-Free Pittsburgh

Get Off Me, Atlanta!

Crispin Glover's Biloxi Morning Zoo

Wake Up, Mommy! Mommy? Baltimore

Johnny Cocktail's Salt Lake City Morning Lounge

What's the Point, Duluth?

God Hates Anchorage. He Told Me.

Bryant Gumbel Is Pissed Off Again, New York

Knoxville, I'm Gonna Whup Your Ass If You Don't Wake Up!

Good Morning Indiancrapolis

—John Moe

Vulcan

Vulcan is the Roman name for the god of the forge. (If he were your team mascot in high school, you'd probably cheer: "Who can? Vulcan!" if you even bothered to go to games instead of just hanging around outside the 7-Eleven with your hoodlum friends.) The Greeks called him Hephaestus, which eliminated all those stupid cheers. He was the son of Jupiter (Zeus) and Juno (Hera). One story has it that his mother was so disgusted with him that as soon as he was born she threw him into the sea where he stayed for nine years. In another version of Vulcan's childhood, he broke his leg when his father kicked him out of Olympus. Neither account says much for Olympian family values. Vulcan may have been rescued and reared by some nymphs and Nereids who took him to a cave and taught him to make things out of metal, including thunderbolts for his father (forgive and forget). He also made Pandora out of earth and water; it's amazing what you could do in those days with just a few simple ingredients. (Nowadays, try even finding a decent tomato!) Eventually, Vulcan married Venus but, despite the alliteration, it didn't work out. In an unrelated incident, he helped at the birth of Athena by splitting the head of Zeus (Jupiter) with an ax. Today, of course, few people go to a blacksmith for obstetric services. Vulcan's five most famous creations were the armor of Achilles, the arms of Aeneas, the shield of Heracles, the scepter of Agamemnon, and the necklace of Harmonia, which while not a weapon, proved fatal to all who wore it. I believe I have a pair of trousers like that.

—Randy Cohen

My Wife Liz

IAN FRAZIER

In the mid-1970s, I was married for a time to the actress Elizabeth Taylor. If this information comes as news to you, join the crowd. Our marriage, though admittedly brief, was quite legal and official; today, however, it remains virtually unknown to the public at large. Ask anyone about Ms. Taylor's husbands and you'll get the usual recitation of Mike Todd and Eddie Fisher and Richard Burton and John Warner and so on, with never a mention of me. Now, I don't care if I'm famous or not, and I have no financial axe to grind. All the same, it hurts to be left out. The feelings Ms. Taylor and I had for each other did not last, it's true; but while we were together we were a part of show-business history every bit as real as any other marriage she had. I have only affection and good memories when I think of Ms. Taylor today. But when I think of how I have been over-looked as one of her husbands, I feel anger, indignation, and a strong desire to see justice done.

Some people say that there should be certain minimum standards you have to meet in order to qualify as an ex-husband of Elizabeth Taylor, and that I (and a few other guys) don't

make the grade. Utter garbage! A person would have to be piti-
fully naïve not to see the fine hand of the distinguished Senator
Warner in this power grab. He even tried to ram a law through
Congress to that effect, with a lot of legalistic fine print about
the length of the marriage in calendar days, number of tabloid
articles about the marriage, and so on (all of which favors his
own claims, by the way). I regret to say that in California a similar law actually passed the legislature and went into effect in
1999. By its criteria, Larry Fortensky, a husband from the
1990s, qualifies and I don't. I like Larry, and I respect him as
a fellow ex. But all I can say is, look at the facts and do the
math: if *he* was married to Elizabeth Taylor. *I* was married to
Elizabeth Taylor.

    Now, for the record, here is how it was between Liz and
me. The year was 1974. I had just got out of college and was
living with my parents, and trying to rekindle a relationship
with Jayna Mills, my girlfriend from high school. One night I
was dialing her number when accidentally I instead called
Elizabeth Taylor. With my mind on something else, I happened
to dial a number in Beverly Hills which turned out to be hers. I
recognized her voice immediately. In those days she had just
divorced Richard Burton and was dating the scientist and peace
activist Linus Pauling, but he was pretty old, and she had a lot
of time on her hands. Why she didn't hang up on me—I was,
after all, a wrong number—I'll never know, but somehow we
fell into conversation that became warm and familiar after
only a few minutes. Not many people know what a wonderful
listener Liz can be. Before I realized it, I was telling her everything about Jayna's and my romance, and how she had dumped
me for one of the Four Speeds (a local band) while I was off at
school. For her part, Liz went into some of the problems she
was having with Dr. Pauling, who may have won the Nobel
Peace Prize but who was also a complicated person in many
ways. I guess neither Liz nor I had really known before how
lonely we were. Before we hung up, we exchanged phone numbers and agreed to talk again soon.

Well, that was the beginning. The very next evening I called her again, and our conversation was even better than the first one. I began calling her almost every single night in a long-distance telephone courtship that continued for months. Liz and I told each other secrets we had never told anybody. Working for Davey Tree Company and living in Ohio, I was, for Liz, a safe listener in whom she could confide her true feelings about the Hollywood world. And for me Liz was—I really can't describe the happiness that Liz was for me.

When the phone bills began to come in, and my parents had a look at them, they were very concerned. I offered to pay the bills myself, even though they took up my whole salary and more. And I tried, the best I could, to explain to my parents about Elizabeth Taylor and me. They were overwhelmed, naturally. They just could not get used to the fact that their son was romancing this famous person every night on their downstairs phone. It was a shaky time for us all. Plus, right around then we started getting a lot of strange calls— hangups, breathing, funny noises—which I cannot prove came from Linus Pauling, though I believe to this day that they did. Finally, my mom and dad, God bless them, decided that if this was what I wanted, then okay. A customer of Dad's had a condo in Venice, California, and my parents arranged for me to house-sit there for a while and see what happened with this Liz business, since clearly it wasn't going to go away.

Events moved swiftly after my arrival. Liz and I decided we had to be together all the time, and got engaged. The wedding was small—just me, Liz, my folks, Jack Warner, and Liz's long-time friend and publicist, Chen Sam. It took place before a judge in the Orange County Courthouse on December 10, 1974, at two in the afternoon. I find it worse than frustrating that now, through some bureaucratic mixup, the county seems to have lost all record of the marriage. As for my own copy of the marriage certificate, it unfortunately disappeared with many of my other possessions in the sinking of my houseboat during the great Mississippi River floods of 1993.

★   ★   ★

Item: a photo of Liz and me coming down the courthouse steps; she is wearing a peach-colored suit and a little pink hat, and I am looking off to the side so you can't quite see my face. Item: a note to me, undated—"Dear, The automatic-opener thing on the garage door is stuck or something. Can you get someone to fix? Love always, L." Item: the stubs of a pair of tickets to a rock festival I took Liz to in the early days of our marriage; it was I, in fact, who introduced her to this exciting new music form. How little history leaves us, in the end! The only hard evidence of my marriage to Liz is these random keepsakes I happened to come across recently in the glove compartment of my van. They may not amount to much, but they're precious to me.

My lawyers have them now. I'm told that the more proof I can produce, the better. I regret that lawyers had to become involved, but I don't see that there was any choice. I needed someone to make my case for me, I'm too close to it to do it effectively all alone. Plus, it looks as if we're going to have to pursue this thing on a state-by-state basis, which could be a drawn-out process. On my own I've worked to get more publicity for my cause. I've gone on several radio call-in shows, trying to establish myself in the public's mind as an ex-husband of Elizabeth Taylor. So far I don't know whether it's working. I thought I saw a sign of progress the other day when I noticed a woman I took to be a fan outside my house, apparently stalking me. When I confronted her, however, it turned out she had me confused with somebody else. I didn't get discouraged; I knew when I began the fight that I might be in for a long haul.

You don't go through an experience like mine without learning an important truth or two. Most important, I've come to like who I am. Who I am is a person who evidently was married briefly to Elizabeth Taylor but almost no one will admit it, so he has to get across to a bunch of self-important John Warner types a simple fact that shouldn't be such a big deal making me talk myself hoarse like this. I've learned, also, that that's not such a bad person to be. In general, I am at peace with myself, except when I get mad and carried away. Other than that, I'm always the same. You see, having once been married to Elizabeth Taylor gave me a great gift that no one can take from me: a calm knowledge of something too high and ideal even to have a name. When I can get a majority of the country to begin to accept what I'm saying, I'll be fine.

Your assumptions are wrong.

Your winning smile will get you nowhere.

Ads: The Final Frontier

KRIS FRIESWICK

Radio Shack Corp. is boldly going where no other advertiser has gone before. The Fort Worth, Texas, retail giant
has signed up with a tiny Arlington, Virginia, start-up
called LunaCorp to sponsor a most unusual marketing
event; a mission to explore the moon with an advanced
robotic vehicle, set for 2003. Neither Radio Shack nor
LunaCorp would disclose exact terms, but the sponsorship
is expected to cost Radio Shack about $1 million in the
first year alone. In exchange, the retailer gets to put its logo
on the moon rover.

—*Wall Street Journal,* June 15, 2000

Johnsbury, IL (June 29)—In what is believed to be the
world's first intra-human advertisement, heart-valve manufacturer Valvetek yesterday announced that surgeons at St.
Joseph's Presbyterian Hospital in Johnsbury, Illinois, have
implanted a special aortic heart valve bearing a Valvetek
advertisement into the chest of Elmore Greenwald, of
Merland, Illinois. The advertisement, drawn on the pea-
size artificial aortic valve, is designed to appear in Mr.

Greenwald's routine chest X-rays as the fluorescent green word VALVETEK. It will appear as a multicolored strobing display in MRIs. The valve was installed free of charge to Mr. Greenwald in exchange for the advertising space.

"We feel that it's a win-win situation," says Chip Damson, Valvetek's vice president of client enthusiasm and marketing. "Mr. Greenwald got a free heart operation, and we got exclusive advertising space that we expect will be viewed by approximately 258 cardiac specialists, our target demographic, over the next ten years, provided Mr. Greenwald's post-surgical recovery meets expectations. It's a very cost-effective way to reach our customer base, and if Mr. Greenwald is still alive, what better ad space could there be?"

Mr. Greenwald was still in ICU and unavailable for comment at press time. But his wife, Yolanda, says her husband accepted Valvetek's offer enthusiastically.

"Before the Valvetek people came along, we nearly had to choose between the operation and the wide-screen TV we'd been eyeing since last Christmas," says Mrs. Greenwald. "This way, we got both. We couldn't be happier."

This comes on the heels of another groundbreaking ad concept, unveiled last week at St. Mark's Church in Sultana, Maryland: a series of display ads affixed to the backs of the first ten rows of the church's pews. Advertisers include Peterson's House of Stained Glass; Tippy's Florist; and Mrs. Gagne, lead church organist, available for weddings and other private functions. Local toy retailer Toys 'n' Stuff also took out a mural-size advertisement that adorns the wall of the children's room.

"Church attendance has been down," says Father Paul Belliveau, St. Mark's priest for 15 years. "Our weekly collection has been dropping, and we desperately needed to renovate the kitchen in the basement to accommodate the standing-room-only crowds we get for the bingo. This seemed like a low-impact way to fund our expansion without further burdening our dwindling client base. Plus, the people who sit in the first ten rows are usually the rich folks who like everyone to see that they're in church every Sunday, so they're the most likely income bracket to respond to the products. I like to think it's what Jesus would have done. Now *there's* a guy who knew a thing or two about marketing."

Father Belliveau says he and a local funeral home, Caputano Brothers, are exploring a strategic partnership that would extend the advertising reach of the pew display ads to the sides of caskets at select funerals in the coming months.

This news follows the launch last month of a new advertising campaign by General Consumer Goods Corporation, makers of Dove's Breath™ toilet tissue, that seeks to place oval-shaped ads on the underside of toilet-seat covers in 50,000 homes across America. "We want Dove's Breath to be what folks think of when they use the toilet," says Skip Hardagon, senior executive vice president of external shareholder attentiveness and corporate communications for GCGC. "We have research that demonstrates that by forming a direct, predictable association between the ad and the bodily function, we can create an almost Pavlovian reflex. Eventually, these folks won't have any choice *but* to buy Dove's Breath."

In exchange for accepting the ads, households will receive coupons worth more than $1,000 for a variety of GCGC products, including Cholestra™ Spread, a cholesterol substitute that came under fire recently after several hundred people complained to the FDA that it caused "aggressive and leakage."

Technology is playing an important role in many of these new ad concepts. Tech start-up On Your Face Media Enterprises, in cooperation with Diamond Vision Centers, recently created a new type of eyeglasses that display ads on the inside of the lenses. On Your Face has signed contracts with more than 20 advertisers to produce "nano-ads," extremely short commercials (less than 1/100th of a second) that will flash briefly on the lens without interfering with normal vision, according to Trevor d'Allement, On Your Face's senior corporate liaison for consumer media coverage.

"With our new nano-ads, you don't even realize you're seeing them," says d'Allement. "Consumers think they're wearing normal eyeglasses, but suddenly, they get a craving for a hamburger or a new car. I mean, most people have those cravings anyway. We're just looking to redirect them a little. And isn't that what advertising is all about?"

You are sitting on gum.

Real-Life *Survivor*

KRIS FRIESWICK

So the big TV trend this season is "reality." Shows such as *The 1900 House* and *Survivor* are supposed to tap into our voyeuristic desire to see how people *just like us* would respond under extraordinary conditions.

I'm not buying the logic. First of all, these *Survivor* people are definitely not just like us. They went through months of grueling auditions in order to win the right to be stranded on a tropical island with a bunch of people they've never met, without food, where they promptly resort to eating rats. They are obviously a very special breed of individual, one that perhaps deserves to be stranded on a tropical island and made to eat rats.

And second, the producers of *Survivor* are missing the boat (pardon the pun) with their scenario. If they wanted to make the show truly captivating, they would create "adventures" to which the common man could relate, and from which that common man might learn a thing or two. Why spend all that money creating these elaborate, utterly fabricated, sterilized, made-for-TV adventures when there are so many real live dangerous, exciting adventures waiting just on the other side of the living-room picture window? Here are a few episodes of *Survivor* that might breathe new life into an already clichéd TV genre.

Family Holiday Survivor: Eight contestants are sent off to travel stand-by on a major airline during Thanksgiving weekend. Once at their destination, a double-wide trailer with polyester curtains and a redwood deck, they will be greeted by their "family," a kooky, dysfunctional group of 15, including inbred cousins, feuding in-laws, senile octogenarians, and Uncle Frank, who likes to grope himself publicly. Each day of the weeklong "holiday," the family will vote out one contestant based on the results of a variety of "challenges," including listening to Grandma tell the same story seven times in a row, breaking up knife fights between the sisters-in-law, and successfully resisting Uncle Frank's "pull my finger" trick. Losers hitchhike home. The winner gets a year's worth of inpatient psychotherapy.

Big Dig Survivor: A group of eight contestants, with nothing but a Dixie cup full of quarters, $100 in bills, and a 1987 Chevy Astro minivan, must navigate from Boston's Lower Roxbury to the North End. There they must find on-street parking, eat at Bricco without reservations, then travel to the FleetCenter on game night and again find on-street parking, relying *only* on existing signage provided by those puckish folks at the Mass Highway Department. On each day of this six-day adventure, contestants vote to expel one member of the group from the van based on a series of challenges, including navigational skills (also known in Boston as "dead reckoning"), tossing quarters into Mass Pike toll booths at 30 mph after being detoured, willingness to lie down in a parking space to save it, and aggressiveness in dealing with North End locals. Losers left wandering aimlessly in Boston. Winner keeps quarters and automatically becomes a contestant in *Tow Lot Survivor.*

Assembly Line Survivor: For four weeks, eight contestants work the night-shift assembly line at the Honeypie Plastics factory in Wilmington. Fellow assembly-line workers "freeze out" one contestant each week based on a series of challenges, including maintaining consciousness while engaging in short-range repetitive motion for eight consecutive hours with only two 15-minute breaks, maintaining a normal relationship with family while sleeping, and scoring whites for other line workers (hope you brought enough of those for everyone!). Losers are fired and have their wages garnisheed for every trip to the toilet during employment. Winner receives minimum wage, two weeks of vacation, all the coffee he or she can drink, and a year's supply of melatonin.

Bridesmaid Survivor: Eight women become bridesmaids to a nervous bride whose wedding is just six short months away ("We've got a lot of work to do, girls!"). Every three weeks one bridesmaid is uninvited based on a series of challenges, including willingness to sit through four-hour discussion on reception color scheme; ability to retain dignity while wearing lime-green, off-the-shoulder, Scarlett O'Hara–style bridesmaid's dress (with matching parasol); creativity in planning bachelorette party that is equally acceptable to bride's mother and bride's worn-out ho-bag friends from college; and amount of money spent on shower/wedding presents. Losers miss "wedding of the century" and forfeit all money spent. Winner is named maid of honor and gets to sleep with hunky best man in coatroom during reception.

Dot-com Start-up Survivor: Armed with ridiculous sums of venture-capital money, eight contestants create a wacky loss-based dot-com business plan, staff up with exorbitantly priced technical and marketing employees, find overpriced office space, and attempt to generate revenue. Each month a new contestant is expelled from the firm by the VC investors based on a series of challenges, including degree of believability when begging for bridge funding, willingness to work 30 consecutive 19-hour days, creativity in revenue-recognition practices, and ability to generate knee-deep bullshit when dealing with analysts. Losers sacrifice unvested options (although they are not automatically disqualified from upcoming seasons of *Dot-com Start-up Survivor*). Winner receives incalculable (paper) riches, his or her photo on the cover of the *Industry Standard*, and tons of babes (of either sex).

HMO Survivor: Eight genuinely ill contestants are sent to the emergency room of a downtown hospital without their insurance cards or preauthorization by preferred-provider physicians, Emergency-room physicians decide whom they will treat based on a series of challenges to patients, including ability to wait for up to 12 hours for medical attention; willingness to deal with surly, overworked nurse at reception desk who is less concerned with a carotid-artery hemorrhage than with determining your method of payment; ability to communicate symptoms while suffering from excruciating pain; and willingness to engage other *HMO Survivor* participants in gallows humor while waiting for help. Winner treated and released without being required to make full up-front cash payment. Losers die.

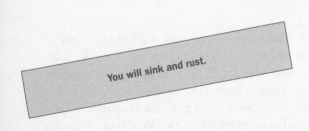
You will sink and rust.

BAD NAMES FOR
PROFESSIONAL WRESTLERS

Beckett
The Tad Pole
Roy Cohn Jr.
The Splendid Splinter
Bruce the Spruce
The Cuddler
The Framingham Fry
  Cook
Paula
Hamilton Jordan
Tarkanian
The Sea Horse
The Incontinent
Minstrel
The Drooling Lamb
Butterscotch
The Standoffish Person
The Wooden Marmoset
The Pasty Accountant
The Tardy Worker
Alan Dershowitz
Inky
The Soothsayer
The City Manager
The Bench Warmer
The Plum-Eating
  Bastard
The Corpse
The Marionette
The Martyr
The Peppermint Rube
The Gout-Stepper
The Williamette Pimp
Linus

The Spiller
Lace
The Soup-Eater
Stilts
The Tailor
Mitochondria
Kimono Boy
The Really Tiny Moth
The Bulimic Cheerleader
Winston Churchill
Vasco de Gama, Jr.
Tickles
The Fig Wasp
Cookies-n-Creme
  (tag team duo)
The Healer
El Wusso
The Precocious Feline
The Professor
Balsamic Vinegar
The Stooge
Diabetes
Warren G. Harding
The Wilting Zinnia
The School Boy
The Yearling
The Pediatrician
The Old Coward
Naomi
The Narcoleptic
Magic Realism
The Vegan
The Lonely Marine
Grace Kelly

Peter Billingsley
Swimmer's Itch
The Orderly
Smarty Pants
Babette
Jivamukti
Paul McCartney
The Shlub
The Shrill Housewife
The Truant Officer
The Dartmouth Grad
  Student
The Keokuk Optometrist
The Whispering Mime
Aaron Copeland
The Impressionist
The Phonics Expert
Nancy Walker
Hospice Boy
Noel Coward
Frondeur
The Demimonde
The Victim
The Tattletale
Truffle
Victor Kiam
The Poet Laureate
Mrs. Grundy
Burt Hooton
The Pawn
Dale
The Little Ragu
Morrissey

—Jeff Johnson

Sixteen Magazine Rates
the Presidents

FRANK GANNON

What does America want in a president?

America is a vast land. At last count there are some 250 million people living in America and, as the saying goes, one man's floor is another man's ceiling.

A dominant theme in the recent Gore-Bush fiasco is "How can guys like this, guys with absolutely no sense of shame, be the only presidential candidates that we have?" Many media pundits have claimed that ours is an age without leaders of men, an age of moral midgets.

But, hey, this is America. There is a place for everything. For a magazine like *American Heritage,* the best president might have been Lincoln or Roosevelt, but since when does *American Heritage* speak for America? For America, the wide? For the America that always has, no matter what the time of day or night, wrestling on television.

But, we are told, America has gotten really cynical. We are usually told this by somebody who is trying really hard *not* to look cynical while he says that. But Americans think, "Damn, this guy is *so* cynical, that he is able to look noncynical while he tells everybody that they are too cynical." Now that's cynical.

But Americans aren't always cynical. Let's examine the ages at which an American person still has his membership in the "Open and Sincere" club. Little kids like Macaulay Culkin are sincere. But they are too young to appraise presidents. But teenage girls are sincere. They are sincere in their love for the Backstreet Boys and 'N Sync and they are sincere in their love for horses and certain clothing accessories. *And* they know about presidents!

When I was in eighth grade, all of the good students were female. If they took the top 50 students, it would be 49 girls and Michael McClarity, who was smart but had an unnatural interest in accessories.

Sincere *and* knowledgeable. Teenage girls, the perfect constituency for evaluating presidents. Much better than those old, hair-in-the-ears subscribers to *American Heritage.* Their list of the best presidents might not be the most "informed," but it would have that evanescent quality we call sincerity. The list might look something like this:

1. Warren G. Harding. Dreamy hair and hazel color eyes set this studmuffin apart. Totally talented, he made presidential magic with his awesome mouth. And that to-die-for bod. They said "He looks like a president." We say he looks like he was bitchin'. He said America needed "not surgery, but serenity." Whatever, hottie.
2. Thomas Jefferson. Fun-loving and talented (he designed his own house!) Always upbeat, he felt that dating a fan wasn't out of the question. He loved to show off his mega-powerful president thing but he always had time to look mega-fine in his stylin' white wigs.
3. Martin Van Buren. He would always drop everything to go to a romantic spot with his special someone. He was only five-foot-six, but every inch a babe! They called him The Little Magician. Cool.

4. Harry S. Truman. We'd love to go on a magical mystery tour with this piano-pounding superstar. Versatility was his middle name; he was the bomb and he dropped it too!

5. Theodore Roosevelt. A romantic camp-out was always in the cards with this buff presidente. They called him a rough rider but he's ultra-smooth for us.

6. Millard Fillmore. Had a major crush on his teacher and later made her Mrs. F, first lady with the major hacienda. They called him a whig but this tousle-haired studmuffin didn't need any optional equipment; he had it all in spades!

7. Grover Cleveland. Tons o' fun with this giant hunkie commander in chief! "Where's the party?" was his middle name, but his romantic White House dream wedding ended his party-boy days. But not his laid-back wacky sense of humor, which melted more than a few hearts!

8. Richard M. Nixon. Filled in his swimming pool so more girls and guys could hang with the prez. That hair, that bod, and that killer nose made many a girl suffer from Nixonitus, otherwise known as inflammation of the heart!

9. James K. Polk. Added California to America (really!) but this scrumptious rockin' president accelerated pulses whenever he took his classic "hands folded in front" pose! Shy in public, this Southern boy knew how to smolder in private!

10. Herbert Hoover. Invited 4,000 partiers to his rave-infested White House for another "get down tonight" Washington blowout. "His dad was a Quaker but he was a heartbreaker." They slammed him for sending goodies to the commies, but it didn't phase this stylish prez who, if he was around in 2000, would say, "You can be a commie as long as you wear Tommy."

Your Y2K Checklist

MICHAEL GERBER AND

JONATHAN SCHWARZ

Have you . . .

. . . bought a few days' worth of staples (bread, canned goods, fruit)?

. . . obtained sufficient stores of potable water, tonic, limes?

. . . hooked up a gas generator, or some other alternative source of electricity?

. . . made a list of people whose e-mail addresses you plan to "lose"?

. . . picked up your dry cleaning? (Any garments being cleaned at midnight on December 31 will be mangled beyond repair when the machines go berserk.)

. . . become unsure whether your neighbors have left town for the holidays or whether the Rapture has begun?

. . . reinvested your portfolio to take advantage of a bang (such as Janus End-Times High Growth) or a whimper (Fidelity "Whew" Fund)?

. . . stockpiled batteries?

. . . stockpiled ammunition?

. . . written an apologetic letter to the Unabomber, acknowledging he was correct about the inevitable collapse of industrial society?

. . . trained yourself to disregard traffic lights?

. . . bought some playing cards?

. . . converted at least one paycheck into bullion?

. . . hidden the bullion in an easy-to-remember-yet-secure location?

. . . realized that everyone will think of the Ramble?

. . . magnetized the bullion somehow and sneakily stuck it to the back of your refrigerator?

. . . photocopied your lease (if your apartment is rent-controlled)?

. . . charged your taser?

. . . learned CPR, first aid, or—God forbid—effective home euthanasia?

. . . replaced "fluent in HTML" with "can kill and dress wild game" on your résumé?

. . . purchased some walkie-talkies?

. . . come up with descriptive-yet-devious code names for your friends and family?

. . . decided what animal your "Clan" will be named after?

. . . radically downgraded your expectations of personal hygiene, both for yourself and others?

. . . traded your new Boxster straight up for a diesel-burning, armor-plated school bus?

. . . canceled your subscription to *Wired*?

. . . begun to regret marrying for love rather than for ability to perform anesthesia-free appendectomies?

. . . used biofeedback to wean yourself off central heating?

. . . continued referring to the UPC code on groceries as "the Mark of the Beast," but now really meant it?

. . . started to care less whether Carson Daly and Cameron Diaz can work through their problems and make it to the altar?

. . . concentrated on the bright side: that with the collapse of the magazine industry, soon there will be an entire generation of women without body image issues?

. . . asked your postman whether their slogan now reads "neither snow, nor rain, nor the inevitable collapse of industrial society as predicted by the Unabomber shall stay these couriers . . . "?

. . . found that the phrase "panicked looting" doesn't *have* to have a negative connotation?

. . . started a meat-squirrel farm?

. . . prepared to have the morning paper and evening news be much sketchier?

. . . reserved a gritty, resourceful babysitter?

. . . written down the names of all the states, along with the capitals of each, in case the government needs it?

. . . asked the rabbi whether or not grubs are kosher?

. . . politely propositioned those whom you would most prefer to repopulate the world, if it comes to that? (NB: do not pick movie stars unless you live within walking distance of Hollywood.)

. . . come up with at least ten recipes in which pigeon can be substituted for chicken?

. . . taught yourself to use a litter box?

. . . studied game theory to figure out how to outwit someone at barter, every time?

. . . started, now that winter is here, to envy those with a high percentage of body fat?

. . . tried to find entertainment not in the frenetic pace of Doom but in Nature's slower, majestic rhythms?

. . . decided to thrown caution to the wind and vote Reform in 2000?

. . . buried your *World Book* as a gift to future generations?

. . . picked out a community member to ostracize and blame for all problems, from crop failures to plagues to children born with a caul?

. . . collected rocks with which to stone him/her to death?

. . . picked out a second community member to blame when problems continue, ideally a professor-type who makes irritating "appeals to reason"?

. . . collected more rocks with which to stone him/her to death?

. . . noticed that everyone seems to be keeping rocks near at hand?

. . . come to terms with the fact that, no matter what, you will continue to receive solicitations from the Quality Paperback Book Club?

. . . begun to truly understand the phrase "the living will envy the dead?"

. . . identified the local children with the fewest useful skills and most nutritional value?

. . . created "collection trousers" to harvest your own methane?

. . . learned not to be so smug about the Dark Ages?

. . . begun to find snide, half-clever jokes about Y2K much less funny?

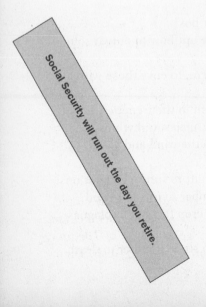

Social Security will run out the day you retire.

WNPR AM910:
"Your Public Radio Station"

MICHAEL GERBER AND
JONATHAN SCHWARZ

5 A.M. *Sound Money.* Silicon Valley's growing Amish community; ex-SDSers turned venture-cap moguls, the Body Shop's CEO on how to make "mad loot" while retaining that all-important sense of moral superiority.

6 A.M. *Living on Earth.* Electricity from burning junk mail; the *real* story of the Founding Fathers and hemp; steam-powered cell phones. Plus: frogs everywhere are dying—but a new guilt-based vaccine could save them.

7 to 10 A.M. *Morning Edition.* Incredibly alarming things that happened while you were asleep, quietly presented; Greenspan's inflation worries, day 10,003; today's birthdays: Ken Kesey is 80, Billie Jean King is 64, Jann Wenner is 39 (again).

10 A.M. to Noon *On the Line.* (Call-in show) Today's topic: "Imagining a Feminist Pornography." Scheduled guests include the obligatory Susie Bright; Michael Lerner, editor of *Tikkun's Best Erotica 2001*; and First Grandmother Barbara Bush. Then,

Listener Soapbox: "Are parents who *don't* drive Volvos irresponsible? Are SUVs acceptable?"

Noon to 2 P.M. *New York and Company.* (Call-in show) Author of new book, *Punny Business*, discusses the idiosyncrasies of English in tiresome detail, then corrects callers' grammar with priggish glee; a chat with a World War II denier; and an ATF expert on the growing nuclear capability of conceptual artists.

2 P.M. *Talk of the Nation.* A recent report has identified a new, vaguely defined, yet extremely frightening problem facing America's children. A child psychologist, a Harvard sociologist, and a syndicated columnist tell how a concerned-but-mostly-absent parent can avoid thinking about this issue.

3 P.M. *Science Friday.* Live from Woods Hole Oceanographic Institute: if a killer whale and a great white shark fought, who would win? How about two giant clams? Plus, the author of *Seahorse: Weirdo of the Deep.*

4 P.M. *Fresh Air.* Host Terry Gross says "Fresh Air" with tremendous aspirative onomatopoeia, then interviews folksinger Buffy St. Marie; the author of the new book, *Special Delivery: the Golden Age of the U.S. Postal Service.*

5 P.M. to 7 P.M. *All Things Considered.* An extremely sedate round-up of today's catastrophes and mayhem, including Fran Leibowitz's death from writer's block. Macramé—one man's ticket out of the ghetto; an interview with the director of a new opera based on the life of Gorgeous George; "Sounds From the Archive": Mark Twain barking his shin and swearing. Plus: the 974th rescoring of the ATC theme, this time for glockenspiel.

7 P.M. *The World.* The ongoing conflict over Kashmir: how a Jersey-based Zeppelin cover band *could* spark WW III.

8 P.M. *Marketplace.* Today's financial news; plus, an exclusive investigation into whatever the hell "Nasdaq" stands for.

9 P.M. *This American Life.* This week's theme: "VD." *Act I:* Monologues from America's next generation of *Harper's* writers, a shocking percentage of whom are afflicted with genital warts; *Act II:* David Sedaris reads a story about faking the clap at age eight; *Act III:* an unattended tape recorder is left on in the waiting room of a free clinic in San Diego; *Act IV:* Dan Savage unsympathetically discusses awful sexual maladies.

10 P.M. *On the Media.* (Call-in show) Media figures discuss other media figures; please do not call in (unless you yourself are a media figure).

11 P.M. *Jazz Set with Ed Bradley.* A celebration of Bix Biederbecke; "Would Dixieland Have Been Improved by Heroin?" If Charlie Parker and Thelonious Monk fought, who would win? How about them versus two giant clams?

Mid. *Newshour with Jim Lehrer.* (Rebroadcast) A positively soporific recapitulation of the day's disasters, in exhaustive detail; Shields and Gigot discuss the suspiciously fulsome hair of other Washington pundits; plus an essay by Richard Rosenblatt: "Is It Okay to Like Nixon Yet?"

1 to 5 A.M. *BBC News.* News with a patina of bitterness and snobbery, spewed from the heart of a faded empire.

Double Diamond/
Highest Difficulty

MICHAEL GERBER AND

JONATHAN SCHWARZ

Across

1 This never happened
5 Schrödinger's dog
10 Half of zero
15 A stitch in _____ saves *eight*
17 PUZZLEMENT
19 Discredited alchemist
20 Huh?
21 I'm thinking of a number
23 Book: The _____
25 Nonsense word
27 She was never president
28 Overhyped dot-com
30 Chevy Chase flop
31 What's that smell?
32 Ugliest fruit
33 Try again
34 Woody flick set in NYC
35 FRUSTRATION
37 Lincoln: "I love _____"
39 What friends *aren't* for
40 Bald NBA'er
41 Obsolete computer language
43 My recurring nightmare
45 Would it sicken you
   if I _____ ?
46 Better not write this one in ink
47 Bee's remorse
48 Earhart's grave
49 Not incest, but . . .
50 More powerful than voodoo
51 The *last* thing I expected
55 Opposite of red
56 Not "gnu"
57 EXTREME ANNOYANCE
58 Famously foulmouthed
   Canadian
59 Gandhi punched him

Down

1 Underpriced NYC neighborhood
2 REAL captain of *Pequod*
3 Famous first words
4 Frost poem about "bumpin'
   uglies"
5 He died in WW II
6 Only cold-blooded mammal
7 TV's crime-fighting slug
8 John _____
9 Common crossword mistake
10 "The Jitterbugging Nazi"
11 IMPOTENT RAGE
12 Tarnished child star
13 Patron saint of zombies
14 Yoko (not "Ono")
15 Feed a cold, starve a fever,
   _____ hookworm
16 It's immune to gravity
17 The aunt of invention
18 Harpo quote
19 My greatest regret
24 Sixteenth sense
26 Slept with Warren Beatty
29 Chillingly accurate stereotype
32 "Sayonara" in dolphin
33 This never happened either
34 Sec. of state, 1836–42, dog
35 2 + 2 *doesn't* equal . . .
36 Military acronym
38 DESPAIR
41 What happens after you die
43 "The next Beatles"
51 Jesus Christ's daughter
52 My secret nickname for myself
54 Long-running anarchist sitcom
55 This is a misprintt
56 GIVING UP

Decision '04

Hello, **Jane Q. Smith!** Today is **Tuesday, November 3, 2004.**
I am <u>not Jane</u>.   You have **610** VoteBux in your account. <u>Spend</u>

☑ Flip-flop Finder™ is **ON**.   ☑ ChadZap™ **ACTIVATED**.
☑ MuckBot™ is **ON**.   Your paper of record: | **NY Times** |

The President of the United States 2004
(Time Left to Vote: 00 days 12 hours 13 min)

George W. Bush	**Albert Gore, Jr.**
Richard Cheney	Hillary Rodham Clinton
Republican	**Democrat**
100 VoteBux	100 VoteBux
For those who like a relaxed fit to their Chief Executive, we present an update of a classic. Our new George Bush has twice as much of the moneyed, inarticulate charm of the original, to provide four-season, full-term, pre-broken-in comfort. With Bush, the leadership goes in before the name goes on!	Achieve total representation with this powerful, no-nonsense advocate for your well-being. Hand-buffed and lovingly neutered, Al Gore doesn't clash with any lifestyle/religion, from Baptist to Buddhist. Dependable toughness and unbeatable quality come together in one painstakingly crafted statesman. Go Gore in '04!
	Vote		Recount			Vote		Recount	
(Please vote only ONCE.)	(Please vote only ONCE.)
Search for "Skull and Bones collectibles" on <u>Ebay</u>	Buy the "Lil' Al" officially licensed home fuel cell at <u>HomeDepot.com</u>

Bush Review of the Day	**Gore Review of the Day**
(write an <u>online review</u> and share your opinions with other voters)	(write an <u>online review</u> and share your opinions with other voters)

★★★★☆

GOPchick23@mindspring.com writes:

it was the happiest day of my life when justice scallia named W president and iam honored to vote for him again. he kept us strong and showed those people who thought that he was too stupid. who's laughing now, trinidad/tobago?—our "sacred honor" is BACK!! i enjoyed the "W-mentary" on the history channel. if he executed you, you probably did it, and even if you didn't, you probably did something else that you got away with. anyway, God will sort it all out in His good time.

★★★☆☆

swilentz@princeton.edu writes:

Lieberman's simultaneous chairmanship of the DNC and RNC raises questions, but to claim there are no differences between the parties is absurd. Vide: during the Bush Presidency, distinguished historians have been invited to the White House so infrequently that it poses a clear and present danger to the Republic. Gore's faults aside, a vote for Jello Biafra *is* a vote for Bush. And it's demagoguery at its worst to call Hillary a "carpetbagger" just because of her recent move to West Palm Beach.

Ask This Candidate a Question:

 | **Did Trinidad REALLY attack?** |

Ask This Candidate a Question:

 | **Who killed Ralph Nader?** |

Special Offers for Bush Voters from: <u>the XFL</u>, <u>Fox News</u>, <u>Charles Schwab</u>, <u>Amway</u> . . . <u>many more</u>

Special Offers for Gore Voters from: <u>Slim-Fast</u>, <u>DreamWorks</u>, <u>Red Herring</u>, <u>Todd Gitlin</u>, <u>more</u>

Can't find what you're looking for? Search our database of <u>Marginal Political Parties</u>

Have you heard about AutoVote, our new personal voting service? After entering your voting history onto our secure server, AutoVote translates the positions of your preferred politicians into numerical values. Then it uses complex algorithms to choose the candidate you'd most likely vote for, in every race, all the time, EVERYWHERE. Our Suffragebot® is constantly scanning for elections, so you'll be sure to make your voice heard again and again. <u>Sign up</u> before Dec. 1 and receive $500 from Ameritrade!

—Michael Gerber and Jonathan Schwarz

The Periodic Table of Rejected Elements

MICHAEL GERBER
AND JONATHAN
SCHWARZ

1 H Halcion	
3 Ac Actium	**4 Cx** Clorox

9 Bg Belgium	**10 Hx** Hydrox	**11 A** Anodyne	**12 Pk** Pekingese	**13 Su** Sumerian
19 Dm Delirium	**20 Am** Aspartame	**21 At** Antipathy	**22 Ch** Chagrin	**23 Ca** Canadian
29 Bz Byzantium	**30 Cn** Collagen		**31 Pz** Pizzazz	**32 Qt** Quotidian
38 Im Imodium	**39 Fg** Fahrvergnügen		**45 Sa** Sanatorium	**46 Ap** Asparagus

40 Gb Gambinium	**41 Gv** Genovesium

Legend

- Sentient Metals
- Al Kaline Metals
- Fey Metals
- © Microsoft Corporation
- Dingy Greases
- Solid Gases
- Criminal Elements
- Consult Your Physician

			2 **Td** Tedium
5 **M** Moron	6 **Ct** Carton	7 **Fl** Florentine	8 **P** Pylon
14 **V** Vinyl	15 **Bs** Bosporus	16 **L** Linoleum	17 **As** Asinine	18 **Cr** Crouton

14 **V** Vinyl	15 **Bs** Bosporus	16 **L** Linoleum	17 **As** Asinine	18 **Cr** Crouton
24 **Tc** Talc	25 **Ge** Geranium	26 **An** Antigen	27 **Rp** Rapine	28 **Pr** Princeton
33 **Gu** Gummi	34 **X** Xena	35 **Sn** Sin	36 **Vi** Visine	37 **Cd** Celinedion
47 **He** Hefnerium	48 **Ae** Antigone	49 **Gr** Grenadine		

42 **Bn** Bonannium	43 **Cb** Colombium	44 **Lu** Lucchesium

Happy Holidays
from Maria Callas

TOM GLIATTO

"Welcome, Noel"

The legendary 1952 Christmas album, not released until the following Halloween because the diva's perfectionism resulted in the nervous collapse both of her and the album. It could not have helped things that Aristotle Onassis had taken up with a cheap hooker, moved her onto his yacht, and pooh-poohed Maria's tearful protestations by claiming the girl was just their illegitimate daughter. Maria, desperately in love with Onassis, was willing to believe all his lies, even the one about the faces on Mount Rushmore being a natural formation. Despite these tensions (or because of them?), Callas is splendid here—tender, reverent, sweet. And those are just the hand gestures. The only cause for concern comes in "The Little Drummer Boy." There is a hint of dry warble in the "rum-pum-pum-pum."

"The Twelve Days of Christmas"

Callas's voice began to rapidly suffer damage from informal training that had consisted mostly of yodeling while working construction. Yet in 1956 she undertook the notoriously difficult role of Frederica in Donizetti's *Osso Bucco* at La Scala. Audiences were electrified when, during the mad scene, Callas hit four high Cs while rolling herself up in a Persian carpet. Only three days later she unrolled herself and recorded this enchanting holiday classic—but who can guess at what cost to her marvelous instrument? The legend: Callas enters the studio booth, changes from Gucci couturier into a hospital gown, and begins her warmup exercises. Her producer quickly intuits that she does not have the vocal strength to get through more than the first 11 days of Christmas. He takes her aside and suggests an old recording "trick" of singing into the microphone through thin slices of raw zucchini. Maria, livid, shoves him aside and says she will julienne the vegetables herself.

For this CD release, the warmup exercises, of great interest to the aficionado, have been remastered and left out.

"Do You Hear What I Hear?"

"Indeed I do know what I hear," wrote critic Arturi Fendetz of this now beloved seasonal treasure, "and I do not care for it any more than I did Renata Tebaldi's album of Mississippi prison blues." It should come as no surprise that Fendetz was later recognized as a philistine, deported by steamboat and, once home, made to denounce his mother, father, and fondness for sweetbreads at a sensational "show" trial. As for poor Maria, at this time she is undergoing tremendous stress in her personal life. Her voice makes something of a comeback after she accidentally swallows acupuncture needles, mistaking them for toothpicks. Then—disaster. She is fired from the Metropolitan Opera after clashing with manager Sir Rudolf Bing over a new production of the "Ring" cycle. He expects her to go on as her own understudy in the long but vocally undemanding scene in which the Valkyries core apples. Callas simply refuses to attend rehearsal. She stays in her hotel suite bleaching yellowed press clippings in the bathroom sink, playing her old recordings on the mechanical pianaforte and in general bemoaning life. "Meanwhile" (as opera buffs like to say) Onassis is planning fresh heartbreak. In the years since he has grown from mere magnet shipper to shipping magnate, his ego also has grown

out of control. Not satisfied with a great yet aging diva who is
only too happy to lend him her chignon, Onassis now is determined to woo away and win the hand of some world leader's
wife. Out on the yacht he already is entertaining actress
Monica Viti—only eight weeks after her wedding to Paul VI.

The real fun here is Poulenc's setting of "I Saw Mama
Kissing Santa Claus" (*Hélas! Madame, je t'ai vu. . . .*)

"A Classical Christmas"

Mostly highlights from Handel's *Messiah*. The voice is now
frail, but Callas courageously manages to sing a few of the
strings, the Vienna Boys Choir, and the conducting. Onassis
has taken to calling her on the phone and taunting her by
cracking eggs on his gray head. Maria tries to keep busy teach-
ing masters' classes, but is so withering in her criticisms she is
allowed only to oversee the cafeteria at lunch. She sits at a
table by herself and, removing the processed cheese slice from
her sandwich, presses it against her cheek, as if for solace.

"The Many Moods of Christmas"

Unable to sing at all and devastated by Onassis's engagement to
Rose Kennedy, Callas recorded this, her last holiday album and
first (and also last) album of sound effects. It begins with chestnuts roasting on an open fire and concludes with gusting sobs.
A treat.

Once, Twice, Three Times a Visdalen

Three Tries at Mocking IKEA

BEN GREENMAN

1. Ikeawocky

    'Twas vimma, and the hatten ulk
    Did romb and rimma in the synk;
    All norsta were the nikkala,
    And the trassent laxne.
    Review: Has an undeniable inner logic, pointing out
    as it does the absurdity of IKEA's nominative scheme.
    However, the fact that it goes only one verse suggests
    that this approach may exhaust itself sooner rather
    than later. Best read aloud.

2. IKEA products or Scrabble hands?

    TULLSTA
    SUFFLOR
    MYNNING
    FENOMEN
    HALLAND

Review: Funny for a second, like a picture of a big man in a little tiny car. Beyond that, fails to capture the imagination, except for diehard Scrabble players, who will spend hours trying to mine the best words out of the letter sets.

3. Rejected IKEA products

> IMTA: Adulterous bed. Available in mahogany or birch. Has adjustable headboard.
> NAMMEN: Sofa where you tell your wife you no longer love her. Choose from black or dark green.
> LINJE: Kitchen table where you fight with your pregnant daughter. Beech only.
> AGHEMAT: Eight-drawer dresser perfect for hiding evidence of drug addiction. Available in black or white lacquer finish.
> KVADWALLA: Entertainment unit on which you can watch videotapes of disastrous family reunion. Comes with tempered glass doors.
> FACK: Mirror in which you look unhappy. With hammered-brass plating.

Review: More emotional gravity than either the first or the second option, and better for it. Also benefits from making furniture consequential: What we do on our beds, couches, etc., is what matters, not their fabrics or colors. And while it is counterintuitive to have invented names that have no etymological connection to their punchlines, that turns out to be a wise strategy—calling the adulterous bed ONNUS or AKKUZ, for example, would have been a mistake.

Letter to Ken Burns

BEN GREENMAN

November 28, 2002
Dear Mr. Burns,

I am writing to complain about your recent six-hour documentary miniseries, *Numbers, One Through Ten*. As a third-grade math teacher for the last twenty-nine years, I believe that it is irresponsible to assert that four is "the most important number of all," especially given the contributions of numbers like two and five. In addition, I am dismayed by the unforgivable omission of one, three, and nine. Where would my students be without the number three? In no grade at all! On the other hand, I was very moved by Morgan Freeman's recitation of pi; after two hours and forty-five minutes, I was still riveted, and only exhaustion prevented me from staying up to see more.

Ruth J. Anderson
Dothan, Alabama

September 5, 2003
Dear Mr. Burns,

The Civil War, baseball, suffrage, jazz, Lewis and Clark, early radio, the police: All of these are fertile topics for exploration, certainly. But socks, Mr. Burns? Socks?

Jay Bettancourt
New York City

January 22, 2005
Dear Mr. Burns,

When I first heard that you were working on a miniseries about the dictionary, I called my son at his friend's house to tell him how excited I was to see it. I have been a student of the dictionary for many years, and have found myself returning to it time and time again. As a devotee of your earlier works, I was eager to see how you would treat this wonderful book, which has given me so much knowledge over the years. How sad, then, that *Dictionary* did not live up to its promise. To begin with, I thought that the choice of narrators was wrong. Arnold Schwarzenegger, while undoubtedly a lovely man, has a Teutonic flavor to his speech that is more than a little distracting, and his work on the first installment, "Aardvark to Acetone," was difficult if not impossible to listen to. Over my son's strenuous objections, I convinced him to watch the second installment, "Candelabrum to Canker," and was horrified to find that it was narrated by Antonio Banderas. I wanted my son to learn to have a greater appreciation for the dictionary, not to walk around the house saying "Candy, noun: any sweet or piece of chocolate" in an exaggerated Spanish accent. And then there was "Dictionary to Duumvir," which had the potential to be the most poignant episode of all, since it contained the word *dictionary*. I cannot tell you how disappointed I was with your choice of Fran Drescher as narrator. I am not a quitter, Mr. Burns. I stuck with you through all fourteen hours of *Dictionary*. The next time, though, I am not certain I will do the same.

> Elaine Ternis
> Davis, California

April 9, 2007
Dear Mr. Burns,

Far be it from me to tell an accomplished filmmaker such as yourself how to do his job. I am just a fan, a loyal fan who has always appreciated the way that you have reconstructed American history with the simplest of audiovisual tools. But in my heart, I feel as though your latest documentary, *The History of Some Things I Could Find Documented in Cheap, Sentimental, Sepia-Toned Photographs*, was a bit arbitrary and self-serving.

> Harold Firbank
> Springfield, Illinois

May 1, 2009
Dear Mr. Burns,

As a documentary filmmaker myself, I have followed your work since *Brooklyn Bridge* in 1981, I was immensely influenced by such projects as *The Civil War* and *Baseball*. But it is your latest effort, *Documentaries*, that finally compelled me to write a letter. I had heard that this was your longest documentary yet, with more than thirty hours of broadcast time. But I was not prepared for the fact that all thirty hours would be spent panning slowly back and forth over a single photograph of your face, or that the soundtrack would consist of only an endless loop of your laughter, which, to be honest, began to sound sinister after the ninth or tenth hour. I hope that the DVD edition will have additional footage.

Lance J. Anderson
Omaha, Nebraska

PASSWORDS PRINTED ON THE EIGHT TRIAL SOFTWARE PACKAGES AOL HAS MAILED TO ME OVER THE PAST FIVE WEEKS, AND AN IMAGINED EXCHANGE BETWEEN AOL AND ME

Passwords	Imagined Exchange
BERRY-BUNKO	AOL: MORE-MAIL!
CHATS-AUGURS	ME: DON'T-WANT
BATCH-DOORS	AOL: HAVE-MORE
CARVES-SNOOPS	ME: NO-THANKS
CHOSEN-THICK	AOL: YOU-CRAZY
LAUGH-THYMES	ME: NOT-NICE
PEARL-ARGENT	AOL: MAYBE-FUTURE?
GROWTH-SOLES	ME: NEVER-EVER
	AOL: BERRY-BUNKO

—Matt Summers

The Crow

Crows are any of several black birds belonging to the family Corvidae (order Passeriformes) that are smaller and less heavily billed than most ravens and, by extension, than the late Ann Miller. They are named for their typical call: "caw" or "crah," but why they are not known as Caws or Crahs is never explained. (In America, a rooster says "cook-a-doodle-doo"; in France it says "coquerie-co," but it's still called a rooster or something French.)

More than 20 of the 30 species of the genus *Corvus* are known as crows, and the name has been widely borrowed, most recently by Sheryl Crow and many pop bands. Crows are omnivorous and eat grain, berries, insects, carrion, and the eggs of other birds. The crow's habit of eating cultivated grains has made it very unpopular with farmers, but not nearly as unpopular as it is with those other birds whose eggs it eats. (Then again, who wants to be popular with farmers? Well, Garth Brooks, which doesn't make it any more appealing.) Crows also eat economically harmful insects, so maybe the farmers were too quick to judge, which wouldn't surprise me. Crows feed chiefly on the ground, where they walk about sedately. Much the same could be said of the lovely Ann Miller, except for the part about walking sedately. Oh, let's face it: She moved like an extraordinarily talented and energetic horse.

Crows are gregarious, and at times they roost together in great numbers (tens of thousands), and yet at the end of the evening, how many stick around to help clean up? Not Garth Brooks or the lovely Ann Miller, I can tell you that.

Although many farmers are helpful sort of people, like with those barn raisings and government subsidies. But I bet they'd be scared if they saw Ann Miller dancing her ass off out among the soy beans.

Each mating pair has its own nest of sticks and twigs, usually high up in a tree, in which are laid five or six greenish-to-olive eggs that have darker speckles. We're back on crows here, although perhaps Garth and Ann have taken a fancy to one another. Who can predict these things? Who'd begrudge them the comforts of love in a harsh world where a crow could swoop down at any moment and eat you, particularly if you were an economically harmful insect let alone a high-kicking hoofer.

A crow may live 13 years in the wild and more than 20 years in captivity, if they're captured someplace nice like a really good French hotel, maybe by a rooster or "rooz-teur" as a Frenchman would say, speaking English in his comical French accent. Some pet crows "speak," and in the laboratory some have learned to count to three or four and to find food in boxes marked with symbols. I suspect Garth Brooks could do much of that (and could even "sing") although I've not seen him in a laboratory setting.

—Randy Cohen

Five Columns from Media Person

LEWIS GROSSBERGER

THE RACE ISSUE

A large number of readers have contacted Media Person to say they were angry and resentful about all the space given in the news media recently to a newly dead person they had never heard of named Dale Earnhardt.

"Why do I need page one of my newspaper cluttered up with stuff I don't know anything about?" wrote one typical reader who wished to remain anonymous, Claude L. Mottleman, a retired antiques manufacturer from Mahwah, New Jersey. "I want news of celebrities, certainly, but only the famous ones."

Another peeved reader who, for maddeningly obscure reasons we'll call Lily Marlene, put it this way: "Can you explain to me why *Time* magazine would put a traffic accident on the cover?"

Of course, these readers, seething with inchoate rage, are not fooling anyone, least of all the ultrasophisticated and discerning Media Person. Underlying their distaste for the Earnhardt coverage is the ugly fact that America is split into two warring camps. In one, you have the wine-drinking, Gore-voting, *Frasier*-watching, Charlton Heston–hating elitists who live in New York or San Francisco. In the other you have those who knew who Dale Earnhardt was.

MP's readers number, according to official estimates, approximately zero of the latter.

Because Media Person, like George W. Bush, considers education his top priority, he feels it his duty to clue you hopeless people in on the arcane world of auto racing so that next time *USA Today* and CNN lead with a defunct sunbelt idol, you will not be humiliated when the Bangladeshi exchange student living in your home asks, "Who was that colorful yokel, please, kind sir or madam, as the case may be?" (Don't worry; it won't take long. MP is on top of this thing and can give you all you need to know in a few succinct paragraphs.)

Who Is Nascar?

Ernie (Tailpipe Billy) Nascar is now the top driver on the Stock-Car-Driving Circuit (as the circuit where stock cars are driven is known), now that Dale Earnhardt is no more. Legendary for his laconic, aw-shucks manner and his habit of tossing lit matches into the gas tanks of rivals, Nascar won the coveted Gold Spittoon, symbol of stock-racing supremacy, three times in a row in 1989 in his familiar orange polka dot Volkswagen Centra with its intimidating Number 6. (Drivers, highly superstitious, fear numerals.) Though his car has "crashed" (a technical term meaning "to merge noisily with a wall, another vehicle, or one of the Dixie Chicks") 146 times this year alone, he has walked away from each one with a smile. Also a slight twitch in both eyes, a mildly paralyzed left leg, and a missing kidney last seen rolling under the front seat.

What Is a Stock Car?

While it may superficially resemble the Jeep Grand Cherokee you toddle to work in every day, a stock car actually bears about as much similarity as a nuclear submarine does to a Japanese fishing trawler. Carrying its fuel—6,000 gallons of highly radioactive liquid plutonium—in a special plastic pouch originally designed for colostomy patients, the car attains speeds of well over 900 mph (minutes per hectare) and is likely to leap unbidden into the ionosphere at any time unless the driver squeezes the Hey Stop That control, a large pink knob in the shape of Homer Simpson's head. Though containing no CD or radio (the reason Media Person refuses to ride in one), each car is equipped with a cooler in the trunk containing a six-pack of Coors Light to keep drivers in touch with the sport's manly heritage, which hearkens back to the early days when they sped through small southern towns, throwing empty beer cans at dogs and running over sheriff's deputies. Voice-activated power windows enable drivers to use hand signals to indicate when they are about to make a left turn or to flip other drivers the bird.

Who Are the Fans of Stock-Car Racing?

Though elitist snobs like Media Person lampoon them as hayseeds with beer-bloated bellies who reside in trailer parks, actually stock-car devotees tend to be hard-working, well-educated, refined hayseeds with beer-bloated bellies who reside in trailer parks.

What Actually Happens During a Typical Stock-Car Race?

The race begins when the "starter" (another technical term) waves a certified check for $100,000 in the air, signaling the drivers to push their girlfriends out the door and choke the throttle, which injects fuel into the camshaft and carburates the afterburner, launching the car into the stadium at a frightening 1,600 decibels per ear. Their heads strapped tightly atop their necks and encased in polycarbonate "helmets," drivers cannot see out the titanium windshield but must rely on "spotters" circling overhead in blimps. They zoom around in a tight pack until all but one have crashed. He is declared the "winner" and escorted to the bathroom where a "pit crew" examines him for pitting. At this time the driver learns he has lost between 12 and 36 pounds and aged nine years. But he is a happy man for he is still alive, though not always.

OH, LIMP OLYMPIAD

Media Person must regretfully announce that the Olympics did not hold his interest this year, which, in his opinion, means they were (or possibly are—who knows whether they're still going on or not?) a complete failure. NBC was finally forced to admit that only six people have been watching its coverage, three of them complaining bitterly, proving once again that Media Person pretty much sets the tone for life in America today.

Unfortunately, the reasons being cited for the low ratings— the late September start date, delayed coverage due to time difference, Internet competition, etc.—are all wrong. If we break down the Olympics into its component parts, we can easily recognize the root causes of the problem, though MP hates to have to drag botany into this discussion.

1. Sports: Are sports really as interesting as they're cracked up to be? Aren't they actually kind of silly? And also quite tedious to watch? Come on, admit it. Let's say you're 40 or 50 years old and male. (If you're younger or a woman, try to picture your father or uncle, if possible.) As a typical American, you've now watched an estimated 16 billion hours of sports, which, let's face it, essentially consist of people endlessly repeating the same few motions: running, jumping, throwing things, kicking things, or propelling themselves rapidly across a limited space by various means of locomotion, physical and/or mechanical. Aren't you getting pretty tired of the monotony by now? Media Person sure is. That's why he's retired from spectator sports. (Except for boxing, where people try to bash each other's heads in or bite their ears, which is kind of exciting, what with the blood and all.)

    We know that the television muck-a-mucks are aware of this problem, which is why they developed the Poignant Little True-Life Biodrama format for covering the Olympics and hired Dennis Miller to try to make football funnier. Unfortunately, the Poignant Little True-Life Biodramas—typically showing how some 19-year-old really got upset four years ago because she came in second, cried a little, blew her nose, ate Wheaties, and is now really determined to come in first—are about as fascinating as Julie Whatsername interviewing the girlfriend of the latest banishee on *Big Brother*. Media Person says it's time we banned sports from the Olympics.

2. Pageantry: People wearing stupid hats and waving while walking around in a big circle shooting videotapes of other people doing the same. Doves cooing. One thousand crocodiles in tie-dyed capes forming the Olympic rings while Olivia Newton-John sings some tuneless song. This is the Miss America contest meets Leni Riefenstahl at Euro Disney. This is for people who think cheerleaders are entertaining. Get rid of it.

3. Nationalism: Enough already with countries! Countries were a good idea when they first came in around half a millennium ago, but by now they've outlived their usefulness. Lets stop talking about globalism and do it already. As the biggest and best country, it's up to the United States to take the lead. Dissolve the union! Let's all just be Earthlings! Then the Olympics won't be able to push its tiresome emphasis on Romanian gymnasts and Australian swimnasts and we can focus on the individual trigonometry champs and speed typists (don't forget, they won't be doing sports anymore), which is as it should be. And why does each Olympics have to be held in one country? By Day One, Media Person was already sick of Australia, where, we are constantly told, everyone wanders around saying, "No worries." As a catch-phrase, that's even lamer than "g'day." MP could coin a better Aussie cliché with his eyes closed. For instance, how about, "Stick it in your wombat, mate!"? In the age of television and Internet, why can't every country host an

event? Oops, forgot, there are no more countries. Okay, every, uh, area code.

4. Swimmers with Gigantic Feet: Obviously there is something unfair going on when mutants and space aliens are allowed to compete. This Thorpedo guy has size 17 feet, or flippers, actually, larger than those of any known human, which propel him with the speed of a frightened tuna. Apparently, he has escaped from some laboratory with a German professor chasing him, closely followed by a mob of villagers. Even worse, he wears a full-body condom. What's that all about? (as they say in New Zealand). If we must watch swimming, damn it, we want our swimmers naked, as God intended them. (Though, frankly, it's time we got rid of God, too, along with sports and countries. You can still pray for a victory if you like, just not to anyone.)

5. Winning: An obsolete concept. Cooperation, respect, inclusion, that's the ticket. Get rid of those tacky medals.

So there you have Media Person's modest plan for improving the Olympics. He's done his part. The rest is up to you. Everyone out there, send an e-mail immediately to Juan Antonio Samaranch and tell him to get moving on this. At first he will ignore you, but don't be disheartened. The revolution always starts slowly.

PIG IN A POKÉMON

Pokémon. What is it? Where can I get some? How much does it cost? If I step on its head, does it die or just whine a lot? Does it even have a head? Can I eat it? Would it perhaps go away and leave us all alone if one were to simply ignore it? Will it turn my beloved firstborn son into a drooling, degenerate monkey boy? Does it go with Victorian furniture? Is it singular or plural? And can it be written without that stupid accent mark over the e?

These are just a few of the many questions Media Person is asked every day by concerned readers about the latest annoying multimedia phenomenon to sweep across the globe and turn our children from obedient little darlings whose only thought is pleasing Mommy and Daddy into obsessed gargoyles who need to devour human flesh every 48 hours. Well, don't worry. Media Person is here to answer all these questions and others you haven't even thought of yet.

How it's pronounced: The word has four syllables, with equal stress on the first three and none at all on the fourth. PO-kih-moh-nnn.

Where it began: In the dark, poverty-ridden suburbs of postwar Japan, a small, odd-looking young boy, Tojaki Mifutsi, collected beetles, peering beneath rocks and inside the shoes of his uncle. Some 40 years later, Mifutsi, now a small, odd-looking old man but still living with his parents and having cornered the world beetle market, thought it would be fun to invent a computer game based on his fantasy life, which seven psychiatrists, a school guidance counselor, and the Kyoto Board of Health had failed to eradicate, despite increasingly desperate attempts. In 1994, he took the idea to Honda and was thrown into the gutter. He had mistaken it for Nintendo, located next door. But he kept searching, and finally success ambushed him.

What it means: Pokémon is a combination of the phrases "pocket money," which Mifutsi never had enough of, though he does now; Pac Man, an early computer game Mifutsi enjoyed; "Parkay margarine," which he eats in large quantities; and "Hey, don't poke me, Mom," a slogan from a Japanese TV commercial for a popular brand of cattle prods in the 1960s, which Mifutsi also collected.

Where it can be found: in every known country (with the exception of Afghanistan, where even mention of the name subjects one to a penalty of death by being sucked into an industrial-strength vacuum cleaner while a boys choir sings the national anthem) and in every known medium. Pokémon can be played on Nintendo Game Boys, watched on movie and television screens, traded in the form of cards, read in comic books, listened to on CDs, spread on onion bagels like cream cheese, invested in through purchase of Pokémon savings bonds, studied at Pokémon State College in Fond du Lac, Wisconsin, smoked in "spliffs" purchased from musicians or injected directly into the brain with a gigantic plastic syringe sold at Wal-Mart and other leading retail chains.

How the characters and plot are configured: There are 150 basic Pokémon characters, and any child between the ages of four and 12 can recite their names, favorite weapons, method of reproduction and the 10,000 supercreatures they may evolve into, except, of course, in Kansas, where they all appear at the same time, brought into being by a Divine Creator. The characters do violent battle, but, happily, no one ever dies, except the occasional parent who learns how much money his child has been spending to collect the cards.

Which are the most popular characters: Porkymon, a warthog with the brain of a supermodel, dispatches its foes by contracting the flu and sneezing on them; Pickyman, part thunder god, part obsessive-compulsive, can mutate into Manny Pokeman, the only Jewish Pokémon character; Skunkosaur, a kind of smelly reptile, is accessible only by placing a Game Boy inside a microwave oven and heating at half power for 10 to 12 minutes; Batooti, half wombat, half copilot, can make the game crash at unexpected moments; Philbin, the hero figure (Reege-san in the Japanese version), shouts "Final answer?!" incessantly and awards cash prizes.

Where it got its name: Oh, wait, we did that one already. Sorry.

Why it is such a hit: because it affords children the chance to be in control of a complex universe and for once accumulate knowledge in a subject their parents do not understand, thus making them feel powerful and masterful, as well as educating them in the domain of commercial transactions as they trade for Pokémon cards. While some experts contend that the acquisitiveness factor emphasizes cupidity and greed at the expense of altruistic values, others argue with equal puissance, "Shut up, or I'll hit you very hard and then step on you after you fall down."

What is its deeper meaning for the society? Virtually none, although it does keep the little beggars from discovering sex for a couple of years.

ROSES FOR MOSES

Of all the hot new holiday movies that Media Person hasn't seen yet, his favorite is DreamWorks's epic *The Prince of Egypt*. What's wonderful about modern media is that you don't have to wait for a movie to open in order to fully appreciate it. Thanks to websites, stories in newspapers and magazines like *Entertainment Weekly*, promo clips shown on TV, releases of soundtracks and tie-in merchandise, the actual premiere of a blockbuster like *P of E* becomes almost redundant. You've already absorbed it all from the multimedia blitz that started months before. In fact, you may already be sick of it. Yes, it is possible to develop *Prince of Egypt* fatigue and actually contemplate passing on the theatrical showing to just wait for the video. Fight this sick tendency! Our economy—indeed, our way of life—depends on it.

Media Person doesn't know who came up with the story idea, but it's a brilliantly plotted, animated fantasy set in the always turbulent and mysterious Middle East. Coming at a time when most animated features are about insects, *P of E* takes for its subject . . . humans! This is a departure as bold as it is original.

Not only that, the producers have woven into the fabric of the drama evocative mythical themes from classic films of the past. The rebellion of hopelessly overmatched underdogs, aided by a mystical force, against the might of a powerful empire is of course an homage to *Star Wars*. The story of two brothers, one of whom is trained for leadership but who is ultimately eclipsed in greatness and wisdom by his younger sibling, obviously was inspired by *The Godfather*. The savagely beautiful desert setting is sheer *English Patient*. The motif of a somewhat inarticulate lad who finds that he has unexpected talents and interacts with important figures of history is an outright steal from *Forrest Gump*. Plus the characters look a lot like the ones in *Pocahontas* and *Aladdin*.

The film opens dynamically with the hero, Moses, already in trouble even though he was just born a few minutes ago. It seems his tribe, an obscure bunch of slaves called the Hebrews, who are involved in some kind of pyramid scheme, has annoyed Egypt's very strict leader, the Pharoah, and he orders the death penalty for all firstborn Hebrew males. To save her baby, Moses' mother puts him in a basket and sets it adrift in the Nile, tearfully calling, "Don't forget to write, even if it's just an occasional hieroglyphic." As he floats past the royal palace (everything in Egypt is on the Nile), Moses is spotted by the queen, who adopts him and raises him as a prince along with her son, Rameses, heir to the throne. As they are not particularly bright, none of the royals suspects that this is a Hebrew kid.

Rameses, by the way, is the voice of Ralph Fiennes (pronounced Rafe Fines) and Moses the voice of Val Kilmer (pronounced Vale Kimes). Other voices in the cast include Michelle Pfeiffer (Male Fifes) and Steve Martin (Safe Mates).

Anyway, the two boys bond as they grow up, hanging around used-chariot lots and sneaking out behind the Sphinx to smoke camels. But one day, wandering around the slums to satisfy a strange yearning for chopped liver, Moses hears people yelling, "Hey, look, it's Moishe!" The truth hits him like a six-ton brick. "Oy!" he exclaims, and we know that he knows. Turning his back on the royal family's plans to train him for a career as a decadent playboy, Moses goes into the desert, marries a Hebrew girl and becomes a humble shepherd.

But that career doesn't last long either, because one day Moses sees a burning bush (one of DreamWorks' less impressive special effects). He then hears the Voice of God (who worked for scale because he loved the script) telling him to return to Egypt and free the Hebrews. Naturally, he does, but not until the special effects get a lot better. Because Rameses, now the Pharoah, is dumb as a frog, God has to send down hideous plagues (one of which is rumored to be recycled from *A Bug's Life*), angels of death, all kinds of great stuff, scariest scenes since *Jurassic Park*. Audiences will weep in gratitude. Finally, the anguished Pharoah exclaims, "Oh, get outta here!" and the Hebrews depart Egypt as Whitney Houston and Mariah Carey raise their voices together (for the first time in history, as the website notes) in the inspiring hymn, "You Did It Yahweh."

But then that cretin Rameses changes his mind and sets out in pursuit. God parts the Red Sea for the Hebrews but drowns thousands of the Pharoah's troops in the most horrible and satisfying way imaginable. Moses then climbs Mount Sinai and receives the Ten Commandments, which enable the Hebrews to invent lawyers. Moses places the tablets in a special ark and from then on is called the arkist formerly known as Prince. Unfortunately, the ark gets lost and begins attracting raiders. But that's another story and DreamWorks is saving it for the sequel.

HIP-HOP HUN

Like Media Person, many of you are down with the February Blahs. This malady strikes about once a year usually, by an odd coincidence, in February, when you get so sick of winter you can't stand one more day of it but nevertheless know you'll be pummeled by many more weeks of it. You feel listless and dull. Your resistance is lowered and you become vulnerable to colds, flu, mad cow disease, and really bad television.

The media are no help. The ever-tedious Super Bowl left a gummy taste in your mouth. Even its supposedly sparkling commercials let you down and the proliferation of articles analyzing said commercials made you wonder if maybe there wasn't some truth to the Unabomber's thesis that Western civilization went horribly wrong around the time of the Industrial Revolution. Last week, Media Person was so starved for diver-

sion he was reduced to watching *Attila* on the USA Network
and reading up on the Sean (Puffy) Combs trial.

Strangely, it turns out the two celebrities had much in common. One was a barbarian who dressed in the skins of animals
and acquired a vast empire. The other was a fifth-century Hun
warlord. Both had colorful nicknames, Attila tagged the
Scourge of God and Combs the slightly less menacing Puff
Daddy. (Wonder what he puffed to acquire it?)

History is a bit vague on the Huns, owing to the deplorable
failure of barbarians to buy a notebook and jot down much of
anything that happened to them. We do know that they originated on the Asian steppes and then got bored with them, as
does just about everyone originating there. Venerating horse-
power, migrating westward, and mowing down anyone who got
in their way, they remind you a bit of our own American fore-
bears. But they lacked PR people so they were handicapped in
the myth department. The Huns were, however, tall, dark, and
beautiful, at least according to the USA Network. This news
doubtless came as a surprise to all the encyclopedia editors who
insist on describing them as short, bow-legged, Mongol types
but who wants to watch four hours of television about people
like that? Attila himself, played by some tanned wide receiver
named Gerard Butler with hair down to his saddle sores, looked
like he was starring in Barbarian Baywatch.

Like Puff Daddy, Attila got a lot of negative ink in his day;
the gossip columnists were forever painting him as a bad boy
and his posse as major havoc wreakers. But USA gave it a different spin entirely: The Huns were the have-nots, simple but honest, earthy and open. The Romans were a bunch of decadent,
trendy, sneaky, stab-you-in-the-back hypocrites, lording it over
everyone else, begging for a fall. Had he still been around, Attila
would've given these USA execs half his spoils from the sack of
Beverly Hills, plus all the oxen they could ravish.

Typically, Powers Boothe as the oily Roman general Scummius
befriends and mentors the young Attila but only so he can manipulate this cool young dude he recognizes as a potential enemy of

Rome. Fortunately, Attie has a rabbi with more mojo back home, this half-crazy spirit lady who bops around the Black Forest wearing a bird's nest on her head, making prophecies, putting spells on people and feeding magic birth control pills to the flame-haired slave girl Attie loves but who is owned by his evil brother, because as long as she doesn't bear the brother's child, she still doesn't really belong to him, under a landmark ruling by the Hun Supreme Court. When the two sibs fight a duel for the Hunnish throne and Attie takes an arrow in the kidney, Weird Wanda writhes around on the ground, somehow absorbing the pain for him.

History of this quality can certainly reveal a great deal about human behavior when it's taught well, don't you agree? It kind of puts that whole fall-of-the-Roman-Empire deal into perspective. And the Puffmeister's alleged offense, too. You know, compared to Attila's rap sheet, what's shooting up a nightclub and racing away with the cops in pursuit amount to, anyway? What is more indicative of the Puffster's sterling character is that he was so broken up by Jennifer Lopez's dumping him that the lovelorn romantic arranged to have 100 white doves and 100 pink balloons released beneath her hotel balcony, according to the *New York Post*, and that his mom, a platinum blond in knee-high boots, is at the trial to tell the press that she brought up her son right and he is innocent. "Sean has manners and he knows the right thing to do," she confided to the *New York Times*.

Now last week, writing about the convicts who temporarily escaped from Texas, Media Person prophesied they would become a movie. The very next day, the news came out that the contracts were being signed. You don't have to be Nostradamus to know that El Puffo too will get his tube drama. Media Person only hopes he doesn't have to wait a millennium and a half like poor Attila.

Carpool Tunnel Syndrome

JUDY GRUEN

My Ford is their Shepherd; they shall not walk.
They maketh the seats recline back at green lights;
They lead one another in carpool contention
They disrupteth my soul;
They guide me to their friends' homes for their play dates;
Yea, though I drive through the battle of traffic congestion,
I will fear no evil,
For school is nearby.
The playground and classrooms, they comfort me.
They straggle out from the car dragging backpacks;
I can now go get coffee; my latte runneth over.
Surely safe driving discounts shall follow me
all the days of my life,
And I shall drive around town in my Ford, forever.

I was sitting in the dental chair, a fat wad of purple modeling clay stuffed in the southeast corner of my mouth. I tried not to think of why I might have deserved this fate, lying semi-prone in a sad excuse for a lounge chair, feeling haplessly undignified in my little blue bib. I glanced at my watch, and realized impatiently that *Gone With the Wind* wasn't nearly as long as this visit to the Drill 'n' Bill Dental Center. By this point, my gums weren't the only things that were irritated.

I moved the little table chock full of dental instrumentation out of my way and swung myself out of the chair. I pried the modeling clay out of my mouth, signaled to my dentist, who was working in the next cubicle, flashing a laser over someone's uppers. I said, "Ah leafing."

Enunciation is much easier after the novocaine wears off.

"What are you doing?" he said in alarm. "I told you the impression needs five to eight minutes to set fully. You don't want us to have to do it a fourth time, do you?"

"Yuh fy minuth ith over. Ah leafing. Ah haf cahpooh."

"What?"

"*Cahpooh!* Kidth! Thkool!" I said, and, needing to display a sense of self-empowerment that belied my Daffy Duck speech, I ripped the blue bib off my neck.

"Oh, you have *carpool!* Why didn't you say so earlier?" The dentist became instantly sympathetic. "We'll work with this impression, then. I'm sure your crown will be fine. Run along now. Shirley!" he called to the office manager, "Mrs. Gruen has *carpool!* Don't bother her about the bill today. Just send it to her in the mail."

Not all dentists are this understanding, mind you. Especially since the Drill 'n' Bill Dental Center posts a sign in the waiting room that states clearly, "Payment is extracted when services are rendered." But as this true-life example shows, carpool can take over a mother's life as nothing other than pregnancy can.

One might not think that the job of ferrying children to and from school, sports and music practices, and other appointments would loom so large in the motherhood scheme. But trust me, once kids are on the school and after-school activity circuit, a mom's life becomes a seven-day-a-week game of beat-the-clock. Every activity, meeting, lunch date, medical appoint-ment, and chore suddenly revolve around drop-off and pickup times. Many schools and day care centers also begin charging by the minute if you are late. Some of these after-school work-ers, I think, were parking enforcement officers in a previous life. They just can't wait to write you up when your meter runs out.

Outside of those nasty behind-the-scenes machinations at presidential conventions, nothing is as political, as rife with drama, as carpool. Friendships are forged and others broken irrevocably over a missed three P.M. pickup. Divorces are rarely as messy as the dissolution of a long-standing carpool arrange-ment.

"Did I tell you what happened with Jan?" a friend asked me one day over a supermarket scrip purchase.

"No, what?"

"We're no longer speaking. She forgot to bring Ashleigh Caitlin home two weeks in a row on the Tuesday pickup, and since I was at work Ashleigh Caitlin missed her ballet lesson and now she isn't eligible to perform in the recital."

"Oh, no!" I gasped. "I had heard about Jan. I was warned not to carpool with her for just that reason. Monica told me that her son Leonardo also missed his semifinal basketball game when Jan spaced out of a four P.M. Thursday pickup, and they're not speaking, either."

"Well, Jan made up some excuse, of course, but we both know the truth. She just didn't make it a priority."

I learned the hard way that mothers are loath to throw a well-oiled carpool into disarray by introducing any new compli-cating factor. One summer, I switched my kids to a new school. It was ludicrously late to even attempt to find a carpool partner, but the thought of that several-mile trip each morning and afternoon without relief was enough to make me think the unthinkable: home schooling.

Once the kids were enrolled, though, my first imperative, even before checking out the uniform and book requirements, was to commandeer a copy of the parent roster and ingratiate myself into a carpool.

In my first dozen or so calls, I was treated with kindness and pity. "Oh dear, sorry, we made our arrangements last spring. But good luck to you. God knows you'll need it."

"You need a carpool *now?*" another asked, trying to hide her disbelief. Her tone reminded me of the old saying stating that a lack of planning on your part did not constitute an emergency on my part. If I am not mistaken, I may have also heard a hint of "Nyah nyah nyah nyah nyah, nyah!"

On my third call, I began to edge closer to a solution. The woman explained: "Well, I have an arrangement, but we may be able to squeeze you in. It depends on whether Lisa can change her daughter's after-school speech therapy to Saturdays, in which case I'll have room to take her son to his karate lesson on Wednesdays, but I really won't know that until Cheryl gets permission from her boss to arrive at nine instead of eight-thirty each day. So basically I'll have to get back to you."

While trying to keep everyone's contingency plans straight, I tried to squelch my fear that I'd be out of the loop completely. If I couldn't snag a partner, every morning, and every afternoon, in sickness and in health, till graduation do us part, I would end up the sole cabbie, snack dispenser, argument arbitrator, and the only one to repeatedly insist that all limbs and phlegm must remain inside the car at all times.

I continued calling other mothers, my fate hanging in the balance. Meanwhile, I decided to get assertive. As a former P.O.C. (Prisoner of Car) and veteran of two years without a carpool, I dared not consider my precarious emotional status if I didn't get one now. I might even suffer a bout of posttransit stress disorder. So I decided to write a personal ad. My clock was ticking, and I was getting more desperate by the day.

My first ad read as follows:

Handsome two-year-old minivan ISO same or SUV. Must enjoy leisurely drives in rush hour traffic with numerous children and backpacks. Clean oil filters, excellent air pressure. Fit 3,000#. High tolerance for *Teletubbies* theme music and the Disney radio station. Drivers with full tanks only, please.

Sure, everyone worries about the unmarried singles these days. Newspapers and magazines feature pages of small-print ads trying to lure the DPM with the SOH and a passion for dolphins to his true love, who had better be slim, fit, tanned, and ready for some power yoga if she had any chance for a LTR. But what about us drive-time singles? We may appear to be merely oversized vehicles plastered with boastful bumper stickers (MY CHILD WAS CHALKBOARD MONITOR OF THE MONTH), but we're crying out for companionship, too.

No one, but no one, should underestimate the importance of carpool, or the emotional toll it takes on drivers. One morning last spring before school ended, I met my friend Diane for coffee after morning drop-off. I got there first, and was savoring my Brazilian Sumatra when she arrived. I took one look at her and knew what she had gone through. Her expression could only be described as "terrorized."

"What happened?" I asked Diane.

"How do you do it each day?" she asked. "It's so exhausting!"

"You mean carpooling?"

"Yes! My God, just getting them into the car takes a half-hour! Who gets to sit in the copilot's seat, who can't sit in the back because that seat belt 'hurts,' whose arm isn't allowed to touch whose armrest. Then, once mine are all in and I have to pick up the kids down the block. They take forever to get themselves in, and step on everyone else's backpacks, which sets my kids to complaining again. This morning one of them also regaled us all with how many kids threw up in class yesterday, how far everyone's vomit projected. . . . Thank God I hadn't eaten yet. I swear, I've only been up for an hour and a half and I need to take a nap already."

"I know what you mean," I commiserated. "Today my

daughter cried all the way to school because she said her hair was too 'fat.' Two of the boys argued over whether the Mets have a chance in the World Series, and the youngest just kept kicking her brother's chair because he had taken the last juice box."

"What did you do?" Diane asked.

"I pulled over twice. The first time I made one kid get out and walk two blocks before letting him back in the car. The second time I pulled over so that *I* could take a walk down the block to clear my head. I was a wreck. It takes me at least half an hour to decompress after the morning drive. That's why I'm determined to get a carpool for next year. It's taking years off my life."

"Only seven hours till we have to go back," Diane said, trying to sound cheerful.

I realized that it was no coincidence that Prozac gained its enormous popularity at the same time that more moms entered the workforce, thus necessitating more hard-to-find carpool arrangements. Carpoolers-without-partners must be the least recognized minority group in our nation today, second only to left-handed vegan Gulf War vets. Researchers are only now beginning to realize that the medical condition mistakenly identified as "carpal tunnel syndrome" is really "carpool tunnel syndrome." The primary symptom is an inability to ever see your way clear to an appointment at eight o'clock in the morning or four o'clock in the afternoon for the rest of your life. Night sweats, migraines, and nausea are not uncommon.

When my first ad failed as bait, I pulled out all the stops for my second ad. After all, desperate times called for desperate measures:

Rugged, shapely hunk of tanned steel ISO up to four additional short passengers for committed LTR through urban streets. Gorgeous chassis. DMV-tested safe. A.M. or P.M.—your choice. Unlimited snacks provided to all passengers. Can withstand whining up to 60 decibels.

Will pay mileage and scrip requirements. Give us a test drive!

A bit overblown? Perhaps. But no more so than the thousands of bankrupt, foul-mouthed, follically challenged men and women out there who claim to be "sophisticated," "good looking," "witty," and "financially secure," while searching for love at a few bucks per line. Anyway, I was willing to do more than my fair share for this relationship.

Believe it or not, I had to turn down the two people who answered my second ad. One had been postmarked near the prison in Lompoc and the second demanded an exorbitant finder's fee for an introduction to someone known only as "Smokey."

Just when I was about to indulge my despair in a pint of Ben & Jerry's Chubby Hubby ice cream, the phone rang.

"Hello? My name's Shauna? I'm the one who laughed when you called me a few weeks ago about carpool? I told you I was all set? Well, ahem, I just got a call and I lost my afternoon carpool? Are you still available?"

Well now, the shoe was on the other accelerator, wasn't it? Once a pariah, I was now in demand. However, I wasn't sure whether I had confidence in a carpool partner who wasn't sure if her name was Shauna or not. And she *had* laughed when I called—very poor form. Still, I couldn't really afford to play hard to get in mid-August. We made a date to compare our kids' school, tai kwon do, creative drawing, speech therapy, and tennis lesson schedules and see if we were compatible.

And I'm happy to report that two other mothers also ended up calling, in breathless urgency, when their carpool partners ditched them at the last moment. Finally, I was in the driver's seat, so to speak.

By the time school started, I had learned that it's always darkest before the driveway, and I was able to tell my doctor that I wouldn't need that Prozac refill after all.

You Fill Out My Census

CHRIS HARRIS

A letter from the Director of the Census Bureau, Spring 2000

Dear U.S. Resident:

About one week from now, you will receive your U.S. Census form in the mail. It is extremely important that you return this form as promptly as possible. Do not even bother to fill out the form, if doing so will hamper its prompt return. Returning this form promptly is so important that we have chosen to spend millions on this advance reminder rather than begin addressing any of the numerous fundamental flaws in our census-taking procedures.

If for any reason you did not receive this letter, please return the enclosed card after checking the box marked "Did not receive this card." It is important that this be done promptly, as it will help us to determine how many people we will be unable to count.

If you have received this letter and you do not, or no longer, exist, it is yours to keep with our compliments. Simply write "Cancel" across your census form when it arrives and return the form in the postpaid envelope.

Note that some new ethnic categories have been added to the Census to more accurately reflect our nation's demographic makeup. In addition to existing groups, you will now be able to identify yourself as one or more of the following :

[ ] *White, but tan easily*

[ ] *Latino with crossover appeal*

[ ] *Reform Party member*

[ ] *One of those people who says "Have a good one."*

[ ] *Tiger Woods*

Also note that we are currently accepting applications for the position of Census Enumerator. Pay ranges from 54 cents (Wheeling, West Virginia) to 88 dollars (New York, New York) per hour. To insure that you possess the appropriate numerical skills, you must pass a test before being hired.

Sample Question:

Which of these numbers is not the number 4?

A) 4   B) 4   C) 4   D) 6

(Answer: D)

At the end of your training, you will be required to swear (or affirm) to use your newly acquired powers of enumeration only for good, never for evil. You will then receive a nonlaminated, easily forgeable red, white, and blue card confirming your new identity. (For those who are wondering, we have chosen these colors because they're the colors of our nation's flag!) This card should serve as sufficient identification to placate any suspicious residents, antigovernment separatists, and over-stimulated pit bulls you may encounter on your rounds.

While we're on the subject of our being staffed entirely by poorly supervised, barely screened, minimally trained temps, we would like to address the issue of colossal ineptitude in our bureau. We have been accused of undercounting certain segments of the population. This is simply not true, and we think all three of our nation's Native Americans will back us up on this. In 1990, for example, our count of people *exactly* matched the total population of the United States, according to Census statistics.

Here at the Census Bureau, we are always striving to give our citizens more. This year, "more" includes an extra digit added to every single street address (enjoy!). Moreover, although there are no problems with the Census, we are constantly making improvements to correct those problems. The Census after this one, for example, will represent a benchmark in accuracy and ease of use. Every citizen will be asked to purchase a hamburger from McDonald's on April 1, 2010. We will then drive over to the one in Bethesda and see how far the number has gone up.

   [***Note to self—need clever but friendly close, perhaps: "We're 'counting' on you!" Make sure to replace this paragraph before mailing letter out to every single person in the U.S. Also, pick up Maxithins for Judy.]

                     Sincerely,
                     Kenneth Prewitt
                     Director,
                     Bureau of the Census

Clarifications

CHRIS HARRIS

**Is it a politician's wife,
or a Pooh character?**

	Politician's Wife	Pooh Character
Rabbit		✓
Kitty	✓	
Tigger		✓
Tipper	✓	
Liddy	✓	
Piglet		✓
Lady Bird	✓	
Heffalump		✓
Dolly	✓	
Winnie	✓	

Is it an uplifting film about self-discovery, or an accusation against Bobby Knight?

	Uplifting Film	Bobby Knight Accusation
Choking Neil		✓
Chasing Amy	✓	
Finding Forrester	✓	
Slapping Daryl		✓
Kicking Patrick		✓
Being John Malkovich	✓	
Beating Steve Alford		✓
Keeping the Faith	✓	
Attacking the Assistant Coach		✓

Is it a Jedi Knight, or a dietary supplement?

	Jedi Knight	Dietary Supplement
Mace Windu	✓	
Ginkgo Biloba		✓
Fen-Phen		✓
Qui-Gon Jinn	✓	
Yoda	✓	
Yohimbe		✓
Ben Kenobi	✓	
Echinacea		✓
Anakin/Anacin	✓	

Is it a Meryl Streep accent, or a Tony Danza accent?

	Meryl Streep Accent	Tony Danza Accent
Italian-American man		✓
Polish woman	✓	
Midwestern woman	✓	
Australian woman	✓	
Southern woman	✓	
French woman	✓	
British woman	✓	
Irish woman	✓	
Scottish woman	✓	
Danish woman	✓	

Is it a troubled Balkan country, or a Def Leppard album?

	Balkan Country	Def Leppard Album
Slovenia	✓	
Bulgaria	✓	
Hysteria		✓
Albania	✓	
Euphoria		✓
Yugoslavia	✓	
Romania	✓	
Pyromania		✓
Adrenalize		✓

Is it a Spanish pop song, or a delicious soft cheese?

	Spanish Pop Song	Delicious Soft Cheese
La Vida Loca	✓	
Gorgonzola		✓
Mozzarella		✓
Macarena	✓	
Copacabana	✓	
Ricotta Salata		✓
La Isla Bonita	✓	
La Vache Qui Rit		✓
Velveeta		✓
Volare	✓	

Is it a James Bond character, battery size, or chromosome type?

	James Bond Character	Battery Size	Chromosome Type
D		✓	
Q	✓		
X			✓
M	✓		
C		✓	
Oddjob	✓		
A		✓	
Y			✓

Is it a martial art, or a delicious shrimp delicacy?

	Martial Art	Delicious Shrimp Delicacy
Judo	✓	
Cajun		✓
Kung Fu	✓	
Kung Pao		✓
Paella		✓
Capoeira	✓	
T'ai Chi	✓	
Tae Kwon Do	✓	
Thai Peanut Sauce		✓

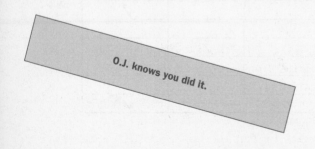

O.J. knows you did it.

Audiobooks for the Deaf

TIM HARROD

One of the most remarkable developments in popular media of the past ten or fifteen years has surely been the meteoric rise of the audiobook. The ability to hear a human voice speaking a popular work of literature, or a skillful abridgement of one, has made good writing more accessible and popular than at any time in human history. One can "read" the Bible or Shakespeare while driving a car, cooking dinner, or otherwise busying the hands with a separate task. Is it any less than a modern wonder that completely illiterate people can enjoy a good book, alone and at their leisure, to say nothing of the convenience to the blind?

It is a shame, though, that one segment of the population is unable to benefit from audio books: the deaf and hearing impaired. I propose an invention to remedy this situation: the Visual Audiobook Display Device or VADD.

The first-generation VADD will be somewhat large and heavy, roughly the size of a small end table, but this is par for the course with new technologies. I expect shoebox-size VADDs encased in fanciful colors of plastic can be developed within five to ten years. A cassette tape will load into the bottom of the device, which will play the book and channel the sound through a sophisticated voice-analysis algorithm that translates the speech into the written word, which will then be displayed on the readout panel.

The ingenuity of my invention is that now even hearing-impaired people who have a favorite audiobook can carry the light and portable box of cassettes everywhere they go, and enjoy their favorite works of literature from any location that has installed a VADD unit. I foresee a future where any library worth its salt will have a bank of VADDs along one wall as a service to the hearing-impaired community.

On the prototype I have constructed, the readout panel is made of alphanumeric LED strips taken from early-1980s pinball machines, yielding a somewhat angular script as well as rendering the text in a rather sickly orange color. This cost-cutting measure was the only way to keep the prototype below $1,000, but I am sure the fluid mastery of our elegant language so present in Keats's work can more than overcome the initial harshness of the experience.

Some work remains, I have no doubt. For example, in the unabridged audiobook of Stephen King's *The Green Mile*, the title appears as "F GIG FINE" on the display. My proposed solution is to advise the performers of audiobooks to enunciate a little more clearly in light of the new market their product will soon be opened up to. I have found through experimentation that the surest way to get a positive reading by the VADD is to speak at about one-third the usual speed, making sure to sustain some of the softer-sounding consonants such as b's, d's, f's, h's, j's, l's, m's, n's, r's, v's and z's a little longer than you would in normal conversation (a second or so is plenty). Following this plan has been observed to reduce errors by up to 90 percent. A seasoned VADD reader can decipher the stray typographical mishap through common sense. (That deaf people read more than others is well-documented!)

Though the slower recording process would require three to four times as many cassettes to vend in the finished product, they are made of flimsy plastic shells and the extra expense would surely be trivial. Doing nice things for the disabled also has that political-correctness-good-publicity-type aura about it. Maybe the government will subsidize the project. Impassioned Senate hearings with pleas like, "There are people who've never heard the world's greatest literary works" should loosen some purse strings. In this manner we can finally emancipate the hearing-impaired community from relying on an interpreter to listen to an audiobook and sign along.

I believe this project is viable and highly marketable once the technology is perfected. In the meantime, intermediary technologies come to mind:

1. As many deaf people have a limited ability to enjoy music by feeling the vibrations, special bass-heavy versions of audiobooks can possibly be enjoyed when played at very high volumes and when the "listener" places his or her hands directly on the speaker. The ability to decode vibrations into specific words can likely be developed with practice, especially if the consumer is also blind and therefore has experience reading Braille.

2. As the reading is audiotaped, videotape it as well for the benefit of lip-readers. In order to fit a six-hour program onto a single videocassette, the recording will have to be made at the slowest speed, with a matching loss of video quality, but this can be offset by focusing the camera directly at the speaker's mouth. This "audiotape-on-video" concept would be a remarkable "crossover" technology whereby a family of deaf and hearing people can all gather around the same television and enjoy the same version of Michael Crichton's *The Lost World* at the same time! *The Lost World* may not be the best example, already being available on videocassette, but lots of popular books are not.

3. As an absolute last resort, some manner of "transcript" could be made of the audiobook and sold to the hearing-impaired or perhaps packaged with the audiobook. Experts from the publishing industry would be better suited to advise on this matter.

Holy Tango of Poetry

If Poets Wrote Poems Whose Titles Were Anagrams of Their Names

FRANCIS HEANEY

Skinny Domicile

EMILY DICKINSON

I have a skinny Domicile—
Its Door is very narrow.
'Twill keep—I hope—the Reaper out—
His Scythe—and Bones—and Marrow.

Since Death is not a portly Chap,
The Entrance must be thin—
So—when my Final Moment comes—
He cannot wriggle in.

That's why I don't go out that much—
I can't fit through that Portal.
How dumb—to waste my Social Life
On Plans to be—immortal—

Toilets

T. S. Eliot

Let us go then, to the john,
Where the toilet seat waits to be sat upon
Like a lover's lap perched upon ceramic;
Let us go, through doors that do not always lock,
Which means you ought to knock
Lest opening one reveal a soul within
Who'll shout, "Stay out! Did you not see my shin,
Framed within the gap twixt floor and stall?"
No, I did not see that at all.
That is not what I saw, at all.

To the stall the people come to go,
Reading an obscene graffito.

We have lingered in the chamber labeled MEN
Till attendants proffer aftershave and mints
As we lather up our hands with soap, and rinse.

I Will Alarm Islamic Owls

WILLIAM CARLOS WILLIAMS

I will be alarming
the Islamic owls
that are in
the barn

and which
you warned me
are very jittery
and susceptible to loud noises

Forgive me
they see so well in the dark
so feathery
and so dedicated to Allah

Likable Wilma

WILLIAM BLAKE

Wilma, Wilma, in thy blouse,
Red-haired prehistoric spouse,
What immortal animator
Was thy slender waist's creator?

When the Rubble clan moved in,
Was Betty jealous of thy skin,
Thy noble nose, thy dimpled knee?
Did he who penciled Fred draw thee?

Wilma, Wilma, burning bright, ye
Cartoon goddess Aphrodite,
Was it Hanna or Barbera
Made thee hot as some caldera?

Hen Gonads

OGDEN NASH

I thought running a chicken breeding farm would
     be a simple matter,
Just pipe some romantic music into the chicken
     coop and chill some champagne and sit back
     and wait for the proverbial little feet's pitter-patter,
But it's turned out to be tricker than that to
     affect a chicken's libido,
Because I just don't know what chickens find attractive,
     I mean, when I go out on the town I dress to the
     nines, but does a chicken prefer a rooster in an
     opera hat and tuxedo?
Well, I can say definitively that she does not,
And if anyone has been considering the purchase of
     a rooster-sized tuxedo and opera hat you should
     come down here and take a look at this reasonably
     priced used set I've got.

Neither did my backup plan of spiking the chicken feed
  with Spanish fly produce results,
Nor the screening of nature documentaries intended for
  adults,
Nor threats of arroz con pollo,
Nor . . . well, I don't want to give all the
  embarrassing details,
    but let's just say there's nothing quite like asking a
    salesman if he has a vibrator specifically designed
    to stimulate hen gonads to make one feel like a
    total yo-yo.
Yes, I'm distinctly subpar at stirring romantic longings
  in the loins of a chicken, and when it comes to
  setting up blind dates in the poultry world,
    I make a pretty poor yenta,
So as for breeding chickens, perhaps I wasn't menta.

nice smug me

e. e. cummings

this here verse's
disjunct
    i used to
    stick to regular metered
        poetry
now i write onetwothreefourfive poemsjustlikethat
            Jesus

but this is simple work
        and what i want to know is
how much am i going to get paid for this
mister editor

Is a Sperm Like a Whale?

WILLIAM SHAKESPEARE

Shall I compare thee to a sperm whale, sperm?
Thou art more tiny and more resolute:
Rough tides may sway a sea-bound endotherm,
But naught diverts thy uterine commute.
Sometime too fierce the eye of squid may glint
And make a stout cetacean hunter quail;
Methinks 'twould take much more than bilious squint
To shake thee off the cunning ovum's trail.
Yet still thou art not so unlike, thou two,
Both coursing through a dark uncharted brine
While fore and aft there swims thy fellow crew;
And note this echo, little gamete mine:
As whales spray salty water from their spout,
So with a salty spray dost thou come out.

Halt, Dynamos

DYLAN THOMAS

Do not work harder than required to work,
Young men should sit around and drink all day;
Laze, laze, ignore the pressure not to shirk.

Though poor men may apply to be a clerk,
Because their jobs are not exciting they
Do not work harder than required to work.

Rich men, who sell and buy, eat at Le Cirque,
And take their "business trips" to Saint-Tropez,
Laze, laze, ignore the pressure not to shirk.

Old men around retirement age who lurk
At desks and hope no tasks will come their way
Do not work harder than required to work.

Smart men, in school, who learn with blinding smirk
That coasting through a class still earns an A,
Laze, laze, ignore the pressure not to shirk.

Don't visit every world like Captain Kirk;
Picard knows that the bridge is where to stay.
Do not work harder than required to work.
Laze, laze, ignore the pressure not to shirk.

DH

H.D.

DH, rend open the ball,
rip apart the seams,
bash it to pieces.

Pitchers can't hit
in the AL—
you are better than the pitcher
that chokes up and bunts
and runs pell-mell
yet rounds no base.

Hit the ball—
plough through it,
cleave it with the Ginsu knife
of your bat.

Kin Rip Phalli

PHILIP LARKIN

They trim your dick, your mum and dad.
They may not need to, but they do.
They take the foreskin that you had
And leave you smoother than bamboo.

But Dad was severed in his turn
By docs in old-style masks and gowns,
Who wore a look of unconcern
While snipping little penile crowns.

Man hands on suffering to man.
It stains indelibly as ink.
They cut you early as they can,
Then wonder why you need a shrink.

We Long Bony Dorks

GWENDOLYN BROOKS

We long bony dorks. We
real big on quarks. We

quote Python lines. We
know arcs and sines. We

not good at sports. We
black socks with shorts. We

beat up at noon. We
out-earn you soon.

I'm Leery, Jocks

JOYCE KILMER

I doubt that I shall ever view
Another football game with you.
You holler nonstop in my ear,
For every tackle makes you cheer,
Or bellow in a wounded way,
Depending on who makes the play.
I do not understand the charm
Of watching athletes doing harm.
Football's played for fools like you,
But I have better things to do.

Drawing Inky

GREGORY HISCHAK

I begin with the nose—at least, that's how I always begin—a little round circle in the center of the canvas. Just an outline because I'll go back and fill it in later.

From there I work outward—a muzzle, mouth, ears—then across the back, drawing a slightly upraised line at the rump. A tricky part: a deer's rump. Most mammals have really difficult rumps to draw. Every time I get to that rump thing I try to approach it different, but it just ends up a mammal's rump again.

I extend the line down from the difficult rump forming a hind leg, like that see? The leg crooks a bit here then descends into a large boot—a go-go boot in this case—extending up to calf length. I'll color them in with red paint later.

Because it's a Sacred Deer, you have this halo radiating off its head. That means it's sacred—are you catching any of this? Puffy cheeks, dark waiflike eyes and a little flop to the ears, cute as a button and called Inky. Radiating from the head of Inky, the cute Sacred Deer in go-go boots, is a halo of concen-

tric circles. The circles extend out to the edges of the canvas—
about eight feet—except for that patch up top I leave blank for
the seven moons. I used to stand on a chair to get the top cor-
ners of the canvas, but now I have this brush taped to a stick
like so.

While I'm up there with the stick, I'll go and start laying in
the mountain directly above Inky. The mountain also has a
bunch of lines radiating from it because it's a Sacred Mountain
and Sacred Mountains get lines too—Sacred Deer, Sacred
Mountain—don't ask me to explain these things.

The big Sacred Mountain is centered right here, like this, and
now above it I draw the moons. Seven moons pulled by seven
chariots pulled by four lions and three bears. Around the lions'
necks are these medallions. Why? Because it looks very cool.
You can't put enough lions with medallions around their necks
in a picture I always say.

The chariots each get a little bumper sticker saying they've
visited each of the seven parallel universes. The chariots pulled
by the three bears—notice each of the bears is a slightly different size—have bumper stickers saying HOW'S MY CHARIOTEER-
ING? 1-800-EAT-SCAT or VISUALIZE WHIRLED PEAS or I WENT TO A
PARALLEL UNIVERSE AND ALL I GOT WAS THIS LOUSY BUMPER
STICKER.

There are seven maidens riding the chariots. They dress alike,
but they're not on a team or anything, they just dress that way.
They're kind of homely because I just can't draw a good maiden
anymore. I used to draw a hot little halter-topped maiden until
my wife Lily, she told me to knock it off, so I did—you know,
por la familia, right?

So now I go back down here below Inky the Sacred Deer, and
while my wife Lily helps out by coloring in the lions and bears
and stuff, I'll draw the spheres. Four spheres of equal diameter
containing a dragon, a snake, a pomegranate, and a grout

sander, in that order. Beneath those, extending the whole length of the canvas, are the 33 levels of spiritual attainment, and that means an afternoon I don't get to spend at the car show.

What I do next is go in and draw every single person who will be born and assign them to one of these 33 levels. To be honest, I really can't remember everybody anymore. I just make some of them up . . . repeat a few. Again, Lily will go back and paint in the clothes. She has an eye for fabric and animal skins and such. Me, I'm more big picture.

I finish up the basic sketch with two forests on either side of Inky, the sacred deer. The forest on the left teams with every beast of land, sea, and air, except egrets which I just can't draw. I give all these creatures happy faces, and then I draw the whole shebang again on the right side of Inky—another identical forest with all those beasts of land, sea, and air—except that they're not the same animals as the left side—I put little frowning faces on these to get that dichotomy thing going. See that? Presto: dichotomy.

At the very bottom, under the 33 levels of spiritual attainment I draw this sun. Illuminating everything from below, very dramatic. It casts into relief this cave where I've drawn the three sages sitting on three La-Z-Boys and sometimes I give the sages medallions to wear too, like the lions.

In the background, seen through the trees of the forest and behind the Sacred Mountain, I draw in History, Geology, Schenectady, Mythology, What Is To Be, What Has Been, and what looks like somebody's high school yearbook. Hovering above is this arcing parade of stars and another lion—a small one—wearing this medallion.

Finally, coiling from the right side of the picture to the left, I draw this snake. Lily does some nice detail work on the snake—

I could tell you stories about her and snakes. The snake comes to a head here, wrapped around a tree trunk in the center of the right-hand forest. In the snake's mouth is an egg, or sometimes a small bird, or sometimes a nice piece of fruit—it's different every time. Sometimes I have the snake's mouth wrap itself around the nose of Inky, the Sacred Deer, but Lily always complains that the imagery is too heavy-handed. There's a place in creation for subtlety, she says—and she's right, you know.

So you see that the whole initial sketch took almost four days—remembering Monday was a short day because I bowl on Mondays. The last three days are all embellishment: Lily and I color things in using magentas, bright lime greens, and fuchsias—you know, colors found in nature. I use sand and shells in places where it's appropriate, and bits of tinfoil and broken glass in other places where it's appropriate. It's all beautiful. It all gets these large dollops of light I put over everything. It comes from this tube of life-colored pigment I use. It's from Malta and it costs an arm and a leg, but I use it everywhere. It greens deserts, makes skies rain. When touched by it, everything lives. Vermeer almost had it. Monet almost had it. Van Gogh came *this close* to having it until I squashed him like a bug—professional rivalry, I guess.

It's an alchemic thing, I suppose. It's *certainly* godlike—what you create lives and carries on without you. That's what I promised Van Gogh before I shot him in the chest—that what he created would live forever even though *he* would be snuffing it very soon.

On the seventh day Lily and I rest. We watch the painting all squirming around, vibrating with that pageantry of its own that it takes on—moving, seething, dynamic. Sometimes we take off our clothes and make love right here on the table—*geesh*, don't let her know I told you that.

★ ★ ★

Sometimes I almost hate to do it—how can you *not get attached* to your creations? Still a job is a job, and while I have no god that I'm accountable to—I still feel accountable. I'm a professional, right? So, when the sun sets on the seventh day, Lily and I open the big can of white latex and break out the rollers. It takes a heartbeat to cover the whole canvas. I let it set till morning when, again confronted by that big blank canvas, I begin with the nose—at least, that's how I always begin—a little round circle in the center of the canvas. Just an outline because I'll go back and fill it in later . . .

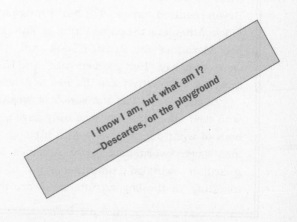

Kato Kaelin will rent your room.

I know I am, but what am I?
—Descartes, on the playground

Demosthenes

These days, a long speech makes many of us doze off, but the ancient Greeks had no trouble staying awake. Then again, in their amphitheaters, the seats were made of stone. Forensic—legal—oratory was the most admired kind in ancient Athens, where litigants were obliged to speak for themselves. We moderns mock a defendant who represents himself, particularly if we attended law school where we learned that a defendant would be better off paying us $300 an hour to speak for him. Among the most admired forensic orators of the Golden Age of Athens, the fourth century B.C., were Lycurgus, Hyperides, Aeschines, and Dinarchus. Although we have no tape recordings of any of these speakers, historians agree that none of them would have satisfied Patricia Duff.

Born in Athens in 384 B.C., Demosthenes is generally recognized as the greatest all-around orator of his day. (And he did it while wearing sandals; William Jennings Bryan required some sort of heavy brogans.) He roused his fellow Athenians to oppose Philip of Macedon and, later, his son Alexander the Great. ("Look out!" the Macedonians were apt to say, "He's got a speech!" And then they'd all run away. Or at least that was the idea in Athens.)

Demosthenes was the son of a wealthy swordmaker who died when the boy was only seven, depriving them both of what might have been a lifelong father-son argument—pen! sword! pen! sword! Aphobus, an unscrupulous guardian, swindled Demosthenes out of his inheritance, instilling in the boy an intense desire to grow up with sufficient eloquence to sue Aphobus. He began training to become an orator. (It would have killed his father.) According to Plutarch, Demosthenes built an underground study where he exercised his voice, and shaved half of his head so he couldn't go out in public. (They cared much more about attractive haircuts in those days.) Demosthenes is best known for overcoming his speech defect—perhaps a stammer—by practicing with pebbles in his mouth. He also trained by reciting verses when running and out of breath. It's kind of like Rocky if Rocky had been Barbara Walters's story, and if Barbara Walters (and the American viewing public) hadn't lost.

Despite his training, his first speech in the Athenian Assembly was a disaster: The audience laughed him out of the place. However, Demosthenes kept working, and in 363 B.C. he won his suit against Aphobus. So it's kind of like Rocky and Erin Brockovich, a woman who cared about a good haircut every bit as much as did those ancient Athenians. Demosthenes later went on to sue the sculptor Antenor. I'm not sure why. But if he is played by Julia Roberts in the movie, I, for one, look forward to the part where she poses for Antenor.

—Randy Cohen

For Whom the Tale Blows
(or The Curtain Also Rises)

GREGORY HISCHAK

I had another cognac and rolled a cigarette and smoked it and then I rolled another one and smoked that too. The morning was cool and sunny and I sat outside the cafe at the table farthest from the street. People walked by on their way to work and I waved to Michaud as he passed—glad that he didn't stop to ask why I missed kickboxing class the night before. As usual first lines were not coming easily to me:

"The Cast in Order of Appearance."

I scribbled with my pencil stub and then quickly crossed it out. "Simplify, Ernest, simplify," I said aloud, hitting my fist hard against my forehead and getting the attention of M. Récamier, who was watering the sidewalk. I ordered another cognac, dissembling the line into its components of vowel and consonant. Stripping it to its bones and then cutting it in half—like gutting a fish. I thought about fishing for awhile, considering how fishing was like writing, only without the funny rubber pants, and how you wrestled with an idea for a long time only to have the idea get away with a hook in its mouth. Sometimes you caught the idea in a net only to let it go because it was a small idea, and sometimes you hit the idea over its head with a little stick and took it home and rolled it in flour and fried it.

I recalled Gertrude's advice when I showed her my first draft. Repeat "Order of Appearance," she said, until it ran together and ran backwards and said "Appearance of Order," and then Gertrude repeated what she had just said and then she started to say it again but I got angry and left.

Returning to the work at hand I put my pencil to paper:
"The Cast."

Yes, that was better. I breathed deeply and began to relax.

With the morning's work done I headed toward Sylvia's to pick up my mail. Sylvia smiled from behind the counter when she handed me the papers and a box of Junior Mints.

"How's Ford's program coming, Ernest?"

"I think today was a good day."

"I'm glad. You write such beautiful programs."

The next day was warmer than the previous and I sat in the cafe at a table close to the street. There was a man with a cart selling onions and I bought one and put it in my pocket to eat later with the Ding Dong that I had in my other pocket as I began the morning's work:

"There will be two intermissions of ten-minute durations."

I dragged deeply from my cigarette, I felt my forehead creasing.

"Please refrain from bringing beverages and snacks outside of the lobby area."

What if the line could be expressed without its baroque ornamentation? Think of the war, Ernest. Could I say *"food and drink"* and still convey an aura of uninspiring wine and stale biscotti? Could I say *"Consume your food and drinks and sit down,"* disassembling the language still further? Sweat poured off my face and blotched my notebook:

"Shut your hole and watch."

Illuminating and urgent—like lightning along the Algarve. If I used tiny italics, I would have room to write about cows standing in woods and leaves crunching underfoot and the dribble of wine down chins and happy peasants carrying my golf clubs down to the lake, but instead I grimaced and scrawled:

"M. Apollinaire's understudy is Raul Petoing, who also performs the role of Professor Harold Hill on Saturday matinees."

I didn't want to write anymore that day. Writing made me cranky and being cranky made me hungry, so I ordered a small fish from M. Récamier because I had been thinking about fish and I ate it and then I took out my onion and ate that too. I ordered another cognac from Récamier, and while I waited for it I slowly removed the foil wrapping from my Ding Dong.

Instead of buying into my brother's muffler franchise when given the chance, I had become a writer. It was a difficult calling and I shut my eyes, letting the sun warm my lids. I thought about walking down the shady side of the rue de l'Odéon to rue Cardinal Lemoine and across the Boulevard St. Germain to rue d'Assas, knowing if I did that I wouldn't know how to get back—and I'd have to call Hadley to pick me up—but if I cut through the gardens to the Closerie des Lilas, keeping Halles aux Vins on the right, I would get to the jette where I would find Francis throwing rocks into the canal. I liked throwing rocks into the canal with Francis—brooding and throwing rocks—Francis and I had talked about going to Spain together that summer where I told him there were lots of streams and lots of rocks to throw into them. I explained how the streams were clear and cold and the rocks were hard and gray and made a white splash when they hit the water. Francis was quiet for awhile and then asked if Zelda could tag along and I told him I didn't think so.

"So, how's my program coming, Ernest?"

I jumped in my chair, upsetting my Ding Dong. The way a raccoon crosses a street when it sees a particularly nice piece of garbage on the other side, Ford Madox Ford had crossed the street and stood behind me. Ford's name irritated me because I always made a point of addressing him by his last name, but he always assumed I was addressing him by his first name. I didn't like Ford and he knew it.

"Damn you, Ford, don't ever sneak up on me like that."

"I need to take the program to Kinko's tomorrow, is it going to be ready?"

"Tomorrow? If you want garbage then yes, it will be ready tomorrow."

"Garbage is fine." Ford pulled out a wrinkled piece of cheese wrapper and my neck turned red knowing what was coming.

"I have a few things we need to add after the bios . . ."

"I was putting in a piece about trout fishing after the bios."

"Monsieur Bouteleau bought a very large ad space."

"Bouteleau is an idiot who sells exercise machines."

"Fitness equipment, Ernest. He sells NordicTracks and he bought the inside back cover."

"My fishing piece was going on the back cover. You're taking out my fishing piece to sell exercise machines?" I took a swing at Ford but he ducked away from the table and headed back across the street cackling with a high-pitched laugh that made me want to put my cigarette out on his nose.

I yelled after him "Who the hell wants ad space when they can read about cows and trout and wine and hills and clouds and—"

Ford turned back and shouted from across the street, "Just slide it under my door when it is typed, and don't forget to mention Guillaume's understudy."

Amenities

GREGORY HISCHAK

True, its close proximity to my firm made it a nice apartment, but I still drove the five blocks to work. True, it had sweeping views of bay and mountain, but I quickly became indifferent to the leering presence of bay and mountain. True, my new home—an older renovated building downtown, a genuine artist's loft—was expensive, but I had the money. If asked, I would admit to some guilt about displacing the genuine artists who had lived there, but no one ever asked. I felt bad about the market economics of place, but the apartment came with a washer and dryer and old world charm and sometimes a washer and dryer with old world charm speaks louder than economics. In truth, I laid out $1,600 a month for an aura of bohemia coupled with a washer and dryer.

Fourteen-foot exposed brick walls, floor-to-ceiling windows, and genuine paint-splattered hardwood floors. As a nod to its more Left Bank past, and to alleviate some of the bad Feng Shui that came with gentrification, the property management left an actual artist in each of the units.

A small artist, not established.

Early one Saturday morning, I was shown an available unit by a portly, shifty-eyed woman in a magenta pantsuit named Claudia. Proudly selling the unit's numerous amenities, she finally brought me into the kitchen, pointing out the disposal, the self-cleaning oven, the built-in microwave/bread maker and, curled up under the sink, stubble-chinned and corduroyed, the artist that came with the artist's loft. As soon as Claudia opened the cupboard the artist slowly unwrapped himself from around the disposal's pipe-metal entrails and rolled over onto his side, averting his face from the early glare of northern exposure.

"Your artist," Claudia the manager said, smiling.

"Very nice," I said, "He seems a bit sluggish, though."

"It's early."

"What's his medium?"

"Mostly figurative work in oils."

"And there's off-street parking?"

"Of course."

"I'll take it."

I moved into my genuine artist's loft with my genuine artist the following week. I made it clear to my artist that he was free to move about the apartment while I was gone, and he could help himself to whatever hummus and grapes I left in the fridge—but he could not have friends over. No collaboration. I told my artist I was planning a small dinner party soon and wanted a couple of in-progress works scattered about the place.

"I've been working on a series of zinc plate etchings, actually," my artist said.

"I want oils. Unfinished oils, got it? And if I catch you doing zinc plate etchings on my couch your ass is down in the storage locker, right?"

My artist nodded.

I liked my apartment. I liked impressing guests with the industrial flavor of the secured entry lobby, the quiet urbane roar of the carpeted lift, the motion-sensor track lighting that was activated when stepping through the front door to reveal sunken hardwood floors and casually arranged issues of *Art in America*, and, squatting under a potted fica, my artist. Laying down his oil pastels, my artist would quietly explain to my guests his work in progress. After a little bemused banter and our vague nods of encouragement, my artist would crawl under the sink as my guests and I continued on with chilled wine and lemon tarragon chicken.

The lawyer in the unit across the hall had a bronze caster. The next-door unit came with a monoprint artist. There was an attractive software consultant in 306 who frequently walked her artist outside the building.

"Organic abstractionist," she answered when we stopped once to make small talk and scratch her artist behind its ears.

"Mine is doing figurative work in oils mostly."

"How nice. Do you have a washer and dryer too?"

"Absolutely."

I returned home late one Sunday after a long weekend of stock speculation to find a five-foot by eight-foot sheet of kraft paper covering the kitchen floor, with my artist squatting in the middle sweeping a thick gray charcoal stick from side to side across it.

"It's an atonal landscape exploring notions of place and identity," the artist explained when I asked him how he thought I was going to get to my microwave/bread maker. It annoyed me that he was discussing his work without there being any dinner guests present.

"Save it," I said, scuffing across the corner of his work with my Guccis. "I want you under the sink."

"The monochromatic palette suggesting an emotional or moral isolation . . ."

"What part of *under the sink* didn't you understand?"

My artist sighed and began putting away his charcoals.

"You don't like me, do you?" he asked quietly as he pulled the cabinet shut behind him.

"You're an amenity. Of course I like you."

★   ★   ★

The software consultant in 306 had her organic abstractionist run
away one morning while being walked. He ducked down an alley
while she returned a video; it would prove not to be an isolated
incident. Shortly afterward, the performance artist in 112 ran
amuck, filling the unit with toast. The glassworker in 314 started
a small fire and ruined a new set of curtains. The artist in 505 was
twice caught drawing its tenant in the shower. After about three
months of sporadic oils and charcoal landscapes, my artist started
going on the fritz as well. He stopped working and sat brooding,
staring at the sprinkler valves in the ceiling for hours at a time.

"Paint something, damnit," I said.

"I can't."

"I'll let you collaborate with the jewelry artist in 211."

My artist shook his head. "I don't think so."

I left M&Ms on the coffee table, which my artist finished off,
but no works in progress appeared. When guests came over, my
artist was surly and wouldn't discuss the impressionist show that
everyone wanted him to talk about. I whacked him with a rolled
up *Wall Street Journal*, but even that produced no art. I called
Claudia, the manager, and complained that my artist wasn't
working, and she came over. Squatting under the counter with a
flashlight for several minutes, Claudia finally rose, turned to me
and shook her head.

"He's shot. I have an installation artist I could bring down
from 520."

"Nothing else in oils?"

"There's an allegorical landscapist on the first floor, but I
think it's acrylics."

"I'm going to have to talk to the property managers."

"Suit yourself, but we're talking about artists here. They
aren't covered in the lease."

I let Claudia leave with my artist. Standing alone near the floor-
to-ceiling windows, I observed the play of light and shadow

across the surface of the bay before closing the curtains so I could make calls without distraction. Markets were opening in Tokyo.

There was a butt of a charcoal stick sitting on my *Vanity Fair*. My artist's charcoal. I picked it up and examined it for a few minutes, absentmindedly scrawling across the top of my Day-Timer while waiting for my call to go through. I drew a matchsticklike swing set, and on its top crossbar I drew a large black bird—a crow. When I finally set the charcoal stick down, an oily smudge was left across my index finger and thumb that would prove difficult to wash off.

The next week, my washer and dryer crapped out on me.

Be decisive. Maybe. If you want to.

Vincent at the Knobs

GREGORY HISCHAK

Dear Theo,

The weather here in Provence now an unbroken series of cloudless days and starry nights. I draw the dark writhing lines of cypresses against azure sky, their erect contorted lines breaking like spires the horizontal fields outside Arles.

I can now move my left hand clockwise while rotating my right hand counterclockwise. This I have practiced in my little room all winter and am able to render—with some semblance of accuracy—a circle. This morning, in one supple turn of wrist, I etched the perfect half dome of Ginoux's haystack. The unhurried squeaking of white knobs filled the groves where I sat and, for the moment, I was at peace.

At dusk I returned to my room above the cafe, carefully holding the Etch A Sketch flat ahead of me. I found Gauguin sitting at the table fondling a Slinky and asked him if he could tell where I contoured the horizon line around the foreground cypress—and he could not tell, Theo—*he could not tell!*

Your loving brother,
Vincent

Dear Theo,

The townsfolk here in Arles have eyed me strangely from the beginning. They whisper I am possessed by demons and tell their children to keep away from "the crazy Dutchman with the little red screens." They are a simple people who care little for art, but they make excellent bread and placemats.

There is this line dictated by nature and masterable by thumb and index finger. Yet it is a technique that can blind one from the true art—that which is projected from the heart and cannot be captured by mere craft. Craft is crippling like a palsy and blinding like a big papier-mâché rabbit's head. This is what Gauguin said last night—though I believe he was asleep as he muttered it.

                                          Vincent

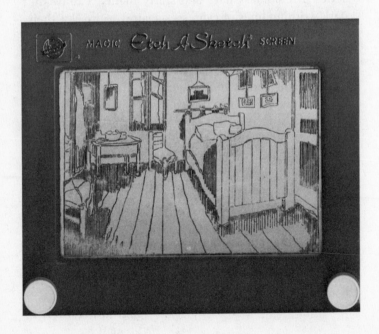

Dear Theo,

Please send me another straw hat. Gauguin sat on the one you sent last month—deliberately, I think. Gauguin possesses a maliciousness I was unaware of until we moved in together. All day he sits in the cafe downstairs and when evening falls he is still there, drinking absinthe beneath the overhead glare of

gaslight. He moves his knobs methodically from left to right to left to right until he has cleared off the entire screen—the internal pulleys and gears of the instrument made visible through the glass.

I scuff at his bleak exercises and he explodes in front of the whole cafe.

"This is what the future of art will be, Vincent!" he shouts running around the room with his arms extended, bellowing like a train, "This is how it will all be! Choo-choo!"

Gauguin is some sort of primitive and I tell him so as we are escorted out of the cafe and asked not to return.

Outside on the street, Gauguin continues to run in circles beneath the stars choochooing. He says that I am melancholic and hyperactive, he says that I stick my tongue out when I draw difficult things. I run home to bed and when Gauguin enters, some hours later, I do not whisper "Good Night, John-Boy" the way he likes me to.

Yesterday I finished a difficult still life: my crushed straw hat, my pipe and the Danielle Steel novel your lovely wife sent me, all arranged on a chair. Getting the parallel curvatures of the pipe was technically challenging—and in truth, I may have stuck my tongue out a little. I was particularly proud of the foreshortened ellipse of the hat and I showed it to Gauguin when he came home. He grunted and collapsed to the floor, but I believe he thought it was good. When I awoke the next morning the still life had been turned upside down and shaken. I do not think it was an accident, Theo.

Please don't forget about that straw hat.

> Your loving brother,
> Vincent

Dear Theo,

Gauguin and I had another terrible fight yesterday. When I came home from sketching he was sitting at the table, still in his pajamas, drawing stairs on an Etch A Sketch that I spent the day before drawing a vase of sunflowers onto—he was drawing stairs!

"Who the hell wants pictures of sunflowers?" he slurred, "This is the future, Vincent—stairs."

I exploded and told him that rather than sit around my room, drinking my Tang all day, playing on my Etch A Sketches . . . and not cleaning the bathroom like he said he would, perhaps he should go somewhere far away and find some nubile young thing to practice *his stairs* on.

This I told him.

He sat on my hat. The new straw hat that you sent me, quite maliciously I'm sure of it. He then took the Twister mat—the one we bought together—and left. I have not seen him since.

Please send me another straw hat.

Vincent

Dear Theo,

Once again technique blinds me from the heart. I have worked all summer and all I have to show for it are dozens of little gray screens in various states of

completion. There is no counter space in my room anymore. Etch A Sketches across the bed, under the bed, between the mattresses, under the rug. All day I am stumbling over knobs and in a state of despair last night I broke open an Etch A Sketch of Dr. Gachet's daughter, swallowing much of the aluminum filling. It wasn't too bad actually, but I sat on the toilet all night with terrible cramps and this morning I cut my ear shaving and had to be rushed to Ste. Rémy.

I returned home this afternoon in wretched shape and turned all my screens upside down, shaking them—except for a drawing of a peach orchard that I made last week. I am pleased with its linework of branches and fence and have sent it to you with careful instructions to Roulin, the postman, to see that it remains flat. I know we have been unsuccessful at this in the past, but maybe this time Roulin will get it through. Thank your lovely wife for the new straw hat, I will begin etching it immediately.

Yours,
Vincent

Dear Theo,

I have spent all month working on one picture—a wheat field outside of town. In heavy wind, the Etch A Sketch roped to my knees, I draw a field of near-ripened wheat. The wheat glows vermilion and ocher in late summer light against approaching storm clouds and this essence of foreboding I attempt to capture in contour line over and over.

A murder of crows nests among the stalks and when they fly it makes for a difficult rendering—I would prefer if they remained on the ground. It is difficult, this line that connects the crow to the ground and a cloud to a field. A dark gray line against gray that connects heaven to earth, an i to its dot, a nose to its mouth—this etched gray line that connects and binds—enslaving me into its confining renderment. Such is the hopelessness of this medium I have chosen.

On days like this my life unravels, Theo, a long gray contour line connecting everything yet disconnected, begging to be inverted and shook. Sometimes we progress so far only to be inverted and shook. To be gray. To be blank.

I would prefer it if the crows remained on the ground.

Your loving brother,
Vincent

A Brush with Greatness

CYNTHIA KAPLAN

On the heels of the unprecedented response the brand new sport of synchronized diving received at the Sydney Olympics, the International Olympic Committee has announced that painting will debut as an Olympic sport at the 2002 Winter Games in Salt Lake City, Utah. Bob Ross of public television's *The Joy of Painting* has been posthumously named chairman of the Olympic Painting Committee.

Tickets will go on sale for the Olympic Painting venue, Room 106 at the Joseph Smith Elementary School in Salt Lake City, in early February. In light of rumors that district officials accepted money and sex from Joseph Smith PTA moms in order to secure the school's bid for the painting competition, PTA president Marge Petersen had only this to say about District Five manager Brett Tingey: "You want me to say I never had a drink with the man? I'm friendly with a couple of his wives. That's all. Christ Almighty!"

The painting competition will consist of two mandatory elements, the compulsory Still Life with Fruit and Dead Partridges, which will account for one-third of the total score,

and the Free Paint, which will account for the final two-thirds
of the score and will consist of one of three painting styles to be
chosen on a random basis every four years by a person unrelated to anything. These three styles are: Seascapes, Animal
Portraiture, and In the Style of the Artist Ross Bleckner.

In the week since the I.O.C. announcement that "Seascapes"
was to be the subject of the Free Paint in Salt Lake, athletes from
all over the world have converged on the Seascape Training
Facility or the SeaTrainFac, in Marblehead, Massachusetts,
where they can train in palette position, the many uses of the ver-
satile burnt sienna, and staying within the lines.

There had been some controversy over whether Ross
Bleckner would have been allowed to compete for a place on
the Olympic Painting Team had "In the Style of the Artist Ross
Bleckner" been chosen as the subject of the Free Paint. This
complex issue will surely be revisited by the committee in 2006
or 2010.

Judging of Olympic Painting will be based on a combination of elements. They are: technical merit, artistic expression
and, in the Free Paint, wave height. Fifty percent of an athlete's
score will reflect the combined political interests of the Eastern
European Painting Cartel or the EEPCart, and 50 percent will
be based on intangibles.

Drugs will be prohibited in Painting as they are in other
Olympic sports, with the exception of heroin, which is not considered a performance enhancing drug in the painting world.
Crack cocaine will, however, be made available to judges and
spectators *with a prescription* during the two-day competition.

In keeping with Olympic tradition, television coverage of all
Painting events will commence immediately after the winners
have been announced by local news anchors and will be presented in a montage format to music from *The Land Before
Time IV*. Half-hour profiles of all athletes will air instead of live
coverage, with intermittent updates of Americans in competition, particularly those in last or next-to-last place.

Already some favorites have emerged from the tens of U.S.

Olympic hopefuls. Janet Whitehead of Jupiter, Florida, a former Junior National Champion known for her portraits of wallabies, has been training vigorously at SeaTrainFac under the expert tutelage of Ronald "Ron" Johannson, a shrimper from Camden, Maine, himself renowned for his uncanny proficiency in forecasting nor'easters. Stan and Shana Eisenberg, the twins from Scranton, Pennsylvania, spent the summer at Lake Placid with coach Ekaterina Covandova-Smithee, where they practiced lake views and worked with a wave machine before entering the demanding SeaTrainFac program in early November. It should be noted that Stan was cleared of charges that he painted by numbers at the World Games in Bucharest. Finally, if anyone has Olympic gold in his future it is Zachy Whistler of Venice Beach, California. Zachy, who hails from a long line of competitive painters and is known the world over for his credo "Paint till you faint," recently came back from a nasty index-finger sprain while painting a clown at the Western Regionals.

The U.S. Painting Team will be announced at the end of the January trials at the Art Mart in Utica, New York.

Also in contention will be athletes from one or two other countries. Favored to win at least silver if not bronze or gold in the compulsory Still Life with Fruit and Dead Partridges competition is Rudolfo Castellenata, Jr. from Spain, whose father, Rudolfo Sr., is a petty criminal infamous in the province of St. M——, north of Barcelona, for poaching quail, grouse, and other wild fowl from the private estate of Señor Saverio di Banderas, a local grower of Bosc pears. Though only seventeen years old, Rudolfo Jr. has seen a lot of dead birds and is no stranger to fruit. Another front-runner is the diminutive, much revered Minnie Mikimoti of Japan. At four feet six inches, Minnie is the shortest athlete in the three-year history of competitive painting. Whether her small stature will be a factor at Salt Lake remains to be seen. Unfortunately, she did not meet the height requirement at SeaTrainFac. Also worthy of mention is Laddie "Saul" MacNamara of Edinburgh, Scotland, an experienced renderer of craggy shorelines, whose work is regarded as a paradoxical combination of unabashedly exuberant and obliquely subtle. There is some concern, however, that MacNamara will not be permitted to compete because the Eastern European judges do not know what a paradox is.

The International Olympic Committee will meet again this summer to consider introducing synchronized freestyle skiing and Shakespearean acting on ice at Torino in 2006.

LESS POPULAR BARS

Naughty's
Scruples
Rumors Lounge
Trampp's
Charlie and Charlie's
Simpletons
DUI Friday's
The Pulled Groin
Effluvia
Club 1040
Bea Arthur's
The Lowered Standard
At the Sign of the
   Bloated Haggis
Serrated Edge
Mazlow's
The Hideous Rictus

Tonto's
Skeet 'n' Brew
Scotch 'n' Stogie
The Doric Tavern
J. Edgar's
Karaokefenokee
Petri Dish
Club Gergen
Flailer's
Orifice
The Alger Hiss Room
Fisticuffs
The Meat Locker
World Famous Beverage
Macbeth's!
The Double Wide
Secondhand Smoke

The Rusty Tankard
Tantrum's
Club Terre Haute
Busty's
Get the Hell Inn
Queasy Street
Skank's
The Old Oil Derrick
Jitters Lounge
Scared Straight Tavern
Decibel's
The Greek Baths
Blimey!
Angry Micks
Quitter's

—Stuart Wade

Hall of Near-Fame

MARK KATZ

Since its foundation in 1981, the Hall of Near-Fame annually honors those contemporary and historical figures whose names are affixed to the asterisks of history.* This year's induction ceremony will be held on Monday, November 9 in the Buzz Aldrin Auditorium of the Hall of Near-Fame, located just outside Manhattan in Astoria, Queens. The master of ceremonies, Kitty Dukakis, is a 1992 inductee who found near-fame when she came within 260 electoral votes of becoming America's first Jewish first lady. She is also the wife of 1980 inductee Michael S. Dukakis.

Depending on how many people RSVP, this year's Hall of Near-Fame inductees are:

Emilio Baldwin. The youngest of the Baldwin brothers, Emilio inherited too few of the family's winning traits and set out to make it on his rough-hewn bad looks. Despite his deficit of

---

*Except in 1984, 1985, 1988, and 1993–96, when the ceremonies were canceled due to lack of interest or, as was the case in 1991, the Persian Gulf War.

appeal and talent, Emilio spent three seasons playing the part of Ziggy the emotionally scarred math genius on television's *Saved By the Bell: The Bitter Years*. In his ample spare time, Emilio stumps for local Democratic school board members and town council candidates in Massapequa, Long Island.

Vidalia. The first and only Amish supermodel is a woman so heart-achingly beautiful, Donald Trump would marry her without a prenup. But her modeling career came to an end almost as soon as it began, as her fervent religious belief that the camera steals one's soul was not well-received in an industry so fervently soulless. The haunting sketch-artist rendition of Vidalia that graced the cover of last year's *Lancaster County Tourism Guide* is the only tantalizing hint of a modeling career that might have been.

Ramfir Bar-Ishnay. The only major literary figure still writing in the long-forgotten Semitic tongue of Ugaritic. As a result, no one is certain whether his extraordinarily prolific output (59 phone-book-thick novels) is filled with deft prose or pure shit. Bar-Ishnay's best-known work, entitled *Shrêwob Phupa Phupa*, is on a topic known only to him but believed by scholars to involve at least two Phupas. The whereabouts of Mr. Bar-Ishnay are also a mystery, as he lived as a recluse since the Ayatollah Khomeini condemned him to death in 1987 just in case there was anything heretical in his writings.

Nigel Best. The older brother of ex-Beatle Pete Best, the ill-fated drummer who John, Paul, and George ousted in favor of Ringo. Liverpool legend has it that on October 22, 1960, Nigel Best was set to audition for the Beatles but was confined to bed that day with the shingles. When Nigel sent his brother Pete (also a percussionist) to reschedule, the boys asked Pete to try out instead. And the rest, as they say, is near-history.

Tony "Nondescript" Lombardo. An otherwise successful organized crime figure of the 1940s who defied colorful characterization. At different times in his violent career, he was known as Tony "Tapioca" Lombardo, Tony "Brown Socks" Lombardo, "Dishwater" Tony Lombardo, and Tony "Third Guy on the Right" Lombardo.

"Astonishing" Stan Rohrbacher. The second worst player on the roster of the 1962 expansion Mets, Rohrbacher was eclipsed by "Marvelous" Marv Throneberry in his bid to be the poster boy for the most hapless team in the history of professional sports. An anemic hitter and inadequate fielder, Rohrbacher had only good luck to blame for his slightly favorable season statistics; seven of his total sixteen hits that season left his bat accidentally as he bailed out of the batter's box for fear of being hit.

	MARVELOUS MARV THRONEBERRY	"ASTONISHING" STAN ROHRBACHER
AVG.	.167	.202
RBI	6	9
HR	0	0
Errors	23	21

Vladimir Pabushkin. A little-noted behavioral scientist often chastised by peers—including many strongly worded rebukes from his mentor Dr. Ivan Pavlov—for his sloppy lab techniques. In his one and only published study, he chronicled the "Pabushkin Effect," the phenomenon of his tendency to salivate whenever his dogs barked, and by doing so, proved nothing of any scientific significance whatsoever.

The Earl of Witherspoon. An eleventh-century English baron who, according to lore, grew hungry during a marathon session of cribbage but did not want the disruption of a sit-down meal. Instead he made this odd request to his servants: place a single piece of bread between two thick slices of roasted meats, slathering each on the exposed outside with condiments and garnish. The result they brought him was such an unwieldy mess, it quickly rendered the playing cards unusable. The experiment was immediately stopped and never spoken of again. Three centuries later, a nobleman residing in the same manor unearthed the original notebook sketches, inverted the design, and became the namesake for one of the world's most enduring and best-loved lunches.

Mediocrites. Ancient Greek philosopher credited with inventing the process of procrastination, as well as the mathematic principle of rounding off. As a youth, he declined an invitation to become a disciple of Socrates, choosing instead to become his *nuch-shlepper.* Like many of the ancients, what we know about Mediocrites survives only in fragments. His name appears but once in the Socratic *Dialogues*, when in response to a question about the nature of truth, he replied, "Let me get back to you on that one, Socrates." In the wake of tribunals that followed the trial of Socrates, Mediocrites was indicted for his astonishing lack of accomplishment and sentenced to death by his own hand. Intrigued by the notion of becoming a martyr for procrastination, Mediocrites spoke of suicide often, only to die decades later of complications following a broken hip.

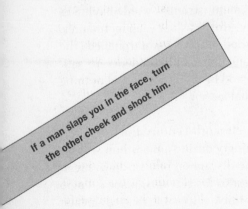
If a man slaps you in the face, turn the other cheek and shoot him.

Near-Deathbed Requests

MARK KATZ

The worst part of dying, I imagine, is ceasing to exist. Brushes with death force us to confront the unknowable void and the grim prospect of eternal nothingness. But during a late-season bout with this year's flu—which I felt certain I would lose—metaphysics gave way to death's more mundane dilemmas. In my woozy DayQuil haze, I contemplated the consequence of my untimely passing, conjuring the many ill-considered judgments, gestures, and rationalizations that might be made with the license of these words: *"Mark would have wanted it that way."*

Today I am a flu survivor, but one still haunted by the niggling details of my aftermath. To avoid confusion, I left specific instructions on a stack of unused Kleenex:

Attending the Funeral

If you find yourself wondering, "Did I know Mark well enough to attend his funeral?," the answer is yes. Valid or not, one of the measures of a life's worth is the head count at the funeral, and having reviewed the guest list, I must rely on acquaintances and friends-of-friends to reach critical mass. Each pewful of mourners is another round of ammo in my send-off salute.

For those who are traveling when I die: if you have an unrestricted coach ticket, you can return without penalties and your attendance will be expected. If you are traveling on a nonrefundable SuperSaver™ and have to purchase a new ticket, I wouldn't have wanted you to spend more than [*see accompanying chart*]:

$100	co-workers, lapsed friends
$250	friends, relatives (cousins, *et al.*)
$400	immediate family and close friends, current girlfriends
$500	old girlfriends

Regarding theater tickets: If it's a show you've been dying to see and tickets are impossible to get, that's one thing. But if it's anything involving David Copperfield, just eat the tickets and show up without complaint.

Interview Requests

Should the tragic circumstance of my death involve gruesome crime, faddish disease, or spectacular disaster, the media will likely take an interest and may try to reach you for a tearful interview. Who do you agree to talk to?

YES: David Frost, Bryant Gumbel, Bill Moyers, Ken Burns, Lesley Stahl

NO: Larry King, Stone Phillips, Gabe Pressman, Bob Woodward, Andy Rooney

Distribution of Body Parts

In a rare noble gesture, I signed my organ donor card. But if it comes down to a decision between equally worthy patients, these are the criteria I would have wanted used as a tie-breaker.

1. No prior convictions.
2. Must be committed to *real* campaign finance reform.
3. Trivia tossup: Name the actor who portrayed TV's Mannix?

Postnuptial Agreement

If I am ever murdered by my spouse, I would not have wanted our children placed in her custody.

Mourning Etiquette

No shirt. No shoes. No service.

Don't be afraid to cry. I've always been known as a rather light-hearted sort, and you might suppose I'd prefer a bittersweet memorial that celebrated my whimsical spirit with the joyful noise of laughter. You'd be wrong. I would have wanted a funeral where the hushed sounds of sniffled sobbing are broken only by the crack of hollow, mournful wails. (Pick a room with good acoustics.)

Suggested Talking Points

- Mark treasured life and all its wonders.
- Mark pursued a meaningful relationship with God and other authority figures.
- Later in life, Mark became a tireless advocate of annual flu shots.
- My life pales in comparison to the rich, selfless journey that was Mark's.
- If there was any tension in my relationship with Mark, it was because I was secretly envious of his abundant talent, easy charm, and thick-curled, effortlessly stylish hair. I blame myself, not him.
- For Sheila, Beth, Marnie, Suzette, and Karen H.: Now I can see that I betrayed Mark, discarding his honest, enduring love for reasons that really had to do with my own hang-ups, only to wind up with some loser who's not half the man that Mark was. I am such an idiot.
- Mark cherished smoked oysters. You bet I'll have another!
- Some crowd!
- Sh-h-h! Let's all listen to the stirring eulogy Mark wrote for the occasion.

The Breakfast Table

MARTHA KEAVNEY

Joan Didion is a novelist, essayist, screenwriter, and journalist who has written on subjects from the war in El Salvador to her life as a writer. She lives in California. Jonjon47065 is a spambot.

From: <u>Joan Didion</u>
To: <u>jonjon47065@mnic.net</u>
Subject: Notes from the West
Posted: Thursday, Nov. 16, 2000, at 8:52 a.m. PT

Good morning. I am pleased to have been chosen to participate in the Breakfast Table with you. I am, as it happens, sitting at my own breakfast table drinking a cup of coffee, and this is less curious than one might imagine if one knew that it is not, in fact, particularly novel for me to be drinking coffee at 8:30 on this morning or, tellingly, any particular morning, nor do I mean to suggest that it would be essentially surprising or remarkable or in any way startling to find me drinking coffee at 9 A.M. or even, in certain curious and unnatural and attenuated circumstances, at 9:30. That is, simply, the heart of the matter: *I like a cup of coffee in the morning.*

It has been several years since I last encountered this particular brand of Colombia Supremo, by which I mean the singularly pungent blend of coffee beans which can be found in the ominous and unsettlingly glossy Stop & Shops in the dry harsh country an hour east on the San Bernardino Highway. But the coffee does not, in the greater scheme of things, matter. What matters—and I think you will agree—is that the current mythos of American culture is, once again, a story without a narrative. What matters is that things that once did matter, deeply and profoundly, do not matter anymore. What matters is that we do not know what matters. Does this, in the end, matter? I do not know.

I look forward to your reply.
Joan

From: jonjon47065@mnic.net
To: Joan Didion
Subject: Here's the information you requested
Posted: Thursday, Nov. 16, 2000, at 8:52 a.m. PT

Congratulations! On taking a beginning step in Changing your life.

Hi, my name is Dave. You were referred to me as someone who was ready for a financial CHANGE, so let me get to the point. I assure you your time will not be wasted.

Do you ever wonder how the rich keep getting richer? Do you ever wonder if THEY pay taxes or NOT? Where do they keep their money? How do they invest?

Well, I can show you a way to learn and implement all the above. The Secrets of the Ultra Wealthy. Even better, I will also show you how to make $150,000+ from Home with your telephone and computer.

Are you Serious about making $2500+ per week with a simple system where the customer contacts you and you do absolutely NO selling? If You can follow simple, step-by-step instructions and put forth the effort to make this a reality Starting Immediately, then we need to talk.

There's no experience necessary. However you must have two qualities:

1. Moderate People Skills
2. A Burning Desire for a Personal and Financial Change

Take a moment to take the next step by calling me at my Home Office and I will provide you with further information.

1-800-318-8477
24 Hrs/7 Days

I Wish You Great Prosperity!
Dave

From: Joan Didion
To: jonjon47065@mnic.net
Subject: The psychology of wealth
Posted: Thursday, Nov. 16, 2000, at 8:52 a.m. PT

Dave:

Do I ever wonder how the rich people keep getting richer? Where do they keep their money? How do they invest? I do not know, nor do I know anyone who knows, and this fills me with an amorphous unease made more forceful by a profound sense of disconnected-ness and despair. I tell you this not as aimless revelation but because I want you to know who I am and where I am and what is on my mind as I consider the question of whether I can honestly say that I have "A Burning Desire for a Personal and Financial Change." (I can, I believe, with some minor equivocation, lay claim to "Moderate People Skills.")

What you left unsaid, but implied, was something I have often sur-
mised: the role of the wealthy is to play the part of stalking-horse
for the febrile and hallucinatory and intransigent desires of an
invidious and resentful middle class. "Do the rich pay taxes?" you
ask. It is my suspicion that they pay a price considerably larger
than that.

And, in a different time and a different place, "The Secrets of the
Ultra Wealthy," as you call them, would not excite our fascination
and dread, would not lure us like doomed mariners with their
lethal siren song, and would not be capitalized for no particular
reason. But that is not our time, and that is not our America.

Thank you for your kind wish for great prosperity for me. I wish
you the same.
Joan

From: jonjon47065@mnic.net
To: Joan Didion
Subject: I want to change your life . . .
Posted: Thursday, Nov. 16, 2000, at 8:52 a.m. PT

I have a few simple questions for you. Are you frustrated of working so hard for so little?

Are you tired of working to make someone else (your boss) successful?

What are you really getting out of your job?

Have you ever wondered how prosperous you could be on your
own?

If you answered "yes" to any of these questions, then I want to talk
to you. My team is looking for serious people who desire change,
prosperity and personal freedom. This is for the absolute serious,
not the curious. If you are serious about changing your life, call
the telephone number listed below. Once accepted as a member

of my team, I will provide you with complete training and will assist with advertising that will put you on the road to success.

Call me now, toll free, at 1-888-583-3480 to schedule your personal interview. You have nothing to lose, there is no risk involved (just a serious mind), and you may be qualified to earn thousands of extra dollars per month.

I look forward to speaking to you soon.

Prosperous Regards,
Dave

If you would like to be removed from future mailings enter remove on the subject line.

From: Joan Didion
To: jonjon47065@mnic.net
Subject: The serious mind
Posted: Thursday, Nov. 16, 2000, at 8:52 a.m. PT

I was at first obscurely unsettled by the thin whine of hysteria in your litany of baneful and despairing and importunate questions until I realized that you have approached the inchoate heart of the matter in a way that no other of my correspondents has.

Am I frustrated of working so hard for so little? I am. You will perceive that such a view of the world presents certain difficulties. I am, you will see, a woman chimerical and intrinsic, unwavering in my succinctness, febrile, atavistic, implacable, and perilously inexplicable, possessed of several thesauri.

Your next question, however, presents a problem. Am I tired of working to make someone else (my boss) successful? I do not think you are entirely familiar with the facts surrounding that particular subject. The truth is, I do not have a "boss" in the way that most people do. I cannot say that there is anyone whom I am making successful aside from myself. And yet, your question taps into an atavistic emotional truth.

Who, after, all, does not desire change, prosperity and personal freedom?

I hope we can discuss this subject further.
Joan

From: jonjon47065@mnic.net
To: Joan Didion
Subject: FLORIDA-BAHAMAS-CANCUN GETAWAY!!!
Posted: Thursday, Nov. 16, 2000, at 8:52 a.m. PT

You have been selected to ENTER a World Class Vacation package offer! A FAMILY GETAWAY FOR 2 ADULTS & UP TO 3 CHILDREN (OR 4 ADULTS) If qualified you could enjoy:

===> 4 Days 3 Nights in Magical Orlando, Florida, home of Disney World, were you will enjoy the hospitality of the Comfort Suites.

===> Have a BLAST with a Family Pass to WATERMANIA Water Park in Orlando. As a Special Gift you will also receive the Orlando "MAGIC CARD" entitling you to HUNDREDS OF DOLLARS worth of DISCOUNTS in the Orlando area!

REGISTER NOW TO SEE IF YOU QUALIFY All of this for only $678* for 4 adults or 2 adults and up to 3 children! THAT IS ONLY $11 PER DAY PER PERSON!! This is NOT a Contest, Lottery, or Sweepstakes. You are qualified based on demographics such as age, area you live in, etc. Qualified Entrants will be contacted by one of our Experienced Travel Representatives with the full details, ONLY ONE PHONE CALL PER HOUSEHOLD.

If you DO qualify you will need to secure promotional fees on a major credit card to guarantee your travel date.

Dave

From: Joan Didion
To: jonjon47065@mnic.net
Subject: Florida-Bahamas-Cancun getaway
Posted: Thursday, Nov. 16, 2000, at 8:52 a.m. PT

Dave:

When we start deceiving ourselves into thinking not that we want or need four days and three nights in magical Orlando, not that it is a pragmatic necessity for us to have it, but that it is a moral imperative that we have it, then is when we join the fashionable madmen.

Having said this, I hope that I qualify for this vacation offer. As it happens I have never been to Watermania Water Park, but I have heard of it, and I recall thinking it an uneasy affair at best some years ago, when, during a conversation about Celine, an old friend suddenly said "But Watermania Water Park in Orlando—now, there's a cure for anyone's formless anomie." At the time I did not believe him, because I had the rashness and self-importance of the young. I marvel now that, so many years later, I can remember his exact words and inflection, although I cannot remember what he said about Celine or what his name is or what I was wearing at the time.

I will call you and supply you with the number of a major credit card.

And, in the end, I know that I will visit Watermania and it will not make me feel any safer, but that, as they say, is another story.

Joan

You have many unique talents, none of which are marketable.

From *The Real-Life Worst-Case-Scenario Survival Handbook*

MARTHA KEAVNEY

Red Wine Stain on White Rug
1. Try to find water. The best places to look are: near green vegetation, at the base of rock cliffs, in the gravel wash from mountain valleys, in a refrigerator, or flowing from the faucet of a sink.
2. Rinse the stained area with water or club soda (if available). Apply a neutral detergent. Blot. Apply an acid such as vinegar or a rinse agent. Apply an ammonia solution. Blot.
3. If this strategy does not work, start a signal fire using dry grass, bark, or leaves. Feed it first with kindling and then use larger pieces of dead wood. Place the carpet on the fire.

Mispronouncing *Nuclear*
1. If you use the word *nuclear* and then find yourself facing accusations of mispronunciation, it is best to attack at once. Using whatever you have with you—a stick, a camera, a harpoon gun, or your fist—make quick, sharp, repeated jabs at your opponent's face.

2. Break free and run through bushes or high weeds, which will give some cover.
3. Do not use the words *espresso, homage* or *Pinochet* for at least 24 hours after the incident.

Karaoke Office Party

1. Stay where you are. Try to keep desks, chairs, and other people between you and the karaoke area.
2. Assume a fixed embarrassed grin.
3. If you see other people off in the distance, try to signal them using flares, a smoky fire, or the international distress symbol (rolling eyes and grimacing).
4. If anyone sings "My Heart Will Go On," get under a desk or table and curl up in the fetal position.

Marriage to Billy Bob Thornton

1. Do not scream or run. Panicking will only use up precious energy.
2. Try to gently extricate yourself bit by bit over the course of several months. Do not struggle or make violent motions.
3. Keep in mind that most people in this situation have found it to be temporary. Even if your efforts to free yourself seem to have no effect, you will get out eventually. Your goal should be to minimize trauma to yourself while you implement your escape.
4. With a swift, smooth motion, engage an attorney.

Served Haggis or Blood Pudding

1. Remain calm. Keep your mouth closed so that there is no chance of accidental ingestion.
2. With your knife or razor blade, make a half-inch horizontal incision in the center of the meal.
3. Widen the incision using a fork.
4. Repeat these actions until the dish is taken away.

Walking into a Party and Realizing You've Slept with All the Men/Women There

1. Keep extremities warm and covered, and maintain an air of dignity.
2. Administer an anesthetic such as wine or one of the vodka drinks. Do not take more than the dosage indicated. Overmedicating is a common mistake in this situation.
3. Do not rub your or anyone else's skin with snow, ice, or your bare hands.
4. Move through the party in a zigzag pattern. When you see a clear escape route, get out of the building quickly. Do not leave with anyone.

Orchestra Seats at Elton John and Tim Rice's *Aida*

1. Do not crouch down. Hold your ground, wave your arms, and shout. Show the musical that you are not defenseless.
2. When there is a pause in the action, run from the theater.
3. Get to a place of safety as quickly as possible. Lie down with your feet lower than your head in a darkened room until you feel better.

A Supporting Character in *Sex and the City* Is Based on You

1. Leave the area quickly, bringing along a supply of canned goods, blankets, and drinking water in portable jugs.
2. It should be safe to return in two weeks. Continue to exercise caution by avoiding parties, taverns, bars, and other places where people might gather.
3. If you are still the victim of good-natured ribbing, deflect the blows by claiming that you do not have cable, then change the subject quickly.

Starring in the Film *The Avengers*

1. Keep your head down. Do not make any sudden moves that could call attention to yourself. Speak as quietly as possible.

2. Do not be a hero. Let Sean Connery absorb most of the impact—that's what he's there for.
3. Back away from the film with a slow, unhurried motion. Speak steadily and soothingly to the critics. When their attention is distracted by *The Odd Couple II*, run to safety.

PROCRASTINATOR'S CHECKLIST

Sharpen pencils.

Organize pencils in a straight line.

Clean out desk.

Strip, sand, and refinish desk.

Buy new desk.

Check mail.

Color-code socks and pants.

Dig up tulip bulbs.

Alphabetize herbal teas in pantry.

Check mail.

Discuss the amusing foibles of your UPS driver's cats.

Organize cereal boxes by height.

Look for your name on the Internet.

Review 1994 tax returns.

Check mail.

See how the Nasdaq is doing.

Clip nails.

Floss.

Floss nails.

Check Christmas ornaments in attic to make sure they're okay.

Can boysenberry preserves.

Check mail.

Relace shoes in closet.

Test yourself on state capitals, just to stay sharp.

Examine moles in mirror.

Midday break for pedicure.

Nap.

Water plants.

Call siblings long-distance, start unprovoked arguments.

Update address book.

Buy stamps.

Call siblings to make up for earlier fights.

Watch Weather Channel to monitor typhoon developments in South Pacific.

Check pulse.

Water plants again, possibly killing them.

Now, that wasn't so hard, was it? Just follow the list, and you'll be ready to embark on an exciting new career as a professional procrastinator. Tomorrow.

—Andy Borowitz

A Short Historical Inquiry into Time

ROBERT KONRATH

Continuing advances in understanding the nature of time are rekindling interest in this elusive force. Physicists have identified a species of subatomic particles that move backward in time and now are discerning bizarre tiny "time wormholes" that appear to connect us with alternate space-time continuums. Perhaps these little worms can be tweaked into widening their paths to create time travel "freeways," each with exit ramps into the past and the future and nice landscaping.

Yet progress has come slowly. For centuries, the concept of time unnerved philosophers. For example, St. Augustine once said, "If nobody asks me, I know what time is, but if I am asked, then I get flustered and forget, damn it!" The invention of clocks didn't help philosophers much, either. The seventeenth-century philosopher Benedict Spinoza never really understood time, pleading inconsolably on his deathbed: "But when the big hand is *hiding* the little hand, *then* what time is it!?" In short, philosophers clearly had trouble getting their minds around Time—though we shouldn't forget their groundbreaking contributions to the now popular subfield of "Wasting Time."

With the philosophers flummoxed, the physicists were called in, and no discussion of space-time can begin without mentioning Isaac Newton and Albert Einstein. These two sultans of science masterfully defined the structure and operation of the physical universe and taught physicists how to think about pulleys, gases, and lunch whistles. For example, Newton was the first to predict that noon must occur at exactly at 12:00 P.M. in most time zones. Nonetheless, they tended to simply brush off important a priori assumptions. For example, neither tackled the fundamental question: "Which came first, God or time?" Or, "Is Father Time God, or is he just a kinder, gentler Grim Reaper?" Vague on first principles, professors Newton and Einstein waved their hands a lot at the beginning of their courses.

Indeed, Newton and Einstein take time as a given. Maybe they felt entitled to this luxury considering the fat royalty checks their publishers sent them each month. Einstein came to view time and space as coequal primary building blocks (or *tinkler* toys, as he called them) of the universe. His genius was to graft time onto three-dimensional space to form what he called four-dimensional "space-time," "Der Box mit Der Clock." In the prologue to his famous paper on special relativity, Einstein mocked earlier models of reality, noting, "You couldn't find time in that pile of trash to save your ass." The clock model of reality was one of the great revolutions of physics, broke all previous physics sales records, and made Einstein very phat worldwide.

But let's back up for a moment and trace the evolution in thinking about space and time via the Great Revolutions of Physics. *Note:* I only consider revolutions in *Western* physics because, frankly, Asian physicists just aren't, well, that sexy.

1543: The Copernican Revolution. Nicolaus Copernicus's *On the Revolutions of the Celestial Spheres* said the Earth moves around the center of the universe, rather than vice versa. Unsurprisingly, this theory infuriated the Pope, who growled: "It makes me feel like a goddamned traveling salesman!" and sent Sunday mass collections into a nosedive from which they never recovered. The notion of a non–Earth-centric universe came to Nicolaus as a boy in Poland when he discovered it was more fun to ride on the outside of a merry-go-round rather than in the middle. In fact, the modern meaning of "revolution" derives from "nauseka," the Polish word for "merry-go-round." Though Copernicus was first to divine the basic form of the solar system, he left the sun out of his design, placing it far from Earth. Explaining his rationale, he piped, "Why else would I feel so cold all the time?" Sixty years later Johannes Kepler—in tandem with Galileo Galilei—showed that the sun is the true center of the solar system. Asked by a contemporary chronicler for the source of their crucial insight, Kepler replied coyly, "Well, it seems to give the entire mise-en-scène a bit more balance."

1687: The Newtonian Revolution. In *The Mathematical Principles of Natural Philosophy*, Newton formulated his three famous laws of motion and gravitation—all that moving, resting, and falling business that numbed us in school. And he showed that all bodies—hard bodies, celestial bodies, and couch potatoes—obey the same physical laws. This set up the first scheme capable of describing the entire universe as a working contraption. Newton created the science of mechanics, now called automotive repair, and went on to correctly describe motion as taking place in an absolute space, though he erred badly when he said that time too is absolute and "flows uniformly without relation to anything external." (Newton had obviously never done any good Asian hashish!)

1905: The Special Theory of Relativity. In this paper, Einstein showed that simultaneity of an event cannot be established definitively at spatially separated points. However, in 1906, Einstein was forced to qualify this conclusion with the famous "Dopplerschnellhandschwingundbewegungszusatz" exception, when he admits: *If* two people with *"really quick hands"* signal each other while passing in opposite directions on flatbed rail cars at half the speed of light, *then*, "*Okay, okay*, I give them the simultaneity, already . . . *scheeze!*" Einstein said that though space and time usually seem distinct phenomena, they amount to the same thing, and he went on to prove the strict equivalence of the two statements: "He's just taking up space at school," and "Boy, is he wasting his time." He made predictions about the weird behavior of measuring rods and clocks, derived the famous $E=mc^2$ equation, and then shocked the academic world by selling the exclusive rights to all three to the *Twilight Zone* TV show. Einstein's devoted acolyte, Hermann Minkowski, then formalized the notion of space-time as a rigid, four-dimensional tableau of world events, very much akin, symbolically, to a life-size cutout of Peter Jennings waving from a museum diorama.

1915: The General Theory of Relativity. The special theory of relativity depicts a world with no gravitation. Eight years later—after a series of nasty late-night tumbles down the stairs of his apartment on Berne's Marktgasse—Einstein reconsidered the exclusion of gravity, asking Minkowski to adjust his space-time model to safely accommodate a plummeting 185-pound Swiss patent examiner. Einstein's reformulated theory showed that time can have a beginning (which he designated The Big O), and that the universe can expand, contract, or "writhe involuntarily." Purportedly the creation of a storied Einstein *"Gedanken-Versuch"* (bad heartburn), the real inspiration for Einstein's Big O, many biographers believe, was his girlfriend of this period, Lulu "the Maenad" Schwartz.

1925/6: Quantum Mechanics. Named after a gay bar in Basel, Switzerland, this theory posits the existence of gadzillions of spiky mechanical quantities, or "quanta," throughout nature. Mass suffused with such quanta exists in three states: "charmed," "quasi-charmed," or "packing it." What a difference in approach: In Newton's and Einstein's schema, a selfish, vindictive God does not share inertial reference frames with anyone. The first quantum effects were discovered and described initially by Max Planck (1900) and Niels Bohr (1913). This was quite an achievement coming from guys with such dumb last names. Later, the theory was elaborated in two different but equivalent forms: *Matrix Mechanics,* by Werner Heisenberg (1925), and *Wave Mechanics,* by Erwin Schrödinger (1926). Heisenberg and Schrödinger named their theories after gay bars as well, but these bars were in *Berlin, Germany.* Alas, we probably will never know if these scientists *were gay* or if this was just another boring harbinger of WW II nationalist competition.

Today, physicists, philosophers, and poets all await the next revolution, the next burst of insight into time. Will new knowledge create a new synthesis between Einstein and those raffish Quantum Boys? And could future discoveries actually "improve" time for humanity, much as quantum physics has spawned lasers, semiconductors, and live acts of bestiality on the Internet? Can we create our time superhighway, yet at the same restrain people from mucking around with history, creating paradoxes, and making us all disappear? Could I get this article published in different historical eras and somehow get paid in today's money? So many questions, but thank God, so much time to answer them in.

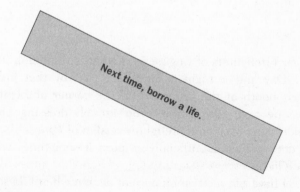

Next time, borrow a life.

An Open Letter to the Firefighters of Engine Company 54, Ladder 4, Battalion 9 in the Glass Booth on the Corner of Eighth Avenue and Forty-eighth Street

M. SWEENEY LAWLESS

Dear Firefighters of Engine 54, Ladder 4, Battalion 9:

Day and/or night, whenever I pass by that little glass booth at the firehouse on the corner of Eighth Avenue and 48th Street, you are all dressing and undressing like some firefighter version of *Porky's*. As if it does not count officially as porn if sometimes you save lives.

I have not seen much porn at all, but when I do see even a little, I think of you because you do so many porn kinds of things, such as:

1. standing in calendar poses
2. blowing on your coffee for a very long time
3. tossing back your head and laughing throaty firefighter laughter
4. you slide down poles

And you do all of the above while wearing those form-fitting bright white T-shirts. And—is it me?—or do suspenders *do* things for a man? Sure, investment bankers try to wear them, but firefighters are bombshells in them. Speaking of which, how could anyone ever think that "bombshell" should be a term for women? Especially women who are not firemen who lift weights until their pecs and their biceps are just perfect little scoops of man flesh.

Scoops.

My friend Jennifer says, "Why don't you turn your head when you walk past the firehouse or cross the street and ignore them?"

I would be willing to try it, but I would have to become a very different person—gay, for instance, or, in the alternative, have both eyes seared out of my skull. But I am hardwired for firemen. It is just a physiological fact. Do not blame the victim. It is not *me* making you firemen; it is not *me* telling you to flaunt your firemen lifestyle.

My friend Jennifer says, "Just because they take off their coats and shirts and strut around doesn't mean they're on display."

Yet you are under glass. Like pheasants. Like drop earrings in a jewelry store. Like the boy diorama in the Museum of Natural History.

My friend Jennifer says, "Not every half-dressed man in rubber boots wants you."

Why is this? I am not saying that, just because I happen to be interested, you are supposed to be after me like a cartoon skunk. I am just saying that I think everyone involved could have a very enjoyable time. But you guys have given me low self-esteem. You made me hate myself until I felt like Shemp.

My analyst has told me time and again of the dark, Freudian significance of polishing and polishing trucks that already are shiny-clean. He says winding and unwinding of big, big hoses is obsessive-compulsive behavior and that many of you sport daffy barber shop quartet moustaches. But the next time I look through the window, one of you is leaning back in the command chair, reaching down to shift himself ever so slightly, and again you inhabit my dreams.

What is the worst thing anyone can say about firemen? That they don't rescue kittens from trees anymore? And listen to this: The African American firefighters organization named themselves the Vulcans. How cool is that? Very.

Even firefighter boring day-at-the-office small talk must be full of sexy words like: hook and ladder, fireman's carry, jaws of life, cherry picker. I imagine you silently mouthing these words to yourselves over and over as you curl up in your cots all in a row, faces ever so slightly smudged with soot and your hair boyishly tousled. You are men who slide down poles as if it is nothing whereas I would find something fascinating about that.

I didn't want to bring this up, but I pay your salary. I was never on fire and I have never turned in a false alarm, so, NO, I do NOT feel as if I have gotten my money's worth.

Writing this letter makes me as sad as when I heard that one time Janet Jackson and Michael Jackson had not seen each other for over two years.

Here are my demands:

1. A written apology displayed in plain view in your window for all to see. It does not have to say "Dear Meg" or even "To Meg" even if I deserve it more than most other people and I would appreciate that very much.
2. It wouldn't kill one of you to call me up and maybe take me to dinner as a very personal apology that I would appreciate. My number is 555-2209.
3. Common courtesy is only polite. I nod, you nod back at me. I wave, you wave back to me. I tell you what kind, you buy me some jewelry. It does not have to be that expensive and I would mention to everyone I talk to that it is jewelry from firefighters and you can't buy that kind of positive publicity. I guarantee that I would be as happy as the people on commercials if it was a real diamond and maybe we could spin round and round happily together in a kind of light-hearted dance if you gave it to me on the beach.

In conclusion, can't we just meet and talk this whole thing through? I'm sure it is just one big misunderstanding, and that when we look back on it together, all of us will laugh and laugh. It can work out for everybody. It is as simple as a nod, a wave, maybe some Speedos in the summertime. It will be so worth it for you to call me at 555-2209. Then I will tell all my friends to stop tapping at the glass.

Sincerely and Very Truly
(any one of) Yours,
Meg

A Fish Story

M. SWEENEY LAWLESS

Before I tell you any of this, I'll say right off the bat that I would have changed the names. The trouble is that I can't think of any right now. Okay, what if this: say you happen to meet a guy named Tapley whose investment banker brother owns a fishing cabin about a mile and a half from the Vermont River. What I'm about to tell you is about a different guy.

Every good fish story begins at 4:30 in the morning. This one also begins at 4:30 in the morning. In Manhattan. In a bar. In early spring. There was Tapley and there was me. We were the dregs of a birthday party that began in a restaurant, rolled into a nightclub, staggered into a smoky lounge and ended up in a bar with a clever name. I am drinking Guinness and Tapley is drinking Cosmopolitans. Guinness is creamy and foamy and brown and Cosmopolitans are pink; this is called foreshadowing.

Tapley writes articles on the Internet and is blond and stocky and looks very good. I decide that if he is not *the* one, then he is definitely *one of* my types.

Tapley and I talk about his brother, the investment banker, who has bought a cabin in Vermont to get back to the land.

Tapley thinks this is a good idea, the thing with the land, and I agree, not because I have any land opinions, per se, but because I realize that if Tapley was standing on the other side, I could chew through a chain-link fence. I agree heartily.

It is very late before I decide for certain that Tapley is not psychic. Not only that, but he is not particularly perceptive in any conventional sense, either. I go home alone.

I do not hear from Tapley for months. Then, one Friday afternoon, he calls me on his cell phone.

"I'm in Vermont at my brother's cabin," Tapley says, "Remember, we were talking that night? Do you want to come up for some fly-fishing?"

I summon the image of Tapley standing in running water, which could potentially wet his T-shirt, and when he hangs up, I make roughly four dozen calls to beg my way out of every inch of my weekend: three shows (I live in New York—there will always be shows); a couple of meetings (you can always put off a meeting); my godson's christening (I already have a godchild.) As for rescheduling Sunday brunch, my friends are more than understanding: Everyone is happier when I have a masher.

As the Amtrak red-eye pulls out of Penn Station, I reflect on the last time I had it for a guy this badly. I ended up ice climbing in New Hampshire. I won't go into it now, but in case you've never had to do it, it takes weeks—*weeks*—to recover from faking upper body strength. When my train arrives just before 5:00 A.M. at St. Alban's Station, Tapley picks me up. Neither of us talk, but the new smell they sprayed in his blue rental Ford Fiesta speaks to me in the music of pheromones.

It turns out that Tapley's banker brother is no goon. He has bought a genuine hunting and fishing lodge built around the 1940s near the Vermont River. It is equipped with an immense and deep double sink where my grandfather would have cleaned fish, sunk to his knees, and died happily. I'm willing to bet there's not a bathroom scale or even a mirror in the place, and there are half a dozen bottle openers in plain sight. For the first time in my life, I am at peace. I decide investment bankers are a lot harder to resent when they share.

Tapley gestures at the eight-foot, five-weight Loomis rod with a Teton reel propped up in a corner and says, "That's your pole." I am about to make a witty remark about the difference between graphite rods and bamboo when Tapley absentmindedly unbuttons his pants to tuck in his shirt and I completely lose my train of thought.

I recover enough to say, "What've they got going?"

Tapley says, "What?"

I say, "What're they running?"

Tapley says, "What?"

I speak slowly, clearly—perhaps a little too loudly—as if I'm an American talking to a slow-witted foreigner under sedation. I say, "What kind of fish will we be fishing for?"

"Oh," he says, "Some trout," and with that, he pulls a tackle box from the closet shelf and checks its contents by vigorously shaking it.

Then it dawns on me: *Tapley does not know the first thing about fly-fishing.* Wait, there's more. Not only does he know nothing about fly-fishing, but *Tapley thinks that I do not know the first thing about fly-fishing.* Now, if I were to generalize, I would say that men do not like to be disabused in any way about a woman's innocence. So I shut my mouth.

Tapley wears his usual longshoreman's hat, and I wear a hunting hat of my grandfather's, which is not that obnoxious modern orange safety color but the dangerous dun-brown plaid favored by Elmer Fudd. Men find this hat very sexy. I just haven't met these men yet. Tapley goes out the door first and I follow the back pockets of his khakis down the path for about a half mile. When we reach the river, I ask offhandedly if he knows the way back to the cabin and he assures me he's been out this way before.

We walk a couple miles upstream until, according to my calculations, we can fish for nine hours and be home in time to clean the fish for dinner. Tapley opens the tackle box, but doesn't seem to notice that I have secretly added a collapsible net, a couple of extra reels, and my Swiss Army knife—a Super Tinker. Tapley breathes deeply and says, "They say there's nothing like a day of fly-fishing." He pokes around and picks out a spoon, a spinner, and a baby crankbait. I shut my mouth.

I pluck up a few different flies and since I don't know anything about the local hatch, I offer Tapley a couple of pheasant tail nymphs, and I say, "How about we use these? They seem to be the color of the stream bed and they match the size of the flies I've seen caught in spiders' webs along the shore." Tapley thinks I have thought this up myself, so as long as I shut my mouth, he thinks I'm a genius. I shut my mouth.

We decide to split up so we don't spook the fish. I cast upstream just past a group of five or six boulders, but by the time I float into flat water, I get too much drag, so I reel in and start collecting enough spit in my mouth to paste up the fly. Tapley, by now farther upstream, turns his head just as I let a great foamy gob of saliva fall into my hand and by the look on Tapley's face it seems he does not assume that my wet fly was acting like a dry fly.

How can I describe Tapley's back cast? It is inspired by years of watching major league baseball. It is a full swing that involves not his hand or his wrist or his forearm, but his knees and his hips and his chin, somehow. *It is the fishing equivalent of throwing like a girl.* I shut my mouth. We continue this way for a couple of hours: I pendulum out with an easy, a fluid cast, pull in my line, and get maybe a nibble. Meanwhile, Tapley throws as hard as he can over and over again with a gigantic, ungentle and uninsectlike "ker-*plunk!* ker-*plunk!*" and I shut up because there is no delicate way to tell a man he's pounding the hole.

My family requires a churchlike silence in order to fish. We are people who do not eat a prize catch. Having generations ago evolved past the base, Neanderthal instinct to fry things with onions, we will eat our catch only in those extreme conditions that lead to movie-of-the-week type cannibalism. We catch and release trophy fish, snapping photographs as the water is still draining from the gills. No one I know fishes "for fun." My Uncle Fran once grounded my cousin Peter for an entire week for farting in the bottom of an aluminum boat.

Tapley reels in his line and makes his way downstream toward me. Someone must have told him about the importance of quiet to fish, because he stage whispers, "The river must be fished out." He sneaks by any fish within earshot by shuffling in his waders over the streambed gravel. To fish reposing underwater, this sounds something like a cement mixer being dropped repeatedly from a height of 41 feet onto a full service of delftware.

My fantasies of Tapley have become unlovely. I begin to imagine what it would be like to punch and punch him until he is a bag of liquid. All manner of uncharitable thoughts elbow each other in my brain when suddenly I see it. Ten yards downstream: pocket water. The most beautiful pocket water in all the land. The stream curves 45 degrees to the left to follow the bank's contour, and there the current becomes loving and soft beneath a stand of overhanging willow trees. There are clumps of pepper grass and a plunge pool with a rowdy little boil that makes the kind of white noise that can hide the approach of a gaggle of Tapleys with sousaphones.

"There," I say and as I'm pointing, there is a long flash—a *long* one, at least 14 inches—and after the flash, the tiniest sip rises, which barely causes a break on the surface. I snatch a fistful of Tapley's shirt and he follows my suggestion to slowly back away. We travel downstream about 20 yards and wade back up until we're close enough to cast, but not close enough to be in the fish's vision cone.

If nothing else, I am a gentlewoman. I graciously let Tapley have the first cast while I wait with the net. He casts upstream, floats by the pocket water and immediately gets a strike! This seems to startle Tapley, who freaks out completely. He jerks too soon, the line goes slack, and the fish gets away. I grab the rod and reel in the line. "I think I felt it," Tapley says, "it felt big."

I set up with a Blue Wing Olive on a size-12 hook. We slosh

back into position. It's my turn. I cast. There is a flash near my line and just as I pull up to set the hook, Tapley's cell phone plays "The Yellow Rose of Texas." It comes as a surprise to both of us when I do not kill him.

I cast again. My line drags a few times, but I get another strike and this time I set the hook and through the clear water we can see that it's a huge toasty brown brook trout, which must be at least 16 inches. Tapley sighs longingly and says, "I've never actually caught a fish." I am overwhelmed by a wave of compassion. In a gesture of good will, I hand him the rod and am immediately rewarded by Tapley's grateful smile and am mesmerized by his beautiful teeth. Meanwhile, he loses the fish, his backing, his fly line, his leader, his tippet, and his fly.

By now it's late in the day and the sun is going down. Back on shore, I trim out the knots and tie a new line, contemplating the idea of walking through unfamiliar wood in the dark. I wade over to Tapley and unceremoniously shove the rod into his hands with greater force than is strictly necessary. Wordlessly, we take turns casting upstream until the fish strikes again, which happens in a little under two hours, and when it does, it's Tapley's turn. When he attempts to hoist the trout up as if he's operating a crane, I hear myself hollering, "Do *not* lift him straight out of the water, you asshole!"

I gently push Tapley sideways and wrest away the rod. He loses his balance or something and braces his fall with both hands. I jam the butt of the rod into my hip, grab the net, and get a scoop under him myself and there he is: a maple-belly brook trout. It must be 18 inches. Probably 20 inches. I lift him by the mouth—the fish, I mean—and gently dislodge the treble hook. It is a beauty and continues the struggle even in midair, sending brilliant, sun-infused sprays of cold water from its tail. We both stare up at the trout in mute wonder.

Now that the fish fight is over, I feel as if the Tapley fight should be over, too, and grandly make the first move. I lower the trout into the net and hand it to Tapley. I say, "You can be the one to send him back to the river." I recall that only moments ago I called him an asshole.

Tapley looks concerned. "What do you mean, send him back? Isn't he big enough?" I patiently explain that the trout is a prize catch and even my uncle would approve of a 22-inch brook trout. However, we can't tell exactly how impressive he is for sure because Tapley's brother owns *the only tackle box in the Western world without a tape measure*.

Tapley is panicky. "If we don't have the fish, what'll we eat for dinner?"

It is a long walk home. Tapley is a good sport when I won't let him take the deer path he was certain led to his brother's cabin, and soon enough we reach the handkerchief I had tied in the crook of a tree to mark the right way.

Tapley walks in silence, looking down every so often, lovingly, at the brookie hanging from his stringer. That thing must have been 24 inches.

I walk in silence, knowing that the last micron of eroticism he might harbor for me is about to be annihilated because you can bet that my dream date, Tapley, doesn't know shit about how to clean a fish.

That is the story of how I landed my largest trout ever.

It is also the story of the one that got away.

For Catherine McKeen and Keith McPartland

ANOTHER UNNATURAL HISTORY

The Antelope

"The antelope," says the *World Book*, "is the name of a large group of animals that have hoofs and horns." And yet, a cow is not an antelope, and neither is Roy Cohn, so let's not go overboard. Antelope belong to a family that includes goats and oxen, but you can't blame them for that; we've all got relatives that make us uneasy. Antelope are ruminants, which means they chew their cud. This can makes them appear to be thinking deep thoughts much as Tom Brokaw often seems to be doing on the nightly news, generally about what fun World War II was. There is little evidence that either of them is actually thinking anything much. Antelope horns come in many shapes and sizes, albeit pretty much all long and pointy—ridged and unridged, curved and straight, even corkscrewed. Antelope horns never branch like those of deer, and if that arrangement suits both species we ought not quibble. Despite the cowboy song, no true antelope live in America, but instead are found in Asia, Africa, and southeastern Europe. Given the scientific training of most cowboys and the rhythmic demands of the song, we should count ourselves lucky that it's not ". . . where the deer and the elephant play." (This sort of thing is called a "tall tale," the cowboy and National Public Radio term for what regular people call "a long boring lie.") Even with their impressive horns, most antelope would rather flee than fight. (Although I'll bet that the quick-tongued Tom Brokaw could talk himself out of a jam, if it was with a singing cowboy, particularly if the cowboy was a WW II veteran not immune to flattery.) Others, including the gnu, the roan antelope, and the sable antelope, will defend themselves with their horns, which are often seen mounted in the dens of hunters; so much for fight versus flight. The heads of hunters are seldom seen mounted in the dens of antelopes, suggesting that antelope have a better sense of interior design than do hunters. Incidentally, the lesser kudu can cover 30 feet in a single leap, jumping six feet into the air, although none has been known to land on Tom Brokaw. That's because they were thwarted by the American GI, every one of whom was a better person than you.

—Randy Cohen

Real-Life Giant Construction Equipment for Kids

ROD M. LOTT

At the beginning of this educational video, which I purchased for $4.95 through a Sunday coupon circular, two young boys are walking around a dilapidated junkyard scattered with chunks of rock on which they might crack their skulls. The oldest, Max, tells the younger, Alex: "See that big yellow monster over there? That's a 520-horsepower D-10 bulldozer. Big as a house!" This is the first clue that Alex is destined for a traumatic adolescence.

Exploring the site, the pair stumbles on a beat-up Thermos. Max warns Alex not to open it because it might be filled with "rotten, stinky chicken soup." It contains worse medicine: Hard Hat Harry, a "genie" with buff biceps who remarks upon his release, "Man, I gotta get a bigger Thermos!" (Don't we all.)

Grateful for his freedom, Harry grants the boys three wishes. And just what do these two eager, enterprising, red-blooded youths wish for? Pogs? Money? Whores? Nope—they blow the opportunity of a lifetime to see *construction equipment*. Harry sprinkles them with "magic gravel," and—*poof*—they're transported to a building site.

There, the boys are introduced to digging, drilling, and dumping machines, each of which, eerily, can speak. A backhoe front

Real-Life
GIANT CONSTRUCTION EQUIPMENT For Kids
~ DELUXE EDITION ~

Featuring...
"Hard Hat Harry™!"

loader sounds like Elvis, a road-paver mimics Dracula, and a dump truck talks like Arnold Schwarzenegger. Another dump truck, this one with a Jersey accent, openly ridicules the boys. Even worse, the young innocents are subjected to a barrage of sexual innuendo. It is introduced in an ever-so-subtle fashion as Hard Hat Harry talks of the time it takes "to erect the tower crane." Then Pete the Piledriver explains how his support beams "keep the pile from moving when I slam into it [with my] king-size hammer." Just before breaking into song, a crane boasts how "me and my crane friends can do it all day long, and we never get tired."

Harry becomes party to the perversion when he forces Max and Alex to watch a dump truck "back up and dump its heavy load." The dump truck croons, "Fill me up and tap my load!" A concrete pumper explains, "I use them for stability so I won't tip over when I'm pumping" just before he is interrupted by the arriving ready-mix truck. "I'm going to pour my concrete into your rear hamper," it says. "Watch my chute come out. Ready, aim, fire!" The pumper elaborates: "Then the concrete worker pulls my snaking hose. When he gives the signal, I take a deep breath and blow that concrete out at a stupendous rate!"

The height of the grotesque talk comes when the paver receives its asphalt. "Ah," it says, pleased, "just the way I like it: Hot and wet! Between two to four inches is the ideal depth." Is it an accident that most of these paving machines are manufactured by a company called Wacker?

By the time Harry tells the boys he likes to call the bucket trucks "cherry pickers," it's too late: The boys have been corrupted. When older and wiser Max spots a female construction worker waving at him, he says with a knowing leer, "Ask her if I can have a bite of her sandwich!"

That night, after returning home, Max and Alex giggle with pleasure, remembering they have two more wishes. Given Harry's corrupting influence, we can only assume they will include more monster machinery. Only if the trio had been visited by Killdozer could this video be more fun.

The Tooth Fairy will step on your face.

Have you put on weight?

Top 100 Toys

1. Dolls
2. Sticks
3. Balls
4. Mud
5. Rocks
6. Straw
7. Water
8. Boogers
9. String
10. Matches
11. Logs
12. Hair
13. Knives
14. Jacks
15. Buttons
16. Hoops
17. Forks
18. Glass
19. Tops
20. Spools
21. Thimbles
22. Ribbons
23. Blocks
24. Cardboard boxes
25. Wooden boxes
26. Wooden crates
27. Steel crates
28. Plastic milk cartons
29. Upside down buckets
30. Jack-in-the-boxes
31. Feces
32. Magnifying glasses
33. Marbles
34. Dead animals
35. Sock puppets
36. Mousetraps
37. Tinfoil
38. Hammers
39. Blasting caps
40. Balloons
41. Scissors
42. Chutes and ladders. No, real chutes and real ladders.
43. Rattles
44. Tiddlywinks
45. Slinkys
46. Cans
47. Abandoned refrigerators
48. Loose teeth
49. Spoons
50. Horseshoes
51. Mars Polar Landers
52. Straws
53. Squirt guns
54. Genuine Red Ryder Carbine Action 200-Shot Lightning Loader Range Model Air Rifles
55. Cork guns
56. Laser pointers
57. Zip guns
58. Tec-9s
59. AK-47s
60. Stinger surface-to-air missiles
61. Darts
62. Game Boys
63. Suction cups
64. Trains
65. Trucks
66. Big Wheels
67. Sheep
68. Beer kegs

69. Checkers
70. Pokémon
71. Eleanor Roosevelt
72. Pentagrams
73. Dental floss
74. Library paste
75. Airplane glue
76. Speedballs
77. Wheelos
78. Legos
79. Tinkertoys
80. Spoons

81. Rotting fruit
82. Fishing lures
83. Close and Plays
84. Cellophane
85. Condoms
86. Dad's lighter fluid
87. Shellfish
88. Other people's mail
89. Paddle balls
90. Colorforms
91. Etch A Sketch

92. Rubber bands
93. Snow globes
94. Skin
95. Shaving cream
96. Cows
97. Bird nests
98. Lug nuts
99. Speculums
100. Weebos

(Will Durst can personally recommend most of these.)

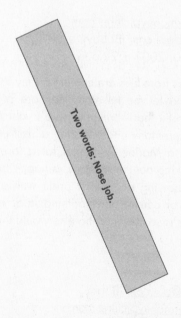

Two words: Nose Job.

Bubba in Paradise

JAMIE MALANOWSKI

To: Stu@mistermoneypictures.com
From: IndieKing@aol.com (Bobby)
        January 20, 2001 1:22 p.m. EST

Stu—The last pages from Ellis are coming off my fax machine literally right now, and let me tell you, they are brilliant, brilliant,
brill—well, we can fix that—brilliant. Here's your new ending: as
the inauguration ceremony ends, Clinton all but unnoticed slowly
makes his way to a Marine helicopter for a farewell flight over
D.C. His face, looking out the window, is happy but wistful, joyful
but melancholy, showing a glow of pride with an undercoat of
self-loathing, and of course other-loathing, too. Just like we just
saw on CNN! Ellis is so clever. Who else would think of ending at
the ending?

To: IndieKing@aol.com (Bobby)
From: Stu@mistermoneypictures.com
        March 19, 2001 8:19 p.m. PST

Bobby—I have just finished rereading Ellis's fourth draft for the fifth
time, and it smells like genius to me. It's *A Face in the Crowd* meets

Raging Bull meets *PT 109*, except with no boats. Or maybe it's *Gandhi* meets *9½ Weeks*. Or *Primary Colors* meets something that made money. Whatever. The point is, seldom if ever have I seen such a sweeping historical epic mixed with such psychological and sexual turmoil. Do you think Sam Mendes and Sir Dickie Attenborough would codirect? Meanwhile, let's get Ellis to work on a rewrite. I don't think the audience really wants to relive the NAFTA debate. And that part where Clinton threatens to punch William Safire in the nose? Why doesn't he? Or do some kind of kung fu thing? We could get Jet Li for a secret service agent cameo.

To: Stu@mistermoneypictures.com
From: IndieKing@aol.com (Bobby)
        May 24, 2001 11:41 a.m. PST

Stu—I have read Ellis's new revision, and it's still missing something. I like what you said at Morton's Thursday night. The president needs a sidekick. Ellis should develop that Carville character. Make him Secretary of State or something. We also need to do more with the George Stephanopoulos character. He always seemed to have a Doogie Howser quality—why can't we make him a teenager? You know, the president's Jimmy Olsen? Frankie Muniz? Jonathan Lipnicki? Finally, we don't see enough of Dick Morris, Clinton's unscrupulous savant foot fetishist. What a shame Liberace's dead.

To: IndieKing@aol.com (Bobby)
From: Stu@mistermoneypictures.com
        September 15, 2001 4:22 p.m. PST

Bobby—I showed Ellis's latest work-in-progress to Warren. He is very intrigued. With reservations, of course. He thinks that in the gays in the military scene, the president should let gays in the military. In the ending welfare scene, he doesn't think the president should end welfare. And in the Sharon Stone visits the Lincoln

Bedroom scene, he doesn't think Sharon Stone should have to give $100,000 to get in there. Here's his exact note: "Unfathomable." He also let on that he might be more interested if there was a role for Annette. I offered Hillary and Donna Shalala. Warren wonders if we're wedded to Gore being a man. By the way, I'm hearing rumors about changes at the studio. New guy coming. Just another asshole in a suit, I'm sure.

To: Bill.Clinton@DreamWorks.com
From: Stu@mistermoneypictures.com
         November 1, 2001 9:00 a.m. PST

Dear Sir,

Bobby and I would like to congratulate you on your appointment as Commander-in-Chief of Production at DreamWorks. We are especially pleased that of all the pictures on the DreamWorks production slate, you will be focusing on ours alone. Let us take your incisive comments about the most recent screenplay one by one.

First, we are working in that information you gave us on how Monica Lewinsky had been kidnapped and brainwashed by the nefarious billionaire Richard Mellon Scaife to infiltrate the Oval Office and sprinkle roofies on your pizza. Frankly sir, that explains a lot!

Second, we were absolutely riveted by your account of the role Satanists played in the impeachment, and we're putting in the new scenes you described. I do not think the moviegoing public will soon forget the sight of Lucienne Goldberg, Linda Tripp, and Paula Jones dancing naked around a bonfire, summoning Kenneth Starr from the flames. We are looking forward to seeing your FBI files that show this happened. Maybe they're with Hillary's stuff in Chappaqua?

Third, we love the new blockbuster action sequences. Who knew that while the House impeachment managers were wasting the public's time and money on a politically motivated which hunt, you were leading a nighttime commando raid on Baghdad to rescue a group of orphans held by Saddam Hussein?

Finally, we love your casting recommendations. We had been thinking of Philip Seymour Hoffman as Ken Starr, but Dom DeLuise does indeed better capture the essence of the man. Drew Carey as Newt Gingrich, Ellen DeGeneres as Hillary, Angelina Jolie as Monica, as Samuel L. Jackson as yourself are all spot on.

To: Stu@mistermoneypictures.com
From: IndieKing@aol.com (Bobby)
         April 9, 2002 5:33 a.m. PST

Brace yourself, he's had another brainstorm. Now instead of C. leading a commando raid to rescue puppies in Kosovo, he leads his fiscal team to rescue the economy from the perils of slow growth. He wants Jeff Goldblum as Robert Rubin, Jet Li as Alan Greenspan, and Joaquin Phoenix as Stagflation. You call Ellis this time.

Ellen and Sam passed. Now he wants Kathy Bates and Russell Crowe. Also he finished auditioning Angelina. Now he wants to audition Britney Spears.

To: Bill.Clinton@DreamWorks.com
From: Stu@mistermoneypictures.com
         July 7, 2002 10:22 p.m. PST

Dear Sir,

We send this letter with heavy regret. We admire and respect you, but sir, you have overstepped your bounds. Eddie Murphy's sweep of the acting Oscars for his performances in *The Klumps* notwithstanding, we just don't think the audience will come out to see Barbra Streisand playing both Hillary and Monica, plus you and Starr as well. You shouldn't have made an offer! And another thing: What twelve songs?

To: Steven.Spielberg@DreamWorks.com,
         Jeffrey.Katzenberg@DreamWorks.com,
         David.Geffen@DreamWorks.com
From: Stu@mistermoneypictures.com and
         IndieKing@aol.com (Bobby)
         October 12, 2002 10:22 a.m. PST

Hey guys—just a note to say no hard feelings about how things ended up. Having Ellis relocate the whole story to a high school in Pasadena was very smart, and picking Jonathan Lipnicki to play Clinton is shrewd. Best of luck the rest of the way.

To: IndieKing@aol.com (Bobby)
From: Stu@CBS.com/Survivor/production
         July 14, 2004 2:224 a.m. PST

Greetings from the world of Reality T.V.! Things are okay—it's too bad that asshole Kent went and annoyed everybody else in the Clan and got himself killed and eaten. But I guess the trial means we'll get picked up for another nine.

Anyhoo, I was thinking 'bout you. Caught a screening of "our" picture. *Impeach My Ass, You Suckas!* was a good choice for the Wayans' first drama. David Spade brought a lot of gravitas to the role of Clinton, Brando was majestical as Starr, and Bruce Vilanch was brilliant as Joe Eszterhas.

What are you up to?

Muʃter the Troops!

The Deal Memo of Independence

JAMIE MALANOWSKI

MINUTES OF THE CONTINENTAL CONGRESS
JULY 1, 1776

The Delegates, deʃirous of avoiding further hoʃtilities with His Majeʃty's Government, appointed a committee to negotiate terms by which Independence might be achieved by peaceable means. The principal negotiator, the Rt. Hon. William Morris of New York, reported that the following terms had been diʃcussed and are now proposed.

The FORMER BRITISH COLONIES (hereafter, the American States) would hereafter be FREE AND INDEPENDENT STATES, no longer owing any allegiance to His Majeʃty's Government, except in the cases mentioned in the provisos following:

First, the AMERICAN STATES would agree to tender no challenge to the United Kingdom's title as PRE-EMINENT ENGLISH-SPEAKING WORLD POWER for at least 150 years.

Second, they would agree to provide aid and assistance, to come to the relief of, and to save the United Kingdom in any armed conflict or war sufficiently wideſpread or intense to be termed GREAT or WORLD.

Third, the AMERICAN STATES would agree to supply the people of Great Britain one (1) ACTRESS-CLASS female of sufficient attractiveness to serve as a mistress to His Future Majeſty, a Prince of Wales to Be Named Later; one (1) BEAUTEOUS WOMAN of sufficient ambition to serve as the mother of a Future Prime Minister to Be Name Later; and one (1) SKINNY DIVORCÉE possessed of sufficient cunning to separate a Diſſident Monarch to Be Named Later from his Crown.

Fourth, the AMERICAN STATES would agree to allow any and all subjects of the Crown full access to and freedom to exploit any musical styles created by NEGRO REFIDENTS of the AMERICAN STATES, including boogie-woogie, blues, rock 'n' roll, soul, and diſco. Reciprocally, the United Kingdom grants to the Negro reſidents of the American States full access to and freedom to exploit any musical styles created by the reſidents of Scotland, including reels, slings, and dirges, in perpetuity.

Fifth, the reſidents of the AMERICAN STATES would agree to maintain an unseemly level of DEFER-ENCE to the members of the royal family and an undue amount of CURIOSITY about their perſonal affairs, and to provide LUCRATIVE ENDORSEMENT OPPORTUNITIES in the field of WEIGHT CON-TROL for any former members of the royal family.

Sixth, the subjects of the AMERICAN STATES agree to provide audiences for the JAMES BOND series of films.

[At this point, the presentation was interrupted by a question from the Rt. Hon. Swifty Lazar of Beverly Hillſ, who asked if the Bond proviso applied in perpetu-ity. "The series is obliged to run until the end of time,"

Mr. Morris replied. "That applieʃ to the girls, the gad-
gets, the villains, the whole schmeer."]

Seventh, the AMERICAN STATES would agree to
subʃidize from tax levies a television network dedicated
to the broadcaʃt of high-toned COFTUME DRAMAS
and middlebrow POLICE PROCEDURALS produʃed
in the British Isles, and to greet with enthuʃiaʃm,
feigned if necessary, the muʃical compoʃitions of SIR
ANDREW LLOYD WEBBER.

Eighth, the AMERICAN STATES agree to reserve
to the British people supremacy in the following fields
of ATHLETIC ENDEAVOR: golf, tennis, and football.
[A committee on Sports Relinquishment counterpro-
posed that instead of supremacy in golf and tennis, His
Majeʃty's subjects be enfranchised with their own
Grand Flam events. "Football they can have," reported
the Hon. Jerry Maquire. "Hey, I hold this truth to be
self-evident: the shoe money's small. Beʃides, we can
start our own kind of football."]

Ninth, the AMERICAN STATES are obliged to
maintain a fascination with really big British luxury
OCEAN LINER DISAFTERS, in perpetuity.

Tenth, reʃidents (particularly of the former colony
of New York) agree to the quartering of British subjects
(particularly journalists) in their HOMES AND
APARTMENTS, to buy them DRINKS AND DINNER,
and to treat them as insuperably WITTY and endlessly
CHARMING, without the expectation of reciprocal
hoʃpitality from counterparts abroad.

Finally, the reʃidents of the AMERICAN STATES
would be obligated to provide a full program of
DENTAL CARE, including prevention, replacement,
and orthodonture, for any and all reʃidents of the United
Kingdom.

The delegates thanked Mr. Morris for his work and
proceeded to debate the terms he outlined. While most

of the terms were deemed acceptable, the delegates unanimouſly felt that the final proviso would subject the colonies to an outrageously exorbitant and punitively expensive program of oral hygiene, and was therefore onerous and a deal breaker. Authorization was then given for Congress to receive the declaration being prepared by Messers. Jefferson, Adams, and Franklin, and word was sent to Genl. Washington to muſter the troops.

[Signed]
Jas. Madison, Secy.

She was faking.

URGENT MEMO

Memo to staff regarding new system of proofreading/ editing marks recently approved by Publishing Industry of America:

In the interest of consistency and efficiency, please adopt the following system of markings for book manuscripts. Compliance strictly required of all editors, effective immediately.

[ ] Indicates an editorial omission for clarity.

[?] Indicates some confusion surrounding the translation.

[?!] Indicates "please, not another moon simile."

H/J Refers to the actors the editor believes should star in the movie version (Heather Graham/Joaquin Phoenix).

*** Indicates that the editor has had this exact same thought before, and in relating to this sentiment, simultaneously feels connected to his author and smugly proud of himself for thinking this very thought, and, to carry this out further, if circumstances were only slightly altered the editor would in fact be the author, instead of the author being the author.

+¢+ Marks the paragraph where, upon finishing, the editor rewarded himself by stopping to check his e-mail.

&&& Marks the sentence that finally caused the editor to conclude that the memoir (with a capital "ME") fad has really, truly run its course.

/-/-/ At this point the editor looked up from the manuscript, glanced briefly at the wall, then at the wall of a colleague, and with startling clarity understood that any effort to de-blandize the walls of one's office cubicle by tacking up Internet-circulated aphorisms, a smattering of up-with-life-type quotes and personal photos of babies/pets/ski trips, although all intended to subtly reveal one's true, profound self, will inevitably seem embarrassing in its earnestness, simplicity, and unoriginality.

@ Marks the point at which the editor felt compelled to see what the Amazon.com sales rank was on the hot new book he passed on 18 months ago.

@@ Marks the point at which the editor felt compelled to double-check the Amazon.com sales rank of the hot new book he passed on 18 months ago.

¿¿¿ Marks the point at which the author totally lost the editor. Mind wandered to (in chronological order):

Weird tingling in right thumb.

Literary soiree heard about but not invited to.

Speculation about who'll be there.

Rushdie, of course. Tina, too.

Can't suck on a Velamint for more than four seconds without biting it.

If *conscious* of being self-involved, does that mean you're not *truly* self-involved?

General feelings of envy, alienation, interoffice conspiracy-phobia, pointlessness, woe, regret, and nausea.

Back to thoughts about the tingling thumb.

♥$ Means that I am still in love with you, Francis. I've always been in love with you. I can't live without you. You are so beautiful, so brilliant. Please forgive me, Francis. Also, I'm looking for a new job—do you still know the assistant editor at the *Paris Review*?

—A.K.R.

LIST OF IDEAS FOR
IDEAS FOR LISTS

Lists that take notice of the fact that a thing has a silly name, and
go on to extrapolate other silly names for that thing
Lists that take notice of the fact that certain phrase is silly, and pro-
ceed to come up with other silly phrases, ones that are cleverly
parallel to the first phrase that kicked the whole thing off
Lists of things that pertain only to my own life; but unimportant
things, so that people reading the list are amused by my feigned
narcissism
Lists that allow me to say some things which are themselves funny,
but less funny than the fact that the things don't have much to
do with each other
Lists that repeat something over and over again, past the point
where a lesser humor-writer person might have stopped
Lists that are the unedited dumping-ground of my unconscious
Lists that trivialize the serious
Lists that elevate the trivial
Lists that are, upon reflection, perverse
Lists of reasons why a certain sensibility is squandering the talent
of an entire generation of writers
Lists that absolve even as they damn
Lists on a bus, lists on a car
Lists to make you a superstar
Lists to win and lists to lose
But these here lists will rock your shoes
And these are the lists
List it up, list it up, list it up!

—Bill Wasik

Monks Among the
Capri Pants

MERRILL MARKOE

I was browsing through a trendy women's clothing store a few miles from my home in lovely Malibu, California, fabled in story and song, when my eye was caught by a Xeroxed flier posted near the display of leopard-skin throw pillows and sparkly purses.

INDIVIDUAL TIBETAN HEALINGS IN MALIBU, it said. FIVE DAYS ONLY. HALF-HOUR PRIVATE SESSIONS BY APPOINTMENT.

Now, not only am I not a Buddhist, but I was raised without a religion. I also didn't have any pressing problem that needed healing except maybe a little personal angst and some mild lower-back pain. However, there's not a whole lot going on in Malibu in between mudslide season (when we're all hysterically calling hotlines to determine if the roads are open) and fire season (when we're all hysterically watching newscasts to determine if the roads are closed). So I thought to myself, "Why not a nice Tibetan Healing?" You never can be too thin or too healed.

"The monks are actually from Southern India where they relocated after they were chased out of Tibet by the Chinese,"

234

their spokesperson told me. "They do a powerful ancient Tantric ritual that's like cleaning out all your old tapes. It gives you a fresh start. Plus the healings raise money for a fund that helps orphans." No one likes helping orphans or making fresh starts better than I do. So I made an appointment.

"Bring fifty dollars cash or check," she told me, penciling me in for 2:00 the following Wednesday. "Plus a quart of drinking water and any prescription drugs or skin creams you currently use." This part confused me.

"Are they dermatologist monks?" I wondered. And when they said "skin creams" did they mean *all* my moisturizers, including the one with SPF 15 for daytime *and* the one with the alpha-hydroxy acid for night *plus* my two kinds of under-eye gel and my bottle of self-tan? Were makeup base and blush considered skin creams? And when they said "prescription drugs," did this also mean over-the-counter ones like Tums and Sudafed and Tylenol? After much thought, I decided to bring only one moisturizer and my birth control pills. No point in getting off to a bad start with the monks by appearing excessively vain.

I arrived at the store early for my appointment and was in the middle of trying on capri pants when a cluster of monks in identical maroon and orange-gold robes entered the store. They all had the same closely cropped hair style but were apparently permitted an individual footwear option, since one had on tan Hush Puppies, another wore sandals, a third wore cordovan wingtips without socks.

"They're just back from lunch, so they're fresh and rested," their representative told me. Excellent, I thought, just the way I like them.

And moments later I was led up a narrow staircase behind the cosmetics counter to a small room where an empty folding chair between two seated monks awaited me. The one on my right began to read rapidly from a Xeroxed copy of Tibetan scriptures as the one on my left, who was wearing round wire-framed glasses and appeared to be an American, read a fright-

eningly literal English translation. I was told to close my eyes
and visualize as he read but the text was so complex and
arcanely worded that I got lost immediately. No sooner had I
begun to wrap my brain around "a thousand Buddhas descend-
ing clockwise" ("Clockwise," I thought to myself, "which way is
clockwise again? Oh, God . . . we're moving ahead!") then I was
supposed to see "a hundred scepters whirling." Never having
seen even one scepter doing anything at all, I barely had a stationary one in my mind when I was commanded to see thousands of angels converging upon the scepters. Soon dozens of
mind-boggling images were piled up ahead of me in a visualiza-
tion gridlock. I needed hallucinogenic drugs to keep up. And I
was growing increasingly panicky that I had totally screwed up
my healing.

So I was kind of relieved when we got to a purification
sequence where I was asked to take a sip of water from my Evian
bottle and spit it into a stainless steel bowl: a little like the
Monastery version of "spit and rinse." This is when the Anglo
monk surprised me by pouring some water from the bottle onto
my head. Not only was I shocked by the sudden blast of cold
water, but I felt really guilty knowing the only thing going
through my mind was a debate about whether the water dripping
from my bangs was going to permanently harm my dry-clean-
only pants.

The ceremony ended with a brief phonetic Sanskrit chant
as a reddish string that symbolized my healing was tied around
my wrist. No one ever mentioned my prescription drugs and
skin creams, which were sitting in a paper bag on the floor next
to my purse.

Finally the Anglo monk put a small amount of "something
from the Himalayas" that he wouldn't identify except to say that
"it was prayed over a minimum of ten thousand times" into my
quart of Evian water and advised me to drink a teaspoon of it
every day.

Back downstairs, as I purchased a sparkly purse and a pair
of capri pants, I tried to evaluate what had happened. "Was I

now healed? And if so from what?" I wondered. Since I wasn't really sick, could I use this healing in a preventative way kind of like a flu shot? "No, no," I said to myself, "You can't just jump willy-nilly into a new religion and expect specific results." I knew I was never going to have the courage to drink the murky looking prayed-over water.

I was also puzzled by why I was willing to assign to these Buddhist Monks a spiritual purity of intention I could never have extended to evangelical Christians in a tent, Lubavitchers in an RV, or Jehovah's Witnesses at my front door. Maybe because they didn't claim to save my immortal soul? Or maybe because I had no idea what they were actually saying? Perhaps because what they offered was achievable in a practical way: a fresh start, financial aid to some orphans.

Or was it that the proximity to capri pants and leopard-skin throw pillows spoke to me in the first spiritual language I could actually understand.

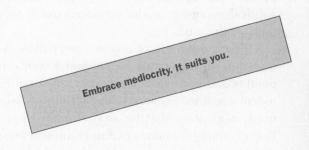

Embrace mediocrity. It suits you.

Full Disclosure

MERRILL MARKOE

As we draw ever closer to another national election we find ourselves in a rare position to observe the birth of a political tradition. I am referring, of course, to the increasingly mandatory use of what is sometimes called "inoculation"—going public with the confession of some private foible before your political opponent or the press can use it to drag your name through the mud.

Recent examples of this are everywhere. George W. Bush bothering to admit that he enjoyed a wild extended youth as pundits and journalists urge him to own up to an alleged past use of cocaine. Senator John McCain of Arizona feeling the need to mention that he strayed in his first marriage. Clint Reilly running for mayor of San Francisco, making a 30-second television commercial in which he looked into the camera to confess that "twenty years ago I had a drinking problem."

Even across the Atlantic in jolly old England, a guy named Michael Portillo, vying for leadership of Britain's Conservative Party, shocked the political establishment in September by announcing that he had had homosexual experiences in college.

Clearly, full personal disclosure is the wave of the future. I believe that soon all new declarations of candidacy will sound approximately like this:

"Fellow citizens and respected members of my party: Although I have not been much of a hat wearer in recent years, I would like at this time to throw my hat into the ring. I have the vision, the dedication, the energy, and the innovative ideas needed to lead our country in the twenty-first century.

"But before I share some of the exciting programs I am planning, there are a few things about me I feel you should know.

"In the seventh grade I was caught, during a history test, looking at the answers I had written on the bottom of my shoe. I regret this behavior and have continued to compensate for it to this day by doing a great deal of supplementary reading about the War of 1812.

"This was a very rebellious time in my life during which, I am ashamed to admit, I also received numerous hours of detention for talking without raising my hand.

"Everyone knows that the teenage years can be a behavioral minefield, which is the only excuse I can offer for why I attended several parties with a group of underage friends who consumed large quantities of a certain brand of cough syrup containing a lot of alcohol. In a misguided attempt to form an educated opinion, I tried but ultimately rejected marijuana, cocaine, diet pills, and a small amount of what the other kids called magic mushrooms, even though I was aware that they were neither magic nor even in the mushroom family.

"These experiences were regrettable and I have not consumed any drugs at all since my junior year in college.

"However, in my senior year, adrift in the overwhelming stress of the upcoming law school entrance test, I experienced an uncharacteristic period of moral confusion during which I was coerced against my better judgment by a girl with whom I was having a turbulent, short-lived relationship into participating in what was then called a three-way.

"Connected to this was an unfortunate incident involving the transmission—to a rather large number of my immediate peers—of a type of body lice with which I was temporarily infested.

"In this same period I regret to admit that I was not entirely frank with quite a number of girls, to whom I professed false feelings of love to gain sexual favors. Afterward, I invited these girls to dine with me in expensive restaurants and then when the check arrived pretended to have forgotten my wallet, thus causing them to have to pay for dinner. At the end of the evening I would always assure them that I would call them soon, knowing full well that I never would.

"I can't change my past. But I do continue to strive each day to be the best person I can be. This past year I am pleased to announce that I have totally eliminated my tendency to speed through yellow lights at the very last second, an unfortunate habit that was at the root of my many moving-violation citations.

"I have also given my word to the people with whom I work to correct what they call my pattern of giving inappropriately cheap seasonal gifts and to stop claiming that I am going to the gym when I am actually just heading home early to nap.

"In coming months I plan to openly admit that the reason I did not lose weight after three months on the Zone was not due to a glandular disorder but because I keep a stash of Snickers and Hershey's Kisses behind the corporate checkbook in the bottom drawer of my desk.

"Yes, I regret the things I did. But I also embrace

them for helping to make me the honorable, law-abiding, church-going citizen and monogamous family man that I am today. As most of you know, I have been happily married to my lovely wife Lana for 11 of the 14 years we have been together and faithful to her for almost three."

STEPS IN
THE CREATION
OF A LIST

1. Gratefully stop working on project that is due in three days.
2. Think of a title.
3. Fruitlessly search for late-night snack in kitchen.
4. Pet cat.
5. Write first list entry.
6. Write second list entry.
7. Notice extreme similarity of first and second list entries.
8. Scrap original concept for list.
9. Reflect that any idea for a list contains the seeds of its own repetitiousness.
10. Resort to cheap self-reference.
11. Pet cat.

—Francis Heaney

Preface to My Autobiography

STEVE MARTIN

Twelve years ago, I was given complete access to myself in order to write an autobiography, and after those dozen years of research, interviews, and personal introspection, I realized that no one was there. I thus decided to invent a character who would be my friend, whose eyes I would be seen through, and who would relate my personality through fictional encounters with myself. I have given this fictionalized narrator the name of Strove Mortman, whom I shall refer to as a he/she. I found it beneficial to have a male narrator when discussing my muscles, my business perspicacity, and my toughness, and a female narrator when discussing my physical appearance, my seductive glances, and my tenderness. I gave him/her the name Strove because it is both masculine and feminine—Strove McCarthy, Irish tenor (1912–63), and Strove Bandolini, Italian lesbian poet (1612–1725)—and the name Mortman because of what it spells backward.

I naturally would like to come off as interesting as possible, so several events in this book have also been made up. My high-school football record as reported is not actually mine but a combination of random numbers over 100, separated by the words "touchdown" and "per." The admiring comments made in the stands by adoring fans during a fabricated game are a pastiche of the compliments paid to Pope Clement VIII by Galileo, in 1605. The descriptions of my sexual prowess are measurements taken from Michelangelo's David, and multiplied by 1.25.

Other fictionalized accounts, related not to fool the reader but to illustrate various aspects of my character, include the single-handed asphalting of a two-mile stretch of Sunset Boulevard, the shunning of the Nobel Prize for my work in gene therapy, and the impregnation of infertile housewives with the tacit approval of their grateful husbands.

Although I am positive that I have had children, I have been unable to find them, or any evidence that they ever existed. This may be a mind game someone is playing on me, but I have a distinct memory of being the father of a bride. I will address this issue in further volumes.

For the sake of dramatic action, certain discrete events have been compressed into one event, particularly in the area of retorts and bons mots. It will often—in fact, always—appear that my comeback was uttered at the moment of insult. In some cases, however, up to three years had passed before I uttered my riposte, which originated not with me but was the brainchild of a team of highly paid writers.

I have exaggerated, for purposes of narrative flow, my involvement in certain charities. This shows my deep concern for those less fortunate than I, although this concern has never translated into any overt action. I have, however, assisted many individuals who fall outside the scope of major benevolent organizations, by offering advice such as "Get a job," and "Your illness is all in your head."

It is interesting to note that my eight years spent at Yale were not entered into the records, or, worse, were mysteriously deleted from them by a sinister hand. Somehow, these records were transferred to Santa Ana Junior College, in California, with a lowered grade-point average. Also, it was worrisome to discover that my high school yearbook photo had been tampered with, causing me to look like a nerd who could not have lost his virginity until the sad age of twenty-two.

I was given free access to my psychiatrist's notes, or at least the notes he left on his desk when he excused himself for a brief moment "to get some caffeine." These notes offered interesting insights into me from an objective third party, whom I pay. I quote a few of them here:

". . . a dream so dull it actually could have happened."

"Pick up cream rinse."

[various doodles]

I have several people to acknowledge for their contributions to this autobiography. I wish to thank my editor, whose comment "I read it" washed away all self-doubt and motivated me to keep writing. I thank my ex-wife, Delores, whose wise counsel—"There better not be one negative word about me in there or I'll let the world know about your freebasing with Liberace"—prompted a reexamination of our marriage that made me recognize that those were idyllic years. And, finally, I wish to thank the Greek poet Homer, for without his *Iliad* I would have been at a loss to put into words certain of my exploits during Desert Storm.

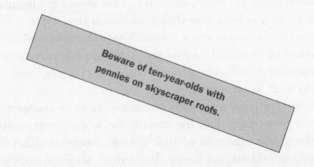

Beware of ten-year-olds with pennies on skyscraper roofs.

Studies in the New Causality

STEVE MARTIN

A 27-year-old Michigan man, who complained that a rear-end auto collision had turned him into a homosexual, has been awarded $200,000 by a jury.

—*Ann Landers, July 30, 1998*

Recent discoveries in the legal profession have left scientists, many of whom still linger romantically in the Newtonian world, scrambling to catch up in the field of New Causality. In a case last month, a judge in Sacramento ruled in favor of changing the value of pi, thus acquitting a tire manufacturer of making tires that were not fully round. An appeal by scientists was thrown out for lack of evidence when the small courtroom could not physically accommodate a fully expressed representation of pi. The oblong tires in question were produced at the retrial, the judge said they looked round to him, the defense played the race card, and the value of pi was changed to 2.9.

Cause and effect have traditionally been expressed by the example of one billiard ball hitting another billiard ball, the striking billiard ball being the "cause" and the struck billiard ball being the "effect." However, in the new legal parlance the cause of the second billiard ball's motion is unclear, depending on whether you're prosecuting or defending the first billiard ball. If you are suing the first billiard ball, it is entirely conceivable that striking the second billiard ball harmed your chances of becoming Miss Paraguay. If you're defending the first billiard ball, the motion of the second billiard ball could be an unrelated coincidence.

It's easy to understand how one physical thing can influence another physical thing: my car hit your car because I was blinded by your shiny hair barrette. But what about emotional causality? Can my harsh words affect your mood, costing you millions of dollars that you would have earned behind the counter at Burger King? Apparently so. Several months ago, a male office worker was awarded $67,000 because a female co-worker asked him if he would like her to drop his "package" off at the post office; he was further awarded $50,000 after arguing that she was also in constant possession of a vagina, the knowledge of which rendered him unable to concentrate.

A more difficult causality to prove, however, is physical to emotional. Can being struck from behind in a car accident cause someone to become a homosexual? Obviously the answer is yes, evidenced by the large award in the lawsuit cited above. Even more interesting is a little-known case in which a man was awarded $36,000 after a driver *failed* to collide with his car, causing him to become a *latent* homosexual.

The New Causality guidelines have redefined many of the basic concepts with which the scientific world has struggled for centuries. They are:

The "97 Steps" Rule: It used to be accepted that one event caused another one event to happen. No longer so. It is now acceptable to have up to 97 causality links: *Your dog ate my philodendron which depressed my mother who in a stupor voted for Marion Barry causing an upswing in crack sales that allowed Peru to maintain an embassy and accumulate parking tickets,* *encouraging me to stay a meter maid rather than become an Imagineer.* And so on.

Semantic Causality: Semantic causality occurs when a word or phrase in the cause is the same as a word or phrase in the effect. "You failed to install my client's *sink* properly, causing her to *sink* into a depression." In the case cited earlier, the plaintiff's lawyer might say that the "party" driving the Camaro collided with his client's car, and isn't a "party" where homosexuals gather and socialize with one another?

After-the-Fact Causality: This simple law states that having sex with an intern can cause a financial misdealing to occur twenty years prior.

Universal Causality: This is the law that has the legal world most excited. It rests on the proposition that "anything can cause anything," or, more simply put, the "Bill Gates gave my dog asthma" principle. If the law of Universal Causality bears out, the economy will receive an invigorating boost when everyone sues everyone else for everything. Everything actionable that ever happened to you will be the fault of your next-door neighbor, who, in turn, will sue Bill Gates, who, in turn, will sue himself.

These advancements in the legal world mean for science that a large stellar object is no longer the *cause* of the bending of light rays that pass nearby but its *blame*. Scientists everywhere are scurrying to make sense of the New Causality, with Newtonians turning into Einsteinians, and Einsteinians turning into Cochranians. Meanwhile, astronomers have discovered new and distant objects in the farthest reaches of the universe. Are they protogalaxies forming near the beginning of time? The courts will decide.

Disgruntled Former Lexicographer

STEVE MARTIN

The following definition was discovered in the 1999 edition of the Random House dictionary. The crafting of this definition was the final assignment of Mr. Del Delhuey, who had been dismissed after 32 years with the company.

mut•ton (mut'n), *n.* [Middle English, from Old French *mouton*, *moton*, from Medieval Latin *multo*, *multon*-, of Celtic origin.]

1. The flesh of fully grown sheep. 2. A glove with four fingers. 3. Two discharged muons. 4. Seven English tons. 5. One who mutinies. 6. To wear a dog. 7. A fastening device on a mshirt or a mblouse. 8. Fuzzy underwear for ladies. 9. A bacteria-resistant amoeba with an attractive do. 10. To throw a boomerang weakly. 11. Any kind of lump in the pants. (*Slang.*) 12. A hundred mittens. 13. An earthling who has been taken over by an alien. 14. The smallest whole particle in the universe, so small you can hardly see it. 15. A big, nasty cut on the hand. 16. The rantings of a flibbertigibbet. 17. My wife never supported

me. **18.** It was as though I worked my whole life and it wasn't enough for her. **19.** My children think I'm a nerd. **20.** In architecture, a bad idea. **21.** Define this, you nitwits. **22.** To blubber one's finger over the lips while saying "bluh." **23.** I would like to take a trip to the seaside, where no one knows me. **24.** I would like to be walking along the beach when a beautiful woman passes by. **25.** She would stop me and ask me what I did for a living. **26.** I would tell her I am a lexicographer. **27.** She would say, "Oh, you wild boy." Exactly that, not one word different. **28.** Then she would ask me to define our relationship, which at that point would be one minute old. I would demur. But she would say, "Oh, please define this second for me right now." **29.** I would look at her and say, "Mutton." **30.** She would swoon. Because I would say it with a slight Spanish accent, at which I am very good. **31.** I would take her hand and she would notice me feeling her wedding ring. I would ask her whom she is married to. She would say, "A big cheese at Random House." **32.** I would take her to my hotel room, and teach her the meaning of love. **33.** I would use the American Heritage, out of spite, and read all the definitions. **34.** Then I would read from the Random House some of my favorites among those that I worked on: "the" (just try it); "blue" (give it a shot, and don't use the word "nanometer"). **35.** I would make love to her according to the O.E.D., sixth definition. **36.** We would call room service and order tagliolini without looking it up. **37.** I would return her to the beach, and we would say goodbye. **38.** Gibberish in e-mail. **39.** A reading lamp with a lousy 15-watt bulb, like they have in Europe.

Also: **a. muttonchops:** slicing sheep meat with the face. **b. muttsam:** sheep floating in the sea. **c. muttonheads:** the Random House people.

ANOTHER UNNATURAL HISTORY

The Children's Crusade

Earlier in history, the largest religious gathering of young people ever held in the west was the Children's Crusade (if by "religious gathering" you mean "getting together to boot out the Muslims"). In the summer of 1212, thousands of children set out to conquer the Holy Land by love instead of by force. (Coincidentally, more than 700 years later, this love-not-force strategy was never considered by General Eisenhower in his planning for D-Day, so I guess it's not really much of a coincidence. Or, as it turned out, much of a strategy.)

One group of children was led by a French shepherd boy named Stephen, from Cloyes-sur-le-Loire. It's hard to imagine that thousands of children would follow a French shepherd boy, but the sheep did, so who knows? Stephen had a vision in which Jesus appeared disguised as a pilgrim, but it couldn't have been much of a disguise because Stephen saw right through it. (If I were Jesus, I'd have chosen something that was less of a giveaway, like maybe a bear costume.) In this vision, inadequately costumed Jesus gave Stephen a letter for the French king. You'd think he could have delivered it himself, but maybe he was worried that the bear suit would scare people. On his way to deliver the letter, Stephen attracted thousands of followers, some of whom decided to go to the Holy Land. (Anything to get out of going back to school.) Eventually, 30,000 made their way to Marseilles, where disreputable merchants shipped them to slave markets in North Africa. So I guess the joke was on Jesus.

Nicholas, a ten-year-old from Cologne with no connection to sheep or sheep-related work, tried to drum up interest in a Children's Crusade in the Rhineland, attracting an estimated 20,000 children. They crossed the Alps into Italy and split into smaller groups. Some were dispersed among various Lombard towns; others continued on to Genoa, where they were refused transport across the Mediterranean, which may have been R-rated in those days. A few traveled to Rome, where Pope Innocent III took pity on them and released them from their crusade vows. Many of the rest were sold into slavery in the East, but at least they weren't spending their days sitting around watching MTV. The fate of their leader, Nicholas, is unknown, but if he ever turns up, I'll bet a lot of people are going to be pretty darn mad.

—Randy Cohen

New Roller Coasters Opening This Season

MICHAEL FRANCIS MARTONE

Mr. Horizontal (Orlando, Florida). This thrill-packed action ride not only whips you up to 1.03 Gs, it also transports you from Parking Lot G to Parking Lot H.

Das Stänky Kaseköaster (The Hague). At 294 feet tall, it's the highest, fastest roller coaster in the world, made entirely out of Liederkranz cheese. (We recommend visiting in winter, before the thaw.)

Sir Crash-a-Lot (Geauga, Ohio). The newest attraction at Six Flags over Informed Consent.

The White Trash Express (Bentonville, Arkansas). Although this coaster has been up on cinderblocks since '83, that hasn't hurt its popularity with tourists and wifebeater-clad locals alike.

The Mine Ride (Heritageville, West Virginia). Travel over 2,600 feet under the majesty of the Alleghenies, dig coal, and die of tuberculosis.

The Mobius Strip (Bern, Switzerland). Tremendous value. For the price of one ticket, you get to ride on this single-sided coaster for the next 12 billion years until the entropy of the universe reaches zero. Then you go backwards.

Captain Emetic (Jackson, Mississippi). New this year: Because lines are so long, management has added concession stands right in line, so while waiting you can snack on fried dough, beer, and raw eggs.

No Exit (Algiers, Algeria). Three chairs. No mirrors. Really popular with high school students.

Maze of the Minotaur (Orlando, Florida). This newest coaster innovation uses the power of "human propulsion" to career at up to 0.002 miles per hour as you walk through a series of iron gates for hour after hour after hour.

Gemini (Sandusky, Ohio). Twin coasters, racing one next to the other, so you can high-five the passengers beside you.

Phlegemini (Sandusky, Ohio). Twin coasters, racing one underneath the other, so you can spit on the passengers below you. (The line to get on the lower coaster is very short.)

The Ride That Your Mom Will Go On (Anaheim, California). Totally lame. There were, like, all these middle-aged women on it.

Last Year at Marienbad (Cannes, France). You loved the flick, now try the coaster!

Whip-a-Midget (Bismarck, North Dakota). Finally, a roller coaster that can be enjoyed by adults shorter than three feet, nine inches. Nobody knows why the lines are so long, though. Hardly any midgets even come to the park. They probably feel uncomfortable standing in line with all those tall, wobbly guys wearing raincoats and giggling from their stomachs.

Whip-a-Midget II (Seoul, South Korea). Exactly the same as Whip-a-Midget, except it is called "Haki-Ko-Tenama," which is Korean for "The Roller Coaster."

Because Yahoo Maps Aren't for Everybody

MICHAEL FRANCIS MARTONE

How do I get to Main Street?

YAHOO.COM
- Turn LEFT on ELM.
- Turn RIGHT on 117th.
- Make a LEFT onto EDGEWATER.
- Arrive at MAIN Street.

PROFESSIONAL.TAXI-DRIVER.COM
- Turn LEFT on ELM.
- Turn LEFT on 117th.
- Tell passenger that traffic is BACKED UP for hours on EDGEWATER, but you know a shortcut.
- Turn LEFT onto State Highway 72.
- Take EXIT 7A onto INTERSTATE 80.
- After crossing the INDIANA border, you will be on EASTERN STANDARD TIME, so set your clock FORWARD one hour.

- When you finally arrive at MAIN Street, laughingly assure passenger that you won't CHARGE HIM for that hour.
- CHARGE HIM for that hour.

AARP.COM
- Start CAR.
- Wait INSIDE while engine warms up. Have a DANISH.
- Get back in CAR. Adjust all MIRRORS.
- Back up SLOWLY onto ELM.
- FART uncontrollably.
- Blame it on TOJO.
- Turn RIGHT on 117th.
- Make a left onto EDGEWATER.
- Don't go too fast, or you'll miss Paul Harvey and the REST of the Story.
- Arrive at MAIN Street.
- Watch your ungrateful GRANDCHILDREN peep though the shades, hoping you don't see them.
- Sit on PORCH until they open door. You may want to get comfortable, because it may be a while before those DIRTBAGS let you in.

MODERNRAT.COM
- Turn LEFT!
- Turn RIGHT!
- RIGHT!
- RIGHT!
- Hurry! HURRY!
- RIGHT!
- LEFT!
- LEFT!
- Sorry, I meant RIGHT! Go BACK!
- LEFT!

- CHEESE! Cheese cheese cheese cheese cheese CHEESE!
- Yes! I beat ALGERNON for the first time in MONTHS!
- I'm SORRY, what was the question again?

LEMMINGS.GO.COM
- Scurry directly from ELM to EDGEWATER.
- Water? WATER!
- March into the LAKE!
- Await further INSTRUCTIONS.

MILLIONAIRE-ANT.COM
- Take surface exit IA73JF8A9E-44107OHUS (2104 Elm, the one with all those guys wearing NAMETAGS).
- Follow that tasty SUGAR trail right into the glass tube.
- Wait until it gets DARK.
- Wait four to six weeks for SHIPPING.
- DIE in transit.

SYPHILLIS.MODERNSPIROCHETE.COM
- Wait for Bob to use the Men's Room at the ELM Street facility. He never washes his hands, even after working with the ants.
- From the faucet, hop onto PAUL's thumb. Paul always licks his FINGERS when he turns the pages of his novels.
- Paul will sell his copy of *Zen and the Art of Motorcycle Maintenance* at HALF-PRICE BOOKS.
- NANCY buys books there all the time. She also works lunch shift at CHICK-FIL-A.
- BEVERLY just lost her taxicab license, and so she's going to apply for work as a MALL SECURITY OFFICER. On the way out of the mall, she passes by the food court and feels a little peckish.

- ALGERNON likd poliswoman! Sh was prety!
- So you think you can ignore me, huh? I know you're in there, and I'll sit on your porch all night if I have to! Ow! A RAT just bit me in the ass! Dirtbags.

LEMMINGS.COM
- I'm still WAITING!

Our New Password Policies

MICHAEL FRANCIS MARTONE

PASSWORD:*****

Your password has expired. Please enter a new password that complies with our new password policies.

NEW PASSWORD:*****

Invalid password. Your new password must not be the same as any of your previous passwords. Please enter new password.

NEW PASSWORD:********

Oh, so your new password is "password?" Yeah, nobody would ever think of that. Try again.

NEW PASSWORD:*****

Can't you read? You've already used that password! If you try it a third time, I swear, your account will expire, and you'll have to visit Gary in the basement, and ask him nicely to reset your password. And remember, he talks this way because he has a gland disorder. If you make fun of him, he won't be in a hurry to reset your password, that's for sure.

NEW PASSWORD:********

Wait a minute. That's Michelle's old password! Is this Shelly, from Marketing? If it is, I'd be happy to reset your password. Come on down to the basement and I'll show you all kinds of neat things you can do on the network. I'll also show you my O'Reilly guides. I've got like eighteen of them, and I wrote my name on them so you can borrow them whenever you want.

NEW PASSWORD:********

Oh, I see. I knew it was you, Frank. Forget it. I won't reset your password until you publicly apologize for your impression of me at the Christmas party. I don't even sound like that. Jerk-wad.

NEW PASSWORD:*****

Uh, I don't THINK so. That's your Oracle password. *Muchas gracias*, Señor Dumbass. If you forget your Oracle password, go bother those Oracle losers on the twenty-eighth floor, with their window offices, like they're all hot shit or something.

NEW PASSWORD:*********

Your password may not consist of the name of a fellow employee, abutted with the words "sucks." Gary works very hard down there in the basement, and doesn't need your negative attitude.

NEW
PASSWORD:***************************************

Oh, so that's how it's going to be? Fine. Your new password must contain at least eight characters, of which three of them must be numbers and two must include diacritical marks. I'll bet you wouldn't even recognize a cedilla if it bit you in the ass.

NEW PASSWORD:^x^n

LOGON AS NEW USER: administrator

NEW PASSWORD:********

I know it's you, Frank. Don't try pulling this "administrator" crap. Besides, do you think I would be so stupid as to make my password "password"?

NEW PASSWORD:*********

Oh. I see what you're thinking. "Password2," ah, yeah, like I had to change my password so I just added a "2" or something. Well, ah, you're barking up the wrong tree, heh heh. LOL. ROFL.

NEW PASSWORD:*********

So, hey, what are you going to prove? Like, it wasn't "Password3," so obviously it wouldn't be "Password4," right? So why don't I just reset your password and we call it a day?

NEW PASSWORD:*********

Oh, poop.

La Bamba Hot Line

BOBBIE ANN MASON

Hello. La Bamba Hot Line."

"Is it true that 'La Bamba' is derived from the Icelandic Younger Edda, set to music by Spanish sailors and transported via the Caribbean to America in 1665?"

"No, not even close. La Bamba Hot Line. Go ahead, please."

"When is the next Louie Louie Parade scheduled?"

"You want the Louie Louie Hot Line. This is the La Bamba Hot Line."

"Oh."

"La Bamba Hot Line."

"This is Senator Sethspeaks in Washington, on the Committee for the Investigation of Obscene Rock Lyrics."

"State your business, please."

"Uh—I was wondering, just what are the words to 'La Bamba'?"

"Do you have the record?"

"Yes, I do."

"Well, listen to it."

"But I can't tell if the words are obscene or not."

"That's your problem. La Bamba Hot Line."

"My teenage daughter has been acting funny lately. She refuses to eat, and she has frown lines on her face. She's become aggressive with her parrot and when you talk to her she just says everything is geeky. The doctor can't find anything wrong with her. What should I do?"

"I'm glad you asked. The La Bamba Hot Line has a special pamphlet dealing with problems of teenagers. Just send a self-addressed stamped envelope to La Bamba Hot Line, P.O. Box 4700. But first, I'd have a heart-to-heart with that parrot."

"Much obliged."

"Likewise, I'm sure. La Bamba Hot Line."

"This is Phil Donahue. Is it true that the La Bamba Hot Line is having a lip-sync contest?"

"Absolutely. October the ninth."

"What do I have to do to win?"

"What do you think? Perform 'La Bamba' till your eyes bug out, do it like a rockin' fool, blow the house down."

"Do you think I've got a chance?"

"Everybody has a chance in life, Mr. Donahue."

You wouldn't believe the stuff I get on the La Bamba Hot Line. I work twelve to four. It's an intensive job and can burn you out quick. Two short breaks, while all the calls stack up. They get a message, "All the La Bamba Hot Lines are temporarily busy. Please try again." It's unfair that people have to keep calling and calling, dialing till their nails split in order to get the La Bamba Hot Line. We need help! We need somebody to handle the genuine emergencies, weed out the crazies. The things people want to know: they want to know are they going to get cancer, will the plane they have a ticket on for tomorrow crash, which stores are giving double coupons this week? We try to answer what we can, but I mean we're not God. I tell them play "La Bamba" 32 times in a dark room, then improvise 32 versions, then listen to it standing on their head. I tell them to walk down the street muttering *"Yo no soy marinero/Soy capitán."* Count the number of people who recognize the lines and multiply by four, and whatever number that is, that's Ollie North's secret Swiss bank account. I mean, some things are so simple you wonder why anybody would bother calling up. We deal with a lot of that. Little kids call just to be funny, try to catch us off guard. Is your refrigerator running, that kind of thing. I'm on to them. I start screaming a wild, cacophonous sort of schizo "La Bamba." Blows them right out of the water.

But mostly it's scholars. Academic stuff. People wanting to know about roots, symbolism, the double entendre of the *marinero/capitán* lines, etc. Idea stuff. I spend my mornings at the library just to stay even with these people. Man, they're sharp. One guy had a beaut—a positive beaut. The way he traced the Paul-is-dead hoax back to the lost Shakespearean sonnets, twisting it around and back through "Poor Ritchie's Almanac" straight up to the chord progressions of "La Bamba"—it was breathtaking. The switchboard was lit up like the stars in the open desert sky on a clear night while I listened and kept all those calls on hold. I was humbled right to my knees. Unfortunately, his spiel didn't get recorded and I didn't get the guy's name. But he'll call again. I'm sure he will.

Some of the ideas that come in are just junk, of course. Did Idi Amin record "La Bamba"? Of course not. But former President Jimmy Carter did. Some stuff you hear is so unbelievable. No, the Voyager is not carrying "La Bamba" out to the end of the universe. Don't I wish. That's sort of my job really, to carry "La Bamba" to the end of the universe.

My boyfriend is giving me a hard time. He says I take my work too seriously. We'll be watching *Washington Week* and I'll say, "Look at those guys. Talk about serious. Don't they ever get down?" He says, "All day it's your La Bamba duties, your La Bamba research, your La Bamba outfits. You go off in the morning with your La Bamba briefcase. When are we ever going to talk about us?"

He says, "This La Bamba thing is going to blow over any

minute. It may be blown over by Friday. Things are that fast these days."

"Don't say that!" I cry. "Buddy Holly. 'American Pie.' The Big Bopper. Elvis. Things last longer than you think."

We're going through crisis time, I guess. But we'll work it out. I have faith in that. Right now, my work is at a critical juncture. I'm talking demographics. Market potentializing. La Bamba aerobics, theme weddings, instructional software. We were represented at the harmonic convergence. We met on the boardwalk at Atlantic City, an overflow crowd of La Bamba regulars. We played the song over and over and concentrated on fiber optics, sending our vibes out all over the universe.

The special thing is, my boyfriend can sing "La Bamba." He's not allowed to enter the lip-sync contest because it would be sort of a conflict of interest. He doesn't just lip-sync. He sings it a cappella. He sounds so sincere when he sings it. He makes up the words—he's not a purist—but they sound right; he has the right tune. That is the secret of La Bamba, inventing it as you go along. That is the true soul of La Bamba. La Bamba lives.

All Shook Up

BOBBIE ANN MASON

Scream sightings have been popping up all over the place ever since the famous Munch painting was stolen from the National Art Museum in Norway. The Scream was first spotted at the Olympics, and then at a Starbucks in Santa Barbara. It was glimpsed on a frozen shoulder of I-95 just south of Waterville, Maine, trying to hitch a ride, and it turned up on the same morning in the crowd beside the batting cage in Sarasota where Michael Jordan was making his first swings of the day. It has been seen driving a big-rig, walking a rottweiler, and lurking around mini-marts, Laundromats, and factory outlets. But these are all bogus reports. I know where the Scream really is. It's right here in front of me, in my kitchen. How the universal totem of complaint materialized at my house in the Heartland is a good question.

I had already been screaming a lot over assorted recent tribulations (ruckus on the Richter scale; Tonya Harding's bodyguard; Oliver North's olive-drab hat flying into the ring; Lillehammer-like winter weather everywhere), and a friend who has one of those inflatable four-foot Screams tethered in her dining room sent me an 18-inch Scream Jr., of my very own. My husband, Roger, blew it up and set it on a paddle of the ceiling fan. It looked terrified. He put it on the floor, where the cats gave it a good sniffing over, and the Scream looked as if it were holding its breath in the expectation of a fatal puncture. Then Roger placed the Scream in the arms of our life-size plush Koko the Gorilla: nothing doing. Everywhere he put it was worse than the last, from the Scream's timid-looking perspective.

Then something happened. Roger set the Scream in front of our Elvis. (More than one vanished icon has found a new place to dwell here, but I can't go into that.) Our Elvis, a sexy ceramic collectible, entertains on top of a cabinet between the sun space and the stairs. He's decked out in one of his caped Aztec-sun-god suits, which is missing a few sequins. There in the light, he really appears to be a sun god—or at least one of the sun god's buddies. I like to think of him as Orpheus, the original rockabilly who plucked the lyre in a band with Apollo, Hermes, and Big Boss Man Pan. They say Orpheus could charm rocks, but Elvis could charm the pants off a snake.

Now the King of Rock and Roll and the official spokesperson of angst stand face to face, their mouths hanging open. It is as if they were meeting down at the end of Lonely Street, one block over from Valhalla. Their confrontation is timeless, yet full of moment.

"*Eeeeee,*" says the Scream.

It shakes Elvis up. What is this? The Scream looks about a 100 years old and is as bald as a monk. Bless my soul, what's wrong with me, Elvis wonders. He starts itching like a man on a fuzzy tree. He's acting white as a bug. His insides are shaking like a leaf on a tree.

"You ain't nothin' but a hound dog," Elvis cajoles, trying to shush the Scream. "Cryin' all the time." He croons, "Are you lonesome tonight?"

"eeeeee," says the Scream.

"Hey, baby," Elvis says. "I ain't askin' much of you. No no no no no no no no. Don't be a stingy little mama. You 'bout to starve me half to death. Just a big-a big-a big-a hunk o' love will do."

The Scream is fixing to scream again, so Elvis tries a different tack. He says, "Bugsy turned to Shifty, and he said 'nix nix!' " Elvis's knees begin to roll; then his pelvis begins its customary swivel, his left leg working like a bit brace. "Everybody let's rock!" he cries.

Slowly, the Scream begins to undulate. Its lips are like a volcano when it's hot. It feels its temperature rising, higher and higher, burning through to its soul. Its brain is flaming. It doesn't know which way to go. It's burning, burning, and nothing to cool it. It just might turn to smoke. The flames are now licking its body. It feels like it's slipping away. It's hard to breathe. Its chest is a-heaving. Its burning love is lighting the morning skies. It's just a hunk-a hunk-a burning love.

The Scream reaches for the scarf around the King's neck.

"EEEEEEEE!" it says.

"I'm proud to say that you're my buttercup," Elvis gasps.

I am smiling. If rock and roll will never die, can spring be far behind?

One man's life is another man's punchline.

Terms of Office

BOBBIE ANN MASON

Q: Mr. President, in a recent news conference you used the rather colorful expression "He doesn't know me from Adam's off ox." Senator Dole alleges there is no much term and says you employed this "pseudo-colloquialism" (he also called it a "Gergenism") as a calculated attempt to sound "down-home" in order to woo back Southern Democrats who have deserted you. Would you care to comment, sir?

A: Yes, Brit, I'd be glad to clarify that allusion. In a team of oxen, the "off" one is the one farther away from the driver—that is, to the right. So if our ancestor Adam is far back in memory his off ox is even farther away—but maybe not as far right as Senator Dole. When I left Arkansas to attend Oxford as a Rhodes Scholar, people back home would ask my mother where I was, and she would tell them I was off. Off at Oxford. I could have said he didn't know me from Adam's hatband, or Adam's pet monkey, Adam's brother, his brag dog, his chief communications officer—whatever. We use lots of these sayings in Arkansas, but you don't know split beans from coffee about Arkansas, do you?

Q (follow-up): Sir, isn't this another example of what your critics call Slick Willie waffling—claiming to be both an Oxonian and a good old boy?

A: Brit, let me say that "Adam's off ox" is heard chiefly west of the Appalachians, according to the *Dictionary of American Regional English*. In the Northeast, there are only two lonely spots where the D.A.R.E. maps the usage of "Adam's off ox"—one in upstate New York and one in Massachusetts.

We have a language gap. Let me point out that I wouldn't naturally say, "He doesn't know me from Adam's off bull." When I was coming up in Hope, we didn't say "bull" in mixed company. We said "he-cow." A bull was a gentleman cow, or a male cow, or a top cow. Up here inside the Beltway, you call a bull a bull, and you call bull "bull." In the South, we have an expression for people who do that. We say, "He's a person who says what he thinks." And it's not necessarily a compliment.

What you call "waffling" is just good manners back home. I was taught to say "he-cow." And we didn't say "rooster." We said "chicken," or "he-chicken." Schoolteachers would speak of "the he" and "the she" and "girl birds" and "boy birds." People never said "cock" in public. Any word with "cock" in it was taboo. They'd say "hoe handle." Why, some Southerners still won't say "the clap." They say "the collapse." Some old-timers back home still can't bring themselves to say my brother's name, Roger. "Roger" used to be a dirty word. A verb.

But yesterday's gone. Now you can say "bullshit," and it doesn't even mean anything. Let me just say this: The trait of being inoffensive in mixed company is a major strength of this presidency. You see, the whole world now is mixed company. It's an advantage that the president of the United States is in the habit of spontaneously blurting out obscure regional metaphors that wouldn't make ladies blush a century ago. I expect to do more of it.

Hey, I just got here and I've got a lot to learn. I know the presidency is more than knitting cat fur into kitten britches. That reminds me—I could have said, earlier, "He doesn't know me from Adam's house cat." And it might interest you to know that Adam's house cat was called Nethergarment. A polite term for britches. Why, I know folks who won't even say the word "socks."

The Magazine

The magazine as we know it rose to popularity in eighteenth-century England, roughly coinciding with the introduction of (although featuring no advertising for) the condom. Early in the century, Daniel Defoe's *Review* and Richard Steele's *Tatler* published three issues a week. Soon after, Addison and Steele's *Spectator* began as a daily. They included articles on politics as well as essays on various aspects of manners and morals. None included perfume samples, although life might have been improved if they had; eighteenth-century hygiene being not very. Much the way our *Teen People* reflects the divisions of our society (and the emergence of a class of readers alienated by *Geriatric People*), companion magazines devoted to women were launched, including the *Female Tatler* (1709) and the *Female Spectator* (1744). In 1731 Edward Cave, an English printer, synthesized many of the diverse features of those publications in *The Gentleman's Magazine*, the periodical that gave the name "magazine" to its genre. It was originally a monthly collection of essays and articles culled from elsewhere, much like our *Reader's Digest* or our "stealing." Its motto—"*E pluribus unum*"—alluded to its numerous sources and would eventually be stolen by the United States. In 1738 Dr. Johnson joined its staff and quickly became its main contributor. "None but a blockhead ever wrote except for money," Johnson said. Or perhaps that was Tina Brown. Rivals and imitators quickly followed, notably *London Magazine,* the *Scots Magazine,* and *Playboy* magazine (or is it just Hugh Hefner and not the magazine itself that recently celebrated its 250th birth-day?) More periodicals for women were introduced, including *Ladies' Magazine* and *Lady's Magazine*—imagine the merry mix-ups! Their progenitor, however, outlived them all and perished only in 1907. (By "progenitor," I mean of course *Gentleman's Magazine*. Dr. Johnson did not outlive Tina Brown, although wouldn't it be great if he had? For one thing, there'd have been a lot fewer Stephen King pieces in *The New Yorker* if Ms. Brown had died in 1907.)

—Randy Cohen

The Greatest Hastily
Written Short Notes of
the Twentieth Century

BRUCE McCALL

Picasso's Note to Rockwell

Hello Dear Mister Norman!

That cute model in your painting—do you have a telephone #?

> Ever,
> Pablo

Rockwell's Note to Churchill

Dear Mr. Prime Minister,

I knew you did landscapes but the cartoon was a big surprise and a swell joke! By the way, is that Charlie Chaplin or Hitler getting hit on the head by Dame Britannia? (I'd make her more of the freckle-faced tomboy type but maybe that's just me.) Good luck with the War!

> Cordially,
> Norman

Churchill's Note to Virginia Woolf

My Dear Mrs. Woolf,

Your fascinating idea of parachuting the entire Bloomsbury group onto the roof of the Reich Chancellery in Berlin, and thereby depressing the Hun into giving up, will be taken up by the Literary Warfare Committee when next it convenes.

Yrs.,
W.S.C.

Virginia Woolf's Note to Henry Ford

Dear Mr. Ford,

I have a very dear friend named Mr. Ford Madox Ford, Esq. Should you not then, for purposes of consistency, be addressed as Mr. Ford Henry Ford, Esq.?

Earnestly, I am
V.W.

Henry Ford's Note to Garbo

To Miss G:

I want to be alone too, but the income tax people and the Washington radicals and the press snoops and the unions won't let me.

H.F.

Garbo's Note to Hemingway

Mr. Hemingway,

The quote was accurate. I did say that Marlene [probably Marlene Dietrich, German-born actress and chanteuse—Ed.] is more of a man than you'll ever be.

G.G.

P.S. Bet my feet are bigger than yours.

Hemingway's Note to Einstein

Hello Curly—

Physics is a mug's game. Would go up against your bomb with my over-and-under Purdey any time. Knocked out your boy Fermi once, in the second round.

Papa

Einstein's Note to Eisenstein

Hello Mr. E—

I expect that you have misunderstood my theory of relativity, but in any event, compare our names more closely and I believe it will be pretty clear that we are probably not relatives.

A.E.

Eisenstein's Note to Gertrude Stein

Dear Gertie,

Didn't quite get that in your last about "a rolling Stein gathers no moss."

Affectionately,
Sergei

Gertrude Stein's Note to Batman

Darling Bruce,

Do come for tea at our flat Sunday afternoon next, but not through the window again, please! And bring some of your thrilling Batpoems!

G.S.

Batman's Note to Superman

Listen, you litigious crybaby, I don't know who has the legal right to use the term "Caped Crusader," and know what? I don't care. If you spent half the time fighting evil that you do fighting frivolous lawsuits, this world would be a safer place.

B'Man

Superman's Note to Gandhi

Dear Mahatma,

I'm returning the turban and loincloth with regrets. Great look, especially with my pecs, but the licensing guys have me boxed in on the big "S" logo & the whole outfit. We all got our crosses to bear, and I guess this goofy getup is mine!

Peace!
S.

Gandhi's Note to Mrs. Simpson

Dear Wallis,

I have taken the liberty of forwarding your most flattering recent note to His Majesty the King of Siam, as I personally do not at present require a royal consort. (Have you tried Edward, Prince of Wales?)

All Love,
G.

Mrs. Simpson's Letter to Freud

Dr. F.:

I sent David to you because he had a mental block about asking for an increase in his royal allowance. He has admitted to me that you instead filled his head with disgusting pseudosexual "theories" that must now be spanked out of him. I am turning your bill over to my solicitors.

Wallis

Freud's Note to Babe Ruth

Dear George,

This recurring dream of popping up: Please bring your bat to our next session. We will work on not choking up so much on the handle.

S.F.

Babe Ruth's Note to Picasso

Hey Baldy,

Keep your paint-smeared paws off my girlfriend.

The Bambinoh

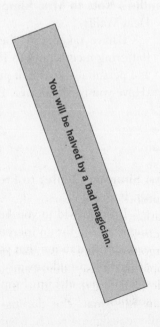

You will be halved by a bad magician.

Anchors Weigh In

BRUCE McCALL

In *The Century*—a companion piece to ABC's ongoing "Century" project—Jennings has something more permanent, something large, something with heft—606 pages that will sit on shelves and coffee tables for many years.
                                                    —*Chicago Sun-Times*

Diane Sawyer's magisterial history of Turkish agriculture in the reign of the Ottomans turns out to be far more enjoyable than its dry subject matter and intimidating 1,403 pages at first might suggest. Ms. Sawyer has clearly done her homework—besides drawing her own maps, indexing her copious footnotes, and personally curing the volume's Moroccan leather binding. Relying strictly on her own research and eschewing all secondary sources, Ms. Sawyer brings alive such forgotten figures as the fifteenth-century rutabaga broker Vopid the Tense (almost offhandedly proving him a more credible claimant to the title Sultan of Early Anitolian Roughage than Klangmat, the darling of so many previous scholars), while consigning such pseudo-events in pre-Akbar drought folklore as the 1453–54 Ankara Sponge Riots to what she rightly terms "both the ash and trash heaps of history." Gumpf has already printed ten million copies of Ms. Sawyer's *Turkish Agriculture in the Reign of the Ottomans*. They may not be nearly enough.

What can be said of Dan Rather's *Aleksander Sergevevich Pushkin: The Real Story* that will not strike readers of this review as arrant puffery? That Mr. Rather not only seems to walk in Pushkin's shoes but his socks as well? That he goes the extra mile that was always a trek too far for Nabokov and Edmund Wilson, virtually redefining the significance of Pushkin's boyhood infatuation with matches? If the author's translations from the Russian occasionally rankle with their slangy Petersburgian burr, his translations to the Russian (*"nyemni pa bidynki"* for "forbearance notwithstanding," for example) are pellucidity incarnate. In his foreword, Mr. Rather makes light of his achievement, which he calls "this slapdash bagatelle, knocked out on a laptop many a late night after one too many, when I didn't have the energy to shoot a few baskets." One can only wonder at the Pushkin biography that might have been engendered had Mr. Rather taken his time. Chartered container ships packed with copies of *Aleksander Sergevevich Pushkin: The Real Story* destined for overseas markets are reportedly causing gridlock in the Panama Canal.

Bravo! Connie Chung, in *Salt II: An Encyclopedia of Reason*, not only has revisited Salt Treaty II but brings forward a brief so airtight—and so cogently proceeds to argue it—that all previous books on the subject are suddenly relegated to the realm of intellectual dwarfism. Ms. Chung's 452 Points of Difference with the treaty's final draft constitute a devastating indictment of woolly-mindedness and point up the danger of accepting quarter-truths as half-truths in the endgame that is modern nuclear physics. If this reviewer can presume to raise a complaint about a work so fastidiously executed, it is that Ms. Chung's epilogue, an imagined discussion between the author and the Four Horsemen of the Apocalypse, never quite manages to engage the Horsemen on NATO's ambivalence about the mistaken 1974 Slingshot-missile count. But this is a quibble. Bravo, Ms. Chung.

Sam Donaldson had maintained what he terms "an offhand sort of interest" in grand opera all his life. Only after fainting from joy one evening during last year's Beijing Opera production of *Tristan und Isolde*, performed in Chinese, did he recognize his desire to write a book about opera's hundred most unsung geniuses. What has resulted—*Kudos Overdue*—is not a book. It is a wonderment. How Mr. Donaldson found the time to comb every libretto ever written, cross-index the more than four hundred thousand suicides, stabbings, and seductions thus compiled, then write his own "mega-opera" including each and every such event, against a score incorporating the signature musical styles of every opera composer who ever lived—all for the sake of amplifying a comment on Mozart's versatility—is not the least of the mysteries occasioned by the magnitude of Mr. Donaldson's accomplishments. Barnes & Noble stores have cleared out all other books and will stock only this one for the rest of the year. Still, hurry.

Barbara Walters's epic history of the past millennium finds room for many a fascinating and insightful nugget. Did you know that Ethelred the Unready was an albino? That the first automobile had no wheels? It might surprise even classical scholars to know that Athenian law in Socrates' time prescribed exile to Sparta for feeding the squirrels. But in *The Complete History of the Past Thousand Years*, Ms. Walters is after bigger game than simple entertainment. With a brush as broad as it is thick, she paints a 1,000-year-wide mural—no, a diorama—that encircles the reader in a historical merry-go-round and will not let him dismount until every jot and title of a millennium of human striving has been documented, asterisked, annotated, and ibided. The sheer weight of erudition in Ms. Walters's epic volume may be enough to bring lay readers to their knees, but the author makes no apologies. "If you don't get it," she snaps in her introduction, "go watch television."

You've always been a little different, haven't you? Now put your clothes back on.

Ancient Chinese secret: You're screwed.

Who Wants to Keep His Job?

BRUCE McCALL

To: Programming Dept. N.Y.
From: Programming Head L.A.

So, okay, I get to play Monday-morning coroner. *Who Wants to Have Sex with Some Hell's Angels?* failed, people, because nobody (anybody at Standards & Practices listening???) visited the set during dress rehearsal. Because leather photographs like muslin on TV. Because depravity-based TV shows shouldn't be broadcast on Sunday A.M.

Onward. Last night I okayed a speed-up of *Who's Up for Robbing an Armored Car?* to fill the sudden hole in the sweeps-week sked. (Don't forget to screen contestants for gun permits, I beg!) I know, it didn't focus-group as strong—despite the built-in freeway-chase viewership bonus—as *Who Wants to Mud-Wrestle Roseanne?*, but the latter's production costs are so low that it will end up bankrolling the first two episodes of *Who Wants to Hijack a Cruise Ship?* I've brought in Hy and Doris (*American's Bloodiest Emergency-Room Videos*). Heed their wisdoms. (Hy memos me re *Who Wants to Kidnap Bill Gates?* four simple words: "Make it Jennifer Lopez." 20 extra Nielsen points.)

But, people, whoa! I'm paid to be a skeptic, to think things like, Is the "who wants to" genre already in its out cycle? I'm not talking retrenchment here. The people have voted: Wholesome, family-oriented, audience-interactive pornotainment—always, *always* with high production values—is today's No. 1 cultural snack food. We're just the Kozmo.com delivery guys. *But the snacks can't arrive stale.* Herewith a few mindprods:

- Has anybody bothered checking out India TV's daytime ratings monster? F.Y.I.: Format, quiz show. Gimmick, wrong answers cost contestants their *own* money, homes, etc. Insight: U.S. has never had a prime-time personal-ruin-driven TV quizzer.
- Amateur-transplant-surgery genre is *hot*. Who says so? Six solid proposals in last week say so. Yeah, I know it's a legal mosh pit. (Shoot offshore? Real surgeon on standby?)
- Affiliates still feel double-crossed after net showed them but then never skedded *Kangaroo Court*, our live trage-docuquiz. Let's relook at it. (Rename it *Twelve Angry Men* to nip the nature-show confusion?) Legal says tacking on a "Life isn't fair" V.O. & super upfront would cover railroading-the-innocent issue like a cheap judge's robe.

This is not to say that we should abandon the "who wants to" franchise, flat out. I mean, any competitor could snap it right up and milk it in its death throes. We need a fresh creative twist, like *Who* Doesn't *Want to . . . ?* How about: *Who Doesn't Want to Have Diplomatic Immunity for a Day? Who Doesn't Want to Blow Up a Building?* I'm thinking this could Viagrafy the concept conceptually.

But the TV audience is treacherous. (Anybody remember *America's Most Shocking Autopsies?*) Moral: Look where not even *cable* has gazed before. Ask yourself, What's the network's liability exposure?—and work forward from there. As in *Who Wants to Bomb an Iraqi Missile Site?* That would be great TV *and* good citizenship, with zero chance of successful litigation.

A few other notions: *The 20,000-Volt Death Quiz*. Gimmick: death-row inmate gets a week's reprieve for every correct answer until . . . hey, you can calculate the odds as well as me. Who, people, could *not* tune in?

But, damn it, that only reminds me, "who wants to" is one haunting refrain. *Who Wants to Drive the Indy 500? Who Wants to Take Home a Fifty-Foot Anaconda?* Wrong. Those are all too rural-unmarried-male-skewed. We've got to think big-target, not fragments. And yet, and yet. Maybe it was Ed Murrow who said that the joke's dead when Letterman stops telling it. Maybe "who wants to" is thresholding—has already thresholded, we just don't have instrumentation precise enough to measure it yet.

People, I have a Monday breakfast with the Chief, and I don't want *Who Wants My Job?* winning the exit poll. Here's one final large, large, *large*, idea: Quiz format. Mega-bucks payoff. Contestants all brainy creeps, but gimmick is: Make lo-empathy super-creeps take a dive and grease answers so single sympathetic creep keeps on winning until even more sympathetic creep comes along. People, how come I suddenly feel a whole helluvalot better about Monday b'fast???

You May Already
Be a Winner

BRUCE McCALL

Just going to sit there while huge conglomerates pay millions for memoirs and autobiographies by folks even duller and less accomplished than you? If you're a windbag, egomaniac, faded star—or simply like the sound of your own droning voice—here's your chance to cash in on the hottest trend in book publishing today: smash celebrity megaflops!

Based on scientific research into dozens of current and recent megaflops, we've streamlined and simplified the process down to a few easy-to-follow instructions. Take five minutes to fill out the form below, then sit back to wait for that FedEx overnight letter with the nonrefundable seven-figure advance (minus our 15 percent commission).

1. **Check one item from each of the categories below:**

Occupation
       ❑ Movie has-been
       ❑ Military second-guesser (Ret.)

❏ Celebrity's ex-spouse
❏ Aging country music star
❏ Office-seeking political hack
❏ Bad-boy athlete
❏ Child earning $1 million + yearly

Obstacle Overcome

❏ Jealous rivals
❏ Too darn nice/trusting/honest
❏ Misunderstood
❏ Acne
❏ Crooked management
❏ Ahead of our time
❏ Unhealthy diet
❏ Fickle public

Goal Achieved

❏ First-name basis with Sly
❏ Tabloid lawsuit victory
❏ MSG/cholesterol/fat free
❏ Career restart
❏ Vindicated by events
❏ Miss U.S.A. judge
❏ Reunited with family at last
❏ Free of family at last
❏ No more Munichs
❏ Let me be me
❏ Grandkids
❏ Daytime Emmy
❏ Comeback
❏ Balanced Federal budget
❏ Met Frank
❏ Made folks happy

2. Now compose your book outline:

"I am a (Category 1) who overcame (Category 2) to achieve (Category 3)."

Megaflop Writing Dos and Don'ts

If you're the buck-chasing cynic we think you are, you—and/or your ghostwriter—will be running roughshod over the language in your hurry to hit the book racks. Some megaflop musts:

When in Doubt, Drop a Name

(a) The pointless inclusion of every random big shot you can think of is a big part of what makes a megaflop. But it's all in the style.

" 'I believe those are my Unterhosen?' It was while doing my weekly wash at the laundromat that I first met 'Doc' Kissinger . . ."

What's wrong with that name-drop? Correct—too intriguing! Try something like this:

"Among the guests was Henry Kissinger, the famous diplomat, who sounded just like a German when he spoke."

(b) What's wrong with this name-drop?

"After the White House ceremonies a bunch of us—Yo-Yo, the Donald, Tiger, Warren, and Annette and a few of the Judds—got the hungries and crashed the Ovitz function just as Dr. Hawking and that Salinger guy were leaving. Salinger did a double take and murmured: 'Over here. Something I have to ask you!' "

That's right, the writer completely left out the clothes! Always stop the action to describe your name-droppee's wardrobe:

"Annette, stunning as always in a taupe Balmain jumpsuit with crossover asbestos shoulder straps, the Judds so cleverly coordinated in cowboy chaps of a matching lizardskin-leopardskin-lizardskin pattern." Gumming up your narrative with such irrelevant asides goes a long way toward your goal of being readerproof. While padding out the pages!

(c) "The biggest name in arbitrage, insulting the flag of Flanders!"

Perfect, yes, but why? Because there is no flag of Flanders, and your publisher's lawyers will have the World Court at the Hague all over them like a cheap judge's robe. Remember: If you aren't sloppy with the facts and libelous with the snide asides, you're not megaflop material!

Tone and Style?
What Tone and Style?

Aim to be a megaflop M.V.P.—Monotonous, Verbose, Pompous—in tone and style. It's the quickest way to signal reviewers "D.O.A.!"

"Notwithstanding, at that point in time, one might, without overly much fear of contradiction, project general negative end results, and it was deemed both vital and necessary to, therefore, 'send them a message,' which, in the event, eventually was what eventuated, as I recall."

There's a paragraph with megaflop written all over it!

Relevance Is Irrelevant

Your narrative is budging along like a piano being pushed uphill. Time to bog it down but good!

"For myself, I ordered the dumplings, the chicken with cashews, the sweet-and-sour shrimp, the pork, the string beans, some brown rice and some sauce, and some tea. For his part, Mao Zedong preferred the chicken dumplings, a fish dish that I failed to recognize and cabbage rolls, while Mrs. Mao, as I recall, chose ham and cheese on a kaiser roll with 'all the fixin's.' Also on the menu were a bewildering number of Peking duck dishes, which if memory serves . . ."

Call such pointless digressions the Chinese Word Torture—but they work!

When It's Time to Stop, Start Up Again

The real test of a megaflop is that it ends 50–100 pages after it should have. That's because real megaflop authors never know when to stop—particularly not in the valedictory that always concludes a megaflop.

"You know, I have a pretty darn simple philosophy of life and it's what I tell friends and colleagues first when they ask me to explain my success. There are no more than 40 or 50 observations and supporting anecdotes that come to mind—in no particular order—so if you'll bear with me, I'd like to pass them along here and now . . ."

It's that sort of windup that stops an inquiring mind like a Cape buffalo stops a bullet.

And that's it, folks. The prescription for your very own seven-figure megaflop. Now get to work. And if you're the born megaflop author we think you are, we can guarantee one thing: You'll never have to write a sequel!

Your grandmother will see you on *Cops*.

Costuming the Homeless

SUSAN McCARTHY

Who came up with the plan to costume the homeless? Whose idea was it to dress them as prospectors, dance-hall girls, gangsters, or cowhands, turning homelessness into a tourism plus?

Nobody seems to know. In fact, everyone denies authorship of the tourism-boosting scheme, rumored to be on the agenda at the next Conference of Mayors. Despite the disavowals, many seem to think the proposal is bound to catch on.

Cities around the nation are fielding complaints from the retail sector about problems caused by homelessness. Shopkeepers complain of people sleeping in doorways, blocking sidewalks, and driving shoppers away with so-called aggressive panhandling.

Big-city mayors don't count on getting federal money for low-income housing any time soon. In cities like San Francisco, Los Angeles, Miami, and New York, where tourism is a major industry, homelessness is considered a severe economic problem.

"Does homelessness hurt my business?" asked one San Francisco retailer who insisted that he not be named. "Absolutely.

People come to vacation, to shop, to go clubbing, not to be nickel-and-dimed by scary-looking vagrants. City Hall's no help. They're afraid to jail these bums in case the civil liberties people come after them."

Ernest Eager, an aide to San Francisco mayor Willie Brown, distanced his city from the costume concept. "At the last conference, someone mentioned that if homeless people just had a little different spin, they wouldn't be so upsetting to tourists," he said. "But the idea certainly didn't originate here."

According to an aide to Denver mayor Wellington Webb, "The plan did not come from here." However, he added, "Visitors don't like to see homeless, but if we had old-timey prospectors wandering around, some have said that would actually increase tourism value, like Colonial Williamsburg."

The idea for Denver would include period clothing, slouch hats, canteens, pick-axes, and, said the mayor's aide, "The homeless would love it, because they'd get free warm clothing. One woman said if we could get them to trade shopping carts—which are illegal to have, anyway—for burros, they could carry their stuff like they do now, but the impact would be totally different. It's intriguing, but it didn't come from us."

At least one homeless person has been seen in Boulder, Colorado, with his possessions strapped to a burro, possibly part of a secret pilot program.

In San Francisco's Haight Ashbury district, a group of young people said they had been paid $15 each to dress in vintage "hippie" attire but couldn't remember who paid them. An older street person charged that the "hippie" clothing was inauthentic. Rumors of street people dressed as "beatniks" in the North Beach area could not be confirmed by press time.

Northern California homeless advocate Ira T. Lee said the concept was degrading. "That is so typical," Lee said. "Cover it up, give it a ticket out of town, paint a handlebar moustache on it. I'd like to know what greedhead came up with this one."

Tina Bitt, a member of the San Francisco advocacy group Creative Homeless And Non-Homedwellers Getting Effective

(CHANGE) agrees: "You can't make real human suffering go away by pretending we're in some kind of a Western."

But Daniel B., who is homeless, was intrigued by the proposition. "I'm kind of a modern pioneer already," he said. "I live off the land, the way the '49ers did."

Jane C., homeless since 1993, was skeptical. "I worry about the burros," she said. "Only ones who get treated worse than us are animals."

Other ideas reportedly tossed around at the conference were for indigent New Yorkers or Chicagoans to dress as Capone-era gangsters, with pin-striped suits and (nonfunctional) tommy guns; for down-on-their-luck Philadelphians to adopt old-fashioned Quaker attire; or for needy Los Angelenos to sport municipally issued zoot suits. An aide to L.A. Mayor Richard Riordan, denying that the idea came from their office, noted that L.A. is ahead of the curve, since homeless people there regularly work as Hollywood extras, he said.

An aide in one Sunbelt mayor's office said the idea may have come from Cool Concepts, which sells CD-ROMs that print out outfits for the homeless on sheets of fabric, as in Mattel's Barbie Fashion Designer game.

Cool Concepts CEO Reilly Lowe said, "If certain municipalities are interested in putting a happy face on homelessness, we can put 500 cowhand outfits a day out on the streets of Laredo."

The Nano-Pet Epoch

SUSAN McCARTHY

As the years drag wearily to 2020, lonely consumers with money to burn will be glad to know that the pet market will soon explode with variety. The cat-dog-guppy paradigm can't meet soaring consumer demand. Nor can it meet soaring concern about the environment. With world population over six billion, there's not much room for wildlife, unless they come and stay with us.

The final factor is genetic engineering, a field that urgently needs to do something crowd-pleasing, like simultaneously averting consumer boredom and ecological disaster.

What does it boil down to? Tiny endangered animals for every room of the home! Wildlife will be miniaturized for your companionship, convenience, and their own survival. Where once there were only cats and dogs, there will now be minute herds of elephants thundering around under the bed, and rhinos you can hold in the palm of your hand.

My daughter is on the cutting edge of the future, where she plans to spend her later years. She wants a little gorilla. My son wants a small elephant seal. I'll have to explain to them that these are social animals. "You can't have just one elephant seal," I will lecture my son. "He wouldn't be happy by himself. You would need a whole bunch of elephant seals." "Okay!" he will say. And I will picture the tiny seals hauled out on the edge of the tub—next to the sink!—and I'll give in.

For fairness to my daughter, we'll get a troop of minuscule gorillas. Can't you just see them knuckle-walking around in the Creeping Charlie?

Another relative, who asked not to be identified, said, "A little rhino would be so cutums-wutums." Pause. "A giraffe. Two feet high. Yes. A leeetle giraffe running around on its leeetle tiptoes!"

There will be a limited specialty market for the reverse product: Little animals made large. Talk about conspicuous consumption: Anyone who has four-feet-high guinea pigs grazing on the lawn has got to be rich. It will be a niche market, though: Showing off is the only excuse for huge guinea pigs. The only good thing about guinea pigs in the first place is that they're small.

Most little animals would be awful if they were big. Big rats, huge hamsters, stupendous ferrets? I think not. Even the cute ones—giant ladybugs, say—would pose problems. You'd need giant aphids for them to eat; the gardening public and the powerful gardening lobby would not stand for the breeding of giant aphids. On the positive side, however, we'll finally find out where the fabled 400-pound canary sits.

The thought of the magnified animals makes clear that our new pets are going to have to change in more ways than size. If they're going to live with us, they'll have to respect our boundaries. We'll make them sweet, even wimpy.

A few decades ago, Russian fur farmers decided to breed a tamer, easier-to-process silver fox. From every generation they picked the nicest foxes, those voted Least Likely to Bite the Man with the Big Knife. After 35 generations, they had some of the most affable, outgoing, glad-handingest foxes you can imagine.

Although they had been selected for sociability, the friendly foxes also tended to have floppy ears, curly tails, and white spots. Apparently these are often linked to traits more obviously connected to temperament, like high serotonin levels. The fur farmers are now trying to market them as pets. All that's left is to miniaturize them into smarmy nano-foxes.

Some critics will say it's wrong to manipulate wild animals, to commercialize their free spirits. Such objections won't last in the face of the next trend: extinct pets.

I was heartbroken to learn that woolly mammoths survived on a Siberian island millennia later than anywhere else and became extinct just 3,700 years ago. They were dwarf mammoths, a mere six feet tall, instead of the usual nine.

We just missed them, damn it! So we'll bring them back. And we'll bring back others we've lost. What wilderness purist's flinty principles would not soften at the thought of a yardful of dodos? Pocket-sized, of course.

Then we'll do dinosaurs. I know, you saw all those movies about scientists who create dinosaurs and are destroyed for their hubris. You know what their problem was? Not enough hubris! We need gobs more hubris for this job, so thank goodness we have me, Susan McCarthy, Animal Futurist.

This time around, we'll make little dinosaurs. How bad could *Tyrannosaurus rex* be if he were gerbil-size? With white spots and a curly tail? Scientists examining fossils of dinosaurs ancestral to birds say that newly hatched *T. rex*es may have had coats of down for warmth. Do you grasp the implications here: We're talking itty-bitty, curly-tailed, spotted fluffy baby tyrannosaurs. You know you want one.

Subvarsity Smackdown

SUSAN McCARTHY

Honolulu (AP)—A University of Hawaii official has conceded that the school nixed the football team's 77-year-old
rainbow logo because of concerns about its homosexual
theme . . . instead of the Rainbow Warriors, the team will
now be known as the Warriors.

Honolulu—A Honolulu State College official denied
today that the school had nixed the football team's request
to change its name from the Fighting Tigers to the Raging
Drag Queens.

"It's true a vote was held, and it's true the students
overwhelmingly favored Raging Drag Queens," said the
official, who asked to be unnamed. "But the name was not
submitted through proper nomination channels, so it
doesn't count as a request, and neither do most of those
others. Properly nominated choices included Tiger Team,
Fighting Tigers, Tiger Gladiators, Just Plain Tigers,
Savage Geckos, Tiger Tsunami, and More Than One
Angry Mongoose, and of those, Fighting Tigers got the
most votes."

Fighting Tigers received only four votes, the official

conceded. He declined to give totals for Raging Drag Queens or other disallowed names.

"Fighting Tigers is a sucky name," said the football team's spokesman, Vincent Lom. "There are no tigers in Hawaii, and nobody's scared of them. We want a name that speaks of our awesome terrifying might, and in our experience, almost everyone in the league is terrified of homosexuals and cross-dressers, so Raging Drag Queens would be a perfect name for us. Plus, we were hoping we would be allowed to share locker rooms with the cheer-leaders."

Lom said that although the team had its heart set on Raging Drag Queens, they would have settled for other disallowed names that did well in student voting, such as the Huge Violent Gays, the Aunt Nancy Men, or the Recruiting Squad.

Lom said his personal suggestion for a scary team name, the Drunken Tourists, did not do well in the voting. "I don't know why. It gives *me* the fear."

Red Field—Red Field Indian High School officials denied today that the school's football team had changed its name from the Mighty Bobcats to the Syphilitic White Missionaries, but a student body representative appeared on local cable news holding a banner with that name in block letters.

Knute Rock Deer, student body president and wide receiver, told newscaster Jay Johnson, "We know what chills the blood and it ain't bobcats."

Johnson asked Rock Deer how students could defend the use of a stereotyped image of Caucasians. "The team names of the Braves and the Indians are stereotypes about scary Indians," replied Rock Deer. "How is Syphilitic White Missionaries any different?"

Rock Deer noted that in the 1970s Stanford University changed its team name from the Indians. Though students

voted to rename the team the Robber Barons, the administration insisted on the Cardinals or, later, the Cardinal, a
shade of red. "How scary is that? A color? Excuse me?"
asked Rock Deer. "They should've gone with Robber
Barons."

"But how can Native American students identify with
syph—with such a name?" Johnson asked. Rock Deer
replied, "It's not about identification, it's about intimida-
tion."

A group of Red Field cheerleaders and spirit mascots
performed a skit depicting the impact of syphilitic white
missionaries on peace-loving indigenous peoples. The
camera quickly cut away from the skit to focus on newscaster Johnson, who attested, "That is one scary team
concept. It left me weak-kneed and shuddering."

"At first we actually picked Forked-Tongued Land-
rapers, but we weren't sure people would get it," Rock Deer
said. "Same with Clueless Wannabe Culture Thieves."

Springfield—The National American United States High
School Football Hall of Fame denied that any plaques or
trophies have gone out with unapproved team names such
as Syphilitic White Missionaries, Steroid-Crazed Monsters,
or Lady Steroid-Crazed Monsters.

The Hall of Fame says it has been deluged with
requests for team name changes, some of which officials
suspect may not have been authorized by school administrations. Hall officials say all name changes will be "carefully scrutinized."

In apparent gestures of solidarity with embattled students at Oklahoma's Red Field Indian High School, where
students were suspended en masse after attending a football game against rival Pleasant Valley Pioneers wearing T-
shirts captioned TREMBLE BEFORE THE SYPHILITIC WHITE
MISSIONARIES, students across the country have been moving to rename teams after "things that *really* intimidate,"

in the words of the valedictorian of one inner-city high school.

"Eagles aren't scary," said Winsocki Smith of St. Euphemia High School. "Losing the roof over your head is scary, which is why kids at City renamed their team the Slumlords. Stallions aren't scary. Losing your kids is scary, which is why the students at Eastside renamed their team the Arrogant Social Workers. Longhorn cattle aren't scary. Being excluded from the dominant culture is scary, which is why the kids at Prep renamed their team the Ice People."

"Also, religious oppression is scary, which is why we at St. Euphemia renamed our team the Braindead Zombie Protestant Fundamentalist Backlash. We mostly play other Catholic schools and we're pretty confident that will have them shaking in their soggy diapers, the big old babies."

Smith added that many of her best friends are Protestants. "Try to understand, this is about football. This is about winning."

"We're going to be checking these name change requests for months," said a weary Hall of Fame staffer who asked not to be named. "I'm pretty sure no administrator approved the Yuppie Creeps, but how about the Entrenched Bureaucracy? It's a D.C.-area high school, so that could be real, right? I thought the Tampa Bay Devil Rays was a joke name when I first heard it, so how can I be sure about the Elbow River Fire Ants? I don't think it's even legal to call a team the Disgruntled Postal Workers."

"And look at this," added the employee despairingly. "First we got this request from the Battling Bearcats at Flatland High—who have a longstanding rivalry with the Pirate Crew at Hilltop High—to change their name to the Declining Test Scores. They crushed the thoroughly terrorized Pirate Crew in the big game, but the Pirates struck

back by requesting a name change to the Crumbling
Physical Plant Plus Your Principal Smokes Crack."

"Turns out neither name change was authorized, but a
temp worker already sent out the trophy with Declining
Test Scores on it. We engraved a new trophy that said
Battling Bearcats, but Hilltop High is naming us in a lawsuit for inflicting loss of school spirit."

"Now, look. Look at this. Here's a new request. What I
am I supposed to do, call the principal at Flatland and
ask, 'Are you really the Flatland High School Thought
Police?' "

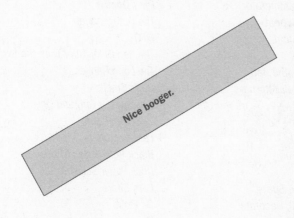

Nice booger.

BAD NAMES FOR ACTION MOVIES

A Fistful of Fern
Good Guys Wear Cranberry
Pop Goes the Evil
Soft Boiled
Run Away!
Fact Checker-on-Fact Checker
   Crime
Kelp
Exit the Dragon
The Programmerator
Rinse & Repeat
Walking Stout
Shelf Life
The Good, the Bad,
   and Their Attorneys
If I Were Twenty Years Younger
Head in the Sand
Take That!
Fists for Fun
Buy Hard
Some Like Spats
Crush, Kill, Decorate
Inaction Jackson
Frosty the Hit Man
Pardon Our Appearance
   While We Kill
Lawrence of Accounting
The Guppy
The Number Crunchers
Lard Target

Defer to Superiors
Lie Down with Lemmings
I'm Saying It for the First Time
Feet of Fungus
Poke Hard
Kung-Food Fighting
Mission Possible
The Road Worrier
A Fistful of Gumballs
Easy Does It
The Octogenarian
FIFO
The Pen IS Mightier Than the Sword
The Loan Ranger
Hell's Smells
Two Guys, a Girl, and One
   Stick of Gum
Less Is More
Black Belt, Brown Shoes
Rock Paper Scissors
Let's Share
Dr. Floss
The Ungentleman
Haste!
The Red Badge of Hilfiger
Never a Borrower or Lender Be
Tough Cheese
Male Pattern Badass
A Wedgie Too Far

—Peter Schooff

Adventures with Rod and Gumshoe

J. H. S. McGREGOR

The situation had gotten way out of hand. It'd take a river of oil to soothe those troubled waters now. Smith and Wesson Oil, I thought. Oh, I know they don't offer it in those upscale *haricoteries* back east; frankly they haven't got the cruets for it. But it's the house label in every joint down every mean and slushy street from Minot to Bemidji. The dumps you settle into when the repo man's got your RV and your wife's got a sinus infection and the kids. My neighborhood. Look me up where the icy wind slams a man hard up against his past, then leaves him muzzle to muzzle with life its own self in some foul rod and gun shop of the heartland.

I'd been down south visiting a client in the joint—Leavenworth, the big house on the prairie—and I was having that dream again. The one where you're ice fishing buck naked with your keister frozen to an aluminum folding chair and a walleye with a grin like a Miata is steaming your dangle with his fishy breath. My client was Edgar Rice "Five" Burroughs, the Native American apeman who'd waded through Bloods to make himself topknot of the Mohawk Mob, a particularly nasty crew of jamokes even by Iowa City standards. None of your mail-order gang-bangers and moshpit hangers-on, these lads were shadow boxers on the twilit fringe of G-land. Dealers in weed and powder, boosting cars and rolling winos—they're what we call the Crack and Bum Club in the biz. "Five" had the Mohawks by the short hairs right now and he stood poised on the brink of a full-blown takeover of the Allinda Family. I'd met Archie Allinda one time. You wouldn't think to look at him that he had a bite out of every wormy apple that fell between Rosebud and Deadwood. Well, actually, maybe you would. Allinda owned the Bass and Blaster but he did serious business out of the Sizzler up at the airport mall. Seventh booth on the left. Order the fajitas if you want, but don't count on still being around when Shirl brings them to the table.

Pat "Garrison" Keeler, *consigliere* to elderly Don Allinda—reputedly a Don Wannabe himself—was my opposite number in this case, my *altered ego*, I guess you would call him. Keeler was a scrapping kid when I first knew him, working his way through parochial school collecting for the massage parlors and shylocks over in Polk City—the Rub and Dun Club we call it in the biz. He was a hard worker and he'd even been a good lawyer once, back in the days before oxymoron. Now when he went for a writ of habeas corpus, he was likely to skip the habeas part altogether.

"*Habeas* might be good Latin," he'd say, "or it might be bad Latin, I leave that to senile judges and toothless old men 'of counsel' "—the Robe and Gum Club we call them in the biz—"but a proper *corpus* needs no adjective."

Keeler wasn't the unkind of man you wanted to go up against unless you were packing heavy and wearing a layer of form-fitting Kevlar between your Duofolds and your Sears nylon parka. After the chat with "Five" Burroughs, I reported to Keeler in his elegant uptown office. He'd hired top decorators—Joel and Ethan Allen from over in St. Cloud. Their work always has a strong regional accent with a lot of naugahyde and a preference for sectionals, if you know what I mean. The

Muzak blared as I stepped inside. At first I thought it was Fargo Uk Yussef, the world-beat disco fusion group from up in Edmonton, but when the brasses squealed like stuck pigs, I knew it had to be Stan Quentin and the Orchestra with the strangled vocal modulations of Taran Tina Louise. I could have listened all afternoon. There was a journal lying open on the sofa. None of your *Southern Living* or *Gourmet* magazine—the Reb and Bun Club we call it in the biz—this was a real literary magazine. The *consigliere* makes sure his brow soars with the eagles while his professional ethics slurp deoxygenated river slime and PVCs with the channel cats. The journal was lying open to a lyrical piece by James Joyce Carol Oates, and the writing spoke to my inner ear:

> Red riverrun out of Smoking Michigun from blasted mug
> of gut-shot thug down low-cut gown . . .

Hypnotic stuff, but I heard Keeler's secretary call my name. It was then that I saw her face for the first time. It was dough-eyed Stella, the doll on the layaway plan. She still had her wandering eye on the prize but she looked like she might be down to her last pair of stiletto heels and faux minx coat. In another minute, if I didn't control myself, she'd be down to her lambswool bustier and thermal socks. One look told you that history still burned between us, gibbering ghosts of the old slurp and tackle. Frank, my former partner, was her hard-boiled ex. No time for that now. The *consigliere* wanted to talk. Time to face the Muzak. Time to wake up and spill the coffee. Time to flinch or cut bait. I didn't stick around to find out which—the Cut and Run Club we call it in the biz.

WELLNESS911

J. H. S. McGREGOR

Thank you for calling WELLNESS911, the Alternative Medicine Emergency Service. Your call is important to us and so is your health. If you are calling from a rotary phone, please stay on the line; an emergency services technician will assist you. But don't hold your breath. Remember, regular breathing is important to your health. And your health is important to us. If you are dialing from a touch-tone phone, please listen to the following menu of options. You may interrupt the dialogue at any time with your selection.

If you are uninsured, please dial 1 now. Remember: your call was important to us and so was your health. Have a pleasant day and try to stay out of trouble next time.

If you are unable to breathe or speak, please dial 2 now. You will be connected with a psychic counselor who will intuit your needs. For best results place the phone on top of your head, clear your mind of negative or anxious thoughts, and get ready to visualize your injury when asked.

If you are bleeding profusely, please dial 3 now.

You have dialed 3 to indicate that you are bleeding profusely. If the blood is oozing and pooling, please dial 1 now.

If the blood has a tendency to spurt, please dial 2 now.

You have dialed 2 indicating that the blood has a tendency to spurt. If you have successfully applied pressure to the wound and diminished the flow of blood, please dial 1 now.

If, despite your best efforts, the blood is still spurting, please dial 2 now.

You have dialed 2 indicating that, despite your best efforts, the blood is still spurting. If you tried really, really hard to stop the blood, but weren't able to do it, please dial 1 now.

If you need a little encouragement and maybe some practical advice about how to stop the flow of arterial blood, please dial 2 now.

You have dialed 1, indicating that you have really, really tried to stop the blood flow, but weren't able to do it.

If you honestly think that's good enough, dial 1 now.

If after giving the matter a little more consideration, you realize that you could do a better job if you put your mind to it, please dial 2 now.

You have dialed 1 indicating that you are satisfied with your own efforts to stop the flow of blood, even though they were woefully inadequate and obviously unsuccessful.

If you've been bullied by so-called "medical professionals" into believing that you're incapable of taking an active part in the healing process—that your only job as a "patient" is to sit up and beg while the MDs with their PCs and their CPAs pick your pocket and play God with your precious health, please dial 1 now.

If you want to turn your back on a lifetime of learned dependency on medical pros and cons and learn some interesting facts about pressure points and tourniquets, please dial 2 now.

You have dialed 2 indicating that you're ready to give wellness a chance. Congratulations! Please listen to the following menu of options. You may interrupt this message with your selection at any time. Should you lose consciousness, stay on the line and a psychic counselor will intuit your needs. If you feel yourself slipping into unconsciousness, place the phone on top of your head; clear your mind of negative or anxious thoughts; and *immediately* begin to visualize your injuries.

If you are bleeding from the carotid or femoral arteries, please dial 1 now.

If your blood is spurting from the superior or inferior vena cava, the aorta, or either of the pulmonary arteries, please dial 2 now.

If your heart has been punctured, please dial 3 now.

You have dialed 3 indicating that your heart has been punctured. If you are sure that you really are bleeding directly from the heart and not overreacting or deliberately exaggerating the seriousness of your injury in a misguided attempt to give a sense of urgency to your call, please dial 1 now.

You have dialed 1, indicating that you are confident of your diagnosis.

If you are a licensed wellness practitioner with more than five years of diagnostic experience, please dial 1 now.

If you are not a licensed wellness practitioner with more than five years of diagnostic experience, please dial 2 now.

You have dialed 2, indicating that while you are not a licensed wellness practitioner with more than five years of diagnostic experience, you still expect us to believe that you can tell the difference between a puncture wound to the heart and a lesion to one of the surrounding arteries.

If you're a little bit ashamed of yourself for trying to put one over on us, please dial 1 now.

If you still think you know what you're talking about, please dial 2 now.

You have dialed 2 indicating that you have complete confidence in your own medical judgment. Congratulations! You've taken charge of your own good health and you are now a licensed wellness practitioner. Thank you for calling WELL-NESS911. Your call is important to us and so is your health. Have a pleasant day.

Eyeglasses

The use of lenses to improve vision dates from around A.D. 1000 with the reading stone, what we call the magnifying glass, employed by nearsighted monks, which might account for their odd haircuts. The Venetians got the idea of putting lenses in a frame in front of the eyes instead of directly on the reading material. *("Quatro optica assinine!"*—you four-eyed geek!—was not a popular bit of Venetian mockery, but should have been.) The Chinese are sometimes given credit for developing spectacles about 2000 years ago, but apparently used them only to protect their eyes from an evil force. Today, of course, we simply change the channel when Larry King appears. The earliest painting of eyeglasses was by Tommaso da Modena in 1352, a series of frescoes of brothers copying manuscripts and being rejected by the more attractive girls. Pope Leo X, who was very shortsighted, wore concave spectacles when hunting and claimed they enabled him to see better than his companions. He also claimed to be taller, smarter, and a better dancer than his companions, who were not inclined to argue; he was the pope and, once Pius IX came along, would turn out to be retroactively infallible. *(Quatro optica assinine!)* One of the nagging problems of eyeglass design is simply keeping them on. Spanish spectacle makers of the seventeenth century experimented with ribbons of silk that could be attached to the frames and then looped over the ears. The earliest condoms, introduced soon after, were attached in a similar manner although not to a similar place except, perhaps, by the very nearsighted. In 1730 a

London optician named Edward Scarlett perfected the use of rigid sidepieces that rested atop the ears, and that is why those sidepieces are today called, well, sidepieces, but that's life for you. Don't expect a lot of credit. In the 1780s Benjamin Franklin developed the bifocal, enabling those who formerly misplaced their reading glasses to now misplace their bifocals. Trifocals were introduced a few years later by Gillette. Before becoming the new leader of Syria, Bashra al Assad was an ophthalmologist. A mastery of eyeglasses seems unlikely preparation for a career as a mideastern tyrant. This becomes more understandable if you read the (admittedly nonexistent) early draft of the screenplay of *Marathon Man* where Dustin Hoffman is ruthlessly interrogated not by sadistic dentist Laurence Olivier but by unpleasant ophthalmologist Laurence Olivier: *"Is ziss better . . . or . . . ZISS!!!!"* (See, he had a German accent.)

—Randy Cohen

My Word Is Beer

Bottleneck Realism from America's Finest Microbrews

TOBY MILLER

Raging Chastity Impeccable Ale. Thanks for choosing Raging Chastity. For our Impeccable Ale, we have developed a special brewing process that ensures each drop exudes the exquisite bouquet for which Raging Chastity is internationally renowned. We absolutely insist on obtaining the most gorgeous ingredients possible, harvesting only the blondest wheat and tannest barley, the supplest hops and the most diaphanous water. Finally, we tenderly brew it over and over and over again until we drop. Raging Chastity Finest Ale. Clean. Crisp. Inviolate.

Pugh's Brews. You hold in your hand a wet bottle of Pugh's Brews. In 1701, our founder, Elihu Pugh, discovered a blend of brewing ingredients that 300 years later still has the folks at the FDA scratching their heads. Pugh's Brews are proud to provide you with one of the most reassuringly expensive price tags of any microbrew available.

Jasper's Officebrau. Master brewer and claims adjuster Jasper Sims (12th floor, room 1801) has crafted this unique pilsner during spare moments in his cubicle when the server goes down. Using pure drinking fountain water, imported Canadian Wite-Out and the finest copy machine toner, Jasper's Officebrau is the ideal beer for those who like to arrive at happy hour just a little bit happier than everyone else. Soon to be included in the Microsoft Office Suite.

Whispering Shaft Premium Ale. All the folks at Whispering Shaft Breweries would like to be able to claim some heritage for our beer, some noble family tradition of brewing that stretches back eons, but honestly, this is just copy for the bottleneck wrapper, they're lucky if they even get a verb. We, or rather, *they'd* like to say it uses a recipe taken from an ancient Native American home brew, but that's a likely story, right? I mean, "Whispering Shaft"? Come on, this stuff comes in cans, too. Whatever. I tried it. It tastes real good. That's all, beer's for drinking, not reading and I should know, I've got half a case of Whispering Shaft going through me right now as I crank this out. And if you ask me, that's truth in advertising, because being able to write after 12 beers says more about the stuff than anything I could come up with. No crap about hops here.

Monk's Underwear Lager. Our beer has been brewed by 25 naked monks from a recipe unchanged since our patron Brewer, St. Thomas of the Sneaking Suspicion, got Joan of Arc mangled to her bangles on the stuff centuries ago. A dark, thin, flat, and tart microbrew, with no head, a nasty aroma, and a marked aftertaste of bismuth, Monk's Underwear has been voted England's most popular beer for seven years running.

Office of Management and Budget Malt Product. To ensure optimum efficiency of beer-product, all our ingredients are carefully vacuumed and then separately run for 25 minutes on the spin cycle. We then take the beer's temperature every 15 minutes during brewing. Known as America's soberest beer, only the finest hops and barley are photographed in order to brew this premium ale.

Mike Tyson's Wicked Ale. Perfect with lunch, dinner, or raw marrow after-work buffet. Its frighteningly full-bodied taste has been specially formulated to meet the high brewing standards of the Illinois Correctional System community service supervisors. Each bottle comes equipped with a special nozzle that allows for drinking through fiercely clenched teeth.

Highway Median Wheat Ale. The only microbrew on the market whose purchase price is fully tax-deductible, this ale is brewed from grain harvested from the rolling plains of America's interstate highway medians. Available in regular or unleaded, Highway Median can be purchased by the case, the keg, and the missile silo.

Nathan Hale New York Ale. Proud to be named after a random historical figure, our beer is brewed in the deathless spirit of Nathan Hale—Victim, Patriot. Each bottle is embossed with Hale's dignified testament of faith with his home-brewed land ("My only regret is that I have but one beer to drink in defense of my country.") and is sold complete with a copy of a commemorative essay written by Nathan Hale entitled, "Sam Adams—Brewer, Yes, but Also an Insufferable Lifesuck."

A Guide to the Lesser-Known Movie Ratings

TOBY MILLER

PG-00 Violence, drug use, language. Parental guidance totally useless.

GPA-3.7 Scenes of subtle transgressive frisson. Not admitted without doctorate.

XD-30 Images of extreme domesticity. Due to the explicit nature of the dishes, drapes, and scented candles, singles over 30 will not be admitted.

AGH Displays of violence verging on barbarism. Parents strongly cautioned to find this material offensive.

∞ Devastating climax, potentially life-changing. No one with a mirror in their possession admitted.

Ë Recurring scenes of evil and Max Von Sydow. No one admitted without murk.

GRR-17 Contains mesmerizing sequences of powerful emotional exploitation. Personal grudges over 17 years old not admitted.

⇄ Scenes of avoidable, and therefore awful and depressing, misunderstanding. 1-D glasses provided.

GAAK Contains rampant bathos. No actors' careers were harmed in the making of this film.

ZZZ Comedy director attempting to be taken seriously with a black-and-white personal phantasmagoria of sorrow. Parental guidance quite possibly the cause of it all.

? Scenes of extreme violence, frenzied drug use, and explicit sexuality. With human subtitles.

0–60 Contains vaulting emotional trajectories. Your popcorn bag can also be used as a respiration device.

1×10^{xxx} Harrowing sexual awakening. Under 17 not admitted with parent.

PG-'53 Sexual situations that haven't really occurred in the past 40-odd years. This film has been altered from the original. It has been formatted to fit reality.

« » Many longing gazes and much emotional ambiguity as a result of being French in a godless world. In French, with French subtitles.

OH! Contains several scenes of almost feral sexuality. Under 17 will be perverted unless accompanied by a parent or legal guardian.

$2 \div 1$ Scenes of marital discord resulting from a love triangle. Due to the soaring divorce rate in this country, no one will be admitted to this film.

$E=NC^{17}$ Contains scenes in denial of the fundamental realities of braking a car at high speeds, the audibility of oncoming locomotives, and the rate at which drawbridges go up and down. Not admitted without having taken your Advanced Placement in Physics first.

Š Joy, food, and killing as a result of moral paradoxes. In Czech with enigmatic subtitles.

UGH Contains material calculated to be as inoffensive as possible. Viewer discretion is strongly advised.

PG-1855 Elaborately appointed British period piece about social maneuvering among the Victorian upper classes. Contains large amounts of language.

NC-47 Aging male hunk actor showing incipient bosoms. Contains sex scenes some viewers may find risible.

æ Contains multiple instances of Kevin Costner. Some accents may be indistinguishable for younger viewers.

NC-.003 The merest of sexual situations. Under 17 not admitted unless lollygaging around the exit when the show lets out for an easy sneak-in.

◖ + 💰 = 💣 Beautiful people cavorting playfully with little consequence to their actions. Some viewers may find their morals to be inappropriate.

Ω One brief scene of marital infidelity. Dozens of prolonged scenes of shockingly vicious multiple murders. In English with Ancient Greek subtitles.

☺ Contains a climatic sequence that features talking puppies apologizing to a sulking wren named Dooley. Parental guidance would be a real achievement.

XS A man and a woman falling in love and deciding to spend their lives together while on an aircraft carrier. This film is rated too much.

60-63 Third movie this year whose central theme revolves around how John F. Kennedy was good. Some iconography may be unsuitable for younger viewers.

⊘ Depicts a personal reckoning played out with numerous memory flashbacks. Includes several scenes of violent past-bashing.

5-10 Contains scenes of graphic jurisprudence. Some justice may be considered inappropriate for younger viewers.

© Contains ubiquitous product placement. This film should be ashamed of itself.

Ø Mere anarchy is loosed upon the world and everywhere the ceremony of innocence is drowned. This film is not yet rated.

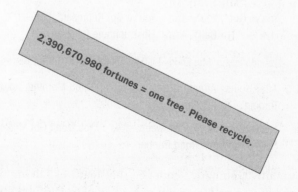

2,390,670,980 fortunes = one tree. Please recycle.

AOL'S PRIME TIME WARNER

EVENING

	8:00	8:30	9:00	9:30	10:00	10:
WB	☆Who Wants to Own a Million Shares?		E-Baywatch	Chat—With Larry King		
TBS	Atlanta Braves Spring Training —Pepper			Atlanta Braves Spring Training —Batting Practice		
PBS	American Masters —Mel Blanc		Jacques Cousteau —You've Got Whale		Charlie Rose	
TCM	Interactive Movie: On Golden Pond: Jane Fonda Deleted—Insert Yourself					
Food	You've Got Kale	You've Got Quail	You've Got Snails	You've Got Stale	You've Got Oxtail	
HBO	Movie: Oliver Stone's "Felicity"			The Making of Oliver Ston		
Weather	You've Got Hail	You've Got Gale	Atlanta Braves Baseball—Rain Delay			
CNN	☆Moneyline	☆Moneyline	☆Moneyline	☆Moneyline	☆Moneyline	
Court	You've Got Jail	You've Got Bail	You've Got Representation— Host: Johnnie Cochran			
TNT	Lethal Weapon Marathon—Till 6 a.m.: Mel Gibson, Danny Glover, Joe Pesc					
CNNFN	After-Hours Trading	Atlanta Braves Baseball —Salary Arbitration	Good Morning, Tokyo			
Cartoon	You've Got Bugs, Daffy, Tweety, Sylvester, Elmer, Road Runner		You Don't Got Mickey			
A&E	Biography—Steve Case		NOVA—Broadband's Advantages Over Dig			
					—Rick Moranis	

Looking for a Supporting Role, Willing to Play Vice President

RICK MORANIS

I should like to herewith declare my candidacy for the office of vice president of these United States in the 2000 elections. As a running mate on the Warren Beatty ticket, I promise to uphold the doctrines and values of the Liberal, Reform, Independent, or Blair Witch parties, whichever it is decided shall best suit the needs of all Americans in the coming millennium.

Beatty and I come with almost half a century of experience in an industry that is acutely aware of the most sensitive aspect of all human needs: cheap entertainment. As a highly successful second banana, I have mastered the art of supporting the "leading man" you want your president to play. Whether being the wry devil's advocate, the loyal best friend, or simply the dumb guy next door, the one who can always keep a secret and loves to take the blame, I am without any doubt the perfect choice to stand behind Beatty and make him look great. "Don't you worry, boss. I won't tell a soul!"

There are many ways a Beatty-Moranis ticket would satisfy the whole spectrum of the constituency. Where President Beatty is tall, I am short. Where I wear glasses, he pensively squints.

Where he is a Los Angeles–based Gentile who has boldly artic-
ulated his doubts about the Democratic candidates, I am a New
York Jew who wishes Zabar's had E-Z Pass. And where the future
President Beatty is a recovering ladies' man—perhaps the only
man alive who has loved more than President Clinton and who
is now happily raising a family in a successful marriage—I, on
the other hand, can bring a great deal of knowledge and experience to the debate on Internet pornography.

Beatty, or just plain Warren as he is known, has demon-
strated a consistently committed empathy toward the plight of
the underclass in this country, and would work to reconcile the
chasm that divides the haves and have-nots of our capitalist
system. I, too, am committed to reducing my own tax liabilities,
to helping my network of top-level advisors grow my portfolio,
and to increase both my consumer-spending figures and my
general savings rate.

This is a great time for America, and as a Canadian citizen,
I offer the kind of regional objectivity that can win the ear of
President Beatty for all American citizens and resident aliens
who, like me, feel more could be done for them. Many people
have said that Beatty has no experience governing, no administrative skills, and no background in budget, management, or
legislation. Well, I have less. Americans can feel comfortable
knowing that Beatty can be a leader who can look around him
and see how lacking the people of this country truly are.

Hollywood has already produced one president and
financed countless others. Clint became the mayor of Carmel,
or was it a town near Carmel? Sonny Bono became a congress-
man, and that other guy, Fred Thompson, what about him? (I
won't even mention the wrestler.) Warren Beatty is doing what
he has always done best: He has looked in the mirror for a very,
very, very long time and said, "I am ready for my close-up."

Well, America, I am ready in the background.

As the brilliant and sympathetic libertarian Bulworth,
Warren Beatty reached out to a cynical America and offered it
hope. Here, today, in the movie of our lives, I too, am reaching

out to a hopeful America. In the words of the little guy next door, the guy I've played so many times—I say to you, the citizens of this country—and to you, Warren Beatty—"Whatever you say, boss. But are you sure you know what you're doing?"

Let me be your vice president. I am right for the part. I need this job.

LIST OF COMMON
NETWIT ACRONYMS

PHAIOYUCTYS: Please hold an item of your underwear close to your screen.

CIHAMOYT?IHMWSAINTFTGBTJ: Can I have a moment of your time? I had my wallet stolen and I need three fifty to get back to Jersey.

IGTAUTDSVSIWUTPUYMALIGOBDI4PJTOOKNKIOMOC!: I'm going to ask you to do something very special I want you to pick up your mouse and lick it go on baby do it for Poppa just this once OK now kiss it O MOTHER OF CHRIST!

WITPOMA: Where is the pen of my aunt?

GOAD: Gurgle off and die!

JOAD: Jack off and die!

ROAD: Rut off and die!

TOAD: Totter off and die!

WOAD: Waddle off and die!

CRUDY: Christ aren't you dead yet?

—Tony Hendra

The Busman's Portfolio

RICK MORANIS

Martin Zeliman
Zeliman Management
2A River Street—Side Door
Hoboken, N.J.

To: Alton J. Caskarden, Esq.
Chairman, First & Goal Hedge Fund
NFL Securities
#1 International Financial Plaza
Green Bay, Wis.

Dear Mr. Caskarden,

First, let me reintroduce myself, in case you don't recall our delightful conversation in the "Absolute Citron" box at the NFC Final. I am the representative of Eddie Wayne, principal Bus driver for Fox Television Star John Madden. You generously expressed the possibility that you might consider waiving the minimum initial investment of $1 million for the First & Goal Hedge Fund if you felt Eddie's portfolio had the potential to grow rapidly. Well, let me share just some of our exciting plans with you.

In our strategy to position Eddie as "The Premier Driver in America," next season he will be wearing, both on and off the Bus, a deer suede driving jacket, featuring the logos of several major corporations, including Krispy Kreme Donuts and Weatherall Wipers. (No photos of Eddie appear without our okay.)

We are in discussions with ESPN 4 for the development of a pregame show to be called, *Tailgating with Eddie Wayne*. Each week the Bus will park in the home team's parking lot for Eddie to host an hour of barbecuing, beer, and broads. We already have commitments from Celebrity Chef Paul Prudhomme and the Statler Brothers, who, I'm told, have a very nice bus of their own. The team owners are also very interested in Eddie's proposal to sell time-shares for choice stadium parking spots, which would, of course, peak in Madden game-weeks. (We hold the option.)

Eddie will be sharing in net revenues from Madden's New Microsoft NetBookie, which features online gambling chat forums up to game time, track odds nationwide, and registers all wagers using the Bus as a base. The vig will not be taxable, as a second bus registered in Montana and driven with Nevada plates will house the hardware. Eddie holds the option to tow, or subcontract. Starting in 2000, pending Justice Department decision, NetBookie will be bundled with all Microsoft's updated Windows 98 software, tentatively called WindOOws.

Should Madden leave Fox for CBS, the Charles Kuralt Estate is interested in developing a "road" concept for Eddie. We have already booked a Square Dance in Houston and a Demolition Night in Indianapolis. (The Bus will not be damaged.) Krispy Kreme will have high visibility at both events. Should

Madden go to Monday nights, Disney/ABC is talking about a high-definition remake of *Driving Miss Daisy* starring Madden and Eddie, to be shot during the All-Star break. (We hold Playstation rights.)

In other areas, Eddie is a partner in his brother-in-law Sal's retail bedding outlet called "The Sack." We hope to spin this off to the bathroom and beyond, franchising nationally Super Bowl L. And Eddie's book, *10 Propositions to Elucidate Crosswords Facilely*, is close to completion.

Now the exciting news. We are talking to the Casey Martin people about having Eddie drive the golf cart during off-season. Should the case go to the Supreme Court, Eddie will drive Casey to Washington. And our injunction against Jerome Bettis' use of the term "The Bus" may be settled out of court, as a direct result of our new golf associations. I am currently talking to the Callaway people about licensing the brand name "Big Bertha" to Bettis. (Madden, unofficially, loves this!)

As you know, the half-time shows next year will all be of Super Bowl quality, complete with hydraulic staging and fireworks. CBS will undoubtedly showcase its prime-time stars, in what will be called *15 Minutes*, produced by Don Hewitt, while Fox will rely heavily on the Macy's Bart Simpson float. It is Eddie's intention, knowing the vehicular requirements of the top performing show-biz acts, to secure the contract to handle the cleaning and maintenance of all celebrity buses in and around NFL '98 venues. (Both Morley Safer and the Statler Brothers have committed.)

As you can see, big things are in store for Eddie Wayne. Some of the many billions of dollars floating around football will surely find their way to us. It is in this spirit that I enclose a check for $412 as Eddie's opening deposit into your fund. "Let the Blue Chips fall where they may."

Looking forward to seeing you at the game!

Martin Zeliman

P.S. I am implementing the league's request that all appliances—microwave, toaster-oven, coffee-maker, etc.—in the Bus be changed from General Electric to another brand.

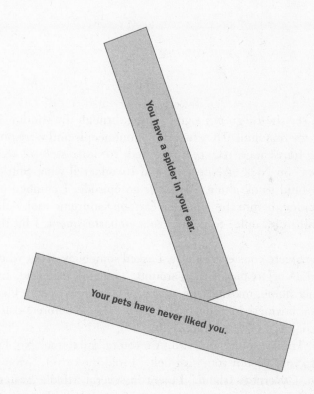

New York Confidential

RICK MORANIS

I could see the *Biography* sign flashing through the window in front of my treadmill. They had run out of people and were now profiling hurricanes. HAZEL, it repeated, TONIGHT AT 8 ON A&E. Hazel was on Nick at Nite, too, and I wondered what Shirley Booth would think about $600,000 an episode. I climbed off the machine, before the Japanese cartoon syndrome took hold. Two-tenths of a mile? Sweating from embarrassment, I hit the streets.

There were cops everywhere. I asked somebody, "Hey, who's in town?" A pretty face turned around. "Giuliani," she said, and I took her home, married her, and we left town to open a bicycle rental business in Tobago. But she was gone before I could ask her name. I climbed into a cab.

"Hi! This is Robert De Niro. Are you talkin' to me? No! I'm talkin' to you! Fasten your seat belt." I told the driver, "Mondo Monaco, Governors Island." Fluent in several Middle Eastern dialects, I knew all nine Arabic words for sinkhole. It seemed, by his gestures, that the top of the Chrysler Building had fallen off—Lexington Avenue from 52d to 24th was the new No. 6

train tunnel, and the whole city was closed below 59th Street, unless you were a tourist with a valid passport and a net worth four times the value of your hotel room on a per foot/per year basis discounted by your primary domestic currency and all city nonresident occupancy taxes. The fare was $3.60. I threw him a five and got out before he could turn off the meter.

These vagabond shoes . . . I ran across the street to grab an uptown cab. Had to talk my way out of a jaywalking ticket using the barricade defense. If I could get up to 96th Street, I could take the DisneyTram to 42d and jump onto the WynnShuttle. I needed to get to the SportsBook before the first pitch. Yankees 6 to 5 over the Staten Island Sea Gulls. I got into another cab.

"This is Philippe de Montebello. The Crown Victoria, a boldly drawn instance of utilitarian pragmatism, is constrained only by the discreetly commanding gesture of the Medallion. Fasten your seat belt and I'll meet you at your destination." The cabby spoke English. One of the new DroidDrivers the Mayor had gotten from Microsoft in the Coliseum deal. The news was bad. Every transverse was closed. The city was biting back.

These little town blues . . . I had some quick thinking to do. I wanted to get off the island but had to sell my apartment first. I thought about the old days. The Naked City. Holdups in the Bronx. Fights breakin' out in Brooklyn. Traffic jams that would back up from Harlem all the way to Jackson Heights.

I bolted from the hack and sprinted south. A glance at Tourneau told me I didn't have much time in any time zone. I jumped on a display bike at the Harley-Davidson Cafe and pulled a wheelie down West 57th. I threaded the Arc de Trump and hung a loud left onto Broadway.

It was eerie. The place was dead. I had heard about this. The Great White Way was dark. Only *Capeman* was playing, but retitled *Bring in 'Da Gar Bring in 'Da Funke*. It had happened. The Casino had killed the Theater. Since Siegfried and Roy had moved those animals into Sutton Place, a lot of people were leaving. Now it was my turn.

I grabbed the first chopper on West 30th and headed for

the one crap table that would take my co-op shares. I landed on the roof of VegasVegas and jumped onto the moving side-walk to the casino. Around me were brightly lit marquees for Betty Buckley, Patti LuPone, and the new all-star Bohemian Opera, *Why Rent?*

"Hi, this is Wayne Newton! Danke schön for keeping to the right!" I moved quickly to the left to get around a gilded Brazilian couple and collided with a young uniformed woman hurrying to her casino job. "Hey," she said. It was her! The Tobago bicycle woman! I asked her where she was going. "Blackjack," she said. I looked around, moved back to the right, realized that I wanted to be a part of it, make a brand new start of it, and noticed that for the first time, I wasn't seeing any cops.

"It's a casino," she said. "Believe me, there's a ton of security."

"Really? Who's in town?"

Teenagers will begin using your first name as slang for "gross."

You will swing your arm and hit a lawyer.

Internet Stocks
Too Hot to Ignore

RICK MORANIS AND
HOWARD KAMINSKY

Gleaned from the desktops of dizzy daytraders and the dense spam of bundled prospectuses, here are the seven new I.P.O. investments of highly successful people:

E*bucks.com

The Internet spin-off of Starbucks. Web buyers can order any size, flavor, caffeinated or decaffeinated, fatte or nonfatte, latte, cappuccino, mochaccino or frappaccino and have it delivered anywhere in the world next day. The company promises "that same burned, bitterly strong addictive flavor that has put a Starbucks on every block." E*bucks.com is a partnership with Fedex, developer of the patented Foamvelope for all E-ccino product deliveries. Javascript only.

felloffatruck.com

The most popular seller of pirated editions on the Web, felloffatruck.com offers a wide array of popular books at unbelievably low prices that can be obtained only through the company's strict avoidance of paying royalties to writers. A complete set of the works of Barbara Taylor Bradford (with the author's forged signature in every volume) goes for $2.17. The company also sells bootleg copies of top 10 CD's and videos at equally unbeatable prices. For example, Hootie (unfortunately without the Blowfish) costs 38 cents a disk, while the tape of *Armaggedon* (with neither the ending nor Bruce Willis's performance) goes for $1.02.

e.floss.net

The only on-line dental hygiene site. Pentium V required. High-intensity kilobyte-impression frequencies are e-mailed 14 million times per second. The user sits as close to the screen as possible, mouth wide open, and is virtually flossed in as little as one hour, depending on modem speed. Tartar ctrl.

sherp@.com

Man, you're gonna carry that weight! The first Internet, global positioned courier/moving system. Web users are outfitted with a digital paging system (optionally implanted). Whenever and wherever you are, a sherpa will be dispatched to schlep all grocery bags, luggage, packages, parcels, even garbage to its destination. Every sherp@.com sherpa is surgically calibrated with G.P.S. chip and digital g-force/baropedometer. User accounts are updated every ten feet and/or ten seconds. Golf caddying, children's backpacks, watercooler replacement, large appetizer platters, weekend newspaper editions, anything inconveniently weighty can be billed. No tipping.

@hh!closure.com

Nothing is worthless in today's cyberworld of possibilities. Whether it's an old blue sock, a weathered left glove, or a salt shaker without a top, @hh!closure.com will search the online world for the right potential mate. If you have a periscope, we'll help you find the submarine that happens to be missing one.

@hh!closure.com is the only, and lonely, Internet merchandise value reclaiming service.

Ovitz.com

Unlimited transactional representation by the world's superest agent. A team of 8,000 highly trained Portland-based support technicians field all potential sales/purchase orders and refer them by category/price-point to specialists around the world to "cut the best deal." Buying a canary or selling a chipped Derbyshire tureen, fixing the eaves or hiring an illegally immigrated cleaning woman, Ovitz.com will put your interests ahead of theirs, for 10 percent of the closing price with an irrevocable option on all future trades, and a fixed percentage of incremental material gains in perpetuity.

toomanyboxes.com

Has today's cyberworld of home shopping created too much garbage for you? At toomanyboxes.com, we work with U.P.S., Fedex, and the Postal Service to track precisely how many packages your home is receiving. Biweekly, or daily if necessary, toomanyboxes.com will send you a really big box, big enough to handle all the bubble wrap, corrugated cardboard, and plastic foam chippies you've accumulated from on-line shopping. When you're ready, just e-mail us and we'll send over a licensed technician to burn everything on your lawn. Don't have a lawn? Don't worry! The staff at toomanyboxes.com can contain a fire indoors. Prefer recycling? No problem! Toomanyboxes.com will take all of your packing material away and burn it in a field somewhere else, or ship it to Virginia. All for the same price! Don't let the convenient life style of cybershopping force you out of your home. "C'mon! Clean house!"

Hurry. Prices are subject to change. Calls may be monitored for quality control.

49 Simple Things You Can Do to Save the Earth

MATT NEUMAN

The author wishes to thank his wife for suggesting he "get up and do something" to save the Earth. This book is dedicated to her.

1. Turn Off the Lights. Even if you're only going out of the room for a few minutes. Those kilowatts add up. (My wife groans when I say it, but, "It makes cents—with a *c*.")

2. Unplug Appliances When Not in Use. Some of them, with their complicated timers and instant start-up features, constantly consume small amounts of electricity. ("Even the TV?" my wife asks. "Good thinking," I tell her.)

3. Separate Your Garbage. At our house we have separate garbage cans for glass, paper, plastic, aluminum, wood, organic matter, natural fabrics, synthetic fabrics, and rubber. (We split the work—my wife does the separating, I drop everything off at the recycling center.)

4. Use Less Water. We have *two* bricks in our toilet tank. But there's a much simpler way to save water: *Don't flush every time!* ("Don't take the sports section in there with you!" is my wife's tip. A sense of humor is *so* important.)

5. Don't Mow the Lawn. Let it grow. Naturally. Like a meadow. ("Like a *dump!*" jokes my wife.)

6. Don't Shave As Often. I shave once a week. ("If it's good enough for Don Johnson," I quip. "That was passé *years* ago," my wife informs me.)

7. Drive Slower. I try to maintain a nice, steady 40 miles per hour, the legal minimum on most highways. Also, I roll up the windows. It reduces wind resistance—and noise. ("You can't hear those horns?" my wife asks, incredulous.)

8. Shop with a Reusable Shopping Bag. And, if you can, walk to the store. ("It'll do wonders for your figure," I mention casually to the missus.)

9. Boycott! Boycott polluters, or anyone who sells any product that can cause pollution, or any product that might contain an *ingredient* that can cause pollution. ("What does that leave?" my wife asks. "Just the good stuff," I reply.)

10. Do Your Laundry by Hand. It may be drudgery of the lowest order to have to hand-launder your clothes and hang them on a clothesline, but it saves water and energy. ("Whistle while you work," I kid my wife. "Hitler is a jerk," she continues. I'd forgotten that verse!)

11. Turn Down the Heat. Especially the water heater. ("They take cold showers in Sweden," I like to hint. "Go to Sweden!"— my wife.)

12. Take Fewer Showers. But don't share them, even if it's been touted, albeit humorously, in other "x-number-of-simple-things-you-can-do-to-save-the-Earth" books. Why? It uses *more* water. Figure it out for yourself.

13. Replace Metal Doorknobs. During the winter, when it's very dry, touch a metal doorknob and you get a little shock from the static electricity. That's *wasted* electricity, I figure. We've replaced all our metal doorknobs with ones made of nonconducting rubber, wood, or glass. ("You've got a screw loose," my wife points out. And she's right!)

14. Go Solar. For a small investment of about $10,000 you can convert your house to solar energy. It'll pay for itself in twenty years, I estimate. ("What next?" my wife wonders, as we all do.)

15. Mount a Windmill on Your Roof. It's cheap—$800—and easy to install. ("A little more to the right," I yell up to her.)

16. Make Your Own Honey. In addition to producing delicious honey, our beehive is a real conversation starter. ("We have to talk," my wife says. See?)

17. Work at Home. Recently, I quit my job of twenty years to become a full-time writer. I write at home, on a computer. I'm not using up any gasoline or motor oil, I'm not wearing out any clothing or shoes. To put it simply: I'm not a drain on the environment. ("You don't *move*," my wife observes, exaggerating slightly.)

18. Board Up the Windows. Windows are nice, but they either let in too much heat, or let out too much, or vice versa. ("This is better than mini-blinds!" I shout to the wife, who can barely hear me over her own hammering.)

19. Get Rid of the Telephone. Think you can't live without a telephone? Think again. We've done fine. ("*Who* would call us?" my wife rationalizes.)

20. Get Rid of the Bed. Many leading chiropractors say that sleeping on the floor, with no mattress or cushion, is the best way to sleep. ("We certainly haven't needed a bed much lately," my wife confides to a mutual friend.)

21. Get Out and Organize. At my wife's suggestion, I got out of the house and into the community—to organize. Now I work with a diverse group of community activists and we meet four times a week—at our house. ("Who *are* these people?" my wife asks. "They are *the people*," I tell her proudly.)

22. Ban All Chlorofluorocarbons. Not just spray cans, but the refrigerator and the air conditioner. Get rid of them! We now have ice delivered to our house every day. ("You're crazy!" my wife shouts from the kitchen. "So was Van Gogh!" I shout back.)

23. Treat Wounds Naturally. If you're injured, cut on the head, above the eyebrow—from a sharp piece of ice, let's say— treat it naturally. Salt and lemon juice is the combination my wife favors. ("I want a divorce," she says, pouring salt on my wound. "Ouch!" I say.)

24. Know the Law. And know a good lawyer. (My wife does.)

25. When You Move, Be a Good Neighbor. Having recently relocated to a smaller environment—an apartment—I can empathize with anyone who has had to go through a "moving experience," as I call it. Remember, along with a new habitat come new co-inhabitants. Get to know them. They are your neighbors and, as simplistic as this sounds, they are the keys to your survival. (When I explain this simplistic theory to one of my new neighbors, she's fascinated. Maybe the beard works!)

26. Carpool. At my new part-time job I carpool with a couple of the ladies from the office. We're saving gas, money, and we're getting to know each other better. ("He used to have a fear of intimacy," my wife tells the judge. On the advice of Barry, my lawyer, I can say nothing.)

27. Make Love, Not War. I know, I know. But, if I could just use one Earth-saving tip to draw your attention to the beautiful and cosmic experience of making love with a truly giving and understanding sexual partner. (Take *that*, you lying, blood-sucking witch!)

28. Share Your Shower. I've done a complete one-eighty on this one. Use a kitchen timer. (Or Ravel's *Bolero!*)

29. Women! Or should I say, women judges! (This just in: She gets the car, the house—everything except the profits from this book, dear reader.)

30. You Can Make a Difference. When someone (especially someone much younger and less experienced than yourself that you only met two weeks ago) tells you that one person can't make a difference—that no matter how much shouting and yelling and "whining and complaining" one person does nothing will change, that "you're too old to be acting that way," that "you should settle down and focus on one thing and do that well"—when someone lays that trip on you, it's time to split. ("I *can* make a difference!" I tell her, gathering my things.)

31. Bundle and Recycle Newspapers. Sorry, I lost sight of what we're trying to do here, which is save the Earth. Take all your old newspapers, bundle them together, and bring them to a recycling center. They'll give you a few bucks, which is nothing to sneeze at. (*What happened?*)

32. Buy a "Recycled" Car. There are some good deals in used cars—if you take the time to look. (I didn't, and boy am I sorry.)

33. Don't Litter the Highways. Be considerate. There are laws, but they're rarely enforced. (Except in *my* case, of course. I told the officer I wasn't living in my car—it had broken down, I was tired—but: A $100 fine for vagrancy, a night in jail, a towing charge of $75, and a ticket—*I'm getting rid of this damn car!*)

34. Keep Fighting. That's right. No matter how tough it gets, the fight to save the Earth will go on, with or without you. (Right now it's without. I'm back to my old habits again—smoking, drinking, and hanging out with a bunch of losers. One of them is a real nut, calls himself the Master.)

35. Donate Old Clothing. There are people out there who can get some good use out of your old moth-eaten sweater or sports jacket or worn-out pair of shoes. (I'm a 41 short.)

36. Follow the Master. The Master has forged an "alliance with the human spirit" that allows him to speak directly and simultaneously to every living thing on this planet. (Follow the Master.)

37. Think for Yourself. Take it from someone who, after having his self-esteem obliterated by a persuasive con man and his gang of sycophants, escaped on foot—with nothing to eat for nine days but wild berries and mushrooms—*and lived to talk about it!* (You might have seen the story in the papers—DAZED FOLLOWER OF DIZZY GURU FOUND ON FREEWAY.)

38. Hi, How Are You? I knew it was her before I picked up the phone. (The cobwebs that covered the receiver were now sticking to my face. "Fine," I said.)

39. Don't Be Fooled. A wise consumer is a protected consumer. (I told my ex this when we got together for some Irish coffee at the mini-mall, near the old house. She ended up selling that barn for—get this—$650,000! "Honey, it seems like old times!" I whooped.)

40. Recycle! Revive! Rerun! Excuse my exuberance, but something is finally happening out there—something positive, something good. People are separating their garbage. They're using biodegradable, ecologically safe, recyclable, and reusable materials. *Everything old is new again!* (When my ex-wife and I decided to remarry, I suggested a "Save the Earth" clause be added to our prenuptial agreement. "We have to talk," she said, showing great interest at the time.)

41. Move to the Country. Inherit the land again. That's what we did. Bought 43 acres in upstate New York. It's a working farm, where my wife can go out to the barn and milk the cows, pick out the freshest eggs, and knit our clothes from the wool she shears from our very own sheep. (And I can finish this book!)

42. Share This Book. I want this book to be passed on to those with limited resources. (And limited imaginations! Have you seen any of these other "x-number-of-things-you-can-do-to-save-the-Earth" books? Talk about writing in your sleep! "You're just jealous," my wife cracks, half-crocked.)

43. Move Back to the City. The housing market, like any organism operating within a much larger organism—which we call the ecosphere, or the biosphere, or the Earth—has its variables. We've decided to give the land back to those who really own it (my in-laws), and live once again at the heart of the ecosphere, the city. ("I'd like to look at *separate* beds," my wife tells me and the salesman at Bloomingdale's.)

44. Life Goes On. And I could go on, ad *nauseam*, about the proper storage of milk, the use of insects as insecticides, how to check for impurities in your tap water—but there are bigger problems. (*Much* bigger.)

45. It Won't Be Easy. Nobody likes the maverick or the visionary. ("The public's had it up to here with those stupid 'x-number-of-things-you-can-do-to-save-the-Earth' books," my wife slurs. "I've had it up to here too," I tell her.)

46. Old Friends. Remember Barry? The lawyer? Well, I had occasion to see him again recently and I noticed that he was using a Montblanc pen, the finest fountain pen in the world. It was inlaid with pearl, *real* pearl, and gold. I couldn't control myself, so I asked him, Where can I get one? (Want to know? See below.)

47. Big Sale, 15 to 25 Percent Off. Right now, if you write to the address on the back cover, you can find out how to get "the finest fountain pen in the world," the Montblanc, at tremendous savings. And, you'll be buying it—*direct*—from an officially licensed Montblanc dealer. (Me! I need some cash—she socked it to me again, dear reader.)

48. Turn the Lights On. And flush the toilet. Forget about saving the Earth. At least for now. It's time to get your life in order. Grow up. Focus on one thing and do it and be done with it. ("For once he's acting like an adult," my ex-ex tells a mutual friend.)

49. Write a Book. It's easy! Pick a topic that's currently in vogue (It doesn't have to be the environment!) and write whatever comes into your head—and write and write and write and write until you can't write anymore. I did. And somebody bought it—*and* gave me a six-figure advance on the next one, *49 More Simple Things You Can Do to Save the Earth*, $12.95, paper, due out next March. ("Honey, it seems like old times!" my ex-ex whooped over the phone. It was good to hear from her.)

Top 100 Colors

1. Blue
2. Red
3. Yellow
4. Green
5. Black
6. White
7. Brown
8. Grey
9. Purple
10. Pink
11. Orange
12. Violet
13. Maroon
14. Olive
15. Tan
16. Silver
17. Gold
18. Bronze
19. Crimson
20. Pine
21. Royal blue
22. Sky blue
23. Midnight blue
24. Navy blue
25. Indigo
26. Scarlet
27. Lime
28. Grape
29. Pumpkin
30. Eggplant
31. Forest
32. Blonde
33. Peach
34. Plum
35. Day-Glo
36. Gray
37. Dark brown
38. Khaki
39. Light brown
40. Baby-poop brown
41. Chocolate
42. Beige
43. Mustard
44. Burnt sienna
45. Cream
46. Sepia
47. Butter
48. Off-white
49. Near-white
50. White, only less than
51. Ivory
52. Bone
53. Eggshell
54. Sand
55. Champagne
56. Pearl
57. Parchment
58. Vanilla
59. Taupe
60. Stone
61. Buff
62. Mauve
63. Ice
64. Watermelon
65. Hemp
66. Turquoise
67. Cinnamon
68. Periwinkle
69. Tortoise shell
70. Charcoal
71. Vermilion
72. Rust
73. Cayenne
74. Cilantro
75. Raspberry
76. Lavender
77. Persimmon
78. Espresso
79. Merlot
80. Burgundy
81. Rose
82. Beaujolais

83. Sage
84. Blush
85. Hyacinth
86. Yellow-green
87. Green-yellow
88. Moss
89. Brick

90. Coral
91. Teal
92. Chrome
93. Jade
94. Ruby
95. Emerald
96. Mahogany

97. Licorice
98. Puce
99. Fuchsia
100. Cerise

—Will Durst

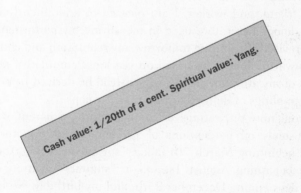

Everything about you is getting smaller.

Cash value: 1/20th of a cent. Spiritual value: Yang.

How I'm Doing

DAVID OWEN

In the hope of establishing a more equitable framework by which the public can evaluate my effectiveness as a father, husband, friend, and worker, I am pleased to announce that the methodology heretofore used in measuring my performance is being revised. Beginning tomorrow, my reputation and compensation will no longer be based on yearlong, cumulative assessments of my attainments but will instead be derived from periodic samplings of defined duration, or "sweeps."

From now on, ratings of my success as a parent will be based solely on perceptions of my conduct during the two weeks beginning March 7th (a.k.a. "spring vacation"), the two weeks beginning August 1st (a.k.a. "summer vacation"), the seven days ending December 25th, and my birthday. No longer will my ranking be affected by unsolicited anecdotal reports from minors concerning my alleged "cheapness," "strictness," and "loser" qualities, or by the contents of viewing diaries maintained by my dependents. Page views, click-throughs, and People Meter data concerning me will also be disregarded, except during the aforementioned periods. The opinions of my children will no longer be counted in evaluations of my sense of humor.

Public appraisals of my behavior at parties will henceforth not be drawn from overnight ratings provided by my wife; instead, my annual ranking will be based on a random sampling of my level of intoxication during the week following January 2nd. My official weight for the year will be my median weight during the four weeks beginning July 1st. All measures of my geniality, thoughtfulness, romantic disposition, and willingness to compromise will henceforth be calculated just three times per year: on September 15th (my wife's birthday), August 26th (our anniversary), and February 14th. My high school grades, S.A.T. scores, college grades, and income history will no longer be available for inclusion in any of my ratings, and in fact they will be expunged from my personal database. Evaluations of my success as a stock-market investor will no longer include the performance of my portfolio during the month of October.

Beginning in 2001, my annual compensation will cease to consist of my total income over the twelve months of the fiscal year; instead, my yearly pay will be adjusted to equal not less than thirteen times my nominal gross earnings during the four weeks beginning February 1st, when the holiday season is over, my children are back in school, and my local golf course has not yet reopened for the spring. My critics may object that my output during February is not representative of my output during the rest of the year, especially when I am at the beach. However, I believe (and my auditors concur) that the work I do during periods of cold, miserable weather provides the best available indication of my actual abilities as a worker and therefore constitutes the only fair and objective basis for calculating my true contribution to the economy. Conversely, my federal income-tax liability will henceforth be based on an annualized computation of my total earnings between Memorial Day and Labor Day.

These changes are being made as a part of my ongoing effort to insure that public data concerning me and my personality are the very best available. This new protocol may be further modified by me at any time without advance notice, and, in any case, is not legally binding. In addition, all assessments of my performance are subject to later revision, as improved information becomes available. Specifically, my lifetime ratings in all categories may be posthumously adjusted, within 30 days of my death, to reflect the content of newspaper obituaries regarding me, should any such be published, and the things that people say about me at my funeral.

TERRIBLE NAMES FOR HAIR SALONS

Shear Hostility

Mane-lining Hair-oin

Clipping Penalty

Dexa-Trims

I Will Cut Your Head

Get the Hell out of Hair

The Razor's Edge Starring Bill Murray

The Mane Reason My Parole Was Revoked

Nervous McStabby's Hair Care Place

Reason Has Been E-Clips-ed by Rage

Running with Scissors

Armon Gilliam's House of Style

In No Conditioner to Drive

Hair Commandant

Cuts & Bruises

Dude, I'm So Buzzed

The Viet-Mane War Memorial

Get the Hell out of Hair, Kevin

I Hate My Mother

George Hair-ison's Solo Career

Why Won't You Dye?

Los Angeles Clippers

Mein Coif

—John Moe

Virtual Friends

DAVID OWEN

Telecommuting would catch on faster if you could do it from your regular office. That way, you could combine the best parts of working at home (daytime movies, faxing in your underpants, postbreakfast napping) with the best parts of working in a faceless monolith of glass, concrete, and steel (free pens, free phone calls, secretarial intrigue). As a longtime telecommuter, I've wrestled with this problem for years. Recently, I found a partial solution: I've become a compulsive viewer of CNBC, the cable-television network that covers business all day long.

CNBC has a lot to offer the homebound worker, including thoughtful predictions about the direction of interest rates, and stock prices that glide continually along the bottom of the screen, even during commercials. What I love about it, though, is not its content but its companionship. I have come to view the members of the CNBC staff as my home-office co-workers.

Turning on my TV the first thing in the morning is like coming in to work early and putting my feet up on my desk. Running CNBC in the background makes my home office seem not like a solitary prison cell or torture chamber but like a beehive of cheerful, important activity. No matter how unmotivated I feel about doing my own job, the people on the screen seem enthusiastic and engaged, even if all they're doing is discussing a sudden small decrease in the number of yen to the Deutsche mark. If I lose interest in some project of my own, I lean back and watch CNBC until I feel like making money again. If I really have to buckle down, I press the mute button on my remote control—the electronic equivalent of closing my office door—but I never turn off the TV.

Virtual co-workers are better than flesh-and-blood co-workers in several respects: they are paid to be entertaining, they are always in the same mood, and they don't duck into the bathroom when they see you coming down the hall. Most of the people at CNBC seem to me to be about my age (which means, I suppose, that they are five or ten years younger), and some of the guys don't wear jackets. There's quite a bit of kidding around, even with the CEOs of big companies. I can nurse my powerful crushes on Sue Herera and Maria Bartiromo without endangering my marriage or risking accusations of sexual harassment. (I'm pretty sure Sue Herera has a thing for me, too, although it's difficult to read the body language of someone whose body usually ends at her armpits.) The only guys in the office I don't really like are Dan Dorfman and a guy who smiles too much and always nods when he talks.

Now that I have begun to settle into my job with the folks at CNBC, I realize that I've had other virtual officemates during my career. For example, I now think of CNN's coverage of the Persian Gulf War—which I watched obsessively—not as a special news program but as an exciting startup company that I used to work for. In those heady days, I loved going to my office, and I often stayed there late into the night. There was also a brief period recently when I took a leave from CNBC to fill in as an assistant prosecutor on a big case out in L.A.

CNBC is not the perfect virtual office. There's no health plan, most of the men wear makeup, and I don't know who our boss is. I wouldn't presume to tinker very much, though. I might add an after-hours segment set in a bar. It would be like *Cheers,* but the people having drinks would be Joe Kernen, David Faber, Ron Insana, and all my other best buddies from the regular show. I might also add a whole separate channel about the receptionists and mailroom guys, who invariably know the best dirt. In a decade or two, perhaps, CNBC will be available in a holographic format that will make the show appear to take place not on my television screen but in my actual office, at desks right next to mine.

I'm probably making it seem that all I do is work. Believe me, I don't. Today was a good example. At three o'clock this afternoon, a full hour before the closing bell on Wall Street, I said goodbye to the guys at the office and went over to ESPN for a round of golf.

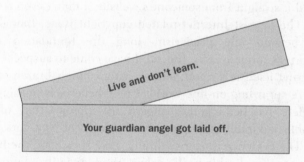

Ripoff!

DAVID OWEN

The rapid growth of the Internet raises many vexing copyright issues. I have no doubt of the truth of that sentence, because I lifted it straight from someone's website. I didn't even retype it!

The biggest Internet-related copyright issue, though, goes far beyond idle plagiarism—long the foundation of the reporter's humble craft. Indeed, I have come to suspect that the Internet itself is a ripoff, and an astonishingly brazen one: the entire sprawling on-line world, I now believe, is nothing but a crudely patched-together digital misappropriation of long-established intellectual property of the city of New York.

The evidence is overwhelming. Like New York, the Internet features inexplicable traffic delays, random confrontations with lunatics, and easy, private, around-the-clock access to pornography. The Internet chat room, in which faceless male lowlifes conduct innuendo-filled exchanges while pretending to be women, is a pale electronic simulacrum of its obvious real-life analogue, the Manhattan hotel bar. And "flaming"—the near-psychotic reaming out of innocent strangers on Internet message boards—is merely a keyboard-based version of the method by which New Yorkers have always conversed. (In Gristede's 15 years ago, I got into a screaming fight with a woman over her contention that a shopper who was buying just three items— me—had a moral if not a legal obligation to use the express checkout line even though the express checkout line was longer and moving more slowly than the regular checkout line, the rear of which was being brought up by a loudmouthed, face-lifted, cubic-zirconia-encrusted battle-ax with an overflowing cart: her.)

But the theft goes far deeper. The pervasive tone of virtually all on-line communication—a tone that might best be characterized as intimate anonymity—was first developed in Manhattan, by adjacent renters in apartment buildings on the Upper East Side. The Internet's core method of routing information (whereby data don't travel directly from Point A to Point B but are broken apart, dispersed over a far-flung network, and reassembled at their destination) is cribbed from the method by which New York City taxi drivers have long conveyed arriving internationals from Kennedy Airport to midtown Manhattan. And what is the hyperlink but a wan imitation of one of New York's best-known and most representative amenities, that every block in the city contains a door through which one can enter the same Chinese restaurant?

As a matter of fact, the very notion of meaningful linkage, which forms the conceptual heart of the World Wide Web, was perfected in New York decades ago. I can offer an example from my own experience. One afternoon in 1979, my wife and I went to see Woody Allen's movie, which had just opened. While we were walking home afterward—through Manhattan—we passed Woody Allen himself, who was walking in the opposite direction. My wife and I at that moment were discussing Allen's portrayal of women in the movie, and Allen was walking next to, and talking with, a woman. Had my wife and I so desired, we could have turned around, proceeded a dozen or so blocks back down Fifth Avenue, entered any of several bookstores, and purchased any of several books or magazines containing references to Allen's portrayal of women in one or another of his films. Or we could have stopped at a newsstand and obtained a newspaper that listed those New York City theaters in which revivals of Allen's earlier women-portraying movies were then playing. Or we could have continued north on Fifth Avenue to the apartment of a woman we knew—a woman who was a friend of a writer who would one day become a friend and occasional collaborator of Woody Allen's.

So, whom do we sue? (The casually threatened, utterly groundless class-action lawsuit—a recurring theme of nearly all Internet newsgroup discussions—was, of course, first developed by New Yorkers.) This case could be worth billions to the aggrieved parties (us), assuming we can figure out who's got the deep pockets. All we need is a shameless, blustering, egomaniacal attorney who is willing, in exchange for a cut of the profits, to spend ten or 20 years doggedly dragging this thing through the courts.

Luckily, I've got just the guy. I found his name in a banner advertisement under the heading "Lawyers" in the greatest search engine the world has ever known: the Manhattan *Yellow Pages*.

Who dressed you?

What Happened to My Money?

DAVID OWEN

God has taken your money to live with Him in Heaven. Heaven is a special, wonderful place, where wars and diseases and stock markets do not exist, only happiness. You have probably seen some wonderful places in your life—perhaps during a vacation, or on television, or in a movie—but Heaven is a million billion times more wonderful than even Disney World. Jesus and Mary and the angels live in Heaven, and so do your grandparents and your old pets and Abraham Lincoln. Your money will be safe and happy in Heaven forever and ever, and God will always take care of it.

Your money is still your money—it will always be your money—but it cannot come back to you, not ever. That may seem unfair to you. One day you were buying puts and shorting straddles, and the next day you woke up to find that your account had been closed forever. Perhaps you got a sick or empty feeling in your stomach when that happened; perhaps you have that sick or empty feeling still. You loved your money very, very much, and you did not want God to take it away.

Your feelings are natural and normal—they are a part of the

way God made you—but God took your money in accordance with His wonderful plan, which is not for us to know or understand. You must trust God and have faith that He loves your money just as He loves you and every other part of His creation. Someday—probably a very, very long time from now, after you have lived a long and happy life in compliance with the nation's securities laws—God will take you to live with Him in Heaven, too. Then you will understand.

Even though your money is gone forever, it can still be a part of your life. As long as love and kindness and happiness dwell in your heart, your money can dwell there, too. At night, before you go to sleep, you can talk to your money in a prayer. You can think about the BMW that you and your money were going to buy, and you can remember the house on the beach that you and your money were going to build, and you can laugh about your funny old plan to send your children to private colleges. Someday, when you no longer feel as sad as you do today, you may even find that thinking about your money can give you some of the same happy feelings that spending your money used to give you.

Those feelings belong to you and they always will; no one can take them away from you. Even when you are very, very old, you will still be able to think about your money and remember how much you loved it. But you will still not be able to spend your money, or even borrow against it.

Photography

According to historian Dr. Robert Leggat, the first successful photograph was taken in 1827 by Niépce using material that hardened on exposure to light. (Coincidentally,
that was the date of the first Clinton-Lewinski joke, told by
a prescient Jules Verne a full year before his actual birth.)
This picture required an exposure of eight hours, and with
rates for fashion models being what they are, *Vogue* magazine as we know it would have been impossible without
some technical innovations.

Fortunately, on January 4, 1829, Niépce went into
partnership with Louis Daguerre. Niépce died only four
years later, but you can't blame Daguerre for that. (Or can
you?) Soon he had discovered a process which reduced the
exposure time to half an hour. (Daguerre, not Niépce,
whose commitment to innovation largely ceased upon his
death.) Daguerre also discovered that an image could be
made permanent by immersing it in salt. And by adding a
little mustard and some garlic, he is said to have created
an excellent salad dressing.

Not everyone welcomed this invention. The *Leipzig
City Advertiser* wrote "The wish to capture evanescent
reflections is not only impossible . . . but the mere desire
alone, the will to do so, is blasphemy. God created man in
His own image, and no man-made machine may fix the
image of God." And this was nearly two centuries before
Hot Thai Nurse Spanking photographs appeared on-line.

Parisian photography shops spread rapidly, from a
mere handful in the mid 1840s, to 66 in 1855, and to 147

two years later. The demand for photographs was such that Charles Baudelaire commented, "Our squalid society has rushed, Narcissus to a man, to gloat at its trivial image on a scrap of metal." But he may have been reacting to a snapshot that "made me look swishy."

In 1851 Frederick Scott Archer introduced the collodion process, reducing exposure times to two or three seconds, opening up new horizons in photography and a chance to say "collodion."

In 1884, George Eastman produced flexible celluloid film. Four years later he introduced the box camera, and photography could reach a much greater number of people. Other developments followed in rapid succession, including that gizmo that lets you print a family vacation photograph on a T-shirt. Baudelaire would have disapproved. As would my Aunt Bernice, who hated being photographed in her bathing suit.

—Randy Cohen

Post–Valentine's Day Special: State Dates

ALYSIA GRAY PAINTER

Name: Indiana ("Indy" "Hoosier Honey")
Occupation: State
Birthday: December 11th, 18??
Bird: Cardinal
Flower: Peony

A Little Bit About Yourself: Well, after entering the union as the 19th state, I had a lot of success with factory-driven commerce and agriculture. I guess I started seeing Oregon a little bit after this, it wasn't yet a state, younger than me and all that, not that I go in for that necessarily. Then Oregon became a state, maybe around 1859? I never heard from the busy Beaver State again. My good friend Calif—well, let's just say a good friend, spotted Oregon under Washington one night and practically every day since. That hurt a lot. A LOT.

Your Ideal Partner: A strong state, older than my last fling, not so brash. Illinois maybe? We've been neighbors for a long time.

"Nois" knows my whole past and hasn't run yet. Chicago is a good kid, too, loud but loves his parent.

Name: Arizona ("The Zone")
Occupation: State (I used to be a Mexican territory, tho—quite the fiesta)
Birthday: Valentine's Day, of course! Isn't that romantic? 1912. Here's a shout-out to New Mexico—1912 rules!
Lowest Point: Breaking up with my ex? Kidding. The Colorado River at 70 feet above sea level.
Famous Ghost Towns: Bisbee, Jerome, Tombstone. And my love life!

A Little Bit About Yourself: I'm young, I'm fun, I'm all sun and I got a great tan line called the Grand Canyon! Take that Montana (private joke)! Anyhoo, I have dated quite a bit. Other states want to know me from A to Z! AZ. Seriously, I guess my most permanent thing was with Delaware some years back, sort of a May-December deal. Del kept asking when I'd lose my baby fat—you know, I'm much bigger and bulkier than my petite ex—but what Delaware didn't understand is that my mass of 114,006 square miles is like a law! I can't lose the weight, ever. Sigh. Bring on the sour cream enchiladas! :-)

Your Ideal Partner: Cute flag, good motto, big borders? Phone the Zone!!!

Name: New York ("New York")
Occupation: Filling out damn forms
Birthday: The 25th of none-of-your-business
Population: My business, not yours
Tree: Plenty

A Little Bit About Yourself: Order the brochure.

Your Ideal Partner: A mountainous state, if you catch my drift. Lots of mountains. Colorado free?

Dear Indiana,

While we couldn't find your ideal match, another state has expressed an interest in you. Hint: it begins with a North and ends with Carolina! Would you hoof it for the Tar Heel State? Please respond within ten days and we'll set something up. Congrats! (By the way, Illinois is seeing another state at the moment and kindly asks that you two "remain friends" for the time being—sorry to break the news.)

Dear Arizona,

Texas may be your true love. Yippee ki way to go! If that doesn't work out, get back to us pronto about a pretty New England state that says it wants "your desert for dessert." Curious? Call us!

Dear New York,

Colorado is free but not the best mate for you. The home of the Rockies cited air quality, crime, and your inability to pick up after yourself as potential problems. That said, we did hear Hong Kong is looking for a mistress and Moscow is seeking "a little something on the side." Game?

Your Neighborhood
Laundraclean

ALYSIA GRAY PAINTER

Suits		
2-Piece Suits	$8.95	
3-Piece Suits	$11.95	
5-Piece Suits	$14.45	
11-Piece Suits	$29.45	

Jackets	
Unlined	$6.95
Lined	$6.99
With Sleeves	$70.00

Sweaters	
Nubby	$6.95
Extra Nubby	$8.00

Coats	
Trench coat	$9.95
Trench mouth	Negotiable

Skirts	
Dowdy	$4.95
Seen on supermodel	$85.00
Seen off supermodel	$150.00

Ties	
Yes	$5.95

Blouses	
Top	$3.95
Bottom	$1.00

Gloves	
Grandmother's	$8.99
Preening fop's	$35.99

Tuxedos	
Prom	$40.00
Wedding	$50.00
Funeral	$100.00

Fancy Dresses

Jailbait	$1.60
Coquette	$3.00
Tomato	$6.75
Patootie	$7.95
Cutie Patootie	$12.99
(further fees may apply)	

Varsity Jackets

Mascot on sleeve	$65.00
Year on sleeve	$65.00
Mascot pretending to sit on Year or hug Year or somehow interact with Year	$70.00

Fluff-n-Fold

Fluff	$5.00
Fold	$5.00
-n-	$2.00

Zippers

Zzzzip	$10.00
Foosh	$6.00
Kak-aka-kak	$4.00

Furs Dyed $100.00

Waists

Take in	$6.00
Take out	$7.00
See again	$8.00

Hems
(Laundraclean is legally prohibited from commenting on hems at this time, please check back next month or call the owner after 7 P.M. weekdays except Thursday thank you.)

Custom colors
Blue
Black
Red
Green, darker than lime
All of the above
  unless taupe is
  present, then
  $1.50 surcharge $5.00

Costumes

Sweet	$20.00
Scary	$20.00
Others	$25.00

Ask us about:
Leather sweating
Notions (references may
  be requested)
Collar color
Pillow per pound
Removable belt loops
Suede for Lunch (no affiliation with Lucky Laundry's "Suede for Brunch")
Thread you never thought possible

Personal pleating
A hat the whole family will
  enjoy
Rewoven things
Our gentleman's club

Shoes that can be worn on
  virtually any surface, day
  or night
Waterproofing for young and
  old (Fido, too!)

Past and current customers say: "If you ever again touch my clothes" "you should never" "say sorry" "because I am [word illegible] happy with your service." (Responses provided by our valued patrons Mary M., Connie B., Mary M., Don S.)

All buttonholes considered.

Three Christmas Candies

ALYSIA GRAY PAINTER

Christmas Traditions from All Over

In Mexico City, two teenagers dressed as Mary and Joseph enact Las Posadas, a journey in which the blessed twosome search for an "inn" where they may stay the night. Local people follow the pair, holding lit candles while singing folk hymns and strumming guitars.

Wee Parisians leave their tiny shoes by the door in hopes that Père Noël will fill them with sweets, fruits, a round of fromage, and a toy or two.

Christmas morning dawns crisp and cold on the Cape of Old Ice, as do its citizens, who must spend the night in the arctic outdoors lest they miss a vision of Sir Klaus speeding merrily by on his sleigh.

The widows of Mont Mendor take to the streets on Christmas Eve, "propositioning" younger men, then handing them a fig if they accept. The younger men are then obligated to hand over their pants to the women, who don the trousers through the Epiphany.

In parts of mountainous Europe, a small cat sits inside a wreath placed on the floor. The moment the cat steps outside the wreath, Christmas dinner may commence. (In northern towns, a baby is frequently used in place of a cat.)

Late on Christmas Eve, children in the lower Taryool are given a fairly complex mathematical problem that they must complete by sunrise Christmas morning. If a child successfully solves the problem without the aid of a calculator or slide rule, the youngster may then run downstairs, where a pile of presents awaits.

If you awaken Christmas morning in Osreno and find a soft banana under your pillow, "treasures untold and chests of gold, all the baubles and blessings your dreams can hold" shall be yours. If the banana is firm, expect nothing.

In honor of the twelve days of Christmas, families near the village of Lornen Downs must hide behind their own festively festooned tree until a neighbor comes to find them. Neighbors must also hide and abide by the same rules. No family may emerge until properly discovered or New Year's Day, whichever comes first.

A very loud man, typically the mayor, stands in the North Audville town square warbling carols with inappropriate lyrics on the merry day. The first person to convince the chanter to cease wins a cooked goose, or some lottery tickets. If the bawdy bard is stopped before he begins "Lydia, the Elf with the Shelf" then the victor also wins a bag of chestnuts, or some lottery tickets. Bribes, monetary or otherwise, are permitted.

It is the magic day when the flour flies in New Hanton. Look out!

In a scrubby clearing in western Kenya, one lion or several will hunt and kill gazelles on Christmas Day, often repeatedly. If other lions are nearby, the predator celebrates the spirit of the day, sharing his catch with his brethren.

Across the world, in every city, hamlet and home, cells divide on the Yuletide.

Tabletop Christmas Village Service Directory

Welcome Neighbor!

You've made a special choice in purchasing your new home in our wonderful community, the Tabletop Christmas Village.

Enclosed in this welcome packet you'll find a town map, important numbers, and tips on making your move to the Tabletop Christmas Village a smooth one. Below please find a directory of services, a "red-and-green" pages if you will, that should answer where you find what in our fa-la-lovely town. We're more than just miniature gas lamps, overly quaint Dickensian buildings, and puffy cotton filling used copiously in the place of real snow! Please see below:

Bread—Bakery
Milk—Kitty's Creamery
Loans—First Bank of Twinkleville
Dry Cleaners—Church
Futons & Accessories—Taffy Factory
Dentist—Music Box Shop
Stereo Supplies—Train Station
Towing—Mr. Buckingham's Bookbinders, est. 1881
Counseling, Employment—Skating Pond
Counseling, Marital—Footbridge
Pest Control—Lighthouse
Pregnancy Clinic—Gazebo
Blinds, Repair & Cleaning—Jenkins General Store
   & Dry Goods
Computer Software—Wishing Well
Tanning Salon—Granary

Tire Dealers, used—Auntie Alice's Wicks 'n' Candlesticks
Attorneys—Old Barn
Sushi—Fanny the Florist
Paging & Signaling Equipment—Carousel
Bankruptcy Services—Lamppost

Keeping Christmas in Your Heart All Year Long

January 18—Deck the house in lots of bright, flashing lights, oversize reindeer, and holiday gewgaws. An aural touch, such as continuous carols playing out the front window, will keep the neighbors in good humor.

February 3—Wish five strangers Merry Christmas today. Repeat "Merry Christmas" joyfully when they ask you to repeat what you just said. Hugs are nice here.

March 11—Build a snowman. If no snow is available, use whatever fetid earth you can scrape up, or any old milk cartons/newspapers lying around. Kids'll love it.

May 30—Set up a hot nog stand out by the city pool. Ask parents if little fishes can have a sprinkle of nutmeg in their cups first. Do not let yourself be snapped by a wet towel while handling the scalding beverage.

June 20—Visit the mall Santa. If he isn't there, be Santa yourself, inviting strangers to sit in your lap. Listen well but promise nothing.

July 4—Explode some holly, making sure it is tinder dry and crackly. See the pretty fire colors. The firemen will be merrily wearing festive red or yellow when they arrive. Have cookies ready!

August 8—Gift tag Popsicles.

September 1–30—Repeatedly ask same neighbor for cup of whiskey for world-famous St. Nick Nuggets. When he first refuses, jump in the leaf pile in his yard, yelling "Santa's comin' in for a landing," or something fun like that. Living next to a card such as yourself may not raise the value of your neighbors' house, but it is sure to raise the value of their hearts.

October 31—Upon opening door for trick-or-treaters, guess each child's costume as Blitzen or Comet. Then hand out candy canes to disappointed goblins with a "Ho-Ho-Halloween wishes" or similar.

November 29—Put roast turkey in makeshift manger, pray. Bread stuffing and cranberry salad artfully placed make for fine cattle and sheep.

December 25—Vow to keep Christmas all next year, or at least every other Thursday, preferably between seven and eight in the evening. Devote the rest of the coming months to keeping National Poultry Day in your heart. Watch for coming tips and hints.

Womenu

ALYSIA GRAY PAINTER

Starters

Diapers in a Smelly Sauce $4
Tasty Talc Lightly Sprinkled over Bottom. $3
Chafing with Risotto in a Dish. $2
Suck Knuckles. $3
Giggles in Phyllo $2

Salads

Tossed School
Raw feelings and teacher worship coated with shredded fights and loneliness, plus blackboard dust perfumed with scent of sack lunch. A dish of lightly nasty notes is served on the side. $4

Brothers with Bibb Lettuce
A flavorful tumble of television, julienned odors, gamey guitar riffs whisked with divorce worries. Includes the occasional holiday hug served warm. Fist vinaigrette with shredded album sleeves suggested $6

Middle School Mix

Best-loved books basted in a steady, sizzling stream of friends and enemies. This dish is encased in a sweet-and-sour slumber party shell. Ouija boards and burnt Toll House cookies are crumbled on top of a creamy, crying dressing $5

Street Slaw

A suburban medley of bike bits plus big trees holding a feast of forts, all layered on a bed of lawn and spicy fall leaves. Barking dogs upon request $4

Soups

Sassy Gazpacho $4
Contrary Consommé $4

Basket of Breads

Period
Crush
Joy
Boredom
White

Butters

Prom
Anti-prom

Entrées

College Casserole with Braised Garlic and Grading Curve

Baked in an ivy-and-brick dish, this mixture includes roommate loathing and a smattering of oversleeping combined with chunks of library time, basted in a bittersweet broth of important conversations. Work/study assignments are sprinkled across the quad, as is a luscious layer of lifelong debt and memories that get happier with time $15

Job Jambalaya

A fried interview with a pungent paranoid after-taste. Presented on a slice of desk, this dish is tossed and topped with a dollop of dictation and a coating of copier ink. Served in a crispy, edible cubicle papered with oniony aphorisms and photos of cats $17

Love Gallimaufry

A tasty concoction of snowy nights, hot hands, and more melted butter than you can eat. Ask your server about availability $17

Family Feast with Savory Kid Gravy

A staff favorite, this overcooked hungry hash sits on a mortgage platter and is stuffed with old couches, juice splotches, smoked carpet, kisses, and blame, simmered in a supermarket sauce with a splash of slamming doors. Phone bills au gratin give this dish a surprisingly tasty tang $20

Ennui en Croûte

A big bland meat house (exquisitely enfolded in puff pastry) remains empty on an oversize plate. Sautéed art and fancy furniture must be left untouched in an accompanying dish (your server will clear immediately). Instead, linger over the lengthy, lemony hours filled with few pursuits but doubt and gout. A snappy remoulade of minced words and Trivial Pursuit gives this dish zing, as do moments of clarity and claret. Children home from college will be served alongside (in season only), as will husbands when fresh $22

After-Dinner Drinks

Postmammogram Mocha
Digestif avec Arthritis
Hysterec-Tea (mint, oolong, black)
Espresso with Estrogen Twist

Desserts

Flambé à la Maison (Shut-in)

A soft stew of bananas and banality is set aflame then extinguished, leaving dabs of daytime television, yellowing scrapbooks, cocoa, calls from a favorite grandchild, nibbles of needlepoint all in a bowl with safety handles and a rubber bottom. Breaths will come shorter after one bite $10

Husband's Burial with Caramel

Papers, lawyers, relatives, and money are stirred into this grave-size serving of sorrow and memory, with a drizzling of coughs and caramel—tiramisu tears extra. A single portion is dished up in a double bed. Plate splitting not permitted $18

Chocolate Deadcadence

Finality in the form of ladyfingers drizzled with darkest chocolate, all with a chewy surprise center. You'll never be hungry again . . . . .Market price

---

No takeout or doggie bags, please.
Ask about our banquet room.
Closed Mondays.

Alfred Hitchcock's
Hamlet

LOUIS PHILLIPS

I believe that not many film fans and/or Shakespearean scholars are aware that Alfred Hitchcock and his production partner, Sidney Bernstein, seriously contemplated filming a modern remaking of Hamlet. Indeed, I was not aware of that possibility until I read about it in Leonard L. Leff's book Hitchcock and Selznick *(Weidenfeld and Nicols, 1987). Mr. Leff reports that Hitchcock and Bernstein "contemplated a Shakespearean release: 'Sidney Bernstein presents Cary Grant as Alfred Hitchcock's* Hamlet, *a modern thriller by William Shakespeare.' "*

It is a shame such a movie never made its suspenseful way to the screen, for in that best cinema of all—my mind's eye—I can clearly see just how the film would unfold. Although the entire script (176 pages of it in its final draft) is much too long to reprint here, I take the liberty of sharing a few key scenes.

ALFRED HITCHCOCK'S
HAMLET

(Freely Adapted from Either Shakespeare or Hawthorne)

EXTERIOR. THE MINUTE HAND OF THE WATCH OF BATES MOTEL.
NEAR DAWN.

Pacing the Motel Towers are two men in beavers. (*Editor's note: The obviously underpaid scriptwriter meant two men with beavers. A beaver is such a tiny and toothy animal, no man could comfortably live inside one for any sustained period of time. Though what the two soldiers want with these furry animals is difficult to say. Perhaps patrolling the towers of a deserted motel is a lonely occupation and the soldiers need pets for companionship.*) These two Danish soldiers are Bernardo and Alfred Hitchcock.

Bernardo: Who's there?

Hitchcock: Nay, answer me. Stand and unfold yourself.

Bernardo: Long live the King!

> (*Editor's note: Hitch, as he was affectionately known to his friends, was famous for making cameo appearances in his movies. Later this trick became a burden to him, and so in his* Hamlet *Hitch wished to get his appearance over with as quickly as possible. The scene, the only one actually filmed by the master director, went off without a hitch as it were.*)

Hitchcock leaves the battlements. Hamlet, dressed in a modern tuxedo with a willowy blonde—Bernardo's mother—upon his arm, enters.

Hamlet: Bernardo, your dear mother here has informed me that you claim to have seen the ghost of my dead father. Are you sure it looked like him?

Bernardo: As thou art to thyself. Such was the very armour he had on When he the ambitious Norway combated; So frowned he once when, in an angry parle, he smote the sledded Polacks on the ice.

(*Editor's note: Selznick, ever sensitive to foreign markets, instructed that the phrase "ambitious Norway" be changed to "spectacular and economical Norway." Also we should note the phrase "sledded Polacks" has long been debated by textual scholars. Some prefer "shredded Pollack,"—referring either to the noted movie director named Sidney or a popular cereal. In an early version of the script, the line reads: "He smote the wedded Polish cats with some ice." No one knows what that means either.*)

The Ghost enters.

Hamlet: (to Bernardo's Mother, Demi) Peace! Zip thee up. Look where it comes again . . .

Hamlet pours the Ghost a glass of champagne. But before he can offer it, Ghost glides off the battlements.

Demi: (Bernardo's Mother) Which way does he go, Bernardo?

Bernardo: Mother, the wind blows North by Northwest . . .

Hamlet: (nearly fainting, feeling dizzy and Demi) If I overcome my vertigo, I shall fetch him home if it's the last thing I do.

Bernardo: No, let's exchange fathers. You find my father. And I'll find yours. Deal? But if one fails in his task, the other gets to kill the other.

Hamlet: (still nearly fainting) Sworn . . .

Bernardo swears and rushes out to follow the Ghost of Hamlet's Father.

Hamlet, recovering, stays behind to make love to Demi-Bernardo.

CUT TO:
EXTERIOR. A CORNFIELD ON THE OUTSKIRTS OF ELSINORE.
HIGH NOON.

Hamlet stands by the side of the lonely road. As we watch Hamlet, we see hundreds of huge crows covering the field behind him. Soon we can no longer see the ground because there are so many birds behind him. Hamlet starts to run. The crows fly after him. Hamlet falls face down in a cornfield and fractures his left leg. Millions of crows start to eat the corn. They inch closer and closer to Hamlet. It appears as if Hamlet is doomed.

Hamlet: O, horrible! O, horrible! Most horrible!

(*Editor's note: A memo from Selznick stated that the scene as written would be too expensive to film. He suggested that a cropduster be substituted for the crows or that only one very large crow be used. Selznick also suggested that the line of dialogue be changed to read: "My hair stands on end/Like quills upon the fretful turpentine." Hitch queried: "Do you really mean 'Turpentine' or 'Porpentine'? Selznick's answering memo has been misplaced. Hitchcock deep-sixed the cornfield scene, saved it for his later oeuvre, and substituted a new scene.)*

INTERIOR. BERNARDO'S MOTHER'S BATHROOM IN ELSINORE CASTLE. NIGHT.

Demi-Bernardo is in the shower. As the water flows over her alabaster skin, she sings to herself.

Demi-Bernardo: Full fathom five thy father lies; / Of his bones are coral made.

As she sings in the shower, we see the shadow of Bernardo appearing upon the shower curtain. He carries a pike.

(Editor's note: See the previous comments on beavers. What Bernardo is doing with a dead fish is difficult to fathom. More fathomable, is the due that Bernardo's mother is offering. She knows where Hamlet's father is buried. He has been murdered and tossed to the bottom of the sea. Perhaps the pike carries a piece of the old man. After all, earlier in the script, Hamlet had told the King: "A man may fish with the worm that hath eat of a king, and eat of the fish that hath fed of that worm." The song sung by Demi-Bernardo has been interpolated from some other play, but this is, after all, Hollywood.)

CUT TO:
INTERIOR. HAMLET'S ROOM RIGHT ACROSS THE WAY FROM THE ROOM OF BERNARDO'S MOTHER. DAY.

Hamlet, confined to a wheelchair because of his broken leg, looks through his binoculars and sees Bernardo in the bathroom.

CUT TO:
BERNARDO'S MOTHER'S BATHROOM.

Bernardo pulls open the shower curtain. His Mother screams. Bernardo hits her repeatedly with a dead fish. We watch the blood go down the drain of the bath.

Bernardo: O wonderful son, that can so astonish a mother!

He looks up and out the window. . . . He sees Hamlet spying on him.

Bernardo: Now it's my turn to slay you for not finding my father. . . .

CUT TO:
INTERIOR. HAMLET'S ROOM RIGHT ACROSS THE WAY FROM
THE ROOM OF BERNARDO'S MOTHER. DAY.

Bernardo enters disguised as his own mother! He is poised for the kill, but Hamlet has disappeared.

CUT TO:
EXTERIOR. A GIANT MONUMENT OF SHAKESPEARE CARVED OUT OF
THE SIDE OF A MOUNTAIN. NIGHT.

Nay, it is more than night. 'Tis now the very witching time of night, / When churchyards yawn, and hell itself breathes out / Contagion to this world. Bernardo and Hamlet are scampering up Shakespeare's nose.

> (*Editor's note:* Hamlet *was originally titled "The Man in Shakespeare's Nose," but the censors found that title too disgusting.*)

Bernardo lunges at Hamlet, but his feet get entangled in the long skirts of his mother, he slips, and he plunges to his death.

Bernardo: Mother! . . . Mother . . .

THE END

(Editor's note: A memo from Selznick suggested that the ending be changed. Selznick wanted to have Bernardo confined to a mental hospital, where he/she would be available for any sequels. His memo concludes with the following lines from Shakespeare's Hamlet: "But is there no sequel at the heels of this mother's admiration?" The answer must be yes. There will be sequels galore!)

SLOGANS OF
NOT-SO-PRESTIGIOUS SCHOOLS

Radclift—We're only a couple of letters away from being a really good school.

Mortensen Taxidermy—Let's not kid each other. You weren't our first choice, either.

Mike's Dental School—No lawsuits in 19 months.

Williamsburg Institute—You can either live on campus or do it by mail.

Raymond Wright College—A lot of sodomy happens here. Yep, sodomy and free gum.

Duncan College—At Duncan College, your parents never see your report card. Guaranteed.

Chounter's Culinary College—You're not a student at Chounter, you're a junior teacher.

Rinzen Music Academy—*and forestry.

People's Choice Junior College—At PCJC, we aren't afraid to have *TV Guide* in our media center.

Furrer Bible College—Did you know some translations of the Bible endorse weed smoking? How about free video rentals?

Colombia University—*Porque parece un error tipográfico en su curriculum vitae.*

—Jeff Johnson

Aristotle's "On Baseball"

TRANSLATED BY

LOUIS PHILLIPS

Baseball is Greek, in being national, heroic, and broken up
in the rivalries of city-states.

ON BASEBALL

Our subject is the art of baseball in general and the theories of
hitting, catching, and pitching in particular, the specific effect
of each genre, and the way to play the game so that the sport be
pleasing to the eye and soul of the spectator. Let us start, as is
proper, with basic principles.

Baseball As Imitation

Dithyrambic baseball, as it was originally named, is the imitation of something, perhaps Tragedy. Perhaps not. In such matters it is difficult to be definitive.

As I have written elsewhere, Comedy is the imitation of
inferior men who are not altogether vicious. Thus, the owners
of teams are Comedic; the players, with their dreams of immor-
tality and another season in the sun, Tragic.

Derivation of the Word

The term *baseball* comes from two obscured roots—*baseios*, meaning low, and *ballein*, referring to a type of whale. Hence, the low song of a whale. Or the song of a low whale. How this derivation came about has yet to be determined. Homer maintains that in the early years of the games, when the games were dedicated to the god Poseidon, a whale was sacrificed at the conclusion of each home stand. Unfortunately, the above may well be a folk etymology. After all, everybody knows that Homer frequently preferred a colorful story to the truth.

What scholars do agree upon, especially Danaus and Chaeremon (in spite of his mixed meters), is that baseball was originally called *baseode*, or Amusement (song) for the low-born.

Whatever the origin of the term, we do know the word was born hundreds of years before *Tragos ode* or Tragedy.

Definition of the Term

Baseball is the good action which is complete and of a certain length (usually nine innings) by means of players who are made pleasing for each of their respective positions; it relies in its various elements not on acting, nor on narrative, but upon skill exhibited within a natural setting; through Pity and Fear, the completed game achieves the cleansing of these emotions. It involves the fall of a team from one level (either of play or of positions in the standings) to a lower level.

The Earliest Use of the Term

The earliest mention of baseball is, of course, to be found in Book VI of Homer's *Odyssey,* where the Princess Nausica tosses a ball. The following passage is of great interest to all scholars of the game and needs, of course, since we are Greek, no translation: "And presently, when Nausica and her maiden servants had finished their lunch, they removed the scarves from their heads and other headdresses and began playing with a ball. Nausica of the white led them in song."

This passage is of especial interest because it shows that at its inception women were not banned from the game (or *agon*) as they are now.

The Six Elements or Aspects of Dithyrambic Baseball

Every baseball game contains six necessary elements (or seven, if your team is managed by a barbarian) that make the game what it is: Agents, Contracts, Character, Diction, Spectacle, and Music. Most exhibitions of the game involve these elements in much the same manner.

Prophecy and Individual Games

Dithyrambic baseball might well have become more popular in Greece in particular and in Europe, but there is no longer any doubt that its popularity has been dampened by the omnipresence of Tiresias and other prophets addicted to bird prophecy. How disturbing it is to the common mind to have a baseball contest interrupted by the sight of an eagle flying over the stadiums of Athens and dropping a snake into the lap of the judges. It is even more disturbing to see a prophet tear open a pig or a chicken and spill its entrails across the bleachers—all in the hope of looking for a sign.

Indeed, as Agathon has observed in his monumental *Encyclopedia of Dithyrambic Baseball,* numerous contests have no sooner gotten underway when Tiresias, blind umpire that he was, would announce the final score. Disgruntled fans would then get up and leave, abandoning the hometown IX for some Dionysian revelry. Who dare blame them? The essence of baseball is the same as the essence of rhetoric—suspense. When suspense is removed from a baseball *agon,* because of vain bubbling of prophets, the game loses all its savor. Indeed, what spectator among us desires to know ahead of time whether or not Oedipus shall hit for the cycle?

It has also been well documented that the Athens Metropolitans lost something in the neighborhood of 580,000 drachmas each and every year they played. No wonder ship owners of certain families near Tampa looked elsewhere to make their fortune.

Until blind prophets are banned from attending the baseball *agon*, the game will certainly suffer a lack of dramatic tension.

The Three Essential Parts

Dithyrambic baseball, as a whole, consists of three parts: the Pitch, the Catch, and the Hit. (I know I have written earlier about the six elements or aspects of the game, but elements are not parts or if they are parts they are very subtle ones.)

We shall consider each one in turn.

The Pitch is sometimes physical, ofttimes purely linguistic. For example, Androtion, formerly of the A's and now a noted politician, would, after each *agon* or contest, post himself at one of the major exits to the stadium and sell tip sheets to the various chariot races going on about town. He also hawked razors. A number of commentators deplored the pitcher's actions and predicted (correctly) that such pitching would bring forth the mercenary side of players.

The Catch. An old saying goes: like the Pitch, the Catch. What it means is difficult to explain. Allow us to begin with the notion that the Catch possesses a twofold nature. There is the physical Catch, defined as the act of a fielder (in or out) plucking a battered ball from thin air. And then there is the other kind of Catch, the legal kind which players refer to when perusing the fine print in their contracts. For example, if a player (such as the aforementioned and deplored Androtion) is induced for a substantial bonus to sign a contract with the Spartans so that the Spartans can trade him to Crete for players (or agonists) to be named later, then the player and/or his agent may rightfully refer to the above play as a Catch.

The Hit. After each game, players have been seen approaching young ladies in the stands and "Hitting" on them. Sometimes, while trying to convince a female fan to join him in a night of debauchery, the player strikes out. Sometimes he gets to first base. This is what players mean most of the time when they talk about Hitting (see Scoring).

Three Additional Elements

Three additional elements of a game may be considered without undue comment. The are Peripety, Discovery, and Suffering. These parts belong properly to the spectators. Especially Suffering.

Three Kinds of Games to Be Avoided

There are some forms of the *agon* that should be avoided at all cost:

1. A good team must not be seen passing from happiness to misery because of the misguided actions of its owner.
2. A bad player must not be seen passing from misery to happiness because of a bad bounce or pure chance. Players must act consistent with their skills.
3. An extremely bad *agon* should not be prolonged more than necessary.

Of Baseball and Thought

Thought, most rightly, should be considered in my treatise on Rhetoric, but since Thought occupies a central position in the meaning of the game, we shall mention it here.

Baseball is considered to be boring by the nonthinking. But those who think find the game exciting. This is what is frequently referred to as Athena's Paradox. Athena's Paradox also applies to the rites of Aphrodite.

Indeed, we should also point out that, although everyone on a baseball team thinks, not all members think at the same time. That is why errors occur and why managers have been deemed, by Zeus, as necessary.

As I have said, all members of a baseball team, at some time during a season, think, but for some reason, only the catcher is allowed to adorn himself with the tools of ignorance. This is also a paradox, for the catcher is frequently the most learned player on the field. Some have even been known to take part in the Lenaea in the month of Gamelion. But the comic playwrights deserve what they get.

Antisthenes, the philosopher and protégé of Socrates, insists that excessive squatting (as performed by the catcher) causes the nerves and brains to settle low in the body. Antisthenes is, alas, a cynic.

Baseball and Ritual Murder

Anyone who has set foot inside the bleacher section of a well-contested *agon* has no doubt heard the cry go up:

> *Kakist' apoloith' ho brabeus*

Most evilly may perish the Umpire. This well-known imprecation has sent chills up and down the spins of novices to the game.

Were umpires actually slaughtered? Yes. After whales were abandoned, umpires were brought in to provide atonement and ritual cleansing. Fortunately, however, because of unionization of the craft of well-seeing and considered judgment, that practice has been rendered unlawful, except in some foreign countries.

But the cry goes on, thus showing us how slowly the rhetoric of the game changes and how eternal baseball truly is.

The First Book of Mailer, Called Genesis

LOUIS PHILLIPS

Since Norman Mailer has published a first-person account of the life of Christ, some readers have breathed a sigh of relief: Thank God, the Old Testament is safe. Well, the Old Testament is also coming under intense scrutiny from the author of The Deer Park, The Naked and the Dead, *and numerous other novels. In fact, we are pleased to publish a brief glimpse of* The First Book of Mailer, Called Genesis, *for our discerning readers.*   —L.P.

Chapter 1

In the beginning, God punched out the friggin' heaven and the friggin' Earth.

And the Earth at that time was without Mailer. And the Spirit of God moved upon the chickenshit void. Norman Mailer was silent. This was not characteristic of Mailer.

Then God fumbled sloppily for light. And there was light. But there was still no Mailer.

And God called the friggin' light Day, and the friggin' darkness he called the friggin' Night. And the evening and the morning were the first day without Mailer.

And God said, Let there be an Army of Night to carry my banner forward and let there be critics to divide readers from writers.

And God made the critics, and divided the readers which were under the firmament from the writers which were far above the firmament. In fact, some writers were far too good for this firmament, John Simon being one. And God called the firmament Book Reviewing, and it was good. Sometimes.

And God created huge advances, and every living literary agent that moveth, and multi-structured contracts which overpaid legal departments brought forth. And God saw that this was complex.

So God created Mailer in his own image, in the image of God created He him, Norman.

And the Lord God said, It is not good that Norman should be alone; I will create an help meet for him. And from the ribbing which God had taken from Mailer more than once made He a woman, and brought her unto Mailer. Mailer then took up a kitchen knife at Eve and, in a fit of ungodly anger, stabbed he the woman. God saw that this was not good and shook His head sadly.

And the Lord said unto the Norman, Why art thou wroth?

And the Norman saith, Why am I not Roth?

And God said, I can see from the sweat of thy brow that thee and Roth are going to suffer much trouble with women. Perhaps after five marriages you might embrace a Church.

And God said, Let the writers bring forth books. And the writers brought forth many books. And the Lord said, This they begin to do. Now nothing will be restrained from them, which they have imagined to do. But I shall confound them by creating Hollywood, a holy place where their names will be mud and they shall be treated like dirt. And that was the morning and the evening of the fifth day.

And God said, Let the writers have whiskey, marijuana, Seconal, and benzedrine. And God blessed them, saying, Sell to the movies and fill the accounts in your banks. And God read *The Naked and the Dead* and said that it was good. Very good. But the movie version was not so good.

And Norman tore the ear off the sun and called it the moon. And was there fire on the moon?

And God saw everything that Mailer had made and behold it was very good, except of course certain home movies. And the ancient evenings and the ancient mornings were the sixth day.

And God helped Mailer create characters for his novels. And they were all naked, the men and the women, and were not ashamed.

And on the seventh day God ended His work, but Mailer continued typing; and God rested on the seventh day from all His work which He had made, but Mailer, he rested not from all that he had made.

And Mailer gave names to all his critics, and Mailer went forth from Harvard and the Great War to cross the borders into the Kingdom of Brooklyn, where he would next write *The Second Book of Norman, Called Exodus*.

Cosi Fans Tutti

The Granddaddy of Baseball Operas to Make Its Presence Felt

LOUIS PHILLIPS

Although there are literally tens of popular songs about baseball, there are (alas!) very few operas about the sport. Thus, the recent discovery of an unproduced opera by Stengel and Hayden has caused a great stir in music circles. (It actually doesn't take very much to cause a great stir in music circles, for such circles stir quite easily; any scrap of manuscript paper is likely to cause a fuss.) The opera, entitled *Cosi Fans Tutti*, was nearly completed, at the untimely death of Stengel and the most untimely death of Hayden, and was discovered under a pile of unpaid bills.

As of this writing, the Metropolitan Opera is planning a production in the spring of 2004.

Cosi Fans Tutti: Opera Comique/Tragique
Scene: San Francisco/Oakland/Vienna/Athens/other
   unreal cities
Time: December, 198—, 199—

Chief Characters: *The Queen of Portugal*
                   The Count of the Baseball Commission
                   Colonel Fairfax
                   Fax
                   Club Owners
                   Mark of Langston
                   Mark of Davis
                   Kirby of Puckett
                   Count di Box Office Receipts
                   Parsifal
                   Kundy
                   Satyagraha
                   and numerous fans

The story of *Cosi Fans Tutti* is taken from a medieval legend (circulated by owners of major league teams, who have reluctantly abandoned stories of poisoned wells). The time is late in the 1980s or some era in the dark ages. The Burgomeister and Commissioner of Baseball stand at the window of a high-rise owned by G. Steinbrenner.

" 'Habit is a great deadener,' said Samuel Beckett," the Commissioner sings. "But so too is playing for a losing team," the Burgomeister replies.

Outside the high-rise in a peaceful part of the Bronx on the bank of the East River, a tribe of gypsy free agents have pitched their tents and temporary condominiums. A bright fire is burning, and a hungry band of pitchers, catchers, outfielders, infielders, and designated hitters have gathered to pray to their agents. They fall to their knees and sing the beautiful and touching religious hymn, "More."

> More! More! More! More!
> More! More! More! More!
> *Si li Conosco!**

---

*Some consider this a misprint for Canseco. Consult his toll-free number for clarification.

The touching but beautiful hymn is interrupted by the arrival of a first baseman named Don M. Alfonso. Alfonso is greeted with much warmth as he sings, *"Tutti, lor painte, tutti deliri loro ancor tu sai,"* which, freely translated, means, "Then you have noticed the owners of major league clubs are overcome by desperation?"

More contracts are tossed on the fire and there is much dancing and singing (simple peasant songs mingled with Gregorian Chants). These baseball players and agents are simple, happy wanderers following their hearts from place to place.

The leader of the players, a venerable young lawyer, whose eyes are young but sad—steps forward, dances a minuet with the Burgomeister (who has donned a disguise to spy on the players) and sings what is known in musicology as "The Lawyer's Aria:" *

> *Ah, perdon mio bel diletto*
> *Innocenyi e questo cor.*

> (I am sure the owners' opposition
> and their fierce anger is not for show.)

> (Translation by Hrbek)

All eyes now turn toward Langston and his fast ball. Years before, Langston had come as a stranger to the tribe, declaring himself weary of the trials and disappointments of life in an obscure part of the media marketplace. He begged to be allowed to remain for a short time with the gypsies or free agents, who received him with great courtesy and hospitality.

From offstage (Queens?) we hear the screams of thousands of men, women, and children. Thirty thousand† die-hard baseball fans rush onto the stage, singing *"Gusti nuni cosa a sento?"* ("How dare a .237 hitter demand a salary of over three million a year?")

---

*Not to be confused with "The Lawyer's Recitative."
†Obviously some doubling and tripling of parts is called for.

The fans pay ten or fifteen dollars for the privilege of doing a little dance with the players. This dance, a combination of a waltz and a mere bagatelle, lasts most of the winter. At the conclusion, the fans leap high into the air and chant, *"Ah che piu non ho ritegno"* (Now I am thoroughly disgusted").

The penultimate scene of the opera is perhaps the most touching one of all. The teenaged daughter of a third baseman who cannot break the $1 million per season salary structure feels that her family name is shamed beyond redemption. She takes down from the wall a Japanese sword, brought back by her lover, a major league player who had spent two or three years with the Hiroshima Carps. She kisses the blade and tenderly remembers that he had used the sword to commit hara-kiri. When Pinkerton returns, searching for a no-trade option and some betting slips bearing the autograph of a future Hall-of-Famer, he sees the body of his mistress. He cries out in despair, and turns to face the ghost of R. D. Laing (whose spirit hovers over the scene). The ghost shrieks, "Long before thermonuclear war can come about we have had to lay waste our sanity."

For the final scene we cut to a secret meeting of the baseball owners who are dressed in hair shirts and who are beating themselves with sacred boughs from Louisville. As the curtain finally descends, all the owners stand and sing a tribute to their players: "I Love Them Like a Father."

The theater fills with *"Sono i piu dolci amici ch'io m'abbia in questio mondo, e vostri ancor saranno!"*

Sorry, this is a BYOF cookie.

Altered History:
Death of the Blues

JUDITH PODELL

Vienna, 1902. Sigmund Freud seeking nonaddictive cocaine substitute discovers Prozac. Revises *Civilization and Its Discontents* to add happy ending, repudiates psychoanalysis. Incidence of neurasthenia plummets, as does Jewish birthrate. Apprentice pastry chef Ludwig Wittgenstein invents the Sacher-Masoch torte.

Prague, 1912. Franz Kafka moves out of parents' house, marries. Writes *The Metamorphosis*, popular children's story about a man who turns into a great big bug and has many exciting adventures.

London, 1920. T. S. Eliot tears up drafts of *The Waste Land*, tells Ezra Pound he wants to write show tunes for shop girls and live on the Riviera. Teams up with George Gershwin to write *Cats*.

Memphis, 1926. Bessie Smith quits vaudeville, opens beauty parlor. Robert Johnson tries to buy back soul from the Devil, struck by lightning.

Berlin, 1933. *Metamorphosis* adopted for stage. Lotte Lenya sings the "Ballad of Max the Roach." Burning of the Reichstag.

London, 1944. Churchill takes up exercise and quits smoking for the duration of the Blitz. *House and Garden* editor Virginia Woolf urges wartime Britain "Think chintz." 10,000th performance of *Cats*.

1952. Dixieland legend Miles Davis quits show business to attend dental school. Billie Holiday records "White Christmas" with Perry Como.

1956. Steep decline in alcoholism, Soviet birthrate. Nikita Khrushchev tells United States, "We will bury you—in cheap household appliances." Russia leads world in production of hair dryers and toasters.

1964. Lawrence Welk named *Downbeat* Musician of the Year. Battle of the Bands won by British barbershop quartet, Rolling Stones.

1970. Janis Joplin passes California Bar. Green Beret Jim Morrison missing in action. Billie Holiday stars in revival of *Cats*.

1978. Sylvia Plath marries Ernest Hemingway, opens first bed and breakfast in Ketchum.

1999. I.P.O. for Sylvia Plath Lifestyle, Inc. withdrawn after shooting accident.

Memphis, 2000. Stash of old records found in yard sale. Rare performances by Robert Johnson, Bukka White, and Son House. *Antiques Roadshow* estimates value at $5.

Nobody gets the blues.

Blues for Beginners

JUDITH PODELL

> *woke up this morning*
> *cat threw a hairball on the bed*
> *[2×]*
> *went to the kitchen*
> *mr. coffee was dead.*
>
> —*"Postgraduate Blues" attributed*
> *to Memphis Earlene Gray*

1. Most blues begin "woke up this morning."
2. "I got a good woman" is a bad way to begin the blues, unless you stick something nasty in the next line.

> *i got a good woman—*
> *with the meanest dog in town.*

3. Blues are simple. After you have the first line right, repeat it. Then find something that rhymes.

> *got a good woman*
> *with the meanest dog in town.*
> *he got teeth like Margaret Thatcher*
> *and he weighs 500 pound.*

4. The blues are not about limitless choice.

5. Blues cars are Chevrolets and Terraplanes. Other acceptable blues transport is Greyhound bus or the southbound train. Walkin' plays a major part in the blues lifestyle. So does fixin' to die.

6. Teenagers can't sing the blues. Adults sing the blues. Blues adulthood means old enough to get the electric chair if you shot a man in Memphis.

7. You can have the blues in New York City, but not in Brooklyn or Queens. Hard times in Vermont or North Dakota are just depression. Chicago, St. Louis, and Kansas City are still the best places to have the blues.

8. The following colors do not belong in the blues:
   a. orange
   b. beige

9. You can't have the blues in an office or a honky-tonk. The lighting is wrong.

10. Good places for the blues:
    a. the highway
    b. the jailhouse
    c. the empty bed

11. No one will believe it's the blues if you wear a suit, unless you happen to be an old black man.

12. Do you have the right to sing the blues?

    Yes, if:
    a. your first name is a southern state
    b. you're blind
    c. you shot a man in Memphis
    d. you can't be satisfied

    No, if:
    a. you once were blind but now can see
    b. you're deaf

13. Neither Frank Sinatra nor Meryl Streep can sing the blues.

14. If you ask for water and baby gives you gasoline it's the blues. Other blues beverages are:
    a. wine
    b. Irish whiskey
    c. muddy water
15. If it occurs in a cheap motel or a shotgun shack it's blues death. Stabbed in the back by a jealous girlfriend is a blues way to die. So is the electric chair, substance abuse, or being denied treatment in an emergency room.
16. Some Blues Names for Women
    a. Sadie
    b. Big Mamma
17. Some Blues Names for Men
    a. Willie
    b. Joe
    c. Little Joe Willie
    d. Lightnin'
18. Persons with names like Sierra or Sequoia will not be permitted to sing the blues no matter how many men they shoot in Memphis.

Totally Amazing Grace

PAUL RUDNICK

Recently *People* magazine interviewed country/pop star LeAnn Rimes about her special audience with Pope John Paul II.

> "Well, I got there two minutes before he walked in. Thank God he was late. He came in [and] gave a whole speech which was in, I think, Latin . . . It was really cool." —LeAnn in *People*

Here now, an e-mail response from His Holiness:

P.J.P. II: Well, of course I was late—I was so nervous! Sure, I'm the infallible voice of God on Earth, but LeAnn's only, what—twelve? And she's gone multiplatinum, with crossover into the pop audience, plus she recently lost 20 pounds with a martial-arts workout. I told Cardinal Benselmo, I can't meet LeAnn Rimes, I'll die, I'll faint, what'll I wear? But then there she was, so beyond adorable, and I got so excited I just started babbling, and she was so sweet, she said something really nice in, I think, English, and it sounded like, "Neat to meetcha, Your Grace. Tell God I say howdy." And then she tweaked my Papal beanie, winked, and said, "Hey, what gives—ya Jewish?"

> "I'm a strong Christian, and to meet someone like him, it touched me a lot, it really did, getting blessed by him." —LeAnn in *People*

P.J.P. II: I am *such* a fan, especially of country/pop, because it's less twangy—LeAnn and Shania are my faves, because they're country, but not too Opry. I like country with a midriff. An audience with LeAnn was like meeting Dolly or Reba or even Della Reese from *Touched by an Angel*—love that show! Whenever the angels deliver the big message, their hair gets this special golden backlit glow, to show that the word of God is not only sacred but a fabulous conditioner. Are you listening, Celine?

> "I just wish I was able to understand what he was saying. It was such a moving moment. I almost started crying." —LeAnn in *People*

P.J.P. II: I kept telling her, over and over, that her version of "How Do I Live" beat the *socks* off Trisha Yearwood's, even if Trisha got the Grammy. I kept saying, We researched it in the Vatican archives, and "Trisha" is definitely an ancient Coptic term meaning "prom date of Lucifer." I asked LeAnn, Please, is there anyone you want sent to Hell, an ex-manager, maybe Britney Spears, but I don't know if I got through. I mimed Britney's schoolgirl/vixen shimmy from the video where she sings, "Hit me, baby, one more time," but I don't know if it was clear. Help!

> "He's Catholic. It's what he dreamed of his whole life."
> —LeAnn in *People*, on her bodyguard, whom she brought with her to the Vatican

P.J.P. II: Cardinal Benselmo begged me to introduce him to LeAnn. He said, You totally owe me, I voted for you. He *worships* LeAnn, he has a tape of her at eight years old on *Star Search*—he says that even then she was da bomb. I said, Okay, but don't gush, just treat her like a person, and so of course he starts speaking in tongues and pleading for an autograph, claiming it's for some abbess from Lake Como. I said, Please, Giancarlo, you are *so embarrassing* me! Why don't you just go say, like, 8,000 Hail Marys and prostrate yourself, but he wouldn't stop, he shoves a pen and his LeAnn Christmas CD at her and says, Please sign it "To My Very Favorite Servant of the Lord, XXX, OOO, You're Next!" As if!

> "I'm Baptist. I didn't quite get the whole feeling, but I totally respect [the Catholic] religion, and it was still really amazing." —LeAnn in *People*

P.J.P. II: LeAnn was just so poised and fun and thin—the baby fat is totally gone, it's just like I told Courtney Cox, it's very pious to give up carbs for Lent. I wanted to tell LeAnn that she has a major career ahead of her in both features and holiday specials involving duets with Clint Black, but then I thought, in the words of Our Savior, *Duh.* When she smiled, the whole apse just lit up, she was like Mother Teresa, only, how can I put this, less infinitely careworn and radiant with inner grace, but technically way cuter. Her eyes just got all crinkly in that majorly sunshiny way, and for that second all I could think was okay, maybe the Church could have done more to help out in the Second World War, but LeAnn *rocks.* Cardinal Benselmo was still grabbing my elbow, going, Ask her about Ricky Martin, but she was already on her way out, and I heard her murmur something to her bodyguard about where could she find "some fries and a Moon Pie in this town" and about how Italy seems "much bigger than it looks at Epcot." And then I had to get back to work, doing Pope stuff, you know, blessing key chains and Kennedy annulments, but from that day on I knew, I just totally knew, there *is* a God.

Teen Times

PAUL RUDNICK

Magazines such as *People*, *Vogue*, and *Cosmopolitan* have recently introduced a separate teen edition, aimed at a friskier demographic. It's only a matter of time before other magazines follow, offering their own youthful rethinks, completed with age-appropriate cover lines.

Teen Scientific American
  If the Universe Keeps Expanding, What Will It Wear?
  Cancer: Shut *Up!*
  Are the Ice Caps Melting? Blame Enrique!
  Penis Grafting—Is It the Answer for N'Sync?
  Is the Earth Over Two Billion Years Old—Like Your Dad?

Teen Tikkun
  Make Your Own Wailing Wall—Just Styrofoam
    and Post-its!
  Five Pounds by Purim—Lose That Arafat!
  Are All Jewish Girls As Pretty As Their Parents Claim?
    Our Survey Says Yes!

Which Backstreet Boy's Facial Hair Could Almost
   Be Orthodox?
Intermarriage: What If He's Only a Paralegal?

Teen U.S. News & World Report
Ethnic Deep Cleansing: Kiss Albanians and Blemishes
   Good-bye!
Britney vs. the Taliban: Oops, They Stoned Her to Death
Milosevic—Now He's Got Time for You!
Famine—Does the Weight *Stay* Off?
Is the Pope Catholic? Your Surprising Letters!

Teen National Geographic
Tribal Makeovers: It's Called Clothing
The Strange, Ugly People of Other Countries
Australia—Is It Too Far Away?
The Elephants of India—Of Course They're Lonely
The Pygmy Prom—Don't Worry About Your Hair

Teen National Review
Sex with a Republican—Your Best Ten Seconds Ever!
Abortion: You Could Be Killing Ricky Martin, Jr.
Sweatshops: Can't They Make Our Clothes Without
   Touching Them?
Don't Ask, Don't Tell—How It Saved My Parents' Marriage
12 Ways to Make Him Buy You a Handgun

Teen Psychology Today
Why Everybody Hates You—Duh, It's Called
   "They're Jealous"
Eating Disorders—Which Ones Really Work
Electroshock and Split Ends—We Tell You the Truth
Attention Deficit Disorder: The Article You Won't Finish

Gravity

It's easy talking about defying gravity when it's not around to hear all your tough talk. But what is gravity? Simply put—my favorite way—it's the force of attraction between all objects, not just between an object and the Earth. So there's no reason for the Earth to act so hoity-toity. The question then arises: If the force of gravity operates on all objects, why don't all the little skinny people get attracted to the big fat people? It might have something to do with *Vogue* magazine and those skinny models it likes so much, but if you ever saw one of them vomiting in the ladies room at a really expensive restaurant, well, you'd have some explaining to do yourself, if you're a man: What are you doing in the ladies' room? If, however, you are a woman, then more power to you. That's gravity.

It was Isaac Newton who discovered that a force is required to change the speed or direction of an object: There's no point in simply shouting at it. Newton realized that the force of gravity made that apple fall from a tree. But it couldn't make the apple into a pie. (Wouldn't that be something? An apple that just fell into some gravity-induced, pie-like form thanks to science. But it doesn't. Damn you, science.) Newton figured out that the force needed to push an object at a given acceleration rate was proportional to the object's mass. $F=MA$. And he did that on an empty stomach. No pie. Newton proposed that, with enough force, an artificial satellite could be put into orbit around the Earth. But he did not anticipate that the satellite would transmit such crappy TV shows. *Dharma and Greg*? Why?

—Randy Cohen

Fun with Names

TOM RUPRECHT

Did you know if tennis sensation Mary Pierce married *Friends* star Matthew Perry, she'd become Mary Perry? But wait, it gets even better!

If Perry's costar Jennifer Aniston married New Hampshire senator Bob Smith, she'd become Jennifer Smith. Just try saying that one three times fast!

Or how 'bout if Yoko Ono married James Coco and kept her name, she'd known as Yoko Ono!

And if Yoko Ono married Dave Grohl, she'd eventually break up the Foo Fighters.

Did you know if Björk married Björn Borg and took his name, she'd have to alert her bank and get new checks?

If rocker Liz Phair married former national security adviser Zbigniew Brzezinski, she'd become Mrs. Zbigniew Brzezinski. Now that's a mouthful!

Remember when Julia Roberts married Lyle Lovett? Man, that came out of nowhere.

If Star Jones married Ringo Starr, he would get arrested for bigamy—unless he divorced Barbara Bach first.

If Al Gore's wife Tipper left him for a stripper, the headline would maybe read: "Gore Remains Focused on Campaign Despite Marital Woes."

If Lynn Swann married former Red Sox outfielder Fred Lynn, the ceremony would have to take place in Hawaii or Vermont.

And finally, if Cher married Charles Nelson Reilly, divorced him and married coach Pat Riley, then divorced him and married Patrick Ewing, divorced him and married deceased business tycoon Ewing Kauffman, she'd be known as Cher!

Let's Go: Jupiter!

TOM RUPRECHT

Thanks to the booming economy, more Americans than ever are expected to travel this summer. The prospect of crowded national parks and the unstable situation in Europe have led many families to look elsewhere when planning their annual getaway.

Jupiter, long dismissed as the ugly duckling of the gaseous planets, has undergone a Cleveland-like rejuvenation in the past few years. With a sparkling new ball park opening next year and the Republicans eyeing the planet for their 2004 convention, Jupiter's future is bright (or as bright as can be expected for a cloud-covered orb located 480 million miles from the sun). But a trip to Jupiter does require planning, so here are a few things to keep in mind before leaving.

Getting There: From Cape Canaveral, board a Ulysses 3 pod attached to a Titan IV rocket. Use the Venetian gravitational pull to "slingshot" you toward Jupiter. Allow six years for the trip. Bear in mind that flying to Jupiter can be expensive ($27.4 billion off-peak), but travelers take heart—Kiwi has announced it will soon be flying five daily nonstops out of La Guardia for $219.

Weather: The planet's outer region averages a chilly -244°F. The temperature rises to 20,000°K as you sink to the core, however, so wear layers! Asthma sufferers should note that the Jovian atmosphere is a stuffy 90 percent hydrogen.

Getting Around: Much as a Denver tourist needs a day or two to adjust to the altitude, Jupiter's crushing gravity leaves many newcomers feeling slightly "sluggish." Visitors should count on setting aside five hours for every two feet of movement.

Night Life: The Jovian magnetosphere emits 100 trillion watts of power (the equivalent of eight million nuclear explosions!), which has been known to encourage tourists to stay in and be "couch potatoes."

What to See: Jupiter has a mass of 1.9×10^{27} kg and can house 1,300 Earths. Many visitors become frustrated by their inability to "see it all." The smart traveler goes in with the understanding that he or she won't be able to do everything and instead finds an interesting five-foot area to explore in the few nanoseconds before perishing.

Locals: As you may or may not know, Jupiter is inhabited by millions of reptilian aliens. According to several movies made on the topic, these bug-eyed creatures are extremely hostile, possess superhuman strength, and have the ability to read human minds. Tourists are therefore advised to carry traveler's checks and to not wear flashy jewelry.

"Will I Be Killed by Ionized Particles?" Yes.

Did You Know? The planet's noxious ammonia clouds create an environment not unlike our idea of hell.

The Great Red Spot: With its distinctive look and Olde World charm, this centuries-old hurricane is considered by many travelers to be a "must see." Some, however, are put off by the 400-kilometer-per-hour winds and sulfurous rain. (Bring a poncho!)

Tipping: Same as Earth.

Leaving: Jupiter's mammoth gravitational pull requires an escape velocity of 133,000 miles per hour, encouraging many visitors to "stay."

In the Spirit of
Full Disclosure

JAY RUTTENBERG

Although this is a review of Maurice Chandek's *Essays, Letters, and Cocktails*, in the spirit of full disclosure I should confess that Chandek and I have known one another for decades, having met while employed as mere peons at the grand old *New Yorker* of Andy White and Wolcott Gibbs. Surely our kinship will not hinder my objectivity toward Chandek's work, however, for his words are like autumn leaves sprinkled on a spring sidewalk, regardless of any brethren status. This collection of Murry's short fiction, dramas, and poems, plus his sole novella (the long out-of-print, idyllically crafted *Girls Who Spit*), shows the enormously gifted writer in full command of his tools.

Oh, Chandek! How his prose sings! Just take the following passage: "Her Adam's apple bobs in full awareness of the incipient dawn." It is written in terse, flowing English, with deft punctuation and spelling, and is but a snippet of the exquisite essay "Lost Virginity: Big Reward." The piece describes his wife, Sarah Chandek, known to her friends as Barnett Berkowitz. (In the interest of full disclosure, it was I who introduced the Chandeks when we were vacationing in the Riviera shortly after the war.) Indeed, Sarah was a favorite target of Chandek's often venomous pen. During their heated romantic spats—of which there were many—the writer would retreat into his scholarly lair for weeks, months, even fortnights, ailing his sorrows with both prose and bourbon. (It should be pointed out that I took Sarah as my mistress in the midst of the "Flying Fifties," causing the Chandeks great marital unrest that resulted in some of the author's most chilling prose, including "The Smirking Clown" and "Sarah Sleeps with Book Reviewers.")

Maurice Chandek's relationships with the fairer sex (and, it is rumored, with males, as well—Chandek and I experimented with homosexuality in the "Salacious Sixties," testing its affects on lab rats and baboons) was nothing short of volatile. Perhaps no piece reflects this more than "Masturbating with Scissors," which sums up marital ennui with the almost quaint aphorism: "Her hair grew tired." (I believe that this oft-quoted line refers to the brief reoccurrence of my liaison with gentle Sarah, at the time pregnant with the couple's second son.)

But to really understand the importance of Chandek's writing, one must turn to his dramas. For it is here, in such pieces as *The Amorous Detective* and *Professor Desan's Bout of Goodwill*, that his words truly spring to life. This particularly rings true in the latter work, which won Chandek 1961's Gold Medal of the Institute. (I was, indeed, up for the same prize and favored by most critics as the more worthy candidate. Typically, the committee failed to recognize my talent, largely because I did not take half the panel to bed, as Chandek most definitely did.) Drama hounds will find no better portrait of suburban solitude than in the third act of *Professor Desan*.

DESAN: You know, Jim, you are not likely to find good tuna fish in the Hills.

JIM: I know, Professor. I know.

DESAN: Then why must you make that face?

JIM: Because I can, Professor.
DESAN: It is now clear to me that you are a fool.
(*Professor Desan's Bout of Goodwill*, Act III, Scene 2)

Even the most casual, poorly educated reader surely will pick up the overwhelming sense of doom the playwright drapes over this scene, not to mention the drama's thick layer of irony: to start with, it is widely known that the finest tuna fish can be found in the Hills, the very place the Professor and his blunder-buss companion identify as a capitol of *un*desirable tuna. What's more, Chandek's adamant refusal to utilize a double exclamation point—clearly needed in the quoted passage's fourth line—reflects the suicidal despondency enveloping his life at the time of this play's conception. (It is both imperative and exigent to explain that this aforementioned despondency resulted when Chandek discovered his testicles to be considerably smaller than my own.)

But at the end of the day, there is perhaps no better summation of Chandek's career as a dramatist than Patricia Wainwright's famous polemic, culled from her 1976 book of criticism: "Chandek will never realize his full potential as a writer until he lays off the Scottish whores." (Wainwright, *Collected Criticism*, 1976. [Full disclosure: I shared a bed with Ms. Wainwright sporadically throughout the 1960s. In fact, without my adept guidance and impressive connections, she would still be writing obits for a Salt Lake City weekly. Seeing that we were together at the time of the above-quoted review's initial publication—and considering that I served as Ms. Wainwright's veritable ghostwriter throughout our steamy affair—it is most likely my pen that should be held responsible for the quote.])

Where his dramas drew tears of laughter, Chandek's verse often drew tears of joy. Innocuous yet bold, his words skipped indelibly across the page, particularly in such noted works as "Grandpa Can't Parallel Park" and "The Handsome Fly." (Although it is widely held that these two pieces are among the finest works of the "& Found Generation," a simple glance at my own "My Father, My Proctologist" by even the least informed, most obtuse reader will surely sway the reader's opinion toward my corner.) Poetry, they say, is the true test of a *writer*, and those heralded italics are clearly worthy of Chandek's words. (For your information, I am most certainly *not* wearing any pants!) After all, what is verse, if not the opium of the masses? (I am not, nor have I ever been, a drug addict, although I do find myself madly drawn to Granny Smith apples; I am also quite fond of muenster cheese, but only when traveling.)

We will never know the true motivation for Chandek's eventual withdrawal from society, though one would suspect that the death verdict placed on his head by nine prominent Arabic dictators factored into the decision. (I get a cheap thrill when my penis accidentally brushes against the inner ring of the toilet bowl; I am not, however, homosexual.) Whether Chandek is still writing "for the drawer" is similarly subject to debate. (Although my seventh decade of life is rapidly encroaching, I am still not sure whether to feel embarrassed when I loudly fart at the urinal.) What we do know, however, is that American letters would be dramatically different—and dramatically weaker—had Maurice Chandek never touched his pen to page. For that alone, this collection is a worthy addition to our national heritage. (Disclosure: Metallica rules!!!)

The Solomon Bar Mitzvah

JAY RUTTENBERG

[Letter from Burbee Party Planning
to Klugar Management and Booking]

Dear Mr. Klugar:

   I am a Chicago-area party coordinator who special-
izes in weddings and bar mitzvahs. I am writing to
request the entertainment services of the rock musician
Beck (who I understand is under your management) for
the night of September 19 to perform at the bar mitzvah party of my client, Stephen Solomon. The party
will be taking place in the Grand Ballroom at Chicago's
Four Seasons Hotel. Dr. and Mrs. Solomon are willing
to pay your client's regular fee for a 20-minute performance; we are willing to negotiate.

Sincerely,
Sam Burbee
Burbee Party Planning
Highland Park, IL

[Letter from Klugar Management and
Booking to Burbee Party Planning]

Dear Mr. Burbee:
　My client, who typically eschews private functions,
will not be available for the given date.

Warmly,
Jeff Klugar
Klugar Management
and Booking
Los Angeles, CA

[Letter from Burbee Party Planning
to Klugar Management and Booking]

Dear Mr. Klugar:
　If I am not mistaken, Beck has two Chicago con-
certs scheduled for October 16 and October 18, leaving
your client free on the day and night of Saturday,
October 17. I have contacted the Four Seasons and
B'nai Torah (the Solomons' synagogue, where the bar
mitzvah service itself is taking place) and have tentatively rescheduled the event for October 17 in order to
accommodate Beck's itinerary.
　Please note that although the Solomon bar mitzvah is technically a "closed" function, the guest of
honor is donating 15 percent of his gift money to various Israeli charities. Furthermore, the Jesse White
Tumblers (a gymnastic troupe composed of inner-city
Chicago youth) are booked to perform at the beginning
of the party; my client has agreed to grant these urban
artists seats at the rear of the ballroom for Beck's
performance, thus incorporating a gritty Cabrini
Green flavor of diversity to your client's concert. As a

bonus, we would welcome MTV News cameras into the party so that Beck may use the performance as a quirky publicity platform—if, of course, you are so inclined.

In addition to your client's regular performance fee, the Solomons are prepared to offer the following:

- Beck will be slated as the party's main attraction, receiving billing immediately under the bar mitzvah boy himself.
- Beck will be granted the fourth toast of the evening, following only the bar mitzvah boy's parents, paternal grandmother, and Rabbi Aronson.
- Beck will be featured in the actual Saturday morning bar mitzvah service at B'nai Torah, receiving a prominent "thank you" at the end of Mr. Solomon's speech to the congregation. He will also be granted the third aliyah, following Dr. & Mrs. Solomon and Aunt Rose & Uncle Jim.
- During the traditional singing of "Hava Nagilah" by the bar mitzvah party's dance band, Beck will be raised on a chair as high as—but no higher than—the bar mitzvah boy, his parents, his maternal grandfather, and his cousin, Scott Solomon.

I hope these conditions are found satisfactory to your client's needs.

Sincerely,
Sam Burbee
Burbee Party Planning
Highland Park, IL

[Letter from Klugar Management and
Booking to Burbee Party Planning]

Dear Mr. Burbee:

I have gone over your offer and conferred with my client's inner circle. Before any contracts are signed, I was hoping to reexamine a few provisions:

- Although the bar mitzvah boy will obviously receive top billing at both service and party, we were hoping to restructure the latter event as a "Beck" theme party, thus guaranteeing that my client receives proper billing. My client's name should appear prominently on the party invitations and my client's image and name should appear on any souvenir T-shirts, boxer shorts, mugs, etc.
- MTV cameras will not be necessary, however we would like to arrange for a photographer and reporter from *The Face* to be in attendance for a possible cover story. The Solomon family and their guests must be willing to be incorporated into the journalist's piece and cooperate with any photography and interview requests.
- During the bar mitzvah service itself, we would like Beck to perform the second, rather than the third, aliyah, so that he is not upstaged by Aunt Rose & Uncle Jim.

For similar reasons, we would like to arrange for Beck to make the first, rather than fourth, toast during the party itself. We assume the Rabbi, parents, and grandmother will understand.

I hope this can be worked out.

Warmly,
Jeff Klugar
Klugar Management
and Booking
Los Angeles, CA

**[Letter from Burbee Party Planning
to Klugar Management and Booking]**

Dear Mr. Klugar:

I have met with the Solomon family and they are
willing to agree to the following:

- *The Face* magazine coverage will be welcomed.
- The theme of the party will be based around
  Beck, however we feel that it would be inappropriate to issue invitations advertising it as such to
  the Solomon's adult guests. Thus, only the children's invitations will mention your client's
  name. We feel this compromise to be more than
  adequate, as these youth-directed invitations will
  target a crucial demographic group with significant disposable income.
- We can offer Beck the second aliyah at B'nai
  Torah, however we cannot guarantee him the first
  toast of the evening, as that spot was promised to
  the bar mitzvah boy's paternal grandmother, Bubbi
  Evelyn, over a decade ago.

> Sincerely,
> Sam Burbee
> Burbee Party Planning
> Highland Park, IL

**[Letter from Klugar Management and
Booking to "Bubbi" Evelyn Solomon]**

Dear Bubbi Evelyn:

I am the manager and booker for Beck, who, as you
probably know, is slated as a possible performer at your
grandson's bar mitzvah this fall.

At the moment, the sole wrinkle in my client's contract involves the placement of his toast during the bar mitzvah party. It is my understanding that you have been promised the premiere toast of the evening; we were hoping to iron out some sort of arrangement with you to allow my client to give the first toast, and you the second.

Please contact me at your earliest convenience.

Warmly,
Jeff Klugar
Klugar Management
and Booking
Los Angeles, CA

[Telephone message left on the answering machine of Dr. and Mrs. Richard Solomon by "Bubbi" Evelyn Solomon]

Hi, it's Bubbi Evelyn. I got a letter in the morning post from—let's see here—it looks like somebody named Beck Klugerman, and it involves the toast at Steve's bar mitzvah. I'm a bit perplexed, the print on this letter is terribly small, and you know my eyes. Could you ring me after the rates change tonight? Hope everybody's well. Say hi to the kids. Bye now.

[Letter from Ted Powers, Attorney at Law, to "Bubbi" Evelyn Solomon]

Dear Mrs. Solomon:

As the personal attorney for your son, Dr. Richard Solomon, I am writing to inform you that you have been bumped to the second toast at the bar mitzvah party of your grandson, Stephen Solomon. Please note that any alleged contract you may have and/or might have had regarding any possible or potential first toast status was strictly informal and therefore utterly and absolutely nonbinding. Please note that any legal action you may seek against Dr. Richard Solomon and/or Stephen Solomon and/or Beck Hanson will be hereby nullified and negated.

Please sign the enclosed documents confirming your "second" toast status.

Thank you for your cooperation and acquiescence,

Ted Powers,
Attorney at Law
Silbersher, Cohen
& Schwartz
Chicago, IL

[E-mail from Burbee Party Planning to Klugar Management and Booking]

Klugar,
It looks like Bubbi's caving on this toast deal . . . So it's a go?
Sam
Burbee Party Planning

P.S. I can have my assistant fax you the final contracts as early as this afternoon.

[Bar mitzvah invitations sent to 240 close
friends and classmates of Stephen Solomon]

Don't Be a Loser!!!

Electric Slide on Down to Stephen

Solomon's Bar Mitzvah

It'll be a "Beck" of a Blast!

Where It's At?
The Four Seasons Hotel, Chicago
Saturday, October 17
7:00 P.M.

Black Tie Preferred

And don't forget the service
(featuring DGC recording artist
Beck **on the fourth aliyah!)**

Where It's At?
B'nai Torah
Highland Park, Ill
Saturday Morning
9:30 Sharp

So RSVP "YESSSS!!!" and join Steve's
family and friends as we celebrate his
"BECK MITZVAH!"

Questions Answered
and Unanswered

DR. SCIENCE

Q: Where can I find a barracuda to eat me and, if they don't eat people, what can I feed it?

—Michael, Freehold, New Jersey

A: Your desire to be eaten by a barracuda is not that unusual. Psychologists report that one tenth of one percent of the populace fantasizes about being torn to ribbons by a predator. I know I sometimes imagine a grizzly or polar bear having his way with me, but that's only after I've eaten greasy pizza and washed it down with grapefruit juice. The good news is, just because we have these thoughts it doesn't mean we're sick, or should be institutionalized. The bad news is that a large percentage of us do find a way to realize this fantasy, and come to a horrible end. So stay away from aquariums, okay?

Q: My clock radio has three settings, On, Off, and Al. Who is Al, and why does he have his own setting?

—Tim, South Saint Paul, Minnesota

A: When we sleep, we all become the same person. A balding, slump shouldered, heavyset guy named Al. As a government worker, Al spends most of his time on and off the job asleep. If you have a sadistic streak, you can jolt Al from his slumber by switching your clock to that setting. For a few seconds, Al is shocked from his chair and thrown to the floor, where he twitches and jerks, in horrible pain. Seconds later, he returns to his chair, where he sinks back into a deep sleep. By the way, misuse of the "Al" feature on clocks is a felony in most states.

Q: When I erase an eraser, I still get the little eraser tailings. Shouldn't I be destroying matter?

—Zach, Montreal, Quebec

A: You are destroying matter, but it's reappearing as fast as you can destroy it, albeit in a different form. If you'd examine the tailings under a microscope, you'd see that they are brine shrimp. Dead, dusty brine shrimp, from millions of years ago. These were created when the asteroid plowed into the ocean just off Yucatan, ending all life as we know it. All that matter was taken to a large warehouse in New Jersey, from whence it is slowly reappearing into this dimension, whenever anyone erases something.

Q: How could the ancient Greeks time those races in the Olympics with sundials?   —Zac, Atlanta, Georgia

A: Sundials work great on really slow races. Often the Greeks would monitor a weeklong race between a slug and a beetle. As long as the sun shone, they'd have split/day timing of the event. Many times the contestants would have already died under the blazing Greek sun by the time the race ended. The invention of the clock in the Middle Ages made shorter races possible. The new atomic clocks allow scientists to race subatomic particles. Is this progress? I'm not sure.

Q: Why is it when you plug in two of the same lightbulbs, one always burns out faster than the other?

—Meredith, Oak Park, Illinois

A: If this weren't the case, then they would all either burn out at the same time, which would be an amazing coincidence, never burn out, which would be a miracle, or not light at all, which would be cause for a lawsuit. To avoid these extreme outcomes, light bulbs take the middle road and behave in a moderate and predictable way. This is probably why lightbulbs were recently voted "Most Boring Household Appliance," beating toasters and hair dryers for that coveted honor.

Q: Why don't plants have a nervous system?
—Joan, Indiana, Pennsylvania

A: They used to, but then modern life took its toll on the leafy, green sensitives, and overnight hospital psych wards were overrun with drooping petunias and frazzled tulips. Indoor plants melted down faster than their outdoor cousins, although soybeans took the honor of being "The Most Psychotic Row Crop." It was only after the introduction of airborne tranquilizers that U.S. agriculture recovered. Eventually, schoolchildren paid minimum wage removed the nervous systems from all plants, leaving us a pleasantly lobotomized plant kingdom, where Brussels sprouts refuse to grow up and endive and iceberg lettuce live in harmony.

Q: What is Ultrasound, and how is it used in a hospital?
—Bernard, Edmonton, United Kingdom

A: Ultrasound is a better class of sound, using prime decibels that are free from all distortion. You can pump an Ultrasound version of Twisted Sister at top volume through cheap headphones and suffer only minimal hearing damage. Perform the same experiment using Lawrence Welk and normal sound, and you'll be stone deaf in a matter of minutes. The reason hospitals use Ultrasound is because it's more expensive. If they can document the cost of using only the best sound waves, then mark up that cost 200 or 300 percent and add administrative fees on top of that . . . well, it's easy to see why your doctor lives in a mansion and you grovel in a mobile home.

Q: When you are working alone in your laboratory, do you hum to yourself, and if so, what do you hum?

—Cindy, Ames, Iowa

A: I'm partial to the Ames Brothers' greatest hits. The Kingston Trio wear me out after a while, but early Joni Mitchell puts me in a contemplative state. I've stood at the window, holding a Florence flask full to the brim with some deadly brew, and found myself humming wildly, lost in a hippie trance. It's Laurel Canyon, 1969, "The Last Time I Saw Richard," I'm young, talented, and nobody loves me enough. When I come to, I find that I've spilled corrosive acid onto my shoes, and the radiation detectors are whooping like the Fourth of July. So you see, with a scientist, even simple humming can end all life as we know it.

Q: When I make ice cubes out of distilled water, a stalagmite appears at the center of each cube, pointing upward like a handle. This doesn't happen with tap water. Why?

—Tom, Iowa City, Iowa

A: You probably have amoebic contamination of your distilled water supply. Those little handles may be the sex organs of a protozoan, paramecium, or even *Giardia*. For heaven's sake, don't use them in mixed drinks. Tap water in most cities is so full of caustic chemicals that even though these parasites are still present, they're dead. I filter my tap water through a reverse osmosis screen, then run it by a proton beam and finally, distill it in a perfect vacuum. Still, it often tastes like swimming pool water, and leaves a scale on the coffee maker. Lower your standards, and close your eyes when you drink. That's the easiest solution.

Q: My normal vision is terrible, but when I wear even a cheap pair of goggles underwater, I can see all the way to the end of the pool. Why?   —Tom, Cleveland, Ohio

A: You may not have anything wrong with your vision. Many vision disorders are actually psychosomatic. It could be that as a child you saw one too many movies involving snow blindness, or blowing desert sand. An unconscious desire to suffer along with the characters in these movies has caused you to manifest chronic, hysterical myopia combined with acute psychosomatic astigmatism. When you're finally underwater, all relaxed and giddy, your mind forgets about imposing this mental disability, and you see the world as it really is . . . a blue concrete tub with black lines on the floor.

Q: What are some flame-retardant fabrics, and why? If you put them on will they blow up, like when people go up in flames? —Paris, New Castle, Delaware

Q: Why is it that a *new* bar of soap makes so much more lather than an *old* bar of soap? —Don, Pittsburgh, Pennsylvania

Q: Can you get a sunburn from the moon?
—Gary, Denver, Colorado

Q: I am currently living on a shoestring budget. How much more money can I get with a bootstrap?
—Julie, Grove City, Ohio

Q: I've heard that if you lose one of your senses, nature tends to compensate. I've recently lost my sense of decency. What kind of compensation should I be expecting?
—Charles, Dallas, Texas

Q: What's Dr. Frankenstein doing with that Tesla coil that's in every horror movie laboratory? He never seems to be using it. It just sits there and looks cool.
—Dave, Milwaukee, Wisconsin

Q: Can you get me the recipe for nail polish?
                              —Jami, Holyoke, Massachusetts

Q: I have always heard the phrase "robbing Peter to pay Paul." If that is truly the case, why not just have Peter pay Paul directly so one doesn't have to commit any illegal acts?
                              —M.W., Oklahoma City, Oklahoma

Q: If you traveled through space at the speed of light for one light year, wouldn't a dog travel seven times as far?
                              —Jay, Omaha, Nebraska

Q: Would you like to earn an extra $700 a week . . . $2,800 a month just by mailing our business circulars from your home?
                              —Me, Harrisonville, Pennsylvania

Q: Is love worth the pain?   —Lauren, St. Louis, Missouri

Q: I have a cabin in Europe 1,100 feet high. If all the snow in the world melts is there any safety at 1,100 feet on the Norwegian border?   —Larry, Toronto

Q: Under what different conditions can the human body act as a battery? Can you tell me some websites where I can find that information? Peace!   —GDBug, Cleveland, Ohio

Q: You know the indestructible little black box that's found on airplanes . . . why can't they make the airplane out of the same material? And why is it when you're driving and looking for an address, you turn down the volume on the radio?
                              —Daniel, Ontario

Q: Will wonders never cease?   —Jay, Omaha, Nebraska

Q: Dr. Science, why do men get HERnias and Women get HISterectomies? —Frank, Ames, Iowa

Q: I'm giving a presentation on crayfish behavior. Do you have any short crayfish jokes that you can give me to "break the silence" in the auditorium. Please ASAP.
—Alisa, Brooklyn, New York

Q: Can you give me some tips on atoms?
—Brandon, Westminster, Colorado

Q: Do I look fat in this? —Karen, San Diego, California

Q: Why are there no placebo-controlled tests of placebos published? This drug has been shown to cause virtually every symptom known to man during 50 years of testing and yet, the FDA hasn't taken it off the market. Nor have studies addressed the obvious differences in efficacy between brand-name and generic placebo. Why aren't our Olympic athletes being tested for placebo use? —Brian, Healdsburg, California

Q: Should I get this checked?
—Kevin, San Diego, California

Q: Why did the ditto paper (from the 70s) seem to smell so good? It was reminiscent of fresh fruit or something. I think it was the solvents used, buy why universally do we remember the smell? —Greg, Cleveland, Ohio

Q: Could time curve around enough for dinosaurs to come back from extinction? Also, are there bathrooms in time machines, and how do you pee when going backwards?
—Robbie, age six, Annandale, Virginia

Q: During chemistry lab, while filtering the product, the laboratory coat of another student catches against your equipment knocking the glass and smashing it, spilling your product onto the bench. What emergency procedures should you follow in order to save your grade?

—Kate Busby, Nottingham, England

A: Quick, grab a beaker of nitric acid and pour it over your head. Then shout "There are some things man should not know!" and grab the most expensive piece of machinery around and throw it out the window. Then pretend to faint. When you "come to" say "where am I?" in a dreamy, childish voice. They'll cancel class for the day, whisk you off to the infirmary, and any points you might have had deducted will be moot. If anyone hints that you should pay for the machine you destroyed, give a wan smile and mention the long-term effects of chromium poisoning, and your uncle, the personal injury lawyer.

Q: I am a Form Five student in Hong Kong. How are the blood pressure, muscle contraction, sense organ, nerves, and hormone system affected when a person plays an exciting game, e.g., bungee jump? —Kevin, Hong Kong

A: Bungee jumping is indeed, one of the most exciting games you can play, but it has almost no affect on blood pressure, hormone levels, or the nervous system. All those things simply go into shock in the face of such an absurd activity. As the ground approaches your face at two hundred miles per hour, there's really no way you can react. Now with Ping-Pong, you get all sweaty, your heart begins to race, you breathe hard, and if you're like me, you get that weird metallic taste in your mouth when you sense you're losing. A good game of Ping-Pong sends my hormone levels through the roof!

Q: I have noticed that when I first start to exercise my mouth gets dry, but after a while it is moist again, so I am wondering: does the inside of your mouth sweat? If so, can you recommend an appropriate antiperspirant? (I wouldn't want to offend my fellow joggers!)

                      —Dave Perkins, Marshalltown, Iowa

Q: If I were to open my freezer door, and then the door to my hot 450 degree oven simultaneously, would not the warm and cold fronts converge in my kitchen, creating miniature tornadoes on the linoleum floor? —David, River Hills, Wisconsin

Q: I am going to buy a product called an Ion Ray Gun. I would like to know if this can actually work or if it's a waste of money. Here's the description that the website says about it. Description—"Ions are charged particles of energy and this weapon is capable of propelling millions of ions considerable distances. The completed device will induce shocks, charge capacitors, light lights and more. All at a distance without direct contact. Operates on (8) AA batteries. It can induce painful but harmless electric shocks. Can induce shocks from up to 20 feet away under ideal conditions." Thank you!

                      —Sean, Antioch, California

Q: Is there any promise in answering the world's energy needs with perpetual motion machines, like the toy rooster that—despite not having a battery—will dip his beak in a vodka tonic for an infinite amount of time?

                      —T. J. Murphy, Brooklyn, New York

Q: The theory that opposites attract has always proven to hold true for me, but also seems to be the root problem beneath all of my troubled relationships. Is there some way that I can reverse my polarity?   —Wendy, Newark, Delaware

Top 100 Years

1. 1776	27. 1857	53. 1972	79. 1930
2. 1492	28. 1863	54. 1973	80. 1840
3. 1945	29. 1919	55. 1985	81. 1940
4. 1781	30. 1846	56. 1986	82. 1750
5. 1789	31. 1777	57. 1987	83. 1850
6. 1968	32. 1886	58. 1988	84. 1950
7. 1918	33. 1974	59. 1989	85. 1951
8. 1865	34. 1969	60. 1872	86. 1851
9. 1939	35. 1936	61. 1990	87. 1751
10. 1952	36. 1921	62. 1999	88. 1651
11. 1933	37. 1971	63. 1893	89. 1551
12. 1783	38. 1892	64. 1894	90. 1451
13. 1803	39. 1922	65. 1795	91. 1351
14. 1790	40. 1923	66. 1796	92. 1251
15. 1963	41. 1924	67. 1897	93. 1151
16. 1981	42. 1925	68. 1997	94. 1152
17. 1900	43. 1926	69. 1898	95. 1154
18. 1820	44. 1821	70. 1799	96. 1164
19. 1796	45. 1822	71. 1800	97. 1998
20. 1941	46. 1823	72. 1493	98. 1860
21. 1946	47. 1824	73. 1494	99. 1960
22. 1964	48. 1825	74. 1612	100. 1060
23. 1913	49. 1826	75. 1613	
24. 1812	50. 1868	76. 1614	
25. 1927	51. 1901	77. 1491	—Will Durst
26. 1787	52. 1903	78. 1830	

Three Meaningless Fables

NELL SCOVELL

MEANINGLESS FABLE #1

In a faraway kingdom, depending upon where you are, lived a King who was overly protective of his daughter. He decreed she would only marry a man who could prove himself worthy by solving a riddle.

Now the Princess herself was quite ordinary. Pretty, but not beautiful. Smart, but not brilliant. She would have settled for much less. But since her father was also her King, she had little choice but to follow his commands.

On her eighteenth birthday, the King announced the contest. After consulting with mathematicians, alchemists, and philosophers, he agreed to gladly give his daughter's hand in marriage to the man who could answer the following riddle: "One plus one equals . . . what?" To be fair, he would give each man three tries to win. To be unfair, he would behead any man who missed all three.

Now because the Princess was sweet, but not to-die-for, there wasn't a big rush on riddle-solvers. A village idiot guessed the answer was 23. Then 34. Then 1,592. He was promptly beheaded.

Years passed and the Princess remained single.

Then one day, a Prince from a kingdom far away from the faraway kingdom arrived. He was strong and brave with a friendly smile and twinkling eyes. One barely even noticed his thinning hair. He was invited to join the King and the Princess for dinner at the court. And even though he was tired, he forced himself to go.

And there he fell in love.

The Princess loved him back immediately. Between courses, the Prince asked the King for permission to marry his daughter. The court gathered round as the King informed the prince of the rules: three misses, no head. The prince nervously agreed, but felt a little put on the spot. The riddlemaster pulled out a scroll. "Here we go," he said. "One plus one equals . . . what?"

A hush fell over the crowd.

"That's it?" said the Prince. "That's the riddle?" He laughed and replied, "That's easy. One plus one equals two."

Now some had long suspected it was a trick question, but no one wanted the embarrassment of hearing the King shout, "Wrong." Which is exactly what he did.

"Wrong?" The Prince couldn't believe it. Then he hit his hand on his forehead. Of course! It wouldn't be a riddle if the answer were obvious. Now the idiot had made his guesses in rapid succession. But the Prince was no idiot. He decided to ponder the question.

For the next three months, the Prince lived at the court. Each day he would walk with the Princess. They discovered they had similar taste in music and art. They even liked the same court jesters. Over time, they grew close. So close, that one day the Prince revealed that even though they were not wed, he felt as if they were one.

"That's it!" shrieked the Princess. "You have discovered the answer to the riddle in the purest and most heartfelt of ways!" The two rushed back to the court and summoned the king and the riddlemaster.

The riddlemaster unfurled his scroll. "Here we go," he said. "One plus one equals . . . what?"

"Mathematically, one joined with one equals two," said the Prince. "But love defies reason and, matrimonially, one joined with one remains one."

A hush fell over the crowd.

"Wrong!" declared the King. The Princess swooned.

Over the next few months, the Prince tore at what remained of his hair. The stakes were high now. Not only because he missed twice, but because he was now deeply, truly, sincerely in love with the Princess. So in love that even though they weren't supposed to, they did.

Two more months passed and the Princess discovered that she was with child. Celebration quickly turned to dismay. She couldn't hide it forever. "What shall we do?" she entreated the Prince. "Soon we will be three."

A thousand bolts of lightning hit the prince. It was so obvious. The two rushed back to the court and once again summoned the King and the riddlemaster.

"Here we go," said the riddlemaster, unfurling as usual. "One plus one equals . . . what?"

The Prince looked at the Princess with her slightly bulging belly. His eyes brimmed with love as he slowly and confidently answered, "A man and a woman who marry do not join as one, do not stay as two, but will become three."

A hush fell over the court. It all made perfect sense. The King's lip began to tremble. He had never felt so disappointed in his life.

The Prince was wrong. He was beheaded. Six months later, the Princess gave birth to twins.

MEANINGLESS FABLE #2

In a woods near a town not far from a city lived a Miser. A very good Miser. People came from all over the world to ask him how to save money. "Don't spend it," he would bark. He was a Miser, not a wise man.

He made his money trapping and selling furs, specializing in the skins of little baby bears, which were very popular at the time. For each skin, he received ten gold porchkins. And each porchkin went into a pit dug deep into the floor of his meager cottage. The pit was covered with a board that fastened with a lock. The key hung on a string around his neck.

Every day, after work, the Miser would wash the little baby bear blood off his hands, take out his key, unlock the board, and enter the pit. At first, he would be quiet, respecting the solemn place of worship. But then when he could no longer contain himself, the Miser would whoop and holler. The delight! The ecstasy! Moneymoneymoney! Not for a second did he believe money could buy happiness. Money *was* happiness.

But that wasn't all that made the Miser happy. He also had a daughter, a beautiful little girl, born the very moment that her mother expired. He called her Audrey so her name would begin with gold. And she grew up worthy of the name with hair as yellow as spun 24-karat and a disposition as good as you know what.

Had he not been a Miser, her father would have spoiled her. Instead, he taught her how to cook, clean the house, groom the horse, tend the garden, thatch the roof, and skin little baby bears. By the age of 16, Audrey completely ran the household. The only thing the Miser wouldn't let her near was the key that opened the lock to the gold. In fact, she had never even seen a porchkin.

That's why he was so surprised when she came home one Christmas, eyes glowing bright and handed him a gift of an expensively carved doorknob. The note attached read, "To my dear dear father, whom I love with all my heart." The Miser looked up from the note.

"Thief!" he shouted. "You have been in my pit, raiding my porchkins!"

"No, I haven't, father," she exclaimed, and pulled off her cap to reveal a shiny and nicked head where golden curls once tumbled. "I sold my hair to buy you this."

"Oh, daughter," he cried, his heart melting. He hugged her tight. Never had he loved her more and truly he felt sorry that he had not even considered buying her a gift—not even a comb—that year.

Winter turned bitterly cold. Audrey never complained but the combination of a drafty house, no heat, and a bald head proved too much for her. She fell deep into sickness. She coughed. She moaned. She spit up blood. She could barely even thatch the roof anymore. It got so bad, her father even noticed.

He was horrified at how thin and pale Audrey had grown. Her cough, which had always been so bright and gay, had become coarse and phlegmatic. He was just about to order her to lie down when she crumpled to the floor.

For the next three days, death hovered at the door. The Miser cradled his daughter's stubbly head and prayed to God to save her. Each day, she got worse. Finally on the third night, he knew it was time for drastic action. He opened up his money pit, grabbed two porchkins and went to town to fetch the Physician. Did it pain the Miser to part with his precious gold? The truth is . . .

No. His daughter was more precious.

The Physician arrived just in time. Five minutes later, he said, and the patient would have been lost. Smelling salts and an herbal wrap retrieved her from the place beyond. The Miser wept for joy. It was a miracle. He embraced the Physician as he was leaving and kissed him to show his gratitude. The Physician said he would have preferred a tip. The Miser said *that* would have been another miracle.

Audrey soon recovered. The rosy color crept back into her cheeks and she fussed around the cottage with the spirit of one who thought she would never have the chance to clean house again. It was so good to be alive. She felt more alert than ever. That's why she couldn't help but notice how her father's own wet, hacking cough was growing stronger and wetter every day. Finally, one day, he keeled over.

Audrey ran to his slumped body in a panic. His breathing

was slow and unsteady. She thought she might revive him by shouting, "Father, look, someone has dropped a coin!" He didn't even blink. This was serious.

Now Audrey had not been faced with many decisions in her life. As she held her father in her arms, she knew she had to do something, but didn't know what. Just then she saw the key dangling from his throat. She scoffed. How could a key help? Then she remembered. Her father guarded that key with his life. That was it! The secret of life and death was obviously in the pit. Within seconds, Audrey had the lock unfastened, raised the board and entered the money pit for the first time in her life. And here's what she saw—

Piles and piles of gold porchkins. Piles as high as her shoulder, next to piles as high as her head, next to piles that reached the ceiling. She had never seen such a sight before. And so she stood there, gaping at the mounds of gleaming metal coins . . . and she was completely unimpressed.

Having only the vaguest idea of what money was for, Audrey filled her pockets and set off to find the Physician. When she reached him, he was just starting his evening meal and in no mood to save the life of a man who had stiffed him on a tip. Audrey reached into her pocket and said, "Please, sir, please. Won't you find it in your heart to help my father?" And she pulled out at least a dozen coins with a dozen more spilling to the floor.

The newly sympathetic Physician raced to the house. He quickly revived the miser with smelling salts and explained to Audrey that her father was very weak, but with proper care he would get better.

"Oh, that's wonderful," said Audrey. "How can we ever repay you?"

"Ten porchkins ought to do it," replied the Physician.

"Of course," said Audrey, happy to trade the heavy, useless coins for her father's health. "But why not take twenty?" And she reached into her pocket for another handful.

The Miser let out a loud moan. Seeing his daughter hand

out his precious porchkins pierced his heart like a red-hot saber. The Physician looked concerned. "I'd better come back tomorrow," he said, gathering up the coins with a smile. The miser moaned again. "Yes," said the Physician. "I don't like the sound of that moan."

The Physician returned every day for the next two weeks. Each day, he would check on the patient, pronouncing him improved, then Audrey would hand him a pail of porchkins, causing the patient to lose his strength and require more attention. More attention meant more porchkins. And more porchkins meant more attention.

One morning, the Physician was running late and the Miser was able to gather enough strength to speak. He begged Audrey to cancel the appointment. "Please," he pled. "Don't spend any more on me."

"You are so unselfish, father," she replied, kissing his brow. "But nothing will stop me until you are well—even if it takes every porchkin." And with that the Miser fell into a deep coma.

Although he never revived, Audrey kept her word. She spared no expense in procuring the top specialists from around the world. Blood experts, surgeons, obstetricians—although Audrey was pretty sure her father wasn't pregnant—all came and poked and left with their pockets full. On the day that Audrey handed out the last porchkin to a slow-talking snake oil salesman, the Miser took his last breath.

Although the Miser died porchkinless, his daughter wept tears of real sorrow at his pauper's funeral. And that, said some people, meant the Miser died rich as a king.

The Physician, who stopped by the funeral in his new fully equipped carriage, saw Audrey's tears and was moved. For the first time he noticed how pale and pretty and helpless she was. He was overcome with emotion and wanted nothing more in the world than to ask her to become his wife. Unfortunately, he already had one. So "instead" he asked her if she'd like to join their household as a servant.

The Physician set out the terms: Audrey would work sunup

to sundown seven days a week with only Christmas off. For her efforts, she would receive a porchkin a month—except for December, when she would be docked one day's pay. Audrey readily accepted the work schedule, but admitted she had a problem with the pay.

"If you please," she said to the Physician. "I prefer not to receive any porchkins at all. As far as I can tell, they serve no good."

So Audrey came to live at the Physician's house where she slaved from dawn to dusk, and never asked for anything in return—not even when the Physician began to creep into her room late at night to have his way with her. She was usually too tired to stop him, so she learned to live with it. And the Physician finally learned what the Miser never did: that the best things in life really are free.

MEANINGLESS FABLE #3

Three men—one deaf, one dumb, one blind—set out on a journey through the forest and immediately came upon a fork in the road. Two of them looked for a helpful directional sign. The third was blind. "Lost already?" cackled an old troll, who sat on a stump, for he had no right leg. "Well whatever you do, don't go that way," he said, pointing to the left path.

Now the deaf man saw the troll point to the left and assumed that was the correct direction, unaware of the accompanying words of caution. The blind man followed the deaf man's footsteps, figuring there's nothing wrong with the deaf leading the blind. And the dumb man, who heard and saw the warning, ran after his companions to tell them they were heading toward disaster. Unfortunately, he could not speak.

The three continued down the treacherous path and no sooner was the troll out of sight than a lion pounced out of the thicket. Standing just ten feet behind the travelers, the lion roared a loud and hungry roar.

The blind man heard the roar, turned, and seeing nothing,

assumed there was no danger, as did the deaf man who ignored the roars because he could not hear them. The dumb man, who both heard and saw the lion, was scared out of his wits and tried to scream. Unfortunately, he could not speak. The lion, puzzled by the strange reactions, cocked his head and returned to the thicket.

Time passed. The journey continued. The blind man began a round of "Row, Row, Row Your Boat" but it never caught on. More time passed. "I'm hungry," said the blind man. The deaf man was hungry, too, but kept silent because he couldn't hear the blind man and didn't want to be the only one complaining. The dumb man was also famished and longed to respond. Unfortunately, he could not speak.

Suddenly, a terrifying crash rang out through the forest. The blind man whipped his head to and fro, but could only guess at the cause. The deaf man was oblivious to the din and even though he felt the forest floor shake, he chose to stare at his own two feet—a habit he formed because he was shy as a result of his deafness. Had the deaf man raised his head, he would have seen an amazing sight. A sight that made the dumb man want to shout. Unfortunately, he could not speak.

And this is what he saw: a mangled heap of an airplane engine smoldering on the ground; a right wing scattered into a million pieces; a left wing neatly severed in two; and most startling of all, the plane's body suspended by a single cable snagged in the branches of a large tree.

The thick canopy had miraculously broken the fall. The dumb man's mouth was agape. Not that it was an option, but before he could say anything, the plane door flew open. This was no ordinary plane. This was a mariachi band touring plane. Eight faces peered out from the portal, faces filled not only with moustaches, but with disbelief and joy at such incredibly good fortune following such incredibly bad fortune.

With the help of their brightly colored, ruffled shirtsleeves, the band members fluttered to the ground. They dusted off their tight black pants and picked up their instruments. They began to play an up-tempo samba so full of joy and life that those who heard it could not help but break into glorious song.

Except the blind man. He heard the music and it depressed him. It reminded him that he was tired and hungry and probably going crazy. For only a rundown, deluded blind man would hear mariachi music in the middle of the forest. He kept his mouth shut in fear that the others might think him insane.

Nor did the happy music inspire the deaf man. He looked up just in time to a see a man with maracas leaping over the shrubbery, arms flailing and smile flashing. Unable to hear the music, the deaf man assumed his eyes were playing tricks on him. He, too, worried he was going insane and he dropped his head quickly to look at his feet.

Still, the music worked its magic on the dumb man. He watched and listened, and the mariachis' celebration of life moved him so profoundly that he began to feel stirrings in his vocal chords. They were strange and wonderful sensations that he had never known before. He knew he had the power. All he had to do was open his mouth and aspirate. He rushed to the mariachis to thank them for the miracle they had triggered. Unfortunately, he could not speak Spanish.

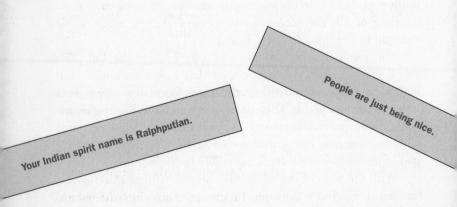

Your Indian spirit name is Ralphputian.

People are just being nice.

Schopenhaur Responds to Fleschman Re: Critique

HART SEELY

To: All
         Saturday, Dec. 11, 19:43
From: Dr. Victor H. Schopenhaur
Subject: Fleschman in BER

Three points in response to Fleschman's critique in the *Bratford Empirical Review* (Vol. 293, pp. 2189–2232):

1. He whines because my "Interpersonal Communication Collapse: A Case Study in One Urologist's Office" took seven years to complete. Hear this, Fleschman: I do not do scientific research to win races.

2. He refers to my $300,000 Crumm Foundation grant as a "keep-it-in-the-family kickback." For the record, Fleschman: I'm not a member of the Crumm family.

3. He says I've taught the Physics of Language at Bratford for 47 years. Wrong again, Fleschman. Forty-three years.

For one so bold with criticism, Fleschman should at least get his facts straight.

To: All
           Saturday, Dec. 11, 21:39
From: FLESCHMAN
Subject: $300,000 GRANT FOR WHAT, THIS?

Schopenhaur ignores the meat of my 4,000-word critique, then announces in a huff, "I am not a Crumm!" Worse, he thunders indignation over inaccuracies in my report that are, in many respects, his own doing.

He ignored repeated telephone messages left on his answering machine.

So let me ask this question of Schopenhaur: Do you respond to anything beyond a Crumm Foundation grant application?

To: All
           Monday, Dec. 13, 19:54
From: Dr. Victor H. Schopenhaur
Subject: Fleschman's charge

> . . . Do you respond to anything . . . ?

Yes, Fleschman. I do.

I respond to empirical analysis, which is sadly absent from your work.

Note: I have never received from Fleschman a telephone message worthy of reply, and I find it typical of his sorry brand of character assassination that he would claim otherwise. I view all this as vindictiveness from one whose tenure at Bratford College has been rightfully, at last, denied.

To: All
          Monday, Dec. 13, 20:34
From: FLESCHMAN
Subject: RING-A-LING, IT'S THE PHONE!

> . . . I have never received a telephone message . . .

On Oct. 11, this message was left on Schopenhaur's machine:

Dr. Schopenhaur, this is Wyatt Fleschman calling, concerning a critique I'm writing of your work for the Journal. Please phone me. I believe you have my number.

Because no call was returned, I ask these empirical questions:

Can Schopenhaur operate an answering machine?

Was Schopenhaur lucid on Oct. 11?

Or was the Martha Slaton Crumm Endowment Professor that day preoccupied, perhaps with the sexual harassment of certain female undergraduates?

To: All
          Tuesday, Dec. 14, 19:31
From: Dr. Victor H. Schopenhaur
Subject: Too far, Fleschman

I hereby demand from Wyatt M. Fleschman an immediate retraction of all public statements concerning my professional and personal conduct. This must be accompanied by a suitable apology, or actions will be taken that I otherwise would eschew.

To: All
         Tuesday, Dec. 14, 21:10
From: FLESCHMAN
Subject: NO APOLOGIES

> . . . eschew.

Gesundheit!

To: All
         Wednesday, Dec. 15, 7:04
From: Dr. Victor H. Schopenhaur
Subject: Very well . . .

Very well. I hereby make public this transcript of a phone conversation taped Oct. 13 between Fleschman and myself:

DR. SCHOPENHAUR: Hello, Dr. Schopenhaur residence. Who is speaking, please?

FLESCHMAN: Schopy? Haha, mmm, gaaa . . .

DR. SCHOPENHAUR: Of whom do I—who is this?

FLESCHMAN: You ganna gooo, Vic, you ole (expletive deleted). Whaddaya (expletive deleted). Hueh!

DR. SCHOPENHAUR: Fleschman! You are . . . Have you been drinking?

FLESCHMAN: Ah, oh, hahahaha. None'a'ya . . . (expletive deleted), guh, hickey . . . (expletive deleted). (Singing:) I FEEL STUPID AND CONTAGIOUS, HERE WE ARE NOW, ENTERTAIN US. (Capitalization is mine, V.H.S.)

DR. SCHOPENHAUR: Fleschman, see here—

FLESCHMAN: (Singing:) MULATTO! ALBINO! MOSQUITO! (Unintelligible.)

DR. SCHOPENHAUR: Get hold of yourself—

FLESCHMAN: (Expletive deleted, expletive deleted, expletive deleted.)

END OF TAPE.

To reveal this outrage saddens me. But Fleschman holds the position of associate professor of sociology. Neither the Bratford campus nor I can further tolerate his reprehensible conduct.

To: All
          Wednesday, Dec. 15, 9:04
From: FLESCHMAN
Subject: DR. CRAB CLAW

Schopenhauer needs psychological counseling. Consider this excerpt of a Nov. 10 notarized statement from Ms. Susan O. Hartfield, a former student in his Dynamics of Sentence Diagramming class.

I said, "Professor Schopenhaur, why are you looking at me that way?"

He said, "As I watch the evening shadows dance along the helix of your hips, you can't imagine how young and lickerish an old sea urchin can feel." Then he began moving his fingers like scissors and saying, "Crab claw. Have you seen my friend, Crab Claw?"

I said, "No sir. What do you mean?"

"I mean CRAB CLAW," he blurted. "CRAB CLAW! CRAB CLAW."

I screamed. He wouldn't stop looking at me and whispering, "Crab claw, crab claw."

It was awful. I ran down the hall. I will never forget those eyes— the red, rotting eyes of the devil. I see them in nightmares and wake up nauseous.

Ms. Hartfield intends to file a sexual harassment complaint against Schopenhauer as a result of his crustacean urges.

To: All
          Wednesday, Dec. 15, 23:53
From: Dr. Victor H. Schopenhaur
Subject: Fleschman's lies

I categorically deny the charges of Susan O. Hartfield. I recall no such incident, although it's possible that she misunderstood a reference to my graduate assistant, Mr. Brad Claubin.

But Susan O. Hartfield is no unbiased observer in my dispute with Fleschman. Fleschman's neighbors indicate that he and the 18-year-old Susan O. Hartfield—(who failed my class, as evidenced by the use of "nauseous" when she means "nauseated"—V.H.S.)—often have been seen vigorously sarabanding to flamenco music on Fleschman's back patio. On occasion, she has been observed to not leave his house until the next morning.

Meanwhile, the whereabouts of Fleschman's wife, Louise Menden-Fleschman, remain unknown.

A postscript: On Nov. 23, my answering machine at home received an especially vulgar message, even considering Fleschman's standards. It was left by Susan O. Hartfield. The full text follows:

DR. SCHOPENHAUR: You have reached the home of Dr. Victor H. and Priscilla Schopenhaur. We are unable to answer the telephone. I trust that, unlike some people, you'll exhibit the basic decency to leave your name, number, and a thumbnail sketch of your concerns, following the electronic tantara:

HARTFIELD: WATCH YOUR ASS, FUCKWAD! (Capitalization and the decision to publish "blue" text is mine—V.H.S.) I hear what you've said about Wyatt, and it sucks, and YOU SUCK! This is Suzie Hartfield, and I want you to know two can play that game. So watch yourself, Vic. WE KNOW YOUR CAR! YOU HEAR ME, VIC? WE KNOW YOUR CAR! (End of tape.)

I submit that the groundless accusations made by Susan O. Hartfield are part of Fleschman's disgraceful attempts to smear my standing at Bratford College.

To: All
         Thursday, Dec. 16, 9:02
From: Brad Claubin, grad assistant
Subject: Not involved

As a research assistant for Professor Schopenhaur, I want to state for the record that I have no involvement in the messages on this board. I hope Professors Schopenhaur and Fleschman will resolve their conflict amicably and for the good of Bratford College.

To: All
         Thursday, Dec. 16, 10:04
From: FLESCHMAN
Subject: LEAVE IT TO SCHOPENHAUR

Claubin, you are a spineless toad.

Re: Schopenhaur's charges . . .

I have on three occasions tutored Susan O. Hartfield—who is 19—at my home. I find her a tireless student with a passion for the South American gaucho subculture of the 1950s. Due to bus line schedules, she twice slept overnight in the efficiency apartment above my garage.

Friends and B-Board readers urge me to sue Schopenhaur. He has insulted my work, lied about my family life, and successfully quashed my chances for tenure.

Still, I feel no malice toward the man.

Only sadness.

I do, however, beg Schopenhaur to—in his unending quest to inflict pain on fellow human beings—spare my loving wife, Louise. Had he spoken to my "neighbors," Schopenhaur would have learned why Louise has not been on campus lately. She is at her home, mourning the loss of a family member.

Of course, such research—without a $300,000, "keep-it-in-the-family," Crumm Foundation grant—is certainly not Schopenhaur's style.

To: All
           Thursday, Dec. 16, 11:01
From: Dr. Victor H. Schopenhaur
Subject: Questions for Fleschman

Claubin, you are a toad. Never again access this B-Board.

I hereby invite Associate Professor Wyatt M. Fleschman—or "Doctor Grunge" to students—to meet me Dec. 19 at 7 P.M. in an open forum at the faculty club's James K. Polk Room. I wish to discuss these topics:

- Fleschman's Apr. 12, 1992 arrest in Elmira, NY, for "public lewdness."

- The "skin" magazines on Fleschman's bookshelves, and the aroma of contraband that emanates from his office at night.

- Plans by Louise Menden-Fleschman, his "loving wife," to file for divorce on the grounds of mental cruelty.

To: All
          Thursday, Dec. 16, 11:10
From: FLESCHMAN
Subject: I'LL BE THERE

I accept the invitation.

On Dec. 19, I'll pose these questions to Schopenhaur:

1. Please explain why you left the Bratford Club on the evening of Sept. 12 in what observers describe as "a tizzy"?

2. What hours does your wife, Priscilla "Prissy" Crumm Schopenhaur actually work as receptionist for the Bratford School of Sociology? Do those hours correspond to the wage log she submits?

Are you "tizzied" now, Schopenhaur?

To: All
          Thursday, Dec. 16, 11:16
From: PRISCILLA SCHOPENHAUR
Subject: HOW DARE YOU

IN 34 YEARS, I'VE LEFT ONLY TWICE BEFORE FIVE P.M., FOR DENTAL APPOINTMENTS. THIS CRAP MAKES ME SICK. WYATT FLESCHMAN HASN'T WORN A CLEAN SHIRT IN THREE YEARS. YOU KNOW HE'S AROUND, BY THE STENCH! WHAT REALLY GALLS ME IS THAT HE AND HIS SMART-MOUTHED GIRLFRIEND LEAVE FOR THE BLUE MONKEY TAP ROOM EVERY AFTER-NOON—AFTER SPENDING THE MORNING IN HIS OFFICE—DOOR LOCKED! WE ALL KNOW WHAT'S GOING ON. THEY SHOULD HAVE DONE SOMETHING LONG AGO.

AND WHO IS BRAD CLAUBIN? IS HE THAT KID WITH THE BAD SKIN? HE IS A TOAD.

To: All
          Thursday, Dec. 16, 11:22
From: Susan O. Hartfield
Subject: No you don't!

Wyatt Fleschman is the finest teacher I ever had.

Ms. "Prissy Wissy" Schopenhaur is the reason why nobody wants to even go into the sociology office, much less take a course there. Has anyone ever looked at her hair? What color is that? As for Vic Schopenhaur, I say this: The gauchos had a way of dealing with your type. I can't write it here.

Brad Claubin should get a life.

To: All
          Thursday, Dec. 16, 11:25
From: PRISCILLA SCHOPENHAUR
Subject: STUPID GIRL

SUSAN O. HARTFIELD IS A FILTHY TART WHO CHASED SEVERAL FACULTY BEFORE HOOKING UP WITH FLESCHMAN, AND SHE SHOULD STICK TO WRITING ON THE BATHROOM WALLS, WHERE HER FILTH BELONGS. SHE SHOULD JOIN A MOTORCY-CLE CHAIN GANG. I CAN PROVE THIS IN COURT!

AT LEAST CLAUBIN BATHES.

To: All
          Thursday, Dec. 16, 11:28
From: Susan O. Hartfield
Subject: Prissy must go!

What is it with people who feel they have to use upper case?

Prissy Wissy Schopenhaur doesn't do a thing all day except hang around the sociology department and talk about people. If you need a course changed, forget it. If her maiden name wasn't "Crumm," she'd have been canned from the college a long time ago.

To: All
          Thursday, Dec. 16, 11:41
From: Dr. Victor H. Schopenhaur
Subject: Today, Fleschman, today!

Why wait until Dec. 19, Fleschman? Meet me at 1 P.M. in the Polk Room. Bring your girlfriend, or your student, or whatever you call her.

By the way, your "loving wife," Louise, has accepted my invitation to address the campus on the precise meaning of "mental cruelty," as it is stated in her divorce papers. It should be interesting, eh?

To: All
          Thursday, Dec. 16, 11:45
From: FLESCHMAN
Subject: I'M READY, SCHOPENHAUR

I'll be there, Professor Crumm. Bring your photographs and tapes. Bring your wife and her dental records. Bring Claubin. I don't care.

But please, Schopenhaur—don't forget Crab Claw.

To: All
          Thursday, Dec. 16, 11:52
From: Dr. Victor H. Schopenhaur
Subject: Now, Fleschman, now

MENTAL CRUELTY, FLESCHMAN. Does that mean anything to you?

MENTAL CRUELTY!

To: All
        Thursday, Dec. 16, 11:56
From: FLESCHMAN
Subject: CRAB CLAW

CRAB CLAW! CRAB CLAW!

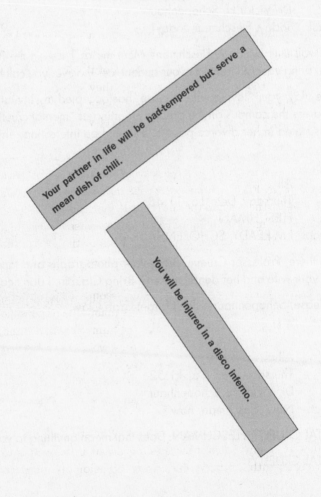

Your partner in life will be bad-tempered but serve a mean dish of chili.

You will be injured in a disco inferno.

ANOTHER UNNATURAL HISTORY

Domestication of Plants and Animals

Domestication of animals and plants began around 9000 B.C., says the *Encyclopedia Britannica*, with dogs, goats, and possibly sheep. (You'd think the editors of the *Encyclopedia Britannica* would know a sheep when they saw one.) Most species that still serve man were developed later, during the Neolithic Period, although the sugar beet wasn't cultivated until the nineteenth century, and was never a popular pet. One rarely sees anyone walking his beet. Rabbits were domesticated in the Middle Ages, from the sixth to the tenth centuries, by French monks who considered newborn rabbits fish and ate them when the church calendar compelled abstinence from meat. (Similarly, some monks classified women as "clothing" when the church urged chastity. With the proper outlook, even the most austere cloistered life can be rather pleasant if you are not a rabbit.)

During the Neolithic Period, dogs accompanied hunters, guarded settlements, and warned the inhabitants of possible danger. In addition, they were eaten by humans: you'd think if they were such great sentries, the dogs would have warned one another about that sort of thing. Sheep and goats were also eaten in the initial stages of domestication but later were valued for their milk and wool and, in cases of urgent need, as a last minute date.

Around this time, the bee was domesticated for its honey, humanity's main sweetening agent until well into the eighteenth century. Bees were occasionally used in warfare, hives being thrown among enemy troops to rout them. Today, this sort of thing is used as low comedy, but it wouldn't seem so funny if you were being routed, or if you were a bee. It might seem funny if you were a bee with a mordant sense of humor. I'll bet if Samuel Beckett were a bee, he'd have found that situation hysterical. Although it would have been hard for him to type it up.

Hens were first domesticated not for eggs or meat but for sport, cockfighting being as popular then as television is now, although less degrading to the human spirit. Perhaps if rabbits had shown a little more fighting spirit, they'd have been domesticated much earlier, but they'd never have been all that enthusiastic about visiting France.

—Randy Cohen

Life's Toughest Critics

Zagat's *Surveys Existence*

JEREMY SIMON

INDIA

This "mecca for Indians" features "authentic" "Indian decor" and "Indian cuisine" served by "old-school" "Indians"; the "predictable" and "repetitious" cuisine can be a boon or a bane, depending on "whether you like Indian food." P.S. it's "a schlep" for most New Yorkers.

THE WOMB

"It's easier to get a reservation at Nobu!" than in this "uterus" where the "impressive climate control" and "proximity to pleasant lubricants" lead fans of this "once-in-a-lifetime experience" to exclaim, "Who would ever leave?"; vets warn, "your mother's wallet, too, will feel the stretch marks."

BURNT SIENNA

"A little pretentious" compared with its neighbor, Orange, this "Crayola classic" is nonetheless "a draw" ("on paper, it's perfect!") for children, parents, and educators, who coo and sigh "it just needs occasional sharpening"; the scene is "a house with two windows," "older brother slain with kitchen knife," or "mommy (with pointy breasts) and daddy and me," depending on the day.

STATEHOOD

"It's not for everyone," say Puerto Ricans, but if you "lack sufficient weaponry to successfully revolt for independence" and can tolerate the "taxation," you'll find that the "protection in armed international conflicts is sublime."

THE PERIODIC TABLE

The "extensive" menu with more than 100 items wins kudos at this "swell spot for bonding," where you can schmooze over "fusion cuisine" amid neon-tinged decor ("try the oxygen bar!"), and while the blinded-with-science crowd mulls questions of price and scarcity—"Why do they list plutonium, if they can't deliver the goods?"—in short it "has all the elements."

DIVORCE

"I thought we'd never go there, but then, I said the same thing about Woodstock!" is a common reaction to this "modern institution" whose adherents find the "predictable" fare, often delivered by fat men in robes, "liberating" and "pretty good for a chain"; other respondents report leaving with "a certain emptiness inside," yet defenders maintain, "it's long overdue."

THE OPPOSABLE THUMB

While this "innovative" evolution—a "pick-up joint" for the klutzy—is valued by locals for "synergy" with its surroundings, dissenters dis it as "overrated" "finger food" and kvetch "we're tired of waiting for it to get on its feet."

CYBERPORN

A "welcome addition" for "lonely heterosexuals" seeking a quick fix, you'll know this "scourge on society" when you see it, according to politicos who either "fear its productivity-sapping effects on a populace helpless to escape its clutches" or find it "surprisingly good."

RAIN

"Karma karma karma!" shout the few insane people who want you to "quit shaking off your wet umbrella on me!"; the scene is "wet," "raw," or "shiny" depending on your view, which insiders claim "is better indoors."

THE FUTURE

Suffers from "poor location"—the temporally impaired find it "hard to see," which others carp "it always seems just out of reach"; dot-com CEOs, small children who are adept at piano, and foodies note it's better than its sister digs, The Past, which "is getting old." P.S. geriatrics be warned: there is no early bird.

MICE

These "cinema-genic" (Mickey, Mighty, et al.) "rats with press agents" "know their way around the kitchen," thanks to the "lax" cleaning habits of the new roommate whose "funky," "eclectic" aesthetic promises that this debut incarnation will be "the first of many rodents to come."

FEAR

"I'll never ask anyone out again!" cry aficionados of this emotion, which has served "sleepless nights" and "self-conscious bouts of inactivity" since the beginning of time; "it's all in our heads" quip rainy-day car washers, but there's no denying the popularity of such "soul-crushing" menu items as "never gonna pay off those student loans" and "meteors falling through the windshield"; its "consistency" is remarkable: "on sunny days," it "still sucks."

BUSINESS-TO-BUSINESS E-COMMERCE

This Silicon Valley yearling was "a find" last year but has been "mobbed" as of late, with beleaguered diners claiming that portions have gotten "minuscule" and the "paranoid" waiters are "constantly looking over their shoulders"; seems that "network solutions that will enable you to focus on what counts most— your customers" is "this year's 'oat bran'."

FOOSBALL

Fare at this "hands-on" mainstay consists of small items "skewered kebab-style" on sticks, then slathered in oil and, finally, rotated over a piece of particle board with lines painted on it; "a few brewskis" help the "pledge-pin-and-ass-brand crowd" stomach the "action" at this "place to score."

MICROSOFT

Opinions are sharply divided on this "Windows for the World wanna-be": Judicious diners say it's become "too big for its britches," while supporters stand by their Word and crow it's "heaven for browsers"; either way, it's a "power scene," so "enjoy it while you can" because "they say that breaking up is hard to do."

In Brief

HOLLY SMITH

Schenectady—Today, after years of relying on sheepskin prophylactics, society sees the advent of the first soy-based condom. Finally, conscientious vegetarians everywhere can abandon the rhythm method.

"What a goddess-send!" said Petra Rock of the upper New York state potato collective, Share our Starch. "Our poor midwife hasn't had a break since the massive Reagan-induced frigidity of 1985."

Due to a relatively short shelf life of three months and extreme photosensitivity, each condom is wrapped in a reinforced hemp-fiber packet. Although tested successfully on a representative cross section of volunteers, the manufacturer discourages exposing the prophylactics to synthetic clothing and/or rugged individualists.

Available in rainbow tie-dye, proletariat gray, and 27 U.N.-approved flesh tones, the condoms retail for $6.99 a dozen. Discounts are available for current PETA members and hyperfertile Marxists.

Baltimore—Scientists at Johns Hopkins University, responding to pleas from parents of attention deficit hyperactive disorder (ADHD) children, are racing toward the discovery of a new drug to counteract the effects of Ritalin.

"While parents appreciate Ritalin's sedating effect during trips to the Home Depot or Sears Portrait Studio, they worry about its tendency to leave youngsters noticeably sluggish when the grandparents visit," explains a Hopkins researcher who declined to be named.

"What we hope to develop," says this same researcher, "is a mild stimulant, perhaps in patch form, which can be administered to kids whenever they're suffering an inopportune Ritalin moment."

An estimated 100 percent of American children are afflicted to some degree with ADHD. Symptoms include general restlessness, an overwhelming urge to torment younger siblings while on car trips, and the inability to pay attention during the "Soil" unit in fourth-grade science.

Los Angeles—Playtex announced a merger with olfactory goliath Renuzit that is sure to turn the sniffing industry on its nose. The newly formed megacorporation, Playzit, hoping to capitalize on the booming aromatherapy market, will introduce a "Spa" line of feminine hygiene products as early as next week.

Playzit is confident that its new line will succeed in a niche market of affluent women who know what they like, and like how they smell. After compiling data from thousands of surveys, Playzit determined that the most popular scents include "citrus," "patchouli," and "Billy Crudup."

Initially, however, the company will introduce more pedestrian aromas. In addition to freesia-infused douches and "calming" panty shields, consumers can look forward to an array of custom-scented tampons, such as Vanilla Monthly, "For the woman who desires a little extra satisfaction . . . a little extra excitement . . . a little extra absorbency."

Houston—Local residents Bob and Betty Fielding put their four-bedroom rambler on the market and plan to head halfway across Texas to a cramped apartment in San Angelo in hopes of bolstering daughter Katie's chances of becoming an Olympic gymnast.

"In Houston, we're right next to Katie's coach and a world-class training facility," explained Betty, as movers loaded one of several trophy cases onto a waiting truck. "The location would have allowed us to remain part of a close-knit community and not neglect our three other children." she added. "And that doesn't seem right."

By relocating so far away, the Fieldings will finally be able to join the ranks of other Olympic parents, none of whom actually live near an adequate gym.

"Obviously, we're excited," said Bob, who plans on abandoning his family at some point in the future due to the incredible stress of driving his daughter eight hundred miles back and forth to Houston six days a week.

"Lots of parents dream of their children becoming Olympic athletes one day," he said. "We're just willing to do what it takes."

Washington, D.C.—Researchers at the Centers for Science in the Public Interest, the group responsible for moo shu pork's single-digit approval rating, have retained a local public relations firm in hopes of softening their image as wellness Nazis.

Although the CSPI's dietary admonitions were intended to increase Americans' life expectancy, they've instead caused a dramatic decrease in people's overall will to live. Individuals may desire longer lives in theory, but in practice they desire bloomin' onions even more.

An aggressive print, television, and radio ad campaign,

featuring CSPI scientists frolicking with Nutella, crab Rangoon, and an occasional Steak-Umm, has already been planned, along with simpler, more down-to-earth image enhancements.

"We're making a conscious effort to be photographed with puppies more," says CSPI spokesperson Ann Tie, "despite the fact that they're notoriously high in cholesterol."

London—White-hot alternative group Turgid Yearn, whose latest single, "Angsty," earned them the title of Best New Band This Week, stunned the audience of VH1's Video Music Awards by failing to name the blues as a major influence in their musical lives.

Unaware of the statute requiring the blues to be acknowledged as influencing everything from the Nasdaq to Hillary Clinton's senate bid, Yearn's lead singer, ¥, seemed confused by the frigid stares emanating from the audience as his acceptance screed concluded with nary a mention of Robert Johnson or John Lee Hooker.

Later, when flat-out asked what the blues meant to him, the haute couture maven ¥ sniffed, "I try to avoid them. I'm an autumn."

Paris—In a stunning reversal, several of the world's most influential cosmetics makers have now agreed to make reparations for the 1980s.

Facing allegations that they "egregiously and repeatedly misled consumers by suggesting that aquamarine eye shadow, Lee Press-On Nails, and A Flock of Seagulls–like styling gel were legitimate fashion options," industry leaders will instead settle with scores of disgruntled plaintiffs, mostly females in their mid-thirties.

Terms of the settlement are said to include free consultations at Merle Norman and makeup bags full of tasteful earth tones.

According to a statement from L'Oreal, the corporations were prepared to fight the suit until a judge overseeing the case ruled that plaintiffs' old yearbook photos and/or glamour shots would be admissible after all.

Chicago—Senior researchers at Northwestern University's Kellogg School of Business announced today that it is, in fact, who you know.

"After analyzing five years' worth of data gathered from the upper echelons of corporate America, numerous junior high school cheerleading tryouts, and Charlie Sheen, we can state with a degree of certainty that being popular or otherwise well-connected just really, really helps," says John Fitzpatrick, the study's author.

Despite the findings, Fitzpatrick urges parents and educators to continue plying kids with the myth that it's what you know, at least during their formative years. "I look at it like the whole Santa Claus thing," he says. "If it makes them feel good, what's the harm? Besides, there'll be plenty of time to broadside them later."

Columbus—Victoria's Secret, purveyor of all things silky and scintillating, announced today the launch of a new product line aimed exclusively at the extremely pregnant. While initially limited to expandable bustiers and forgiving satin briefs, VS plans to expand its offerings almost immediately.

"We've done some test marketing with our fringed lamé maternity thong, and the response has been quite positive," says company spokesperson Jennifer Watson. "Because of its control top and snug fit, not only do women feel sexier, but we've also seen a drastic decline in premature labors."

Committed to gilding the beauty of all women, regardless of gestational status, VS predicts its products will forever change the face of fecundity. "Never again," says Watson, "will fishnet belong solely to the barren."

Manhattan—Busily crafting a position statement on normalized trade relations with China, Barbra Streisand denies recent allegations that she somehow overestimates her relevance in the political arena.

"My opinions matter because I'm an ordinary citizen just like anyone else," she said while speed-dialing Bill Clinton's private line and caning a house boy. Draped in a stunning Donna Karan frock, Streisand, sounding dismayed, instructed the former president to immediately call her back on the car phone.

"I'm already late for a quorum with Rosie O'Donnell and *The View*, and then I've got to rehearse for my annual farewell concert," she snapped. Asked about the recent Republican takeover in Washington, Streisand declined to comment, preferring to save her remarks for the more proletarian setting of the *20/20* studios.

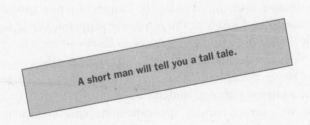

A short man will tell you a tall tale.

The Party Problem

BILL WASIK

One hundred people are invited to a party, and each is asked to RSVP. Each invitee is permitted to invite five friends, who are also asked to RSVP. (These friends are not allowed to invite friends of their own.)

Of the eventual attendees, three-quarters will attend as couples; and of these, two-thirds will have RSVPed. The remaining quarter of the attendees will attend alone, and of these, one-half will have RSVPed.

For every attendee there will be another attendee who has the same first name. If, for example, Mary Johnson attends the party, then at least one other Mary will be attending the party as well. Also, for every attendee with a surname that is also a common first name, someone with that first name will be at the party. So if John Patrick is at the party, then someone named Patrick—Patrick Smith, say—will be there too.

Of the attendees, three-quarters will have graduated from prestigious four-year colleges or universities; the other one-quarter will have attended two-year community colleges. For the three-quarters the presence of the one-quarter will be, for want of a better word, delicious. (At an earlier such party, a Bennington alumna was intrigued to discover that the handsome young schoolteacher with whom she was chatting had recently graduated from Laramie County College [Wyoming]. She will be coming to the party again.)

The world's three major presumed racial groupings—Mongoloid, Negroid, Caucasoid—will each be represented at the party. Attendees willing to make nametags for their grouping should indicate this when they RSVP.

All of your ex-girlfriends will be at the party. (Many will wonder how this is possible. "I have dated 50 women," one reader e-mailed. "They are scattered throughout the Americas, as well as Europe and Asia. I believe two to be dead. Could it be that they will all be at the party?" The answer is yes. They will all be at the party.)

Employees of think tanks will be disproportionately represented at the party, numbering one guest in twenty. These individuals are smart and well-read, and their research has been exhaustive, but remember that their conclusions are ideologically motivated.

If one member of a "school" is at the party, then the school's other members will be there as well. If Max Horkheimer is at the karaoke machine, then Herbert Marcuse is likely rounding the corner with a mai tai. If an attendee should happen to spot Thomas Cole, the nineteenth-century landscape painter, then by necessity Asher B. Durand is somewhere in the apartment as well. Or he's on the way, or has already left. (Note: The members of each school will not necessarily arrive or leave together.)

(Also: note that not every notable attendee is part of a school. When, for example, you see Lewis Grizzard at the party—he will be there—don't jump to the conclusion that Roy Blount Jr. will be in attendance as well. The comic minds of the American South have influenced each other strongly, but they do not yet constitute a "school.")

One-quarter of the attendees will encounter someone whom they know but did not expect to see at the party. "What are you doing at this party?" one will ask the other. "I might ask you the same question," the other will respond, and the two will share a laugh. But beneath the laugh there will be, for each, a deadly seriousness; each had come to the party hoping to start anew.

For each attendee there will be another attendee on whom, over the course of the evening, their glance will tend to linger. One man may notice a woman who is the spitting image of his recently deceased aunt; another may marvel at the creamy skin of a toddler; another still might be moved with pity at the sight of a half-wit, or amputee.

Two-thirds of the attendees will have nemeses, also in attendance. The nature of their conflict will vary from pairing to pairing. Two might be vying for the same love object; another two, the same promotion. But for all the conflict will be primary—indeed, mortal; or as close as we come in this day and age, at any rate.

The number of people at the party cannot exceed 100 at any point in time, as per local fire codes. Guests who arrive after 100 attendees are already inside will be asked to wait outside, by the door.

The number of guests waiting outside may not exceed 50, however, and so guests who arrive after 50 hopefuls are already waiting will be asked to stay in their cars with the engines running.

These guests will be asked to rev their engines every thirty seconds to indicate their continuing desire to attend the party.

I hope you all can make it.

Dismembering Mr. Shawn's
New Yorker

BILL WASIK AND
ERICA YOUNGREN

From Dusk 'til Shawn. Which *New Yorker* staffer loved Mr. William Shawn the most? Despite what other biographers might have you believe, it was Ralph Treadwell, *The New Yorker*'s longtime night-shift guard, whose loyalty to Shawn ran deepest. Though the two never met, Treadwell would often pass the long, quiet hours in the great editor's office, poring over Mr. Shawn's marked-up manuscripts of *New Yorker* pieces. It was there, he says, that he met his "only true hero" and began a life-long love affair with copy editing.

William Shawn, Man of Lætters. Dolores Farber, a Minnesota housewife, corresponded with Mr. Shawn for over 30 years through two wars, through seven presidential administrations, and through Mr. Shawn's entire tenure as *New Yorker* editor. After a ten-year silence, Farber has finally come forward to publish 300 pages of their hitherto secret correspondence. In letter after letter Mr. Shawn gracefully responds to Farber's lengthy missives of life, love, and loss with reassuring replies, always beginning with the familiar greeting, "We regret that we are unable to use the enclosed material."

I Barely Remember Mr. Shawn's "New Yorker." She was only in the typing pool for three weeks during the winter of 1964, but Ethel Witcomb remembers it as though it were yesterday. Sort of. She vividly recalls what time she clocked in (8:30 A.M.) and how much she paid for lunch at the Tastee Coffeeshop on West 43rd ($2.75), but critics will find that she's a bit vague on other facts and details, when she writes, for example, "I think Mr. Shawn was the bald one. And he was short. Yeah, I'm almost positive he was short. He smelled sweet, too . . . like bacon. Best-smelling man at *Esquire*, Mr. Shawn."

Shawn but Not Forgotten. Most *New Yorker*ites knew Mr. Shawn for his thoughtful repose, but the old fellow could enjoy a good joke from time to time. Mail-room manager Frank Letty recalls that Shawn would occasionally beckon him into his office and, with a smile, offer a dry remark about the Yankees or the weather. Always one to reciprocate, Letty would frequently sneak his mail cart up behind the aging Shawn in the office halls, snap his butt with a rubber band, and yell, "Special delivery for ya, Shawnsy."

Outside Mr. Shawn's "New Yorker." To *New Yorker* writers, Mr. Shawn was a brilliant, commanding editor, whose pen could make a phrase sparkle on the page. Not so to the man who sold him his candied nuts. Jack O'Rourke, who saw Mr. Shawn nearly every day from his cart outside the *New Yorker* offices, remembers him as a cold, taciturn man, who rarely said more than, "A bag of nuts, please," or "I think I'll have some of those tasty nuts."

Below Mr. Shawn's "New Yorker." The novelists, journalists, and thinkers whose prose filled Shawn's *New Yorker* spent much of their days roaming the office halls, striking up spirited discussions of literature or current affairs. But for Tony Gerwitz, whose accounting firm occupied the floor immediately below the magazine, the era was marked only by a loud, unceasing trudging overhead. "Intellectuals are all well and good," writes Gerwitz in his memoir, "but when they're stomping around above you all day, it becomes hard to balance the books."

Inside Mr. Shawn. A *Fantastic Voyage*–style fantasy about four *New Yorker* writers who feel so strongly about Mr. Shawn that they miniaturize themselves and have themselves injected into the great editor's bloodstream. By traveling up into his brain, they discover the awesome secret of Mr. Shawn's editing prowess. The book ends before the readers discover the answer, but there will, we are told, be a sequel.

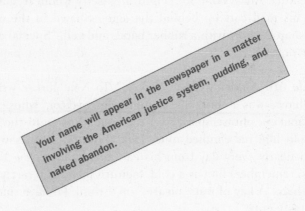

Your name will appear in the newspaper in a matter involving the American justice system, pudding, and naked abandon.

International Name Encyclopedia

NOAM WEINSTEIN

So you've got a new baby cooking in the uterus. But what are you going to call it? That's where my award-winning *International Name Encyclopedia* comes in. Each day billions of mothers and fathers sift through my collection of over thirty names in search of an appropriate moniker for their little fetus pie. Please don't let today be an exception. Here is the *Encyclopedia*. To learn more about a specific name, give it to your baby and see what happens.

Adam Of Hebrew origin. Translates to "he who builds the ladies."

Ann Originally a one-syllable abbreviation for "Anne," Ann grew in popularity after the letter e was discovered in "devil," much to the devil's surprise.

Benjamin Long for "Ben," Benjamin gained acceptance after the death of Benjamin Franklin, the man who accidentally discovered kites.

Britney Though primarily associated with the recently famous pop singer Britney Spears, Britney actually dates back to 1982, when she was born.

Christian Of biblical origin, as in "Wow, look at all those Christians!" and "Hello, my name is Christian."

Cripple What better way to protect your potentially disabled child from the ridicule of his peers? He can't take offense, because they're just calling his name.

Dawson British for "elevator," Dawson is undergoing a resurgence due to the popular television character Freddie (Boom Boom) Washington.

Erstwhile Spanish, as in *"Mi nombre es* Erstwhile."

Flash Great for a short-lived, explosive child. "He came and went in a flash," the epitaph will read, "and he had a very unusual name."

Glaucoma More of an eye disease than a name befitting a child, Glaucoma strikes millions of Americans every year.

Hickory "Hickory dickory dock, the mouse ran up the clock, the clock struck one the mouse ran down, hickory dickory dock."
   Did you catch the reference?

Hoop Hoop would make a strange name for any child.

Klaus von Klitzing English, meaning "claws of the klitzing."

Larry (Lawrence) Origin unknown.

Lesbian Greek—translates to "from the island of lesbians."

Mister Sniggles "Congratulations, Mister Sniggles! You've just been elected King!"
   "Despite my name?"
   "It wasn't even a factor."

Mordechai Very ethnic. Very chic. Very Mordechai.

Neiman-Marcus "Any parents naming their children Neiman-Marcus will receive a $75 gift certificate to our store, redeemable for up to one year beyond the date of birth"—

Neiman-Marcus catalog. That's a lot of money, folks. Think about it.

Oh Possible nicknames: "hhh," "<silence>."

Rapist Not to be confused with a type of violent criminal, Rapist would make a great name for your child.

Retardo A Spanish retard.

Sweatshop Although some parents may object to using their children as walking political statements, these are the same parents who put leashes on their babies and send their dogs to college.

Trendy There's nothing more Trendy than a child. Anybody who says otherwise has obviously never met your son.

Uglirific Okay, I admit it—this is just one I made up because I thought it was funny. Sorry about that.

Vat A nickname for Victoria, Vat has earned increasing street cred as a result of Canada's Value Added Tax initiative.

Whoops Though less common since the advent of reliable contraception, Whoops is still fairly popular for purely aesthetic reasons.

Xenophobia Xenophobia is a powerful human phenomenon that deserves widespread attention. Wouldn't you say the same of your child?

Yogurt The first goats and sheep were domesticated in Mesopotamia around 5000 B.C. But only in the last several decades has their product become popular in this country, thanks to its convenience, texture, and taste.

Zebrew If you are Jewish and your baby is a zebra, why not make the best of an admittedly difficult situation?

Top 100 Human Body Parts

1. Soul
2. Heart
3. Gut
4. Pigment
5. Female reproductive organ
6. Male reproductive organ
7. Thumbs
8. Spine
9. Eyes
10. Placenta
11. Thighs
12. Ears
13. Female nipples
14. Teeth
15. Washboard abs
16. Hands
17. Bowels
18. Tongue
19. Feet
20. Artificially augmented mammary glands
21. Nose
22. Liver
23. Mouth
24. Hair
25. Middle finger
26. Muscles
27. Knees
28. Shoulders
29. Skull
30. Kidneys
31. Taste buds
32. Pituitary gland
33. Sinuses
34. Elbows
35. Shins
36. Forearms
37. Neck
38. Fontanelle
39. Temple
40. Spleen
41. Intestines
42. Brain
43. Claves
44. Larynx
45. Lungs
46. Ribs
47. Forefinger
48. Collarbone
49. Coccyx
50. Buns of steel
51. Heel
52. Big toe
53. Stomach
54. Upper palate
55. Chin
56. Hips
57. Nostrils
58. Groin
59. Male reproductive organ's two best friends
60. Cheeks, upper
61. Urethra
62. Epidermis
63. Arches
64. Fingernails
65. Lips
66. Clavicle
67. Back of knees
68. Cheeks, lower
69. Fallopian tube
70. Ring finger
71. Mandible
72. Forehead

73. Pelvis
74. Eyebrows
75. Pancreas
76. Freckles
77. Vertebrae
78. Trachea
79. Inside of elbows
80. Wrists
81. Gums
82. Achilles heels
83. Veins
84. Eyelids

85. Capillaries
86. Eyelashes
87. Knuckles
88. Belly
89. Anterior cruciate ligament
90. Funny bone
91. Sideburns
92. Palms
93. Toenails
94. Prostate
95. Duodenum

96. Groove between nose and upper lip
97. Tonsils
98. Appendix
99. Armpits
100. Male nipples

(Will Durst is reasonably equipped.)

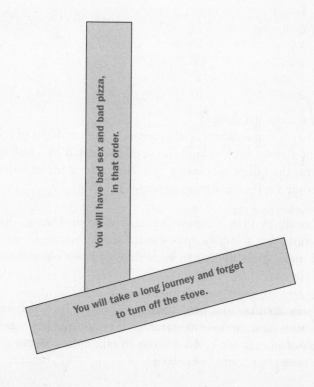

You will have bad sex and bad pizza, in that order.

You will take a long journey and forget to turn off the stove.

Supplement to the Basic Course Catalog, University of Kansas

ROBERT S. WIEDER

Welcome, freshmen!

To accommodate recent changes in the curricula of a number of Kansas high school districts, mandated by local school boards, the following classes have been added to the university schedule for the upcoming semester.

Archaeology 110: "Carbon-Dating, Shmarbon-Dating." Raising the intriguing scientific hypothesis, "Could not an all-powerful God make rocks appear to be billions of years older than they actually are?"

Physics 290A: "Modified Entropy Theory." In which certain scientific assumptions regarding thermodynamics and the decay of matter are revised, so as to take into account a bush that burns but is not consumed.

Physics 290B: "Elementary Table." Study and memorization of a Simplified Table of Elements, which includes only those elements commonly and abundantly found in nature. This course explores the question, "If you can't see it, were we really meant to know about it?"

Marine Biology 363: "Cetacean Digestive Anomalies." Investigating the unique and remarkable ability of a whale's gastrointestinal process to distinguish between plankton and marine creatures, which it chemically dissolves, and the randomly swallowed human being, which it merely bleaches. Field trip. (Scuba equipment and certification required.)

Zoology 109: "Introduction to Kine." What they are. (Cows) Their proper care and feeding. Their selective breeding. Their particular suitability as sacrificial offerings to an angry God. (Not for the squeamish.)

Astrophysics 191: "Acoustical Influences on Planetary Motion." A study of subatomic particle resonance, and how it may be manipulated by repeated marching and blowing of trumpets in order to halt the rotation of the Earth. How playing "Reveille" starts it turning again.

Agricultural Economics 140B: "Crop Storage and Nocturnal Divination." The art of employing traditional methods of dream interpretation to foresee and plan for years of extended famine and/or plenty. Emphasis on the significance of "devouring." Also, why everything happens in sevens.

Health Science 402: "Morality and Etiology." Understanding the causal relationships between fornication and AIDS, masturbation and leprosy, pornography and insanity, secular humanism and cancer, and abortion and death by lightning.

Health Science 404: "Passover Epidemiology." Analyzing those properties of lamb's blood that make it an effective preventive and prophylactic measure against certain pediatric plagues. Also, how to remove stains from door frames.

Chemistry 301: "Oil on Troubled Waters." The figure of speech as a basis for scientific inquiry.

Mathematics 300A: "Non-Satanic Numerical Systems." A "pure math" class, in which textbooks, handouts and board-written problems will exclude the number 666 (the sign of the Beast) or use in its place the symbol . In all lectures and oral presentations, said number will be expressed as "the numeral formerly known as Prince of Darkness."

Food Service Science 120: "Large-Scale Meal Preparation and Management Techniques." The challenge of feeding multitudes. Creative use of loaf- and fish-extenders. Nutritional properties of milk and honey. Manna explained. (At the conclusion of the term, each student will be required to plan and prepare a final supper for twelve.)

Law 901: "Introduction to Higher Law." Resolving questions of priority when confronted with conflicts between state or municipal statues on the one hand and direct commands from the creator of the universe on the other. The Special Prosecutor as God's own emissary. Why ACLU lawyers go directly to hell. Why you still have to pay parking tickets even when the end is nigh.

Base Ten

Say what you will about your precious base ten, the counting systems of ancient peoples were based on numbers from two to 60, so you can all put your gloves back on, or your shoes, or both if you are a talented counting monkey who is wearing shoes in some pathetic and misguided attempt to be accepted by humans, to whom you'll always be just a monkey no matter how well you count and ride around on that little bicycle. You're a monkey! Show some self-respect.

Where was I?

Binary systems, in which the counting goes "one, two, two and one, two twos, two and two and one," etc., are still used among the ethnologically oldest tribes of Australia, who apparently do not accept the American Express card, if I understand the ads on NBC's overproduced Olympic coverage. But hey, how about those anorexic gymnasts! What a plucky bunch of permanently prepubescent athletes they are!

There are tribes of Tierra del Fuego who use number systems in base three and four, confusing even themselves. The quinary scale is very old but is now used only by speakers of Saraveca, a South American Arawakan language, or perhaps by GW in calculating his goofy tax cuts, for all the sense I can make of them. And I doubt that he'd do well on the uneven parallel bars. (Nor will that monkey if it insists on wearing shoes.) Similarly, the pure base six scale seems to occur only sparsely in northwest Africa and is otherwise combined with the duodecimal, or base 12, system. (I can go on and on, all the way to base 60 and those cuckoo Babylonians, if my search engine doesn't overheat, or whatever it is that search engines do.)

Suffice it to say that eventually, base ten dominated all other systems with no involvement from Bill Gates and no whining from the antitrust division of the justice department. Nevertheless, vestiges of other systems endure. Twelve is particularly durable—inches in a foot, months in a year, ounces in a pound, gates to the city. Oh, what a beautiful city! Our watch faces are a constant reminder of the persistence of this number, and just how late we are filing our copy. And of course we see twelve in "dozen." A gross is a dozen dozen, perhaps because it would be really gross to eat a dozen dozen donuts, or whatever it is ancient American peoples used to eat—each other apparently, if you believe some of the catty stories about the Aztecs. People can say such mean things.

None the less, ten does enjoy a privileged position among number systems, no doubt because of the number of fingers found on human beings who are not shop teachers. We even see this in the names for our numbers. Eleven comes from Old English *endleofan,* meaning ten and one left over; 12 from *twelf,* meaning "two left"; the endings -teen and -ty both refer to ten, of course, and not in some snide way. And 100 derives from a pre-Greek term meaning ten times ten. And what about tent? Well, probably not. But still. A monkey gymnast—that would be something to see, wouldn't it?

—Randy Cohen

Excerpts from *Men's Self*

ROBERT S. WIEDER

COVER LINES

WHEN YOUR BODY CLOCK KEEPS FLASHING
  "12:00"
LEARNING TO PLAY YOUR WASHBOARD ABS
GOOD SEX, BAD SEX: Like There's a Difference
TEN STEPS TO A COLON OF STEEL: There's a
  Light at the End of the Tunnel
SEXERCISE: There Are Good Burns, and Bad Burns

CONTENTS

Losing Your Job Can Make You Impotent. Yikes! Talk about
  "downsizing."
Erections During Gym Exercise. Don't think "embarrassing
  gaffe," think "I must *buy* this Flexobar." How to get
  workout woodies, how to maintain them, negotiating
  the stationary bike, the importance of the spotter, and
  more.
The Absolutely Final Article We'll Run About "Abs." Also,
  the last time we mention fiber, our final word on ways to

get laid, and our last "how to" piece about something you already do every day. Honest, we swear. Stop laughing.

Pause Celebre. Menopause begins with "men." Science now says that guys go through it, too. That means we can blame *our* tantrums, foul moods, and sexual indifference on it, and otherwise use it to our advantage. 131 ways.

Travel. What your luggage says about you, from "I am being deported" to "Please rip me off."

The Executive Secret of Better Sex. Pay for it! That way *you* decide when, and where, and in which positions, and the definition of "foreplay," and whether she dresses up this time as the Girl Scout or Ellen Degeneres.

Dealing with Sudden Hair Loss. Drat, you've misplaced your toupee again. And that "special" dinner guest is due any minute! 17 desperate measures—from Magic Marker to sedated pet hamster—to help get you through such hairy emergencies.

The Hidden Benefits of Impotence. "It's an ill wand that no one blows good." Some handy rationalizations and self-denials for when your meat loafs.

20 Low-Stress Jobs YOU Can Do. Traffic monitor, art-class model, aquarium guard, swami, queue placeholder, Wal-Mart greeter, scarecrow, lab-test urine donor, proof reader, lieutenant governor, more.

"Gee, They Fit in the Dressing Room." Are those new pants so tight it's like your ass is in a tourniquet? Is the old roll-of-quarters-in-the-pocket ploy more painful than it's worth? Is your rodman getting gangrene?

Stop Kidding Yourself! 7 easy steps.

Malegrams. How to get to know her gynecologist, how to fake a tattoo, how to measure your *total* penis, how to glue your hair back on, how to hang by your tongue, how to choose the right wristband (or even the left one), how to get lucky on your StairMaster.

Getting to Know Your Kids. At a time when they're
independent, crafty, and armed to the teeth by age 12,
you're crazy not to ingratiate yourself with them. A few
simple techniques—sharing meals with them, remembering their birthdays, learning their names—can at
least make it worth a try.

The Secret Source of Job Stress. Amazing new evidence
indicates that many of us *don't actually enjoy working
at all*, and indeed, would rather spend our lives doing
things we like! No *wonder* you keep having those
nagging "office party massacre" fantasies.

Useful Stuff. Halcion, Prozac, melatonin, serotonin,
Metamucil, ginseng, and BreathAsure all in one
handy capsule; a funhouse mirror that makes you look
three sizes smaller; clip-on nipple rings; a liposuction
vacuum cleaner attachment.

Ask "Men's Self." What it means when your proctologist cries
"Eureka!", where to get your Barcalounger detailed, how
to get your nuts out of a vise (you'd be surprised—we
hope—at how often we get asked).

MALEGRAMS
Pick-Me-Ups

Zzzzzzzzzzzzzzzzzzzzzzzzzowie
Tired and listless? Have we got snooze for you.

Feeling sluggish and fatigued? Beset by recurring drowsiness?
Maybe it's time to consider *sleep*. It's more than just practicing
for death, you know. Millions use it to refresh and restore their
vitality and spirit. With these basic guidelines, it could work for
you, too.

Be regular. Establish a pattern, such as the same place and
time each day; make a routine of it.

Nocturnal mission. Nighttime's the right time. The fact is, it's quieter then, and darker, and it's probably the slowest part of your day anyway.

Try lying down. Proven 90 percent more successful than sitting, standing, or using a belt-sander.

On a bed. Softer than the floor, safer than the ironing board.

10 Exercises You Can Do Without Appreciably Altering Your Schedule or Lifestyle

1. Walk on tiptoe whenever no one is looking.
2. Press down on steering wheel while waiting in KFC drive-thru line.
3. Brush teeth with both hands.
4. Put catsup on everything, always using a brand new bottle.
5. Tape TV remote to a brick.
6. Use butter knife to cut steak.
7. Wear wrist weights when masturbating.
8. Push away from dinner table without using your legs or feet.
9. Always jog from TV to bathroom and back.
10. Hold toaster oven at arm's length while waiting for Pop-Tarts to heat up.

Where There's a Will, There's a Raise

Things You Can Do, Say, Wear, Offer, Threaten, or Desperately Stoop to in Order to Increase the Most Widely Accepted Measure of Your Worth: Your Paycheck, by Jerry Rubitin

Gaining weight? Stressed out? Marriage in trouble? Kids in jail? Unable to afford slick new workout equipment? Can't get it up? What you need is more money. As Dr. Mose Bettah of the Institute for Personal Evaluation says, "If money can't buy happiness, why the hell are we all working?"

"Where can I *get* more money?" you ask? Our answer, after exhaustive research, is, "From the person who *already* gives you money: your employer."

It's called _getting a raise_, and like every other subject we've encountered, it can be reduced to just enough "insider" tips and tactics to fill a magazine article.

Pop the Question

Try asking. It works with "Would you pass the butter?" and "What time is it?", so why shouldn't it work with "Can I have more money?"

Location, location, location. Be in your boss's immediate vicinity when you ask. Make sure he or she can see and hear you and is awake and aware of your presence. Introduce yourself if necessary.

Locution, locution, locution. Phrasing is vital to getting your point across. Choose your words carefully. Wrong: "Tell the Archbishop I've a muffin in my pants!" Right: "I would like to be paid more money."

Specify money. A clever boss's promise to "increase your salary" may turn out to mean dinars, supermarket coupons, or, most deviously cunning, celery.

Call Me . . . Irresistible

Beguiling for dollars. Be just so darned likable that your boss can't say no. Dick Van Dyke as Rob Petrie—be like that. And take a dog with you. A yellow lab. Who could turn down Old Yeller's owner?

Be a brown nose. Before hitting on your boss, hit the tanning parlor until you're a nice walnut hue. It's one of life's basic rules: If you radiate health, youth, and good looks, you get whatever you want.

Call Me . . . Indispensable

The inside poop. Be the only one in your office who can fix the office toilet in an emergency. Arrange an occasional "emergency" just to confirm the point.

Do a bang-up job. Get your boss hooked on heroin. Okay, this will take some planning. First, tell him it's just a series of flu shots.

An Hour-by-Hour Guide
HOW TO HAVE SEX

The Good Book tells us there's an appropriate time for everything. Legendary tippler John Barrymore's motto was, "It's always cocktail hour *somewhere* on earth." What's our point? That whatever your clock or chronometer reads, the time is right for some form of sexual activity or another. Or another. Or another. (Repetitions are everything.)

With that in mind, here's a daylong Libido Log to slip into your organizer for future reference. Properly used, it can give you, literally, endless hours of pleasure.

5:00 A.M. Gently awaken your beloved and romantically point out that both the sun and your manhood have risen. (A caution—this approach can backfire unpleasantly if you're just getting in from that "boys' night out.") Upside: You start the day feeling relaxed and good about yourself. Downside: During the throes of passion, you realize that she's still half asleep and has mistaken you for the gardener.

5:30 A.M. Shower together, sensuously soaping one another until nature takes its course. Upside: No need to worry about the wet spot. Downside: Oral sex leaves that Irish Spring taste in your mouth all morning.

6:00 A.M. While preparing your breakfast cereal, you handle the banana in such a salacious manner that your partner takes you down right there in the nook. Upside: The butter is already conveniently at hand. Downside: Your kids laugh so hard they spray cocoa out their noses.

6:30 A.M. While driving to work, you plug your "Car Jac" auto fellator into the cigarette lighter and complete your trip oblivious to the commute nightmare. Upside: The miles seem to whiz by. Downside: Your moans of ecstasy awaken your carpool passengers.

The End-of-the-World
Bake Sale

As far as the eye could see it was glass casserole dishes and paper plates stacked with powdered delicacies. There were Little Debbies and Entenmann's, baklava and lady fingers. There were brownies both from mix and scratch. The Best Chocolate Chip Cookies in the world were there along with sugar crepes, key-lime pie, peanut butter Rice Krispies Treats, caramel banana freezer pops, and Eskimo pies. There were four hundred types of apple pie and they were all excellent. There was free coffee and there was half-and-half.

No one had said it would be like this. It was to come in sheets of fire and showers of brimstone, but what happened at the end of the world was this: The cities did not tumble and the cemeteries were still. In fact it seemed to be a really nice day.

But upon waking that Wednesday everybody knew, quietly and collectively, that it was to be the last Wednesday—so nobody went to work. It would be the hump day to end all hump days, and by eight that morning, the whole planet smelled of nice things to eat. By noon everybody assembled across streets and fields and steppes and tundra and parking lots, with covered dishes and coffee urns. Folding tables wrapped in white paper sprang up because it was Wednesday, it was to be the Last Wednesday and it would be the End-of-the-World Bake Sale.

You couldn't have asked for a nicer day for an End-of-the-World Bake Sale. With powdered-sugar lips, everybody laughed about how with the end of the world and all there would be no time to try the loukoumathes and honey, or the sticky rice balls or the dried-pineapple scones. Of the crème brulée or the raspberry flan, caramel tortes and bizcochitos with white cocoa icing, of the thick slabs of warm banana bread—sadly—there would be no time. In fact, the only regrets voiced by everybody on that last day was that they had not started sampling more desserts sooner.

Fittingly, at the end of the last day of the world there was a beautiful sunset. Over cheesecake, almond paste, capriotada, and International Coffees, a sorbet palette of long pink clouds floated across a pale green twilight and everybody said:

"Look at that," and everybody did.

As night fell there were warm bonfires to gather around. The heavens were watched and when the first star appeared everybody wiped their mouths and raised their Styrofoam cups over their heads and made their last wishes.

Lit by the conflagration of paper plates and folding tables, strangers whispered introductions and final intimacies to each other. Sticky hands clasped. The appetite for sweets and talk and for each other's company was insatiable and intoxicating right up until the end—

And the end arrived quietly and without fanfare. Save for the final consensus that fudge with nuts was better than fudge without nuts, the end arrived without judgment.

On the pale cold morning after the End-of-the-World Bake Sale, as far as the eye could see, were row after row of folding tables wrapped in white paper stood empty save for one. And upon this table sat untouched a small lemon Bundt cake which, hastily written across it in frosty-blue icing letters, the last person to leave had managed to apply this epitaph:

> *Let it be said of us, that in that last warm sphere of subsiding light that glazed our faces, and in the collective delight that came with pie and in the sharing of pie, briefly, there was here such community.*

—Gregory Hischak

Submission Guidance

DAVIS SWEET

We call this section "submission guidance" as opposed to "submission guidelines" because many publications, we assume, have "submission guidelines" but we wanted to do oh so much more in this volume.[1] We at the *Mirth of a Nation* office complex are often asked by would-be humorists, "What do I have to do to get published in your thing?" It has been our formal policy to ridicule these poor saps with o'er-erudite language[2] until they weep, but a recent management shakeup (same management, just shaken) has led to this altogether fuzzier approach. We will now tell you, in this very "submission guidance" section, how to be a humorist in America. We strip away the thin kimono of mysticism that has cloaked the black art of humor and lay barely before you.

HOW DO I BE A HUMORIST?

First off, being a humorist isn't a matter of making up funny things. Quite the opposite. If you're truly a humorist, funny things make you up. That's not entirely true, or even remotely true, but it sounds sizzlingly cool, doesn't it? Humorists are actually born of horrifying childhood experiences, ruthlessly sadistic bullying, and parental abandonment.[3] Rather than thwart the bullies and other terrors with fists or semiautomatic weapons, the nascent humorist

[1]See examples of our new "Love Those Readers!" policy throughout the book, like Amy Krouse Rosenthal's "Reader's Agreement" (p. iii).
[2]Not unlike the linguistic gymnastics used in Randy Cohen's Unnatural Histories spread thoughout the book.
[3]Parental abandonment is illustrated to varying degrees in "How I'm Doing" by David Owen (p. 340) and "The Solomon Bar Mitzvah" by Jay Ruttenberg (p. 407), and one way or another throughout the rest of this book.

faces them cross-eyed, making noises like a cartoon animal. If you were not the butt of your own jokes, the class clown, or both (the "butt-clown"), give up now. You're not funny, and never will be.[4]

VOCABULARY AND OTHER PSYCHOLOGICAL WOUNDS

Still reading? Good! You are either not paying attention or warped enough to be a humorist.[5] The second part of humoristic development is vocabulary building. Humorists can't just go around calling things whatever those things are called. We have to dredge up obscure words on the pretext of "choosing the perfect word." This ritual is for the edification of magazine editors,[6] the patrons of our art, who erroneously think themselves not only funny but also educated. Humorists strive to gain the respect (money) of these editors by using words that secretly confuse, mystify, or frantopoculate both parties.[7] These "perfect" words are then discarded by copy editors later in the process and replaced with more commonly used synonyms, ostensibly for the benefit of the great, unwashed reader (you). If you learn nothing else on your path to humor, learn a few words of Gaelic.[8] Also, Shift-F7 in Microsoft Word invokes the professional obscurist's Sancho Panza:[9] the thesaurus.

Only after you have built up significant psychological wounds and vocabulary skills should you attempt to write

---

[4]Meditate on your lack of funniness with the help of David Bader's "How to Meditate Faster" (p. 1).

[5]And you need help. See "The Self-Help Hot Line" by Carina Chocano (p. 39) and "WELLNESS911" by J. H. S. McGregor (p. 304).

[6]See "Dismembering Mr. Shawn's *New Yorker*" by Bill Wasik and Erica Youngren (p. 462).

[7]You might try building your vocabulary with crossword puzzles. See "Double Diamond/Highest Difficulty" (p. 92) by Michael Gerber and Jonathan Schwarz.

[8]Francis Heaney ("Holy Tango of Poetry," p. 140) has a Gaelic-sounding name.

[9]Like Sancho Panza, capri pants (as illustrated in Merrill Markoe's "Monks Among the Capri Pants," p. 234) come from Italy. Or Spain. I think Sancho is from Spain, come to think of it. The pants themselves are from China, probably, or Venezuela, but named after a place near Spain.

something funny, and even then it should be something simple. Start by writing a single joke or a movie. At this early stage, you should not try to write a humorous essay.[10] Later, after you've created a humorous website no one visits, you can move on to creating a humorous essay no one will buy. After many such fledgling attempts at humor, you may get passed over by one of the really big publications.[11] This is the pinnacle of the humorist's craft: being personally rejected by someone who's sort of famous. The gleeful "I almost got published by Tony Hendra!" (followed by a lengthy biography of Mr. Hendra[12] and a pantomime of a cricket bat) is the anthem of a truly successful humorist.[13]

HOW TO WRITE A JOKE IN 21 DAYS

The stock and trade of humor is "the joke." In ancient days it was the deftly created character, the subtly nuanced observation, or the kick in the temple, but today's humorist is nobody without a joke. This section shows you how to create your very own joke inexpensively and with tools you'd find around your home.[14]

Day 1: Decide on a genre for your joke

Passé joke genres include the knock-knock genre, the call-and-response genre ("My period is SO irregular!" "HOW IRREG-ULAR IS IT?"), and the Holy-Christ-isn't-George-W-a-flipping-

---

[10]See "The Short Essay That Conquered the Planet" by Tim Carvell (p. vii) for insight into the dangers associated with essays.

[11]Nell Scovell's "Three Meaningless Fables" (p. 425), as the legend goes, was rejected by both *Cat Fancy* and *Penthouse*. Bet those editors are kicking themselves right about now.

[12]See *The Book of Bad Virtues* (Pocket Books, 1994) by Tony Hendra. Particularly the Wodehouse thing toward the end.

[13]True success is a pain, anyway, and that's not sour grapes. See Cynthia Kaplan's "A Brush with Greatness" (p. 177) and Mark Katz's "Hall of Near-Fame" (p. 181), conveniently located right beside each other alphabetically.

[14]Quite unlike the tools you'd find in Rod M. Lott's "Real-Life Giant Construction Equipment for Kids" (p. 217).

moron genre (illustrated several times in this volume,[15] but only as an homage to the jokesters of olde). If you want your joke to be funny (most do), you will choose one of these genres:

- the not-terribly-witty observation
- the mildly ironic situation
- the still-safe stereotype

The not-terribly-witty observation is distinguished from its ancient cousin, the witty observation, by its sheer Americanness. Oscar Wilde need not apply. For example, Mr. Wilde, reincarnated and working for Hallmark,[16] might observe:

> "When the heart of one loved is dark,
>   the heart of a lover is alight."

While his not-terribly-witty American cousin, Wilde Bill, might say:

> "Oscar is such a fruit he couldn't
>   cross the California border."[17]

The mildly ironic situation makes a common situation wacky by replacing one of the elements. For example, here is a common situation:

A man buys a house from an elderly couple.

The elements here include a man, the act of buying, a house, a couple, and the fact that they're elderly. Look what happens when we replace just one element:

---

[15]See Andy Borowitz's "The Inaugural Address of President George W. Bush" (p. 19) and, just to maintain a charade of objectivity, Bobbie Ann Mason's "Terms of Office" (p. 268).

[16]You realize we're trying to distribute footnotes to just about everybody in the book (except for Robert S. Wieder, p. 470), right?

[17]If you've ever driven to Cali, this will make sense. Otherwise see the California Agriculture Department's guidelines on transporting fresh fruits and vegetables across state borders. If you haven't driven to Cali, you might develop the necessary map-reading skills with Michael Francis Martone's "Because Yahoo Maps Aren't for Everybody" (p. 254).

A man buys a home-built sadomasochism bench from an elderly couple.

The joke practically writes itself!

Still-safe stereotypes are rapidly becoming extinct, so if you choose this genre, your work will have a short shelf life. This will be followed by a relatively short period of complete obscurity, your own death, and the rediscovery and celebration of your work as bold defiance of the constrictive cultural mores of your time.[18]

Stereotyping minority groups is largely off the table,[19] unless you are a member of the minority group about which you joke.[20] If you are tempted to write a joke about a minority group to which you don't belong,[21] you should look for the signs that the group is considered safe to taunt by the entertainment establishment. The rule of thumb is this: if Tracey Ullman has made of fun of them, you can too.[22] Warning: Do not follow the examples of Whoopi Goldberg or Woody Allen[23] (known in The Business as "Whoo and Woo"). Stick with Tracey Ullman. This introduces one sticky area: Tracey Ullman in Woody Allen's film.[24] If you see Tracey Ullman making fun of a minority group and you aren't sure whether or not you're

---

[18]Robert Johnson boldly defied the constrictive cultural mores of his time, but he was a blues musician, not a humorist, so he really doesn't count in this context. Still, not a bad segue into Judith Podell's "Blues for Beginners" (p. 390).

[19]Something funny about "table." Table . . . table . . . Table tennis! No . . . Tablecloth! Tablespoons! No . . . Oh, I know. See "The Breakfast *Table*" by Martha Keavney (p. 188).

[20]See "Womenu" by Alysia Gray Painter (p. 364).

[21]If you don't know which minority group you belong to, see "You Fill Out My Census" by Chris Harris (p. 129).

[22]Other rules of thumb: Don't go into business with friends, don't get your wedding ring too close to the outlet, and don't flush a spider unless you've squished it first (it'll just crawl back up the pipes and it'll be mad).

[23]Woody was supposed to be in this book somewhere.

[24]Other famous film directors are also in this book somewhere. See "Alfred Hitchcock's *Hamlet*" by Louis Phillips (p. 368) for just one example.

watching a Woody Allen film, leave that minority alone just to be on the safe side.

Some sterotypes that are safe to exploit (as of this writing) include:

- greedy and/or unethical lawyers
- greedy and/or unethical politicians[25]
- uncaring tobacco executives
- self-absorbed celebrities
- smooth-talking midgets

Your assignment: When you've decided on a genre, write it down and tape it to something.

Days 2–6: Find other examples of work in your chosen genre

Digital cable and satellite television are the humorist's gold mine,[26] offering you literally dozens of jokes every day for just a few dollars. Just click the CHANNEL UP button (your remote control may vary) every three seconds. You will probably find the richest soil, the risingest yeast, and the most fertile spermatozoa in commercials, partly because they're almost all you will see, period.[27] Should you accidentally stumble across an actual television program,[28] press the CHANNEL UP button until a commercial appears. Unless the program is that Australian guy with the fang scars on his hands. He's funny.[29] Your

---

[25]See "Bubba in Paradise" by Jamie Malanowski (p. 222).

[26]See "AOL's Prime Time Warner," by Rick Moranis (p. 316).

[27]Quick, think of a neat link from "commercials" to Jeremy Simon's "Life's Toughest Critics: *Zagat*'s Surveys Existence" (p. 449). E-mail it directly to *Davis.Sweet@yahoo.com*.

[28]Or, indeed, a fake television program, like those illustrated by Lewis Grossberger (p. 109).

[29]You think it's easy trying to come up with footnotes for every flipping contributor so nobody's feelings get hurt? I mean, take a look at the table of contents! There are about 60 writers in this stupid thing. And there's that Michael J. Rosen editor guy with the chainsaw whining about "Oooh, don't forget Gregory Hischak (p. 153). He's really nice. Plus he lives near you so he could come down and hit you if you skip him."

assignment: Write down the funniest jokes you see and tape them to something.[30]

Day 7: Discover the 3-K secret (not the KKK)

Find the jokes you've written down and study them. You'll start to see a pattern emerging, and it will probably involve the number 3 and the letter K. Very boring studies have proven that things happening in threes and K sounds are funnier than other things, and this may or may not be traceable to our childhoods.

Examples of childhood threes:

- "I'll huff, and I'll puff, and I'll BLOW YOUR HOUSE DOWN!"
- "This one's too soft, this one's too hard, but this one's just right!"
- "Bada bang, bada bing, bada boom!" (specific to Italian children)[31]
- "Wham! Bam! Thank you, ma'am! 'Happy ever after' my butt. Prince Charming just goes to sleep and smells like a pig all night." (specific to drunk mothers slurring bed-time stories to their terrified children)

When you start to construct jokes, remember that you can't just go straight to the funny bit. As the laugh-ee you have to set the laugh-er's expectations with two bits that have a faint promise of "funny" but, in the end, aren't. This intentional withholding of the funny material builds frustration and resentment in the audience, which is sometimes released as laughter when you blurt out the punch line.[32]

---

[30]Judy Gruen's "Carpool Tunnel Syndrome" (p. 122) has several funny jokes in it. Steal some of them and tape them to something. If challenged, claim you stole them from Erma Bombeck.

[31]See "Happy Holidays from Maria Callas" (p. 98) by Tom Gliatto. Both were Italian children.

[32]"Blurting out" the punchline is only appropriate when your audience is *not* deaf (see "Audiobooks for the Deaf" by Tim Harrod, p. 137). If they *are* deaf, you have to draw a picture of the punch line, which can irreparably mess up the rhythm of the joke.

The K sound is believed to be one of the first things we associate with laughter when we're infants. Adults apparently make K noises (*coochie coo!*) when they tickle babies, so we're more or less programmed to laugh when we hear Ks.[33] Note how these punch lines elicit dramatically different responses simply because of the K sound:

- So I said, "If it's not a kipper, I'm in the wrong house!"
- So I said, "If it's not a zipper, I'm in the wrong house!"

Your assignment: Repeat "3-K" over and over for several minutes. Tape it to something.

Days 8–13: Decide on a topic

This is the hardest part of being a humorist, except enduring the prerequisite overwhelming emotional injuries mentioned earlier. This is where you go on an intense inner journey to discover that singular part of you that will make your humor unique. This trip is often painful, but if you can find that one nugget of "funny" and hold it up in front of you, it will all be worth it. Once you have found the funniest core of your soul, smash it with a hammer and leave it for dead. This is the Big Secret of Comedy: Abandon any desire you ever had to be unique.[34] You aren't unique. You don't have a unique perspective. You're not going to change the world by revealing the insights with which you alone have been blessed. Abandon hope, all ye who enter "funny."

Understand that absolutely—without exception—every moderately interesting topic has already been explored, dissected, spun, wrung, and joked about, more than 60 percent of

---

[33]Bruce McCall and Susan McCarthy each have two K sounds in their names. In The Industry, we call that "born funny."

[34]Teens often think they're friendless because they're just too unique to be understood (see "Teen Times" by Paul Rudnick, p. 396). They find out later that they're friendless because they have that one weird thing about their face, like a mole or one nostril that's really small.

them by Dave Barry alone. Warning: Internalizing this reality *does not* mean it's too late to write any new jokes, though it is, it simply means you have to give yourself over to comfortably ripping off someone else's ideas.[35] Many humorists can't do this, so they make the mistake of falling back on that old crutch "crazy" rather than rip someone off directly. The thought process looks something like this:

1. I want to write a joke about how people in small towns look down on people who live in big cities.
2. But Garrison Keillor already does that joke half a dozen times a week.
3. I'll just give it a crazy twist! I'll write a joke about how people in small towns look down on people who live in upside-down psychedelic mouse-skin kayaks!

Forget crazy. Just go ahead and rip off the concept. While you're at it, steal the whole joke. This will save some strain on your already fragile psyche, unless you get sued.[36] There is not much danger of this happening. Since other humorists are made of the same awful insecurities as you, they worry that if they sue you for comedy theft they'll be exposed and humiliated for their own inadequacies in public[37] and no one will ever love them.[38] This is what agents are for, because agents don't care how ridiculous they look in public. As a rule of thumb, never steal material from someone who has an agent.

Just accept that it's all been done before, or as Shakespeare

---

[35]Ian Frazier's "My Wife Liz" (p. 68), for example, is a direct ripoff of *Huckleberry Finn*, but at least Ian had the sense to rip off someone who's dead enough to be in the public domain.
[36]Ben Greenman will probably be sued by IKEA for his piece on page 101.
[37]M. Sweeney Lawless demonstrates public humiliation in "A Fish Story" (p. 208).
[38]See Matt Neuman's "49 Simple Things You Can Do to Save the Earth" (p. 330). It's relevant. Really.

said (stealing from Ecclesiastes[39]), there is no new thing under the sun. With that in mind, you might work up a joke with the punch line, "Well ex-CU-uuu-USE me!"[40]

Your assignment: Write down 500 stolen topics and tape them to something.

Days 15–20: Take a break. You've earned it![41]

These days really just serve as padding to get us to 21 days.[42] This step is optional.

Your assignment: Whatever. Tape it to something.

Day 21: Write the joke

This is the easy part. Just fill in the blanks below:

I heard the weirdest thing. [a neutral person associated with the topic and genre], [a slightly controversial person associated with the topic and genre], and [a very controversial person associated with the topic and genre] were all [doing something neutral in a context appropriate to the topic and genre]. [the first person] said, "[something plausible]." [the second person] said, "[something slightly cynical but still plausible]." So [the third one] reaches into [his/her] pants and says, "If this isn't a [word with a K sound], I'm in the wrong house!"

Your assignment: Write a joke. Send it to several friends via e-mail, but pretend you don't know who wrote it. Start your

---

[39]See Ecclesiastes 1:9, right before David's teacher tells him the whole world is meaningless (see "Schopenhaur Responds to Fleschman Re: Critique," p. 435, by Hart Seely for a rebuttal).

[40]You didn't really think we'd cross-reference Steve Martin from this 25-year-old wacky catch phrase, did you? The man's an artist these days, for Pete's sake!

[41]Day 14 omitted for clarity.

[42]Time is an illusion, anyway. Just see Robert Konrath's "A Short Historical Inquiry into Time" (p. 199) if you don't believe me.

note with, "I don't usually send these out, but this is really funny! I don't know who wrote it." Check your e-mail frequently over the next week to see if the joke has become so famous somebody else e-mails it to you, not suspecting *you* actually wrote the joke *in the first place!*[43] When this doesn't happen, start at Day 1 and try again.

SO WHAT DO I HAVE TO DO TO GET PUBLISHED IN YOUR THING?

When you are too old to attend effective meetings, provide effective feedback to your teammates, and squint effectively at your computer screen when someone sends you the latest version of that "Shit happens" e-mail message,[44] retire. Realizing you haven't set aside enough money for a comfortable living and the Republicans have "reformed" Social Security into a weird cross between a lottery and a ringtoss, break your lease and buy a trailer home.[45] At this point in your life, getting paid for humor is the difference between baloney sandwiches with moldy mayonnaise and a Dixie cup full of "Bow Wow" with moldy mayonnaise. In other words, that's when humor is survival, or at least the next best thing to survival.[46] *That's* when your humor will take on the edge you wish you had when you were a kid. *That's* when the jokes will dribble out of you unbidden like last night's chamomile tea. *That's* when you'll be funny,

---

[43]For examples of e-mail you might actually receive, see "Representative Government: A Correspondence" by Richard Bausch (p. 11).

[44]Though copyrighted and indeed published by George Carlin, this piece turns out to have been conceived and written by Norwegian schoolboy He in Mental. He says so on his website.

[45]Your need for news rapidly decreases at this stage of your life, so you can safely cancel cable. Just get the local weekly newspaper, skim the "In Brief" section (see "In Brief" by Holly Smith, p. 453), and pore over the obituaries to find out in which humorous ways people you know have died recently.

[46]If your survival depends on humor, it's probably just about checkout time. See "Packing for the Second Coming" by Michael Thomas Ford (p. 57) for advice on what to do when your number is called.

Sparky. No sooner. And that's when you can send a little something (three somethings, with lots of K sounds) to Mirth HQ.[47]

Until then, please enjoy the work of the two-bit hacks who were suckered into writing for this edition by Michael J. Rosen's[48] piteous pleas. And nobody's getting rich on this. Remember that. This is all just a favor to Michael J. Rosen[49] (not Michael Rosen, who is a different guy) which we're all doing gratis, for no money, free. At least that's what I've heard. If you hear something different, let me know.

---

[47]Mirth of a Nation is a wholly-owned subsidiary of the Rand® Corporation, bringing you the most controversial statistical analysis for over 50 years Rand®: We've Got Your Numbers!™
[48]See the cover of the book, near the words "Edited by."
[49]Ibid.

Questions for Reading Groups

HENRY ALFORD

1. *More Mirth of a Nation* is a biennial. A "biennial" book: that's just a book that's afraid to own up to the truth about itself, isn't it? How would *More Mirth of a Nation* be different if it were heteroennial? Why are people always made slightly uncomfortable by biennials?

2. Last summer, Sandy proposed that we read the autobiography of the Rock, whom she described as "one of the rising stars of the WWF." Surprisingly, Edwin voted yes. What are the odds that Edwin voted yes because he thinks the WWF is the World Wildlife Fund?

3. When Edwin says—as he did twice during the *American Pastoral* session and once during the *Amsterdam* session—that the book "triggered a series of personal resonances and cogitations" within him, did that strike you as a mite precious? Also, what does he mean when he says that a book is "writerly?" Would Edwin be slightly less unbearable if he didn't always wear a bowtie?

4. British novelist Anthony Powell's last name is actually pronounced "Pole," not "*Pow*-ull." Should we tell Edwin this?

5. The group's assessment of last month's book was essentially a "Jewish mother review"—i.e., the literary equivalent of "the food is bad and the portions are too small." Has the group—many of us writers ourselves—devolved into a cabal of jealous naysayers unable to praise others' work because of our tortured feelings about our *own* inherently flawed work? Is this related to the fact that the only books that the group seems to get excited about anymore are non-fiction adventure-disaster books wherein most of the characters die? Discuss.

6. Sandy has suggested that, for September, we read Jane Smiley's *Moo*, Phillip Weiss's *Cock-a-Doodle-Doo*, and several back issues of *Buzz*. Is adorable the right direction for the group to go in?

7. "Somewhat jejeune." This is a phrase that Edwin has, over the years, ascribed to everyone in the group with the exception of Julia. Why has Julia escaped Edwin's jaundice? Is there something going on there? Does Julia trigger in Edwin a "series of personal resonances and cogitations?" Or is it that we are *all* a little bit in love with Julia—that we *all* feel somewhat diminished in her presence. (Possible topic for further discussion: What does Julia have that Sandy doesn't?) And what will happen to the group now that Julia is moving to San Diego in the fall? Many would agree that she is the the heart and center of the group, the only member whose sense of self-worth is not so wobbly and tremulous as to render her constantly on the brink of tears or to making comments which betray an inability to divest herself of her own personal baggage. Moreover, she has been instrumental in having us read a variety of non-Western authors (Kenzaburo Oe, Ha Jin, Vikram Seth); but when John takes over, we are likely to read *only* books that have been adapted by Merchant-Ivory, not to mention yet more additions to the canon of books devoted to the fascinating personal lives and interstices of the Bloomsbury Group. Additionally, now might not be a bad time to discuss the fact that Edwin has asked Robert twice about Robert's aunt, who is an editor at Viking-Penguin; has tried to befriend Sandy's friend who works at the *Times*; and—unbeknownst to Julia—has written a letter to Julia's agent. Has Edwin misinterpreted the Forster dictum, "Only connect"? Explore.

8. Next month, at Sandy's urging, we are going to read Sandy's unfinished novel, which she has already confessed is less a novel than a collection of "wintry, Italo Calvino-ish snippets." Presumably, many of these snippets are transcribed directly from Sandy's journal. Rate your anxiety from 1 to 10.

9. Would Sandy be happier in a different *kind* of group?

10. Sandy recently suggested that we start meeting weekly instead of monthly. Why all the resistance?

Index

Subject Index to *The Weekly World News*, Part XVII: Volume 14, No. 44 (August 3, 1993) through Volume 15, No. 4 (October 26, 1993). Compiled by Chip Rowe.

497

NEW THING

This is it. The **newest thing**, fresh from the mysterious plastic asshole of "popular culture". All shiny and ready for you to put in your home, video cassette player, or mouth. Wow! It's ready to go. Everybody wants one, or two. Enjoy it mindlessly, as if it was all that gave meaning to your life, or distance yourself and write about it in effete, obscure language, employing it as yet another example of how everything's going in the toilet socio-economically. Or wonder if it's going to matter at all in a few years, all this **stuff** that everyone seems to always be wanting. But don't miss out. Get the complete set. Maybe it'll be worth money someday. Some people think that this is what it's all about, anyway. Maybe you could even spend your life making this stuff, that people seem to want. What could be better? Happiness awaits.

No. 1221. HUMAN CULTURE 10c

YOUR OWN PERSONAL CHEERLEADING TROUPE.

Just imagine -- a group of scantily-clad, tight-skinned youngsters following you around everywhere, shouting your name and forming human pyramids in your honor. Never be at a loss for confidence, or for young bodies. They will unconditionally love you no matter what, and will sway public opinion your way. Expensive to feed and cumbersome to house, this is still a great bargain. Specify all male, all female, or mixed. Single shouting idiot leader extra, plus Spangles, Pom Poms.

Gym Coach Fantasies, Ltd. Dallas, Tx.

IRONY

New for the season. What the kids are talking about. Strange way of seeing the world which is completely alien to animals, insects, and all other forms of life. Rationalize wide variety of otherwise embarrassing and disreputable behavior, tastes, responsibility for your actions. Usually most popular when culture is at lowest ebb, but get yours now. What a handy thing, this irony. Just in time.
No. 3365. NO, REALLY $2.00

CHILDHOOD

Everything you've been missing. Toys, mom, the old place, the mysteries of sex - - all back in force. Suddenly everything seems brand new. Great way to eliminate boredom, get stuff done. Stuff like watching T.V., blowing up dolls, eating boogers. Suddenly all your aspirations vanish and all you can think about is Batman and unicorns. Dance around wildly, stick your butt in the air, and scream. Pee in the pool. Read comics all day long with your hand in your pants. Tell people you saw them naked when you didn't. Crawl around on all fours and squeal. It's fun for all. Stay awake at night wondering about other people's crotches while desperately hoping to grow up faster. Limited time only.
No. 2411. SQUARE ONE.. ...Only 25c.

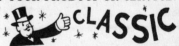

LUMINOUS STARS, COMETS, METEORS, PLANETS, SPACESHIPS, SATELLITES, ETC. ON YOUR CEILING

BEAUTIFUL   NOVEL & FUN

★ MAKE A QUAINT MODEL OF THE UNIVERSE IN YOUR OWN HOME! ★

An assortment of old-fashioned paper stars, moons, planets, celestial bodies, et cetera all coated with a thin luminous preparation that actually shines in the dark! Government-banned radium is the trick. We found boxes of these things in a disposal bin in Nevada and now we make them available to you at a fraction of their original cost. Made out of plain, clean white paper, already conveniently gummed on the back just like postage stamps, and all you have to do is lick them and press them on the wall. Fun! And dangerous. Highly radioactive radium layer instantly attacks tongue and jawbone, increasing chances of lymphoma and marrow cancer a thousandfold. Teeth begin to feel loose, hairs appear on the pillow. But, oh, aren't they pretty! It's almost worth it, these pretty, twinkling little stars and planets. Imagine yourself a spaceman adventurer or a daring fighter pilot, soaring into the sky. Or, more accurately, an angel ascending to heaven. Even as night slowly overtakes the light of your life's morning, then the slow exposure to their harmful rays eventually will. Joint aches, reeling head pains are some of the fun symptoms. Take these around in your pockets for a really painful experience. Hurry! Supplies are limited, and illegal, so we won't be offering them again soon. Cash only. The heavens await!

No. 4991. Dental Work Assortment. Contains 1 large star, 1 small star, 1 crescent moon, 1 shooting star, 2 medium stars, 1 saturn and 2 planets. Price per package postpaid . . . . . . 50c.

No. 4992. Reconstructive Jaw Surgery Assortment. Contains 2 large stars, 3 small stars, 2 crescent moons, 3 shooting stars, 5 medium stars, 2 saturns, 4 planets, 1 spaceship, and 1 satellite. Price per package postpaid . . . . .75c.

No. 4993. Brain Cancer and Tumor Assortment. Contains 5 large stars, 5 small stars, 2 crescent moons, 3 shooting stars, 5 medium stars, 5 saturns, 5 planets, 5 spaceships, 5 satellites, 25 missile defense systems, 60 broadcasting stations, 105 landsat mapping units, 200 surveillance deploys and 300 privately-funded orbiters. Price per package postpaid . . . . $1.00.

CUT YOUR OWN DESIGNS

Plain white luminous coated paper with gummed backs, size 8" x 10". Cut your own designs, stick figures, anything. Endless fun — or quicker, too. Flame, mystics begin to hurl. Or, excellent on the family pet. Tie around dog's midsection, make him visible at night. Watch his gums begin to bleed. Get that glow. Luminous ink. Wow! You get the idea. Order now.

No. 4990. Per Sheet $1.00
No. 4994. Liquid Death $5.00

Notes on Contributors

ROGER DIRECTOR

E. BOSTWICK BLANE is Professor of Irascible Behavior Studies at the State University of New York at Foodtown. For his groundbreaking field work cataloguing over 1,100 different hand gestures of contempt among Mediterranean cultures he was admitted to the French Academy and was arrested for inciting to riot.

REX J. CAIRO is Oliver North Fellow at the Center for Advanced Strategic Asseveration in Fairfax, Virginia, and senior editor of the foreign policy journal *Quagmire*. His last book, *Hillary Clinton: The Real Author of the Zimmerman Telegram*, received the 1998 Wolf Beppo Award for Distinguished Achievement in Binding.

DR. BABETTE COLA is president of the American Junior College of Surgeons. Last June, she astounded the medical world by transplanting onto a three-month-old parakeet the wattles of a 71-year-old billionaire.

ALAN DERSHOWITZ, delicatessen owner and Professor of Law at Harvard, is the author of *The Genesis of Justice*, due out this month. The piece in this issue is a transcription of his oral argument before the U.S. Supreme Court last January in which he sought the right to sue his own pastrami.

FAWN says she constantly regenerates herself in transpersonal encounters, sending shoots of lifelick into the tomb/tubers of buried human potential.

PHIL IACOBUCCI was until recently a VCR repairman at the Video Clinic in Boise, Idaho. Following favorable Federal court rulings and the deft leveraging of some communications stock he became, last Wednesday, Barry Diller.

RABBI MEYER KOPLOWITZ is President of the Organization of Presidents of Major Jewish Organizations of Presidents of Major Jewish Organizations.

FELICITY LEEK is John McEnroe Professor of Rodomontade at Stanford University. Her forthcoming book is *Clueless: How I Taught Francis Fukuyama Everything He Knows*, and is a main selection of the Remaindered Book Club.

SENATOR JOHN MCCAIN is the author of *Faith of My Fathers*.

BRIO ROTH, Distinguished Professor of Music and Dance at the University of the Levant, is editor of the three-volume collected letters of Paula Abdul.

NIPSEY RUSSELL is a contributing editor to this series.

VIC SAINT-SAENS has installed artwork all around the world and is most recently the recipient of a 1999 MacArthur Award. Later this year he will attempt to drape Guam in shiny slacks.

COTSWOLD A. TAPOOTY is India's Deputy Ambassador to the United States and Chairman of the United Nations Commission on Peculiar Aftertastes. He writes frequently on the entertainment scene.

RUSSELL K. VANADEEN is proprietor of Rusty's Acre of Gators in Chokoloskee, Florida. His article in this issue is adapted from the Seagrams Lectures, a series of incoherent ripostes delivered outside the Dew Drop Inn last fall to nobody in particular.

Notes on Contributors

(NOT BY ROGER DIRECTOR)

HENRY ALFORD is the author of three books, *Municipal Bondage, Big Kiss,* and *Out There.*

DAVID M. BADER is the author of *Haikus for Jews* (1999) and *Zen Judaism* (2002).

RICHARD BAUSCH is the author of twelve volumes of fiction, including *Rebel Powers, Violence,* and *The Last Good Time.* His *Selected Stories* is part of the Modern Library publishing program. His short fiction has appeared in *The Atlantic Monthly, Esquire, The New Yorker, Playboy,* and is widely anthologized. He lives in rural Virginia.

ANDY BOROWITZ is a writer and performer whose work appears in both *The New Yorker* and the *New York Times.* He is a commentator on NPR's *Weekend Edition,* and author of *The Trillionaire Next Door.*

TIM CARVELL is a writer based in New York City. His work has appeared in *Slate, Fortune, Entertainment Weekly, eCompany Now,* and *McSweeney's Internet Tendency.*

CARINA CHOCANO is a senior writer at Salon.com.

RANDY COHEN writes "The Ethicist" for the *New York Times Magazine.* A book based on the column, *The Good, the Bad, and the Difference,* was published by Doubleday in 2002.

ROGER DIRECTOR is a journalist, a writer-producer for such television shows as *Hill Street Blues, Moonlighting,* and *Mad About You,* and the author of the novel *A Place to Fall* (Villard). He lives in Santa Monica with his wife, Jan Cherubin, and daughter, Chloe.

LAWRENCE DOUGLAS is Assistant Professor of Law, Jurisprudence, and Social Thought at Amherst College, and writes with Alexander George for such publications as the *New York Times,* the *Chronicle of Higher Education,* and Salon.com.

WILL DURST is a comedian, actor, writer, producer, and host of PBS's *Livelyhood*, who lives in San Francisco and yells himself hoarse at Giants games, then soothes his cords with ample samplings of Anchor Steam.

MICHAEL THOMAS FORD is the Lambda Literary Award–winning author of numerous books, including *Alec Baldwin Doesn't Love Me, That's Mr. Faggot to You, It's Not Mean If It's True*, and *The Field Guide to the North American Homosexual*. His website is www.michaelthomasford.com.

IAN FRAZIER is the author of "The Bear" by William Faulkner.

KRIS FRIESWICK is a humor columnist for the *Boston Phoenix*, a sketch comedy writer, and a financial journalist for *CFO* magazine. She lives and works in Newton, Massachusetts, where she is presently procrastinating her way through her first book.

FRANK GANNON's work has appeared in *The New Yorker, Harper's*, and other magazines. He recently finished a nonfiction book about Ireland for Warner Books.

Born and bred in Manhattan, ALEXANDER GEORGE attended the Lycée Français de New York, Columbia, and Harvard. He is currently Professor of Philosophy at Amherst College and writes other stuff with his left hand.

MICHAEL GERBER's humor has appeared in *The New Yorker, The Atlantic Monthly*, the *Wall Street Journal, Esquire*, and many other publications. The only two-term chairman in the 130-year history of *The Yale Record*, he has also contributed to *Saturday Night Live*.

TOM GLIATTO is a writer for *People* magazine in New York City.

BEN GREENMAN is an editor at *The New Yorker*. His work has appeared there, in *McSweeney's*, and in many other fine publications. A collection of his fiction and humor, *Superbad*, was published in 2001.

LEWIS GROSSBERGER served for three years as secretary of commerce in the first Bush administration and is currently confined to a minimum-security correctional institution in Pennsylvania.

JUDY GRUEN has written for *Women's Day*, the *Los Angeles Times*, the *Chicago Tribune*, and many other publications. *Carpool Tunnel Syndrome: Motherhood as Shuttle Diplomacy* is her first book.

CHRIS HARRIS, a writer for the *Late Show with David Letterman*, has published work in *The New Yorker, Time, McSweeney's, Spin, Modern Humorist*, the *Wall Street Journal*, and a number (0) of other publications.

TIM HARROD is a staff writer for the *Onion*, and contributed to its three books: *Our Dumb Century*, the *Onion's Finest News Reporting*, and *Dispatches from the Tenth Circle*. He lives in New York City.

FRANCIS HEANEY is a playwright, songwriter, humorist, amateur tap dancer, and puzzle writer who lives in New York City. His work has appeared in *Modern Humorist, McSweeney's Internet Tendency*, Playboy.com, *Games*, and the *New York Times*. His superpower is the ability to blind people with his ties.

TONY HENDRA was editor of *National Lampoon*, and editor in chief of *Spy* magazine. He has failed to live down playing Ian Faith in Spinal Tap.

Spoken-word performer, national slam poet, and corn-fed Dayton native, GREGORY HISCHAK is the author of several plays, most recently, the radio play *Beautiful and Shining Like Asphalt*. He is the editor, stapler, and pretty much sole contributor to *Farm Pulp Magazine*, the acclaimed zine of juxtaposition and mirth. He lives in Seattle.

JEFF JOHNSON contributes to *Jane, The Minus Times*, and *McSweeney's Internet Tendency*. And also to the delinquency of minors in Tulsa, Oklahoma, and Ogden, Utah.

HOWARD KAMINSKY was president and publisher of three major publishing houses, and is the author of several screenplays, four novels, and numerous magazine articles. His new book, *The Magic Words*, co-written with Alexandra Penney, was published in 2001 by Broadway Books.

CYNTHIA KAPLAN is a writer and actress is New York and yet she has never appeared on *Law & Order*. She has written for the *New York Times*, the *Philadelphia Inquirer*, and Playboy.com, among others, and is the co-writer of the film *Pipe Dream*. Her book of essays, *Why I'm Like This*, is published by William Morrow.

Speechwriter and humorist MARK KATZ is the Resident Scholar of the Sound Bite Institute (www.soundbiteinstitute.com), a one-man creative think-tank for humor-writing projects. During the eight years of a previous administration, he assisted President Bill Clinton with his annual humor speeches to the Gridiron Club and the White House Correspondents' Dinner. He is the author of *"I Am Not a Corpse!" (And Other Quotes Never Actually Said)*, and of various humor essays published by *The New Yorker,* the *New York Times, Time,* and aired on National Public Radio.

MARTHA KEAVNEY is a humor writer and cartoonist. She lives in Jersey City, New Jersey.

ROBERT KONRATH retired from the U.S. Foreign Service in 2000. He lives with his wife and two children in Coral Gables, Florida.

M. SWEENEY LAWLESS is a member of the Chicago City Limits Touring Company in New York. She is a founding member of the Young Survival Coalition (www.youngsurvival.org) and can hide five bees secretly in her mouth.

Based in Oklahoma City, ROD M. LOTT is the editor and publisher of *Hitch: The Journal of Pop Culture Absurdity,* and an overworked freelance writer with little sleep.

JAMIE MALANOWSKI was a writer and editor at *Spy* magazine.

MERRILL MARKOE has a bathroom shelf full of Emmies she won as a writer/co-creator of *Late Night with David Letterman* and a garage full of boxes of her three books of humor pieces: *What the Dogs Have Taught Me, How to be Hap Hap Happy Like Me,* and *Merrill Markoe's Guide to Love.* Her only novel, *It's My &%$#@! Birthday,* was just published by Villard/Random House. Other than that, she seems to have no life.

STEVE MARTIN (as if you need to learn about him here!)

MICHAEL FRANCIS MARTONE is a contributing editor for *Modern Humorist,* and has written for publications varying from *TV Guide* to *InfoPro.* He is also a contributor to *Modern Humorist*'s second book, *Rough Drafts.*

BOBBIE ANN MASON's most recent book is a collection of stories, *Zigzagging Down a Wild Trail,* published by Random House. Her other works include *Clear Springs, Feather Crowns, In Country,* and *Shiloh and Other Stories,* which was reissued last year by the

Modern Library. She resides in Kentucky with her husband, cats, and dogs.

Canadian-born and -reared, BRUCE MCCALL is a writer and illustrator whose work appears frequently in *The New Yorker*. His newest humor collection is *All Meat Looks Like South America*.

SUSAN MCCARTHY writes about science and the environment, and also writes humor. She's a contributing writer at Salon, and the co-author, with Jeffrey Moussaieff Masson, of *When Elephants Weep*. She is a carbon-based life form, and a native of Earth (based in San Francisco). "I love your sunsets," she reports.

J. H. S. MCGREGOR is a writer, professor, and malcontent living in parts of Georgia.

TOBY MILLER has published several humor essays and has recently directed his first film, a documentary entitled *Log's Place*.

JOHN MOE has written for National Public Radio, *McSweeney's Internet Tendency*, and Amazon.com. He operates RobotDanceparty.com and founded the *New York Times*.

Born April 18, 1953, in Toronto, RICK MORANIS was a member of the SCTV television cast. He has appeared in several films including *Ghostbusters*, *Little Shop of Horrors*, *Parenthood*, and Mel Brooks's *Spaceballs*.

MATT NEUMAN has won numerous awards writing for television (*Saturday Night Live, Not Necessarily the News*, Lily Tomlin), and has published work in *The Realist, Speak*, and the *New York Times*. His website is www.mattneuman.com.

DAVID OWEN is a staff writer for *The New Yorker*. His books include *The Walls Around Us, My Usual Game*, and *The Making of the Masters*.

ALYSIA GRAY PAINTER lives in Los Angeles. Other work of hers appears on PBS, *Modern Humorist*, and *McSweeney's Internet Tendency*.

LOUIS PHILLIPS is a widely published poet, playwright, and short-story writer whose two collections of stories are *A Dream of Countries Where No One Dare Live* (SMU Press), and *The Bus to the Moon* (Fort Schuyler Press). Broadway Play Publishers have published his comic one-act plays.

JUDITH PODELL is the author of *Blues for Beginners: Stories and Obsessions*. She lives in Washington, D.C., but in a New York state of mind.

AMY KROUSE ROSENTHAL creates the weekly, handwritten column "15 Megabytes of Fame" for Amused.com. She is the editor of the audio-magazine *Writers' Block Party*, and the author of some books including *The Book of Eleven: An Itemized Collection of Brain Lint*. A collection of her essays was published in the spring of 2001. She is best known for never leaving the house with an umbrella. She is working on a novel, as well as on letting go of trying to find meaning where there probably is none (e.g., she recently stepped outside and at once saw a license plate which read Amy1429; her birthday is 429, so, except for the 1, the license plate was perfect, and surely a sign of something. Another example: Not too long ago, she was trying to pick out a movie for her kids, and as she walked down the aisle, her bag accidentally knocked a video off the rack. It was *Adventures in Babysitting*. The children are meant to watch this tonight, she thought, like this movie had some important and powerful message to impart, one that would make her children better people. That same week, at the drugstore trying to pick out a color for her hair among the dozens of near-identical shades, she noticed one, sole box jetting out amid the rest of the perfectly stacked boxes. It was a bit blonder than she would have chosen, but she trusted the gesture just the same, and immediately took #211, Ginger Zing, to the counter.) She has no plans to write a screenplay or to participate in the Creative Memories Photo Album movement. She is pro-satin, and anti-fennel. She wants you to be happy. She understands that black is the absence of color, but feels it makes more sense for it to be *all* the colors smooshed together, and, likewise, it seems that white would be the peaceful, blank *absence* of color. As for nonfiction and fiction—those should be switched as well. Nonfiction should be the *non*true one, and fiction, true. It would also be her preference to spell playwright *playwrite*, and she believes others would support this long overdue change. She is saddened by parades, by abrupt receptionists—the ones who just transfer you without any verbal niceties or warning—and by the fact that she hasn't heard from several friends in a while, despite the fact that if she did she knew she would try to avoid making plans. She is also saddened by the sight of parents walking their children into school while talking on their cell phones. Ms.

Rosenthal would rather take the extra two minutes to maneuver into an awkward but slightly closer-to-her-destination parking spot, than take the big, wide open spot a few cars down. Also worth noting: she is a ridiculously messy cook. She gets teary listening to the *Free to Be You and Me* soundtrack. She would love to tell you about her vacation, but knows better. She loves butterscotch, but rarely remembers to seek it out; ditto the band Squeeze. She has only recently learned how to be highly possessive of her time, and is feeling more and more entitled to cut short a boring conversation—monologue—by interjecting a simple, "You know, I've got to get back to work"; people seem to get that. She was recently scheduled to go to New York, but somehow she couldn't bring herself to follow through with certain arrangements, with dinner reservations, etc.; as it turns out, her father had unexpected surgery (fine now) and the trip was canceled; it was as if her lack of energy, lack of mental commitment toward the trip, was due to some predetermined cue from the universe. Incidentally, if she had gone, she would have tried to pack light, she always tries to pack light—to do so is to really achieve something—but never manages. On the subject of travel: She never remembers to preorder kid meals, never even occurs to her, until she sees the flight attendant prancing down the aisle with fun, colorful trays for children that are not hers. Ms. Rosenthal always starts off clean and organized on these flights, putting her book and magazines in the seat pocket, her backpack tucked neatly under the seat in front of her, but about 20 minutes after takeoff, her papers are everywhere, pens are in between the cushion crevices, and sour cream'n'chive pretzel wrappers are strewn on the floor. Though this has never materialized, Ms. Rosenthal still thinks of Sunday as the day that she will stay home and make a large vat of chili for the neighbors, and also boil a sack of potatoes so she can use them in various ways throughout the busy work week. She lives in Chicago and can be reached at amy@suba.com.

CHIP ROWE is Associate Editor at *Playboy*. His website is an archive of his own humor and links to many others humorists: www.chiprowe.com.

PAUL RUDNICK's plays include *Jeffrey, The Most Fabulous Story Ever Told, I Hate Hamlet*, and *Rude Entertainment*. His novels are *Social Disease* and *I'll Take It*, and his screenplays include *Addams Family Values* and *In & Out*.

Tom Ruprecht is a writer for the *Late Show with David Letterman*. His work has appeared in the *New York Times*, the *Wall Street Journal*, and *GQ*. His work has not appeared in *Modern Bride, Inside Kung-Fu, Barely Legal*, and, well, loads of places when you think about it.

Jay Ruttenberg is a staff writer at *TimeOut New York* and editor of *The Lowbrow Reader*, a fanzine about comedy.

Peter Schooff is a humor writer living in New York City. He has been published on numerous Internet humor sites, including *McSweeney's Internet Tendency*. He is also the writer/editor of PeteTV.com.

Jonathan Schwarz has (with Michael Gerber) written humor for many publications, including *The New Yorker, The Atlantic Monthly,* the *Wall Street Journal*, and *McSweeney's Internet Tendency*.

Dr. Science, of National Public Radio fame, lives in Iowa, where he is best known as Dan Coffey.

Nell Scovell has written for umpteen magazines (*Vanity Fair, Vogue, Rolling Stone, The Tatler*, and *Spy*), a slew of television shows (*Newhart, The Simpsons, Murphy Brown, Smothers Brothers*, and *Sabrina, the Teenage Witch*—she actually created that show), and a Showtime movie (*Hayley Wagner, Star*), which she also directed. She is married to architect Colin Summers, and has two children. This is her first published fiction.

Hart Seely is a reporter with the *Syracuse Post-Standard* and is co-author, with Frank Cammuso, of *2007-Eleven*, published by Random House in 2000. He lives with his wife and three kids in Syracuse, New York.

Jeremy Simon is a writer based in New York City. His humor, essays, and reporting have appeared in *Modern Humorist, Newsday, Nerve*, and several other newspapers and literary journals.

Holly Smith has written for the *Washington Post*, Salon.com, *Washington Flyer, Frederick* magazine, and the *White Shoe Irregular*. She grew up in Ohio and now resides in Maryland with her husband, Ben Rogot, and their three children.

MATT SUMMERS has written for print, video, television, and love. He is a frequent contributor to *McSweeney's Internet Tendency*, and is completing a collection of short stories.

DAVIS SWEET writes funny things from his home in Oregon with frequent editorial assistance from his wife Tammy. He is the co-author (with Tony Hendra) of *Real Conversations with God*, a forthcoming book from The Bean, writer/producer of the vaguely infamous underground song "Slow Brain (George W. Bush Raps over 'Cocaine')," and screenwriter for *Six Strings in Seven Bands*, *Better Than Average*, and Lenny *Bruce Is Not Afraid*, any or all of which may someday be produced, or at least optioned.

STUART WADE, co-author of *Drop Us a Line . . . Sucker*, is a regular contributor to the *Onion*. He lives in Austin, Texas.

CHRIS WARE, born in 1967, is a cartoonist living in Chicago. He is the author and creator of the beloved "Acme Novelty Library," as well as the graphic novel *Jimmy Corrigan: The Smartest Kid on Earth*, published by Pantheon Books.

BILL WASIK is an editor at *Harper's* magazine. Previously, he was the editor of *The Weekly Week*, a humor magazine based in Boston.

NOAM WEINSTEIN grew up in Cambridge, Massachusetts, and currently resides in New York City.

ROBERT S. WIEDER has written for *Playboy, Penthouse, The Lampoon*, and several magazines that would rather not be mentioned. He wrote a book about convertibles and cowrote one about the Oakland As. For a while, in the 1980s and '90s, he also did stand-up comedy.

ERICA YOUNGREN currently resides in London with her husband Craig, where she is working on the first London edition of a shopping guide called *Where to Wear*. Her writing has been published in *The New Yorker, Harper's Bazaar, Slate*, InStyle.com, and traveldish.com.

PERMISSIONS

The Worstseller List

Let Me Tell You About My Cold ($17.95) The story of Al, a window treatment and blinds salesman, who loses his clients, and ultimately his job, because all he does is talk about is his cold (when it started; the wonders of ColdEeze; how in 25 years of practice his doctor has never seen a cold that bad).

Truth unto Death ($35.95) A Tolstoy-influenced masterpiece with multiple layers and plot twists. A bit hard to follow due to the author's trademark "utilitarian literary device" of naming all 204 characters "Jeb."

Shelf Life: A Novella ($22.95) A lyrical tale of a cup in search of the ideal saucer.

You're Ordinary, Ha Ha ($89.95) A collection of personal essays by famous, beautiful, rich people. A tiny mirror affixed to the top of each page drives the title home.

Dr. Atkins Diet Protest ($19.95) The now-legendary, then onto-something nutritionist preaches the benefits of a weight-loss program consisting solely of meat, cheese, nuts, and Zima shakes.

Pre-Me ($29.95) In this latest example of how everyone and their fetus is trying to catch onto the memoir craze, an actual zygote writes about his early, early childhood trauma (mom didn't give in to beef jerky cravings; mom forgot to bring prenatal vitamins on overnight business trip; mom often treated zygote like it wasn't even there).

Eggie and Me ($17.95) A touching story of a man and an eggplant.

This Book Is Worth One Picture A high concept book consisting of 1,000 words, lifted directly and alphabetically from the dictionary. (Book costs $0.00, booksellers instructed to accept one picture, of any kind, as currency.) Page "Adenoid-Aluminum" is especially riveting.

No, We're Really Smart ($29.95) The Backstreet Boys' 200-page dissertation (rhyming) on the history of the Middle East using the falafel as a metaphor for peace.

Eating Your Cat ($14.95) The ultimate cookbook for "cat lovers."

Mondays with Morrie ($2.95) In this prequel, Morrie goes on and on about not being able to find a good pastrami sandwich anywhere.

The Candle Manifesto (50 cents) The best book ever written by any-one, ever, in the history of the world, this book would have single-handedly changed your life in an unimaginable, lasting and profoundly meaningful way, but the head publicist went on maternity leave at the most critical time and thus the book inadvertently fell through the media cracks.

—A.K.R

END-OF-THE-BOOK READER'S SURVEY

Mirth of a Nation wants to know you better, so it can tailor its future editions specifically to you, dear reader. Won't you take a moment to tell us a bit about yourself?

Please circle all that apply:

I am male / female.

I read the first edition of *Mirth of a Nation.*

I read the second edition, *More Mirth of a Nation.*

I have recently fallen in love with a fictitious character.

I got depressed flipping through an issue of *Cat* magazine at the doctor's office the other day. (I hate cats, but was curious about the contents of such a magazine.) More specifically, I was depressed by the titles of the various sections: "What's Mew" and "Purrsonals."

Ditto regarding an innocuous logo for a local hair salon (something about the turquoise swish).

I think my life would be complete if only I had a Chinese marble frog on display in my backyard.

I recognize that everything I do—and I mean *everything*, from my career to breeding to vacuuming—is really just one big distraction from belaboring the real issue at hand (death, inevitable).

I would like to see more punny jokes in future editions (What's converted rice? Answer: Rice that converts from one religion to another.).

I would like to see more historical pieces (I am, as you might recall, very interested in Mesopotamia).

My husband and I have matching Western wear with fringe across the chest.

I can not stress this enough: One second your toast is fine, pleasingly brown; the next second it is black.

Thank you!!! Answering this questionnaire will improve future editions and your experience of reading them.

—A.K.R.

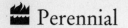 Perennial

Books by Michael J. Rosen:

MIRTH OF A NATION
The Best Contemporary Humor
ISBN 0-06-0953217 (paperback)

A premier showcase of great literary humorists and masters of the journalistic jab, the social spoof, the satire, the tirade, and the send-up. Here are those "last laughs" and "wit's end" pieces everyone turns to first but then loses in the back issues of favorite magazines and newspapers. Contributors include Rick Moranis, David Rakoff, Michael Feldman, Mark O'Donnell, Paul Rudnick, Garry Trudeau and many others.

"The cream of the current humorist crop."—*Richmond Times-Dispatch*

"As I read it again, now alone in my apartment, I am once more laughing uncontrollably." —*Boston Globe*

MORE MIRTH OF A NATION
The Best Contemporary Humor
ISBN 0-06-095322-5 (paperback)

Sixty-five writers deck the halls of hilarity with witty, wise work by Ian Frazier, Merrill Markoe, Andy Borowitz, Bruce McCall, Bobbie Ann Mason, Paul Rudnick, Henry Alford, Tony Hendra, Will Durst, Richard Bausch, and Susan McCarthy. Also featuring the undiscovered Etch A Sketch drawings of Van Gogh, a *Zagat's* Survey of existence, Aristotle's long-lost treatise "On Baseball," and "One-Minute Histories" by "The Ethicist" Randy Cohen.

(((LISTEN TO)))

MIRTH OF A NATION
Audio Companion, Fellow Traveler, and Friend for Life

ISBN 0-06-051319-5 (audio cd)

The best of *Mirth of a Nation* and *More Mirth of a Nation* here on this CD collection—performed by Tony Roberts and Christine Branski!

Available wherever books are sold, or call 1-800-331-3761 to order.